THE VISUAL ARTIST'S MANUAL

A Practical Guide to Your Career

THE VISUAL ARTIST'S MANUAL

A Practical Guide to Your Career

Compiled and edited by Susan A. Grode

EDITORIAL BOARD

Debra L. Fink   Madeleine E. Seltzer   Shari Friedman
David Paul Steiner   Ellen Jacobson

THE BEVERLY HILLS BAR ASSOCIATION BARRISTERS COMMITTEE FOR THE ARTS

EXECUTIVE DIRECTOR	CO-CHAIRPERSONS	LEGAL SERVICES
Maria Luisa de Herrera	Lawrence J. Blake	Melinda Benedek
	Jordan Kerner	

SYMPOSIUM	COUNCIL ON THE DISABLED IN THE ARTS	OUTREACH
Susan A. Grode	Les Jankey	Harvey Harrison
Doug Rosner	Alan Toy	Paul Mayersohn
Steven H. Gardner	Darell Ray	EVENTS
Betty Brown	Julianna Fjeld	Wendy Fishman

First distributed at the Fourth Annual Artists' Symposium: For Visual Artists
at the University of Southern California, November 14, 1981

Chairperson: Susan A. Grode

A Dolphin Book
Doubleday & Company, Inc., Garden City, New York, 1984

Beverly Hills Bar Association Barristers Committee for the Arts
The Visual Artist's Manual

Library of Congress Cataloging in Publication Data
Main entry under title: The Visual artist's manual.
First distributed at the Fourth Annual Artists' Symposium:
For Visual Artists at the University of Southern California, November 14, 1981.
Bibliography: p. 275
1. Law—United States. 2. Forms (Law)—United States.
3. Artists—Legal status, laws, etc.—United States.
4. Artists—United States—Handbooks, manuals, etc.
I. Grode, Susan A. II. Fink, Debra L.
III. Beverly Hills Bar Association Barristers Committee for the Arts.
KF390.A7V57   1984   344.73'097   82-45347
ISBN 0-385-18251-1

WHAT IS THE COMMITTEE FOR THE ARTS?

This book and the Fourth Annual Artists' Symposium: For Visual Artists, with which this book was conceived and published, are the products of merely one facet of the work of the Committee for the Arts (CFTA). CFTA is an ongoing project of the Barristers (young lawyers' division) of the Beverly Hills Bar Association, a nonprofit organization.

CFTA was formed early in 1978 when approximately thirty young lawyers and artists had a series of meetings to discuss how to satisfy the needs of struggling artists and entertainers in the Los Angeles area for affordable, first-rate legal counseling. As enthusiasm for undertaking this project spread among artists and lawyers and as ideas for starting the project began to take concrete form, the Beverly Hills Bar Association quickly embraced CFTA and threw its considerable support behind the project.

CFTA began with two broad objectives: first, to provide educational and information services relating to the interface of arts and law to both lawyers and artists, entertainers and arts organizations, whatever their financial means might be. CFTA's working membership grew rapidly and it spawned several subcommittees, the work of each of which is briefly outlined below, to take a specific focus on those broad objectives.

The Symposium Subcommittee was formed to produce annual, all-day symposia, each for a particular type of artist or entertainer (e.g., actors, visual artists, writers, musicians, etc.), in which well-known professionals working in the subject area would present a series of lectures, panel discussions and workshops on the practical, legal and business aspects of working within that area. The Symposium Subcommittee is also responsible for publishing a reference work, such as this one, in conjunction with each such symposium.

The Legal Services Subcommittee worked for well over a year to establish a lawyer-referral service which provides first-rate, free or affordable legal services specifically to artists and entertainers working in the Los Angeles area. Legal services are furnished on a free, low-cost or negotiated fee basis, depending on the client's ability to pay, which is determined by a simple screening process. The problems which are handled include contract negotiation and drafting, copyright matters and any other arts or entertainment-related problem, excluding litigation. When you call CFTA with a legal problem, you will be referred to one of its many panel attorneys who is experienced in the particular area of law. We encourage you to remember this service when you think you may have a legal problem. Simply call CFTA at: (213) 556-1598.

The Community Outreach Subcommittee was established to serve the same educational function as is being served by the Symposium Subcommittee, but on a smaller, more personal scale. It sends attorneys to meet with arts organizations at their headquarters in the Los Angeles area to present lectures and workshops on legal topics selected by those organizations and their members as being of interest to them. The topics are not limited to "arts law," but include any topic directly related to the artist's ability to engage in his/her profession, such as taxation, zoning ordinances and laws relating to nonprofit organizations, to name just a few.

The Council for the Disabled in the Arts is a subcommittee composed of both disabled and able-bodied artists and attorneys. It is at the vanguard of a growing movement to foster awareness of and compliance with the legal rights of the disabled, to assure the accurate portrayal of disabled persons in motion pictures and television and to integrate disabled artists into the mainstream of all facets of motion picture and television production. To this end, it has provided consulting services to the networks and the major studios on matters relative to the disabled and is encouraging the development of programs to provide training and experience sufficient to develop employable skills among the disabled in the entertainment and arts industries. The CODA has become a clearinghouse for a wide variety of information concerning the disabled and the entertainment industry.

The Events Subcommittee works to provide necessary funds for the development and continuation of all substantive activities of CFTA. It organizes and promotes fund-raising events in the Los Angeles area such as motion picture premieres and "gala events."

The opportunity to experience works of art undeniably benefits every individual in our community. The majority of those in our community who enjoy the vast array of art forms available to them never realize how difficult the road is for a young artist to have his or her creations displayed to the public in any medium or forum. The public interest, as seen by CFTA, will be well served by the fostering in the artists of the greater Los Angeles area an awareness of the legal fabric in which their artistic endeavors are intertwined and by providing them with access to affordable legal services. Our hope is that an informed arts community will have the foresight and knowledge to command fair treatment from the businesses which they help to create. We will all reap the rewards.

This year's annual symposium represents a continuing tradition in the Committee for the Arts' commitment to provide a low-cost forum of practical education to the artistic community.

The Committee's goal in providing these yearly symposia is to present a basic nuts-and-bolts look at a particular category of artistic endeavor at a reasonable, break-even cost. Each year we explore a new category of artistry.

The Visual Artists' Symposium could not have taken place without the tremendous contribution of time and the dedication of the following volunteers. Along with each of our speakers, to each of them must our kudos be addressed:

Ellen J. Jacobson, Esq.
(Program Co-chairperson)

Doug Rosner, Esq.
(Program Co-chairperson)

Steven H. Gardner, Esq.
(Publicity Chairperson)

Maria de Herrera
Andrea Morse
Paul D. Supnik, Esq.
Marilyn Frandsen
Steven Nissen, Esq.
Marilyn Anderson
Barbara Singer
David Paul Steiner
Betty Brown, Ph.D.
Inese Lacey, Esq.
Jordan Kerner, Esq.
Debbie Ross
Norman Beil, Esq.
Debra L. Fink, Esq.
Howard M. Rootenberg, Esq.
Wendy Fishman, Esq.

SUSAN A. GRODE, ESQ.
Symposium Chairperson

PREFACE

O it was impossible to go on! I was on the verge of painting God's finger reaching toward Adam but in my mind there was only the image of my hand imploring a groat from Papa Julius. And if at the mere approach of his hand, the God I conceived could stir dust into life, ah, that was not so with Julius. Nothing seemed to stir him into any awareness that all my efforts to perpetuate his glory threatened to come to a standstill for want of money. . . . He marched out of Roma without paying me a ducat, although he had promised a payment once I had unveiled the first cycle of my work.[1]

You may well recognize the above problem as one to be faced repeatedly in your professional lives as visual artists. What you may not recognize is that these comments were made during the Italian Renaissance by Michelangelo imploring his patron Pope Julius II to live up to their contract for the completion of the Sistine Chapel. This situation is not unique, regardless of whether you are a painter, sculptor, graphic artist, animator or photographer. We operate in a world of rules and regulations imposed on everyone, even the artist. From the moment that you put your work into the stream of commerce, the rest of the world is likely to view it as a commodity and to view your activities as business conduct. As soon as something is created by you the problem of legally protecting that creation becomes a reality as well. In addition, the environment in which it is created must not only be conducive, it must also be safe for both you and your work.

Now, for the first time in history, visual artists can have professional bargaining power, both collectively and individually. This power is the product of an amalgamation of facts and individual rights which must be first understood separately since they affect and influence every facet of your professional life, including the act of creation itself. This Manual is a guide through that unfamiliar but necessary information. We hope it may be used as a reference to help you develop a practical and professional approach to your career.

The Business of Being a Visual Artist deals with the most common professional relationships and the agreements that define those relationships. In it you will find a discussion on what to expect from and what is expected from you in dealing with galleries, reps, attorneys and accountants, followed by sample contracts with detailed and easy-to-understand analyses prepared by attorneys and other professionals in the field.

Legal Protection for the Creator and the Creation illustrates that there are legal and practical means by which artists can protect themselves and their work from use, misuse and abuse. In articles explaining federal and state legislation, the authors demystify the statutory language so that it can be understood and used to benefit you in your work.

Licensing, Merchandising and Publishing Visual Art explores commercial relationships in which the art is reproduced by others. Articles reflect the growing bargaining power of the artist in

[1] The Hand of Michelangelo, by Sydney Alexander (1966), p. 341.

ix

this area and the sample annotated contracts will familiarize you with a panoply of emerging rights and obligations, as well as established commercial procedures.

Money and the Visual Artist. By the time you reach this section you should have secured your work and earned some money. These commentaries will acquaint you with some of the planning and methodology to follow for keeping some of it. Understanding personal and corporate tax, estate planning for your family, valuing your artworks and obtaining funding to support your work through grants are concerns as essential for the artist as anyone else who earns a living.

Practical Safeguards for the Artist, the Work and the Studio completes the profile of the visual artist as a concerned professional by dealing with the heretofore unexplored areas of: dangers in the studio from hazardous substances, art insurance for artists, preserving work in transit and how to transport it, and the urban studio explosion and the laws that make it possible for the artist to combine living and work space.

Finally, we complete the Manual with a detailed resource section listing arts organizations and other institutions that can provide valuable information for visual artists and an exhaustive bibliography for the visual artist.

On a personal note, we believe that the Manual is the first of its kind to combine a broad variety of pragmatic and legal resources for visual artists under one cover. Use it and prosper.

SUSAN A. GRODE, ESQ.

ACKNOWLEDGMENTS

The editor wishes to acknowledge the following contributors to the Manual. They provided the foundation for the successful gathering, coordinating and reproducing of the vast collection of facts and materials that comprise this book. Thanks to:

Marlene Weed and Martin Weber for their tireless efforts in researching, classifying and obtaining sources, materials and reprint rights.

Aki Toyooka for masterful manuscript typing and preparation of contract materials and articles.

Debra L. Fink, Esq., Madeleine E. Seltzer, Esq., Shari Friedman, Laurie Bernhard, Esq., Ellizabeth L. Weller, Esq., Alan Thaler, Mary Anne Gilmour, Esq., Gregory T. Victoroff, Esq., Sue E. Garbowitz, Esq., Richard M. Ross, Esq., Tina Pasternack, Esq., Alan Abrams, Esq., Polin Cohanne, Esq., Steven Nissen, Esq., Norman Beil, Esq., Carl Bressler, and Sharon Ehrlich for editing, proofreading and providing materials.

Special recognition to the law firms of Manatt, Phelps, Rothenberg & Tunney; Kaplan, Livingston, Goodwin, Berkowitz & Selvin; and Irwin & Rowan for their generous contribution of time and skills in the preparation of printed matter for reproduction; and specifically to Lawrence J. Blake, Esq., of the Manatt firm, and Lawrence Rubin, Esq., of the Kaplan firm, as well as the word-processing personnel at the Manatt and Kaplan firms for their polished and professional work.

Personal thanks go to the editors of the preceding three Manuals for establishing excellent models to follow.

Finally, I am greatly indebted to the many experienced professionals who contributed their expertise by researching and writing articles for this Manual.

THE EDITOR

CONTENTS

Part Two
LEGAL PROTECTION FOR THE CREATOR AND THE CREATION

Part Three
LICENSING, MERCHANDISING AND PUBLISHING VISUAL ART

Part Four
MONEY AND THE VISUAL ARTIST

LIST OF CONTRIBUTORS

RON BAKAL is senior partner in the firm of Bakal and Kaplan and specializes in copyright, contracts and litigation in the creative arts field. He is counsel to the Graphic Artists Guild, the Society of Illustrators and many other arts organizations, including West Reps.

ESTELLE BERN received her B.A. in design from UCLA in 1982. She has previously studied art and design at the Cleveland Institute of Art and the Fashion Institute of Design in Los Angeles. Her jewelry designs have appeared in *Cosmopolitan* magazine.

LAWRENCE J. BLAKE, ESQ., practices law with the firm of Manatt, Phelps, Rothenberg & Tunney in Los Angeles, specializing in matters relating to the music and entertainment industries. He is currently also president of the Barristers.

LORIN BRENNAN, ESQ., is an associate with the Los Angeles law firm of Musick, Peeler & Garrett. He is a member of the board of directors of the Southern California Center for the Arts, a California nonprofit corporation.

MARTIN BRESSLER, ESQ., founder of VAGA, is an attorney in New York City. Mr. Bressler has been a distinguished lecturer in Arts Law at the University of Texas, Rutgers University and Columbia University, among others. Mr. Bressler is a 1957 graduate of Harvard Law School. He is one of the initial directors of VAGA.

ALLAN B. CUTROW received his B.A. in 1968 and his J.D. in 1971 from UCLA. He is a certified public accountant in California. He is also a certified tax specialist in California and is a partner in the law firm of Ladin, Kassan, Kurtz & Cutrow.

MARC DARROW is an attorney in private practice at 9255 Sunset Boulevard, Hollywood, California. He is a graduate of Northwestern University (1969) and Golden Gate College of Law (1973). His general practice emphasizes entertainment clients and he is a member of the New York and California Bars.

DEBRA L. FINK, ESQ., is an attorney in Los Angeles. She received her A.B., magna cum laude, in communications from the University of Miami and her J.D. from Loyola Law School.

SHARI FRIEDMAN is a candidate for Juris Doctor, May 1982, at Southwestern University College of Law, where she has served as a staff member for the *Southwestern University Law Review.* She is presently a law clerk at the firm of Irwin & Rowan, which specializes in entertainment law.

SUSAN A. GRODE, ESQ., editor of the Manual, practices law in Century City, specializing in matters relating to creators and their creations in the fields of entertainment, publishing and the visual arts. Ms. Grode is counsel to the Los Angeles Graphic Artists Guild and other arts organizations and has lectured on the visual artist and the law to members of the Bar as well as artists at UCLA and USC. She is a graduate of Cornell University and the University of Southern California Law School.

MARK E. HALLORAN practices law with Filmways Pictures, Inc. Mr. Halloran is co-author of *The Musician's Manual* and *The Musician's Guide to Copyright.*

MARGARET L. KAPLAN is vice president and executive editor of Harry N. Abrams Publishers, Inc., the world's largest artbook publishers. Ms. Kaplan has been with Abrams for seventeen years.

PETER H. KARLEN, J.D., UC Hastings; M.S. (law and society), University of Denver; B.A., UC Berkeley. Mr. Karlen is adjunct professor of law at the University of San Diego, where he teaches law and the arts, and contributing editor to *Art Week,* for which he writes the "Artlaw" column. Mr. Karlen practices art and entertainment law in La Jolla, California. The author expresses his gratitude for comments of Ms. Barbara Roth, Broker, Shores Insurance Agency, La Jolla.

HOPE LONDON is an artist and an attorney currently working as an artist in the animation industry and teaching drawing at California State University at Northridge. Ms. London was a Walter J. Derenberg fellow in copyright law at New York University School of Law.

MELVIN NEFSKY, a graduate of the University of Southern California, is a Los Angeles CPA specializing in the visual arts, entertainment and sports industries. He is a member of the American Institute of Certified Public Accountants and the USC Accounting Circle. He is a director of Pro Talents International.

RICHARD NEVINS is the elected member of the State Board of Equalization representing five-sevenths of Los Angeles County. The Board administers the sales and use tax, many other excise taxes, and promulgates rules for the county administration of property taxes. It is the appeals body for sales, franchise, corporate and personal income tax. Nevins, a veteran, is a graduate of Yale in the field of government. He worked in the insurance brokerage business before his election. He lives in Pasadena.

JERALD ORDOVER, a member of the New York Bar, has been specializing in art-related matters since the mid-1960s.

TINA D. PASTERNACK is Director of Business and Legal Affairs for Embassy Pictures. She received a B.A. in art history from UCLA and her J.D. degree from Loyola Law School.

STEPHEN F. ROHDE, ESQ., has his own law practice in Century City, specializing in entertainment and constitutional law, including First Amendment cases and civil litigation in the areas of copyright, libel and slander, invasion of privacy and unfair competition. Mr. Rohde was graduated from Northwestern University and Columbia Law School. He is admitted to practice law in New York and California. He has written for the Los Angeles *Times,* the *Pepperdine Law Review,* and speaks widely on copyright and First Amendment issues.

RICHARD M. ROSS is an attorney who has practiced entertainment law in New York City and Los Angeles.

ROBERT L. SCHUCHARD, ESQ., is an associate with the Los Angeles law firm of Musick, Peeler & Garrett. He is a member of the Ad Hoc Committee of the State Bar for Revision of the California Nonprofit Corporation Law.

EILEEN L. SELSKY is the associate editor of the *Entertainment Law Reporter* and maintains a private practice specializing in entertainment and corporate law.

MADELEINE E. SELTZER, ESQ., holds a B.A. in art history from UCLA and is a graduate of the University of Southern California Law School. She practices law in Los Angeles, specializing in civil litigation.

DAVID PAUL STEINER graduated from Stanford University (B.A.) and UC Hastings College of Law (J.D.), where he co-founded the *Hastings Constitutional Law Quarterly.* A founding member of the Committee for the Arts, he is currently an attorney in private practice in Century City, specializing in entertainment, business and tax planning matters. Mr. Steiner wishes to give special thanks to Howard Rootenberg, Esq., for his helpful research, without which the article would not have been written.

PAUL D. SUPNIK graduated from UC Hastings College of Law in San Francisco in 1971 and received a B.S. degree from UCLA in 1968. He is a past chair of the Intellectual Property Section of the Los Angeles County Bar Association, a co-editor of the Committee for the Arts publication, *The Actor's Manual,* and has a law practice in Beverly Hills.

GREGORY T. VICTOROFF is an attorney practicing with the law firm of Johnson and Lang in Los Angeles with an emphasis in entertainment and copyright law. He received his B.A. and teaching certification in theater arts from Beloit College in 1975 and his J.D. from the Cleveland-Marshall College of Law in 1979. He is the author of *The Artist's Resource Directory for Greater Los Angeles.*

JAE WAGONER is a commercial artist's representative and has been working in the Southern California area for five years. She represents at this time twelve commercial illustrators and has also represented photographers. Educated as a fine artist and commercial photographer, she also has a broad business background as a department store manager, boutique owner, manufacturer and designer of her own clothing and jewelry line and proprietor of a courier service.

DOROTHY M. WEBER is the executive director of VAGA. A graduate of Brooklyn Law School, she has dealt widely in various aspects of artists' rights over the last four years.

MARTIN WEBER holds an M.A. in art history from the University of Southern California and has done graduate work in art history at the University of Chicago. He was curator of the Pacificulture Museum (former Pasadena Art Museum) and founding director of the Huntsville Museum of Art in Huntsville, Alabama, and founding director of the University of Alabama at Huntsville Art Museum. He is currently studying law at the Whittier College School of Law, intending to specialize in art law.

MARLENE WEED, motion picture screenwriter and senior law student at Whittier College School of Law, attended Baker University, Baldwin, Kansas, and UCLA. She plans a law practice to serve the artistic and motion picture communities of the Santa Barbara area. Weed is a member of the Writer's Guild of America, West.

PART ONE

THE BUSINESS OF BEING A VISUAL ARTIST

CHAPTER ONE

HOW TO HAVE A MEANINGFUL RELATIONSHIP WITH YOUR PROFESSIONAL: CHOOSING A REP, A GALLERY, AN ACCOUNTANT, A LAWYER

Madeleine E. Seltzer, Esq.

Both the fine artist and the commercial artist must rely on various professionals to protect and further their economic interests. The fine artist's work is marketed by the gallery/dealer and the commercial artist's by the representative/agency. Each must also seek guidance from lawyers and accountants for various reasons. Thus the manner in which these professionals are chosen and the structure of the ensuing relationships are of prime concern to all artists, whether commercial or fine, new or established, struggling or successful.

THE ARTIST/GALLERY RELATIONSHIP

Purpose

Unlike other producers of objects or products for sale to the public, the fine artist has generally refrained from marketing his/her work himself/herself. Whether due to disinterest, lack of time or psychological aversion, the fine artist has used the services of a gallery/dealer to reap the financial rewards for his/her work. But it is obvious that the relationship between artist and dealer is unlike comparable arrangements in the marketplace. It is more intense and emotional because the dealer must like and appreciate the artist's work in order to be able to best present it to the public. And the dealer is selling an aspect of the artist's persona; one of the purposes of the relationship is to make the artist visible and to establish his/her credibility in the art community. Sales of work at any one particular point in time may be secondary to reaching the critics and major collectors; sales will naturally follow once the artist's work has achieved recognition. Moreover, the dealer's own reputation is a function of the success or failure of his/her artists; when exhibiting new artists, the dealer puts himself/herself on the line. Thus there is a symbiotic interdependence between the artist and the dealer which is unlike other marketing relationships in the commercial world.

How to Find the Gallery/Dealer

Although some dealers may say that they will consider work presented by any individual who appears at their doorstep, it is suggested that instances where artists have found dealers in that manner are probably few. And it is obvious that one does not choose a dealer as one would a physician or lawyer; there is the aspect of mutual appreciation which must exist before a gallery will take on an artist, especially an unknown one. Paradoxically, then, you must make yourself known in some way to draw the attention of the dealer in the first instance. You should circulate within the art community, associate with other artists, cultivate relationships with critics, writers, curators, academics and others with contacts and influence in the art world. It is perhaps not too optimistic or naive to suggest that the talented artist will ultimately be discovered by a dealer who recognizes the merit of his/her work, but only if that work has become known to the extent necessary to interest professionals in the art community.

The Artist/Gallery/Dealer Contract

Because of the unique and sensitive nature of the relationship between artist and dealer, and perhaps also because, with some notable exceptions, the artist traditionally has had little bargaining power, it is more often than not the case that arrangements between artist and dealer are oral rather than written. This does not mean that the parties are without rights and obligations or that the artist is necessarily oppressed by the dealer. Despite the widespread lack of use of written contracts in this context, the parties do function within the limits of legal responsibility, assuming the relationship is a viable, productive one. If it is not, then no written contract is going to keep the parties together, prevent acrimony or even adequately compensate an injured party for damages arising out of a dispute. Indeed, one established Los Angeles dealer has said that he has written agreements with his artists except two of them, and it is they whom he trusts the most and with whom he has had the most successful partnerships based on mutual trust and benefit rather than written contract. (See examples and analyses of artist/gallery agreements in the Contracts section of this Manual.)

Agreements between artists and dealers should, at the very least, cover the following issues:

Commission to be paid gallery The standard commission split is currently 40%/60%, although this term is certainly negotiable and may vary according to the relative fame of the artist, the length of time the work(s) remains with the dealer, the nature of the artist and other factors.

Term of agreement When the relationship between artists and dealers is good, it can span years, even lifetimes. When artists are unknown, a considerable period of time is needed to develop a market for their work. Yet it is still advisable to be precise about the minimum length of time the artist's work will remain with the gallery. And, in any event, the manner in which the agreement may be terminated by either party should be articulated, including the method and timing of the return of the work to the artist.

Terms of payment and record keeping   Some mechanism should be agreed upon to handle payment to the artist after sale including the time for payment and the accounting of receipts. The gallery's books and records should be subject to review by the artist at reasonable times and places.

Exclusivity   It is obvious that a dealer will want the greatest degree of exclusivity he/she can extract from the artist; and probably such is advantageous to the artist as well, as it follows that the gallery is going to invest more time, energy and money into selling if competition with other dealers is eliminated. Although there is at least one prominent L.A. gallery which does not use written agreements and just "assumes" exclusivity, it is still preferable to discuss the issue since exclusivity can be relative—it can mean a metropolitan area, west or east of the Rockies, national or international.

Control over style of exhibition   Although some galleries demand complete control over the manner in which shows are set up and individual works displayed, it would seem advisable for the galleries and artists to work together. In any event, the decision about control should be agreed upon prior to exhibition.

Expenses   There are several categories of expenses which are attendant to the gallery/artist relationship:

  transportation of works
  exhibition
  marketing advertising
  insurance, if available

If a dealer is granted complete exclusivity and can rely on a continuity of representation over a long term, then it is not unreasonable to expect that all expenses will be borne by that dealer. The amount of the commission will also bear on this issue, as will the nature of the artwork. Furthermore, the nature and extent of the advertising should be discussed as there is a wide range of advertising options available.

Setting of retail prices   In addition to the issue of the regular retail prices of works for sale, there is the question of whether and to what extent certain buyers will receive discounts, e.g., major collectors whose business is coveted by both galleries and artists.

Copyright protection   If there is one matter which should be reduced to writing, it is the artist's right to copyright protection (fully discussed elsewhere in this Manual), which should be acknowledged, at the very least, on the bill of sale.

  The foregoing terms apply to the typical situation of the print, painting or sculpture marketed by a dealer. In these days of concept, performance and electronic art, among other art forms, the division of income may vary; if an artist gives a one-time performance or screens a videotape at a gallery the fee arrangement would differ from the typical 40/60 split when a painting or other object is sold.

THE ARTIST/REPRESENTATIVE RELATIONSHIP

Purpose

Although the fine artist is certainly not averse to being financially compensated for his/her work, there are other, perhaps more important factors which motivate him/her. The commercial artist, on the other hand, is primarily concerned with selling the work which will then be used to sell a product to the public. Because marketing is a full-time job in itself and requires particular aptitude and expertise, the representative/agent is crucial to the commercial artist's success. (It should be noted that there are some artists who represent themselves in the marketplace, though increasingly most do not.)

The goal of the representative (hereinafter "rep") is to sell the work of the artist, to encourage repeat business with existing clients and to motivate new business. Thus the rep "packages" the product by getting the portfolio in selling condition, shows the product to all possible prospective customers and promotes and advertises the product. Further, a good rep attempts to obtain the highest price possible for the work; that is, if an art director has a budget range of $3,000–$5,000 for artwork, the rep will endeavor to obtain the high side of the budget. Finally, the rep negotiates what the fee includes: e.g., reproduction rights or "buy-outs."

Because the rep is intimately involved with the financial survival and success of the artist on an ongoing, daily basis, it happens that a rep may become a financial or business manager. The personal manager is concerned with the total career of the artist rather than just marketing a particular product. Although the line between strictly repping and managing may not always be clear, it is safe to say that one major difference is that the manager will participate in the making of major career decisions.

How to Find the Rep

The following is a partial list of directories of artist and photographer reps:
AMERICAN SHOWCASE, 724 Fifth Avenue, New York,
NY 10010 (national list of reps by geographical area)
L.A. WORKBOOK, 1640 Lindenhurst Avenue, Los Angeles, CA 90048 (list of L.A. reps)
THE BLACK BOOK, Friendly Publications, 80 Irving Place, New York, NY 10003
(sourcebook: consult individual ads)
THE FREELANCER, 4407 Holland, Suite B, Dallas,
TX 75219 (Dallas/Fort Worth showcase: consult individual ads)
CHICAGO TALENT, 310 Melvin, Suite 14, North
Brook, Chicago, IL 60062 (Chicago showcase: consult individual ads)
THE BOOK, P.O. Box 749, Westport, CT 06880 (New
England sourcebook; consult individual ads and talent listing)

It is also suggested that you contact art directors directly to inquire about whom they would recommend. Since the art directors are probably impartial critics, if they think the rep is doing a good job selling, then it is likely that the rep will do a good job representing you. In addition, you should ask other artists about their experience with and/or knowledge of reps in the community.

The Artist/Rep Contract

Because there are special aspects peculiar to the marketing of photography, the discussion of contracts between photographers and reps and agencies will be treated separately below.

Just as with dealers and galleries, there are some artists and reps who operate without written contracts. Whether oral or written, the basic terms of the agreement between artist and rep should include:

Fee arrangement   The standard commission is 25% of the creative fee, that is, the fee paid to the artist. However, some adjustment may be warranted for out-of-town business due to increased costs. And when the rep functions as a business manager his/her fee should reflect the increase in responsibility and time investment.

Term of agreement   There are several issues you should consider with respect to the term of the agreement:

Should the rep receive a fee for work generated before and during the term if it is the artist who acquires it?

Should the rep be compensated for fees paid to the artist after the agreement is terminated? If so, for what period? One local rep uses a 90-day post-termination clause, while periods as long as 6 months, or longer, depending on the length of the relationship, are not unheard of.

Month-to-month terms—that is, termination by request of one party at any time on 30 days' notice—are used often because they ensure flexibility and mutual satisfaction.

Billing and payment procedures   It is imperative that billing and payment procedures be precisely defined and scrupulously followed.

Exclusivity   The discussion above relating to galleries is equally applicable here.

Expenses   No commission should be paid to the rep for expenses which are charged to the client. The artists and reps generally cover their own expenses: the artist pays for his/her studio rental, telephone, art supplies, messengers; the rep pays for his/her office, travel, telephone, entertainment. Promotional expenses, however, should be shared in some fashion between the parties.

For Photographers Only

The photographer has the option of having his/her work marketed by an individual and/or a stock agency. The rep secures jobs for the photographer, while the stock agency handles the work of numerous photographers in bulk for the purpose of licensing the use of existing photographs. Because of the basic differences between the rep and the stock agency, contract terms will differ between them.

Compensation   The agency will usually garner 50% for black-and-white and color photos, while the rep, as with his/her arrangements with other commercial artists, usually charges 25%.

Grant of agency authority and rep's territory   Since the agency deals with specific material, it follows that it should have exclusivity in connection with that material for the geographical area in which it operates. As a corollary, agencies will request that dupes, similars and future stock materials not be placed elsewhere. In addition, since the successful photographer may have more than one rep, their territories should be precisely delineated.

Usage   It is important to distinguish between the right to sell versus the right to lease as to both agencies and reps. Loose language could result in the artist's giving up all reproduction rights to the agency or rep. Also, limitations may be stated with regard to time period or specific uses. In any event, all rights not granted should be reserved to the artist.

Loss or damage and return of black-and-white prints   Agencies and reps will not agree to be liable for loss or damage to photographs since the risk is not insurable. Further, since it is not uncommon for clients to lose or misplace black-and-white prints, the photographer should, whenever possible, retain master prints and provide the agency or rep with copies or repro prints. If master prints are required, the client should bear the cost of their loss or damage.

Term of agreement and return of photos after termination   As with galleries, stock agencies need a substantial period of time to develop a market for their material; thus contract terms are generally several years in length. In addition, they require considerable time to return material to photographers upon termination of the agreement, because of the volume of material they retain in their files. Agreements with reps, on the other hand, can more easily be of shorter duration; immediate termination upon request is quite common.

Warranties re authenticity   Both the stock agency and the rep should be entitled to rely on the authenticity of the work and other information regarding its origin and content. However, inadvertent inaccuracies should not result in liability on the part of the photographer for damages sustained by the agency or rep.

Post-termination sales and house accounts   The use of duplicate material after the termination of the agreement between photographer and agency should be carefully treated so as to ensure that if such use takes place, the photographer is compensated, and the agency has the right to demand return of the material.

With respect to compensation paid to photographers after termination of a rep agreement, generally the rep is entitled to some compensation based on past efforts to secure or solidify the account. Commissions from house accounts—accounts which the photographer established prior to the relationship—are generally at a lower rate than new accounts. The treatment of commissions from post-termination sales and house accounts can be tailor-made to suit the parties and the equities involved.

Again, refer to the Contracts section of this Manual for a more detailed discussion of contracts between commercial artists and reps/agencies.

THE ARTIST/ACCOUNTANT RELATIONSHIP

It is apparent that there are numerous contractual terms confronting both fine and commercial artists which require financial expertise in order to ensure that they are executed correctly and expeditiously. Further, all artists must pay taxes, whether federal, state or local, and must be familiar with estate and gift and sales tax concepts. (Please refer to other articles in the Manual that deal with these important areas of concern.) Thus the accountant is an important professional who must be chosen carefully and with whom the artist must work closely so as to maximize the financial benefit to be derived from his/her work. To best serve the accountant, it is essential to keep neat, complete and accurate records for documentation purposes, particularly with respect to the IRS.

There are numerous accountancy firms in various urban centers. Of these, some do represent arts-related entities and individual artists.

THE ARTIST/LAWYER RELATIONSHIP

The lawyer provides many and various services to the fine and commercial artist alike, including:

1. Negotiation and explanation of contracts between artists and other professionals, between artists and suppliers, between artists and other artists
2. Explanation and protection of basic artistic-legal rights such as copyright, resale royalty, constitutional
3. Basic income tax planning in conjunction with accountants and/or business managers
4. General advice regarding real estate transactions, landlord-tenant disputes, banking relationships, trusts, wills, general business planning
5. General career guidance

To find a competent, interested lawyer, you, like anyone else, can inquire of others whose opinions you value, and use referral services associated with local bar associations. In addition, there are bar organizations whose sole purpose is to serve artists, such as Bay Area Lawyers for the Arts and the Committee for the Arts of the Beverly Hills Bar Association.

Once the lawyer is selected by the artist, the question of fees must be resolved. Lawyers will often require a written fee agreement and an initial retainer (payment). The type of fee arrangement is related to the nature of the work to be done. Whatever the fee arrangement, the artist as client is entitled to a complete accounting of time spent by the lawyer and explanation of the services rendered. On the other hand, the lawyer is entitled to prompt payment upon receipt of statement.

A talented artist's career can only be enhanced by the support of competent professionals. Thus the choice of these experts is of major importance. Once the decision is made, clear and precise guidelines for conduct between the parties should be agreed upon. And remember, you should allow the professional the space to accomplish the stated goals of the relationship. Finally (and this does occasionally happen), if your relationship with the rep, gallery, accountant, lawyer or the like breaks down, work out an orderly dissolution to cut down any financial losses you might suffer, and move on to another professional better suited to help the entrepreneurial side of your career.

CHAPTER TWO
CONTRACTS: GET IT IN WRITING

Compiled by Susan A. Grode, Esq., and Debra L. Fink, Esq.

A publisher makes an offer to do a print edition, prints and sells certain pieces that the artist insists are off register and are of inferior quality. A company art director asks for a slide presentation of designs which the artist submits at a cost of $50.00 for slides, binders and postage. The slides are never returned and the artist later discovers her modified designs decorating the company's most popular products. A patron commissions a portrait/sculpture or photographic study. The sculptor or photographer submits his maquette or proofs for approval and discovers that the patron has lost interest and refuses to pay. A painter executes a massive mural for an office building and later discovers that the mural is to be demolished along with the building.

The visual artist who puts his/her work into the stream of commerce must know how to deal with the business and professional relationships surrounding that work, as well as the potential effects on both artist and work at every stage, even before the creative process has begun. Traditionally, visual artists have relied solely on verbal agreements with galleries, museums, art directors, publishers, purchasers, managers, agents and representatives. But generally such oral understandings lack sufficient detail to constitute a binding contract. More importantly, and all too often, artists unknowingly relinquish important rights and fail to take precautions against injury to themselves, their work and their reputations because they have neglected or forgone the right to the security of a written agreement.

The graphic artist could have requested *written* aesthetic and technical approval of the print edition as a condition of the publisher being able to sell it. The designer could have placed copyright notices on all slides and required a delivery invoice, *signed* by the company (noting the copyright and a prohibition against reproduction), requiring payment for each slide if not returned within a specific time period. The sculptor/photographer could have insisted that the patron *sign* an agreement detailing approvals and payments at each stage of the work. The painter could have prepared a *written agreement* providing that in the event of alteration (painting, redecorating) or destruction of the building, the owner could not paint over or mutilate the mural and that the painter would have the right to remove the mural itself.

Negotiations often take place sporadically over relatively long periods of time, often among many participants, with numerous changes in both the general and specific terms of commitment. It is unlikely, then, that both parties to an agreement will, at any time, have the same recollection and understanding of exactly what the "final terms" of their agreement actually are. It is therefore advisable in most situations to use some form of written document: letter, memorandum, notice, short-form agreement, attorney-drafted contract. When it is not possible to determine all the details before the contract is signed, state *in the agreement itself* that the details included are preliminary and provide that within a certain period of time after signing the agreement, the parties will develop a mutually agreed-upon plan.

A contract may be simply defined as a legally enforceable agreement between two or more parties. It may be oral and it may even be implied by the circumstances (each party fulfilling substantial independent obligations as though an agreement actually existed).

A *written contract,* whether informal correspondence or formally prepared, accomplishes the following:

1. Reduces the risk of misunderstanding by providing a written record describing relationships, rights and responsibilities.
2. Provides a ready reference for settling disputes concerning the intention of each party at the time the contract was executed.
3. Often specifies the procedure to resolve any controversy arising out of the agreement (see sample arbitration clause in this section).
4. Encourages cooperation.
5. Provides tangible, reliable and convincing evidence when attempting to enforce the agreement in court.

In the following Contracts section you will find a variety of "suggested" agreements and forms. Although the materials may be labeled for specific purposes or types of visual art, they can be adapted for use in other situations. You or your attorney must judge whether a particular form or agreement meets your individual needs and how it can be modified to suit them.

Knowledge increases bargaining power! Most of the documents included have been annotated to explain their terms and provisions and to illustrate pitfalls to avoid as well as modifications you should try to obtain in negotiations. If your bargaining position is not sufficient to demand a formally drafted legal document, compose a shorter, less formal agreement. If that doesn't work, write a letter and have it signed as "agreed to and accepted" by both parties. Invoices and printed forms, work orders and project sheets, bills of sale and consignment receipts—all can be used as binding written agreements.

The investment you make in your art is considerable in terms of time, money and emotion. It is up to you to protect it . . . in writing.

ARTIST/REPRESENTATIVE AND ARTIST/GALLERY CONTRACTS

The following agreements illustrate well-thought-out professional contracts between artists and their representatives. Each is tailored to the needs of an "agency" relationship in a specific area of the visual arts and each is annotated to explain the meaning of and the reasons for each point of agreement between the parties.

As noted throughout this Manual, these agreements cannot replace consultation with an attorney and should be used only as information and reference when negotiating or preparing your own contract. Nor can these samples replace adequate investigation of and discussions with the representative prior to signing any agreement.

ILLUSTRATOR/DESIGNER/PHOTOGRAPHER AND REPRESENTATIVE AGREEMENT

Comments and Annotations by Jae Wagoner and Ron Bakal, Esq.

The purpose of this Agreement is to provide a clear working arrangement and a fair method of termination of this Agreement between the Illustrator/Designer/Photographer (hereafter referred to as Artist) and the Representative. The particular Agreement is between:

ARTIST: _____

REPRESENTATIVE: _____

1. The Representative will receive 25% commission on work for clients in town and 30% commission on work for clients out of town. The Representative will pay her own out-of-town travel expenses. The Representative will take a full commission on all work that originates in the Representative's assigned geographic territory that is produced by the Artist and is not written on the House Account list which follows. This commission will be taken on all fees resulting from this artwork including the sale of the original artwork itself whether these fees are negotiated all at one time or over a period of time unless the Artist and Representative have terminated their working agreement and a settlement to the Representative has been made.

Comment: This clause clarifies the representative's commission. This is a standard commission percentage. The reason a rep asks for 30% commission on out-of-town work is that the expenses are higher: telephone, delivery, etc. The rep, whenever possible, tries to get the client to pay the delivery costs on out-of-town jobs, but there is often travel time, additional telephone, promotional mailings and portfolio material delivery costs involved.

If the artist is located out of town, the commission is usually a straight 30% on all work so that the rep can recoup long-distance calls and delivery to the artist.

The phrase "out of town" should be defined. For instance, Los Angeles and Orange County might fairly be described as "in town" in a contract written in Los Angeles.

There is no "law" that the representative's commission should be 25%. Although it is the most common fee charge, an artist in high demand may get a representative to work for 15% to 20%.

There is also a statement made which refers to making commission on all sales resulting after the first sale. Artwork may be commissioned originally for one-time use. Later the client may come back and purchase additional usage and even a long time later ask to purchase the artwork for display, or the same artwork may be sold for a greeting card to a different company, or sold in a gallery. This clause clarifies that the rep is entitled to commission on all revenues resulting from any sale anytime if the artwork is one on which she is entitled to initial commission, unless the artist and rep are no longer working together and have made a settlement according to the later terms of this agreement.

2. The Artist reserves the following clients as House Accounts to be exclusive to him without compensation to the Representative. House Accounts may be turned over to the Representa-

tive under specified conditions and a partial commission paid to her. When full commission is paid, the account is no longer a House Account.

Comment: HOUSE ACCOUNTS

The term "house accounts" should be more specifically defined. For example: all those accounts which are listed by the artist prior to the execution of the agreement as those on which no commission is to be paid the representative.

Some reps expect an artist to turn over all existing accounts to them with the rationale that the artist needs their services totally or not at all.

Other reps do not care if the artist keeps a few long-standing accounts that he has worked to establish. Some reps stipulate in their contracts (not this contract) that house accounts must be active, as in at least one assignment worked on in the last year. Sometimes the artist is happy to relinquish the account at a later date to the rep so the client is better serviced. However, if the artist has a long local list of house accounts that he wishes to keep to himself and for other artists, the representative may decline to represent the artist because the artist does not seem seriously in need of the rep's services and the rep may end up in competition with the artist for certain clients. Another consideration from the rep's point of view is that if the artist has a long list of house accounts, his time may be so booked up he will be turning away the rep's jobs in favor of his own accounts. If the rep does not have a fair chance to make money with an artist there is little reason to represent him.

3. The Representative will actively show the Artist's work and pursue new business. All referrals and leads coming to the Artist directly, and not listed under House Accounts or otherwise restricted under this Agreement, will be turned over to the Representative. The Representative will pursue, negotiate, pick up (when appropriate), provide written Assignment Confirmation forms for (as required), invoice, collect sales tax, and receive full commission therefrom.

Comment: This explains what the rep's responsibilities are. Note that this rep will pick up the job "when appropriate." Sometimes the client may insist on explaining the job to the artist or it may be a rush job and the rep may be booked solid and unable to pick up the job and it may be lost.

Representatives are not lawyers and/or accountants and the artist should not presume that they will handle either legal or accounting problems for the artist in conjunction with the handling of his work.

The clause referring to the artist turning over all leads is important because some artists feel if the call comes directly to them the rep had nothing to do with it. It is impossible to trace where a rep's promotion of an artist stops. Even if the rep has no traceable connection to the job, the account is hers to pursue if it is not listed under house accounts. The rep is entitled to income only on the jobs that come in. Therefore, it is reasonable she lose no opportunity to earn a living.

4. The Artist will be responsible for delivery of the interim sketches and the final artwork unless the Representative's assistance is needed (but the Representative is not to be considered a messenger).

Comment: Some reps pick up and deliver all phases of the job to both the artist and the client, especially if they are new and have fewer jobs and more time. Others pick up the work and have the artist come to their offices to get the work and return it to them so the rep can deliver it to the client. Some reps pick up the work and the artist does the legwork from then on (as in this case). There are endless variations regarding delivery. The most important issue is that the client must be serviced well and that the arrangement between the rep and the artist must be flexible enough to allow for prompt pickup and delivery. Reps more and more are resisting being a delivery service, as it interferes with time allocated to pursuing new business, which is the rep's most important function. This clause seems flexible, as the rep seems to be open to assisting, if needed.

5. The Artist does not discuss or agree to a price or terms of a job without consulting the Representative first.

Comment: This clause is very important because if the rep is not available or the artist is consulted first on a job and agrees to any terms, the rep may not have a chance to get the top fair price. The rep may have information on pricing and usage that the artist is unaware of or may have already discussed the work with the client and the client is trying to get a different deal (usually less favorable for the artist) through the artist. As mentioned before, artists need to support their rep's position as negotiator to the fullest because clients who insist on speaking to the artist directly about the business end (not the art end) when they know the artist has a rep, usually have a hidden agenda.

6. If the Artist actively pursues new work in competition with the Representative contrary to the terms as stated in this Agreement, the Artist is automatically put on thirty (30) days' notice and all the termination procedures will begin to apply.

Comment: This clause makes clear the rep does not intend to compete with her artist in obtaining work for the artist. If an artist is in a slow period and takes his own portfolio out, he may be going to clients already serviced by the rep, thereby weakening the rep's (and the artist's) position with the client. If an assignment or project results from the artist showing his own work, for whatever reason (a legitimate reason for an artist to show his own book would be if his rep is on vacation), the rep is still entitled to full commission. The artist should always inform his rep of these situations beforehand, if possible. Complete candor between artist and rep makes for a long-lasting, trusting relationship.

7. The Representative will solicit work for the Artist to the best of her ability in the following areas:

GEOGRAPHIC TERRITORY OF THE REPRESENTATIVE

FIELDS OF WORK IN WHICH TO REPRESENT THE ARTIST

Comment: Examples of geographic territories are: all states west of the Rocky Mountains, California only, the United States, Los Angeles, Orange and San Diego counties only.

This is especially important if the artist has more than one rep. Some have two or three in the United States, so geographic boundaries should be clearly defined.

Examples of "fields of work" are: commercial photography (not stock photography), illustration (not graphic design), movie poster illustration (not editorial illustration).

It is important for the artist to realize that the more he restricts his rep, the less business he can expect. A thorough discussion should be held on these two areas. A good rep will not take on territories or fields of work she is unwilling or unable to actively pursue.

8. During the term of this Agreement, the Artist agrees not to use any other Representative in the same geographic locations or fields of work.

Comment: This clause makes the rep's territory and fields of work listed above exclusively hers.

9. The Artist will provide updated portfolio material of acceptable format on a regular basis. It will be the Artist's responsibility to pick up artwork and tear sheets from the client, for the portfolio and promotional purposes, after an assignment is completed.

Comment: If the rep shows her other artists' work in slide form or laminated printed pieces or 8 × 10 transparencies, then "acceptable format" would mean the new artist would provide the same. It is very important, no matter how busy the artist gets, that he keep the rep supplied with new samples. It is most logical for the artist to get the samples from the client after a job is completed because he can keep track of his own work better than the rep, who may represent many people and is handling dozens of clients at the same time.

10. The Artist will provide promotional material on a regular basis, no less than once a year, with the Representative's name and phone number on it. On mass mailings of promotional materials to clients, the Artist shall pay 75% of the costs incurred and the Representative shall pay 25%.

Comment: New promotional material is essential in marketing talent. It is appropriately professional to advertise that you have a rep (and that all new business must go to the rep anyway), so the rep's name and phone number are essential. If promotional material is in a catalogue or reference book form reps pay a percentage of the page fee. Some reps pay 25% of the page fee and the artist 75% (or whatever their standard fee breakdown percentage is). Sometimes the rep prefers to deal with this on an individual basis rather than putting it in the contract, i.e., the artist may decide to go into the *Black Book,* which is national, and the rep's territory may be limited to California, so the rep would want to negotiate this out of contract with the artist each time a catalogue opportunity comes up.

The cost of mass promotional mailings is prohibitive, therefore the standard 25%/75% breakdown again.

11. The Representative will exercise great care in the handling and safekeeping of all portfolio materials left with her. However, the Representative will not be financially responsible for loss or damage of the portfolios in her care. To prevent undue loss the Artist will keep all original artwork and will provide the Representative with duplicates or reproductions only.

> *Comment:*   It is next to impossible for representatives to insure work that does not belong to them. It is up to the artist to do so. No artist should show or allow his rep to show original artwork, if possible. There are countless horror stories of theft, accidentally spilled coffee, fire damage, rain or flood damage and other acts of God that have destroyed irreplaceable transparencies and original artwork. Better safe than sorry.
>
> It may be advisable for the rep and artist to take out a personal property insurance policy to protect against lost or damaged materials. The premium should be paid in the same proportion as the fee arrangement (75% by the artist and 25% by the rep).

12. The Representative will provide invoicing and collecting (including sales tax) services for the Artist and will pay the Artist on receipt of the monies after the checks have cleared the bank. If collection or legal fees are involved in the resolving of the client nonpayment, the Representative will pay 25% of the fee and the Artist will pay 75% of the fee for those services.

> *Comment:*   Most professional reps do all the billing so that they can make sure that the prices charged are those negotiated, that the proper sales tax has been added, that the correct conditions of rights and usage and who owns the original work are stated on the invoice. Prompt, professional billing by the rep provides greater control of accounts (including follow-ups on late payment and return of original artwork), which increases the likelihood that the artist will be paid on time. As stated here, the rep should not be required to pay the artist before the checks have cleared. International and out-of-state checks take a long time.

13. The Artist and the Representative must have valid state resale sales tax numbers.

> *Comment:*   Artwork and photography are usually taxable under state law, and both the artist (for his house accounts) and the representative must have valid sales tax licenses in order for the state to allow them to do business.

14. The Artist has the right of approval on fees and assignments and may refuse any assignment before it has begun.

> *Comment:*   The representative is only the agent. The artist should have the final say-so on any job *before* it begins. However, once the work is in progress the artist must continue on the terms as agreed in order to ensure good working relations with the client and so that future work is not jeopardized.

15. The Representative does not acquire any rights to the Artist's work, and will return it promptly on demand.

Comment: Only the artist owns his original artwork (unless the client has purchased it). The rep must return any work the artist requests to have back. The rep, however, does make a commission if the artwork is sold (see clause 1 of this contract). The representative does not have a 25% interest in the copyright to the works of the artist, but merely an interest in receiving a fee for the sale of its uses or a fee for the outright sale of the work (as in a "for hire" contract where the artist conveys the copyright to a third party). The representative has no control of the artwork regarding modifications or changes in it, although some knowledgeable representatives may be very contributive and helpful critics.

16. The Artist and the Representative are independent contractors and their relationship is not that of a joint venture or employer/employee.

Comment: Neither the artist nor the representative is the other's employer and should not treat the other as an employee. Each runs his own business in his own way and their relationship is governed only by this mutual agreement. This clause should also make clear that this relationship is not a partnership.

17. If the Representative or the Artist should die, any monies due either party will go to the heir listed below:

ARTIST'S HEIR: _____

ADDRESS: _____

REPRESENTATIVE'S HEIR: _____

ADDRESS: _____

Comment: This is an important clause. If death occurs and any money is outstanding it is important to know to whom and where to send it.

18. This Agreement is personal between the parties and is unassignable.

Comment: This agreement cannot be turned over from one rep to another or from one artist to another. It is between only the parties who are signing it.

19. This Agreement constitutes the entire understanding between the parties and no modifications will be valid unless made in writing and signed by both parties.

Comment: Any verbal agreement which is a modification or change should be written down, signed by both parties and added to this agreement.

20. This Agreement will be interpreted in accordance with the laws of the State of _____.

Comment: If a rep handles an artist who lives out of state, this clause stipulates that this agreement will be bound by the laws of the state in which the contract has been executed and not the state the artist may live in.

21. This Agreement will terminate thirty (30) days after receipt of written notice of termination given by either party, subject to the following terms.

(a) The Representative will receive her full commission for six (6) months after the termination notice on all the jobs she is entitled to under this Agreement. Commissions to be paid within the six (6) month time period shall include work that has been completed prior to termination notice and not yet paid, and work that is started or completed within the time period whether the fee has been collected by the end of that six (6) month period or not.

(b) The Artist agrees to continue to work with the Representative during the six (6) month termination period unless a cash settlement is made to the Representative.

(c) Any controversy or claim arising out of or related to this contract or the breach of this contract shall be settled by arbitration in the City and State in which it was executed, if mutually agreed upon by both parties, within thirty (30) days after demand for arbitration is received by either party. A settlement will be made before a jointly selected, single arbitrator, the Graphic Artists Guild's Arbitration Board, or other appropriate board, and upon such terms as then agreed upon. In either instance the award rendered may be entered in any court having jurisdiction thereof.

(d) If litigation becomes necessary (as a last resort after arbitration has been completed) to settle any disputes between the two parties, the loser of the suit will pay all attorneys' fees.

(e) An optional cash settlement can be made to the Representative of an agreed-upon amount reflecting the estimated work which might be expected in that six (6) month period and additional fees from resale of artwork usage or sale of the original artwork that may reasonably occur during that time period. This settlement would complete this Agreement and no additional money would be paid the Representative except for the monies due her for work previously billed and not yet collected.

(f) Notice will be given to the Artist at: _____

_____

(g) Notice will be given to the Representative at: _____

_____

_____

Comment: A thirty-day termination notice is necessary because it allows all current business to be wrapped up, and it gives both parties time to mutually decide whether a cash settlement or six months of continued work is acceptable.

(a) This clause explains that when the six-month termination period is over, what is terminated is any business dealings between the artist and the rep and by the rep on behalf of the artist, with the *exception* of the collecting of fees which are outstanding. The rep is still entitled to a commission from these fees if they were earned during the agreement, even if they are collected after the end of the final date of termination.

(b) There have been cases where an artist refused to make a cash settlement with the rep after terminating and also refused all new work, including jobs which had been arranged for and agreed to, thus causing the rep loss of earned income. The phrase "agrees to continue to work with" should be more clearly spelled out to reflect the fact that the artist, during the six-month period, will cooperate in completing work accepted prior to termination and maintain the usual business relationship with the agent regarding that work.

(c) This clause is aimed at preventing costly litigation and providing an *objec-*

tive outside arbitrator or use of established arbitration boards in the community who can provide a fair method of settlement. The non-prevailing party should pay the costs of litigation, attorneys' fees and/or arbitration.

(d) A reason for litigation after arbitration would be if one of the parties was awarded certain monies through arbitration and refused to pay and the other party had to sue to collect.

(e) If the artist has to move or if the artist and rep no longer wish to have any contact with each other this clause assures a quick separation and solution regarding any future money disbursement. Because this settlement terminates this agreement immediately, it releases the artist from six months of commissions to the rep on new work or work not yet completed as of the termination date (see paragraph b above).

(f) and (g) It's important to establish in writing (not just a phone call) that this agreement is being terminated as of a particular date (month, day and year).

22. This Agreement is accepted by:

ARTIST	DATE
REPRESENTATIVE	DATE
CITY	STATE

ARTIST/GALLERY CONSIGNMENT AGREEMENT[1] (Short Form)

Comments and annotations by Mark E. Halloran, Esq.

Between _____
　　　　　　　　　　　(Artist)　　　　　　　　　(Address)

and _____
　　　　　　　　　　(Gallery)　　　　　　　　　(Address)

To begin on _____ and to end on _____

TERMS OF AGREEMENT

This is a short-form agreement. Use it when all else fails in obtaining a formal contract tailored to your situation. In California and some other states you have the added power of artist/dealer relations laws which provide substantial protection for the artist when art is consigned. (See Legislation section in this Manual.)

[1] © N.Y./AEA 1979. Prepared by the New York Artists Equity Association as an Art Community Service.

1.   DURATION: The Artist agrees to be represented by _____
_____ for a period of _____ years at which time the arrangement automatically terminates UNLESS extended by mutual agreement in writing. The Gallery will have exclusive representation of the Artist's work in _____.

(City, Region)

Comment: This clause goes beyond "duration" of the agreement. It sets up the basic agency relationship of the artist and gallery. The gallery is the artist's agent, that is, the gallery represents the artist to potential buyers. The gallery is also "exclusive" in the elected area. As the artist's agent, the gallery has additional legal duties and must always act in the artist's best interest.

2.   OWNERSHIP: All works left in the Gallery on Consignment shall remain the sole property of the Artist until sold and the Artist's share is remitted by the Gallery in FULL. In the event of the Artist's death this agreement reverts to the Artist's survivors *on demand.*

Within this period the Gallery shall arrange and promote (a) a SOLO EXHIBITION of _____ weeks' duration; (b) the Gallery shall provide exhibiting exposure in GROUP SHOWS _____ times during this period.

Comment: We first run into the word "consignment" here. Consignment is the entrusting of goods to another, while keeping legal title, so that other persons may sell the goods for your benefit. This is a typical artist-gallery relationship, and is consistent with the language of the first sentence, which states the artist's work remains his or her property. Since legal title stays with the artist, the consigned works pass to the artist's survivors. This paragraph also sets minimum performance level for the gallery as far as solo exhibition and group shows. This is a good idea but an artist must have clout to get this provision. You might add that if a certain number of works are sold you will be entitled to a one-person exhibition within the next year from the date of the sale of the last work sold, or attempt to include a provision that the gallery must provide a one-person show after a specific period of representation has elapsed.

3.   TITLE: The Gallery shall not be entitled to make or assert any claim or right to any possessory liens against the property of the Artist for any cause whatsoever. Work on Consignment on the premises of the Gallery may not be open to any claim by the Gallery's creditors and continues to remain the sole property of the Artist (or Estate) unless paid for in full.

Comment: The first sentence makes it clear that the gallery cannot assert any legal rights to the work of the artist. The second sentence says that the gallery's creditors cannot go after your work. In California, consigned works of art are exempt from creditors' claims by law. Unfortunately, in other states artists may find their gallery closing down and their artworks snatched up by creditors.

4.   SALES: The Gallery shall be responsible for the Sales price as mutually agreed upon

with the Artist. The Gallery shall, however, have the discretion to lower the agreed-upon price by not more than 10%, especially to museums and institutions.

Comment: The gallery is given the leeway to discount the mutually agreed-upon price by 10%. Add that the discount shall be borne by the gallery out of its commission, with a sharing of the discount only in the event of a sale to a museum.

5. COMMISSION: The Artist and the Gallery agree on commission of _____% on all sales generated by the Gallery's efforts, whether on its premise, or, from the Artist's studio. Prizes and Awards are not subject to Gallery's commission.

Comment: The standard consignment percentage in Los Angeles is 33% to 60% of the retail price of the work. Commissions can vary with the status of the gallery (profit or nonprofit), status of the artist and length of their relationship.

6. PAYMENTS: All payments must be made within 30 days of an individual sale, or within 30 days of the termination of a Solo Exhibition. All credit verification is the sole responsibility of the Gallery.

Comment: Thirty days is fair—the gallery should not have the use of your money for a long time. This clause does point to a potentially sticky problem—credit sales. Even though the gallery has the responsibility to verify credit, what if a credit buyer doesn't pay? Also, you should note that if the buyer pays in installments, under California law the gallery may not take a commission until the artist is paid in full.

7. EXPENSES (advertising, promotion, brochures, liability insurance, mailing, transportation, reception, delivery to Gallery, delivery to Buyer, etc.):

The following expenses shall be borne by the GALLERY:

1. _____ 2. _____
3. _____ 4. _____

The following expenses shall be borne by the ARTIST:

1. _____ 2. _____
3. _____ 4. _____

The following expenses shall be SHARED by the Gallery and the Artist:

1. _____ 2. _____
3. _____ 4. _____

Comment: The majority of expenses should be borne by the gallery. The more established you are, the more willing the gallery will be to pick these up. If you are dealing with valuable items, such as works of art or originals of any type, liability insurance is crucial. Other costs are shipping, framing, installation, publicity and catalogues.

8. ACCOUNTS: (a) A semiannual record of sales shall be given the Artist by the Gallery

the first week in July; and an *Annual* statement not later than January 15 following the previous calendar year.

(b) A complete account of sales from a Solo show shall be given the Artist within 30 days after such exhibition and shall contain itemized record of payment *as well as* the names and addresses of each buyer.

> *Comment:* The timing of the statements is a bit tight, since the gallery has to render a semiannual account the first week after June 30 and the annual account by January 15. The solo show account includes the names and addresses of all buyers—the other statement should have the same information.

9. LIABILITY: The Gallery shall be responsible for theft, loss or damage, however caused while on the premises of the Gallery or in transit arranged by the Gallery. Proof of such insurance, carried at the expense of the Gallery, shall be supplied at the signing of this Agreement.

> *Comment:* Traditionally the gallery has assumed responsibility for theft of or damage to the artwork. This is now part of California law.

10. COPYRIGHT: Reproduction and Copyright rights remain exclusively with the Artist or his Estate.

> *Comment:* This clause makes it clear that the gallery is merely the sales agent and has no copyright rights. Actually, "reproduction" is redundant since copyright includes this right.

11. RETURN OF WORK: At the termination of this agreement all work not paid for shall be returned to the Artist as agreed. The Artist shall have the right to withdraw any work on demand unless it is on the walls of the Gallery as part of an exhibition.

> *Comment:* This clause makes it clear that all unsold work must be returned at the end of the agreement and that the gallery must return work during the agreement unless the work is exhibited on the wall.

12. CANCELLATION: Thirty days' notice in writing by either party may be provided in the contract by Mutual Agreement.

> *Comment:* This clause is ambiguous, as it states "may be provided." The contract should either state that the contract may be canceled by means of thirty days' written notice or not.

DATE:_____   _____
                        GALLERY

                        _____
                        ARTIST

CONTRACTS FOR EMPLOYMENT
by Paul D. Supnik, Esq.

Suppose you are an artist working for an advertising agency. Who owns the rights to designs which you create after hours? What if the designs are made during office hours but are not used by the agency? If you are a cartoonist hired only to ink cels and you develop cartoon characters during working hours, who owns the rights to these creations? Have you ever been "commissioned" to do a portrait? A mural? A sculpture? A monument? What if you are a photographer and you are commissioned to photograph a series for a photographic composite book. Do you retain rights of reproduction? Can an employment contract last indefinitely? Does an artist have any recourse against a "promoter"?

Artists frequently enter into employment agreements and related documents. These contracts may acquire or attempt to acquire from the artist rights to his creations. Some business relationships may have the same effect as a signed agreement even with no written papers. In other situations, a signed agreement may not be effective.

THE ARTIST AS INITIAL OWNER OF CREATIVE WORKS

Assume first that no business relationship exists, whether as employee or as commissioned artist, written agreement or otherwise. The copyright laws state that "copyright in a work [subject to the copyright laws] vests [i.e., is owned] initially in the author or authors of the work." Assume further that you own the materials used to create an artwork. Then (1) the actual original work itself and (2) the exclusive rights to reproduce and do all the other things that copyright allows are initially owned by you. That will not be true if the work is a "work made for hire."

It is often advantageous to avoid having your work become a work made for hire. If you own the copyright, you initially have many different rights in your work. These rights can be granted, licensed or sold, individually or collectively, in one medium or a plethora of media. Licenses may last for a limited period of time or may be concurrent with the copyright term. But you can attempt to base the sales price on the extent and variety of rights which are granted. Even if you assign the rights to the work now, many years in the future you may have the opportunity to terminate that assignment (which can be important if your work in later years becomes particularly valuable) under special provisions of the copyright law. Or you can retain all or some of the rights. But a work made for hire, if not properly limited, may take all rights away, including the right of termination.

WORKS MADE FOR HIRE

The copyright law gives the initial copyright ownership to *other than* the artist in certain situations, even in the absence of any agreement, contract or other oral or written statement. This may occur in the case of works made for hire. Thus the copyright law states:

> In the case of a work made for hire, the employer or other person for whom the work was prepared is considered the author [the word "author" has a broad meaning in the copyright law and can include "artist"] for purposes of this title [the author is the initial owner of copyright], and, unless the parties have expressly agreed otherwise in a written instrument signed by them [the employer or other person for whom the work was prepared] owns all of the rights comprised in the copyright.

This statement hasn't told us what a work made for hire is, but only tells who owns rights when a work made for hire exists.

Employed Artists

A work made for hire has a special meaning under the copyright law. A work made for hire exists in two situations. The first is where the artist is "employed." The law states:

> A work made for hire is—(1) a work prepared by an *employee* within the *scope of his or her employment* . . .

Sounds simple. But how do you know if you are an employee? Some of the following facts may give you clues as to whether you are truly an employee, but may not be the determining factors. Does your employer have the right to control the manner in which you work? What about the place where you work and the times that you work? Does the "employer" withhold income tax? Does he or she pay unemployment insurance and deduct disability and social security from your paycheck? If you can answer yes to all these questions, you are probably an employee within the meaning of the copyright law. But if you have difficulty answering some of these questions with a yes, it is possible that you may *not* be an employee within the meaning of this provision of the copyright law.

If you are not paid for your work, either for supposed employment or in the case of commissioned works, it may be possible that you have not lost ownership in the copyright in your work. The law on this subject is not clear, but it is arguable that either there was no true employment situation, in which case the work-made-for-hire doctrine would not apply, or that the failure to pay is a material breach of the contract, for which you are entitled to rescind the contract.

Not only must you be an *employee,* but the work must have been created within the *scope* of your employment. This is sometimes a difficult question to answer. Suppose you were hired to put together an exhibit and during work hours you created a painting. The painting might not be within the scope of employment and thus not a work made for hire owned by the employer.

What if the painting was made after hours? That might not be in the scope of employment. More difficult questions arise when using materials, time and supplies of the employer. In this situation, the employer may own the canvas and original artwork, but you would own the exclusive rights provided by the copyright laws, such as the right to reproduce the work and to license others to do so.

Commissioned Works

The copyright law provides a second basis for determining if a work is a work made for hire. Generally this involves certain specific *types* of commissioned works. The copyright law provides that a work made for hire is:

> . . . (2) a work *specially ordered or commissioned for use as* a contribution to a collective work, as a part of a collective work, as a part of a motion picture or other audiovisual work, as a translation, as a supplementary work, as a compilation, as an instructional text, as a test, as answer material for a test, or as an atlas, *if the parties* expressly agree in a written instrument *signed* by *them* that the work shall be considered a work made for hire. . . .

Note the various requirements. It must be specially ordered or commissioned. Thus a general agreement to create, but not for a specific purpose, may not fall within this definition of a work made for hire.

Note that the law specifies the words "for use as" before enumerating in detail specific categories of works. If the work is not specially ordered or commissioned for use as one of these types of work, it will not thereby become a work made for hire. Thus if you are a photographer or painter and take a photograph or do a painting of an individual, just for an individual, it will not be a work made for hire. But if the photograph or painting is for a book of photographs or reproductions of paintings, for example, it could become a work made for hire.

Of primary interest to artists are the first two categories specified in the Copyright Act.

A contribution to a collective work may be a painting for a multimedia work, a photograph for a book of photographs or perhaps some aspect of a performance piece. Thus if you are specially ordered or commissioned to create such a work for use as a contribution to a collective work, it may become a work made for hire, and you may not be the "author" or owner of the work.

A part of a motion picture or other audiovisual work may include set designs, photographs, drawings or other artistic aspects of a filmed or taped performance piece.

A supplementary work is defined in the Copyright Act as "a work prepared for publication as a secondary adjunct to a work by another author for the purpose of introducing, concluding, illustrating, explaining, revising, commenting upon, or assisting in the use of the other work, such as forewords, afterwords, pictorial illustrations, maps, charts, tables, editorial notes, musical arrangements, answer material for tests, bibliographies, appendixes and indexes . . ." It is possible that an illustration made for a book jacket or a record album cover could be a supplementary work.

The other specific areas of this act, of perhaps more limited interest to artists, are materials for teaching aids, texts, atlases and the like, which may involve the use of photographs, pictorial illustrations or drawings.

Work Made for Hire—There Must Be a Writing

Note that even if the commissioned or specially ordered work is one of the specific types of works set out in the copyright law, it does not automatically become a work made for hire. It only becomes a work made for hire if there is a *signed written* instrument expressly agreeing that the work shall be considered a work made for hire. The instrument must be signed by *both* the artist and the commissioning person or other commissioning entity. The paper does not have to be formal but must be written down. This has been somewhat of a change in the law to the benefit of the artist since the enactment of the new Copyright Act in 1976. Note that even if a work does not fall within one of the specified categories, if a writing is signed, it may be possible to effectuate a transfer of the copyright to the commissioning party.

Reserve Rights in Your Work-Made-for-Hire Agreement

As long as a written instrument has to be signed, the artist should consider reserving certain rights, such as the right to reproduce the works in other media or the right to reproduce after the commissioning party has had a specified period of time in which to attempt to exploit the work.

Work-made-for-hire agreements may look like routine paperwork. Some may be form contracts and some may be typeset. They can be found in the fine print of purchase orders and stamped on checks. They are frequently found in agreements with newspapers, magazines and the publishing industry but they may also appear in other areas. Photographers have paved the way in negotiating around and out of work-made-for-hire agreements. Try to limit the scope of work-made-for-hire agreements. For example, suppose you wish to use a mark to promote yourself. If you signed a work-made-for-hire agreement, you may need to seek permission to use that work from your former employer. The employer should not have any need to acquire these rights and it should not be too difficult for the artist to negotiate for them. Try to split out or withhold rights for specific purposes and take these out of the work-made-for-hire agreement. The artist's argument is that if the commissioning party does not need the rights, why not let the artist have them? If you are able to carve out rights from a work-made-for-hire agreement, make a very good archival copy of the work. Otherwise, in the future, you will have a difficult time making quality reproductions of the work for other purposes.

The justification for the laws relating to works made for hire are based on the following reasons. In the case of employment, the rationale is that the employer risks the funds, environment and working arrangement and pays the artist and therefore the employer should own the rights in the work. This has greater justification in a large business environment.

In the case of specially commissioned works, the categories specified by the law typically involve group or team situations, such as with respect to motion pictures. It is burdensome to attempt to separately secure rights from all parties concerning such works. And the artist, if he or she has the bargaining power, may agree that the work not be considered a work made for hire or not sign such an agreement.

EDITOR'S NOTE: Senate Bill No. 1755 has amended the California Labor Code Section 3351.5 and Unemployment Code Section 621, to redefine the status of an artist commissioned to create a work of art under a "work-for-hire" relationship as an *employee* for the purpose of workers' compensation insurance, unemployment insurance, and unemployment disability insurance, thereby availing to artists employment benefits previously not allowed under a work-for-hire arrangement.

WRITTEN EMPLOYMENT AGREEMENTS

New employees for various ventures are requested to sign an employment agreement when first hired. Often the agreement is regarded as a mere formality by both the employer and the employee. But it later may have substantial significance in determining what valuable rights are given to the employer and retained by the employee. This is important for artists as to ownership of their creative efforts. The agreement may be signed and forgotten, but later can come back to haunt the artist.

It is important to know what the agreement has to say, even if you have no bargaining power to make changes at the time the agreement is entered into. In that way, you may know what changes to seek if your bargaining position changes. You will also know who owns the rights to your creations before you create something valuable in which you want to retain ownership.

Trade Secrets, Confidential Information, Designs and Copyright

Two types of clauses often present in the employment contract are of interest to the employee-visual artist. The first is a statement requiring that the employee not disclose confidential information or trade secrets of the employer. This restriction should not present significant problems to the artist. That is separate and distinct, however, from a different type of clause in which the employee agrees in effect that everything created in connection with the employee's work is owned by the employer.

A trade secret may include such things as patterns, charts, compilations of information or other materials used in business (e.g., art gallery, design studio, advertising agency) which gives a competitor an advantage over others who do not know of it. It is generally something which is continuously used in the operation of a business. Sometimes, materials are not enforceable as trade secrets as they may be only confidential information which does not have the capability of retaining the nature of a trade secret over any length of time. A customer list (e.g., patrons of a particular art gallery) is also an example of a trade secret. So long as the list is continued to be used in the business and is maintained in confidence, it can function as a trade secret. In fact, a trade secret may be almost any sort of confidential information which may be used to obtain a competitive edge in a business sense.

For drawings, patterns and designs to be trade secrets, they must be treated as trade secrets. Once they are generally exposed and available to the public, or if they are not treated in confidence, they may lose their character as trade secrets and then may not be protectable.

The law protects trade secrets from employee disclosure where there is a contract specifically referring to trade secrets. The problem for the visual artist is to determine what the employer believes is a trade secret. For example, you can specifically question the employer as to whether the pattern you are interested in using in your own ventures is considered a trade secret. You should also try to get a written response to your inquiry. If the employer does not consider information a trade secret, it is doubtful that a court will define it as a trade secret at a later time.

Trade secrets may be protected by the court even where there is no trade-secret agreement. A court can base its decision to protect an employer on a breach of confidence or breach of trust by the employee. The courts consider many factors in determining whether trade secrets have been taken.

As a result, the court decision tends to be subjective, based on a gut reaction as to who was morally right or wrong.

A trade secret can be enforced by obtaining an "injunction." An injunction is a court order generally requiring that certain named persons or businesses refrain from taking certain actions. The failure to obey a court order can result in "contempt of court." This means that the court has the power to place in jail one who disobeys the order. The order can also award a money judgment for damages resulting from the disclosure of a trade secret.

Rights in the Absence of an Employment Agreement

Even in the absence of an employment agreement, the employer may acquire certain rights in the visual artist's work. To the extent that it does not conflict with the federal law, the California Labor Code, for example, states:

> Everything which an employee acquires by virtue of his employment, except the compensation which is due to him from his employer, belongs to the employer, whether acquired lawfully or unlawfully, or during or after the expiration of the term of his employment.

Try to Limit the Scope of Your Employment Agreement

The employment contract may go further and state that everything created during the term of employment belongs to the employer. This may be too broad. It is possible that if a court were to rule on the matter, it could attempt to limit the scope of the agreement to those creations which were conceived during office hours or those which were related to the company's business. It is best that so broad a clause be eliminated from the agreement.

If you have the bargaining power, you may wish to consider limiting the scope of the agreement to creations (1) made during office hours, (2) made with company materials, (3) related to activities currently being worked on by the company and (4) only those which you were hired to create.

Consider the situation where you are hired by an advertising agency to work simply on the creations of another employee within the company. Assume you are promoted a year later to a more creative position. The agreement which you signed a year ago may not have had much meaning at the time. Now it becomes important with respect to various designs and layouts which you may have made on your own time. At this point, you may wish to have the agreement clarified and re-executed.

There may be restrictions in the employment agreement on your ability to engage in other work activity during the term of employment. This could restrict your ability to moonlight on other projects.

The agreement may attempt to prevent you from competing after your termination. Such agreements may be void. To be valid they generally have to be limited to a reasonable period of time and limited to a reasonable geographical area. In California, however, unless drafted to protect trade secrets of the company (including such things as customer lists), that aspect of the agreement may still be void. The California Business and Professional Code states:

> Except as provided in this chapter [which discusses primarily the sale of the good will

THE BUSINESS OF BEING A VISUAL ARTIST

of a business, trade secrets, employment agencies and telephone answering services],
every contract by which anyone is restrained from engaging in a lawful profession,
trade, or business of any kind is to that extent void.

Once again, this does not apply to prevent the dissemination of trade secrets or confidential information, and may not be applicable in situations involving the sale of a business.

However, the law may be different in other states. In such situations, the reasonableness of the time period and of the geographical area should be considered to determine whether it is lawful.

Maximum Term of Employment Agreement

An employment contract is limited to a period of time not in excess of seven years in the state of California. Thus the California Labor Code states: "A contract to render personal service . . . may not be enforced against the employee beyond seven years from the commencement of service under it." Other states may have similar statutes for different time periods. Any options or extensions of this time period may not total more than seven years. Thus, once the seven-year period has elapsed, there must be at least a brief period during which the artist can be on the "open market" to render services for others.

Can the Employer Stop You from Working Elsewhere?

Can an employer prevent you from working elsewhere by an employment contract? Under certain limited conditions, that may occur where the artist has signed an agreement guaranteeing at least $6,000 per year in compensation. To prevent the artist from seeking other employment, the employer must establish that the services of the artist are unique and personal. Words to that effect may even be stated in the employment contract. The employer then must go to court and ask the court to enjoin or stop the artist from seeking related employment elsewhere during the term of the contract (not more than the seven-year period). If the court grants an injunction (an order by the court requiring the artist not to be employed elsewhere), an artist disobeying the order would be in contempt of court. Obviously, this power is not likely to be used unless the services of the artist are particularly important to the employer.

Printed Form Contracts—Are They Always Enforceable?

What if you sign a printed form contract at the beginning of your employment which you are given on a take-it-or-leave-it basis. Assume the contract has lots of verbiage and is not particularly understandable to you as a lay person. Are you going to be clearly bound by it? Contracts of this nature, if particularly unfair and if presented by those in a superior bargaining position, may be considered in the law as a "contract of adhesion" (you are stuck to the contract and don't have any choice in the matter if you wish to work for the employer). It may be possible to find relief from a contract of adhesion sometime after you have signed it. This type of contract will be construed in a manner most favorable to the employee and least favorable to the employer who drew up the agreement. A court may try to find a way to relieve you of the contract if it finds it unconscionable. However, it is not a wise practice to sign an agreement on the grounds that you might possibly be able to get out of the agreement at some future point in time. A better approach would be to know what you are signing, and not sign the agreement if you are not able to live up to it.

AGENTS, CONSULTANTS, MANAGERS AND OTHERS

You as an artist may team up with an individual who seeks to promote and to sell your works, and to take a share of income based on sales. The agreement may be for a significant period of time. You may be requested to sign an agreement, whether it be called a partnership agreement or other document. How legitimate are such contracts?

If you are an artist in the entertainment field, anyone who offers, procures, promises or attempts to procure employment for your artistic services must be licensed by the state of California. Similar provisions exist in New York. However, fine artists and commercial artists do not fall under the regulation of the California Labor Commissioner at the present time.

There are statutes regarding the sale of fine prints and consignments which levy a statutory responsibility on the promoter. In certain circumstances it could be possible for one operating such a business to fall within the bounds of the Employment Agency Act, which is enforced by the Industrial Relations Department of the state of California.

Not being regulated by the law, artists must take special care in dealing with contracts with promoters. One problem area is where the artist gives the promoter the "exclusive" right to promote or sell the artist's works. The promoter may be guaranteed to receive a percentage of the selling price. At times it can be as much as 30% to 40%. This is without the benefit of having a gallery. The promoters may then sell to decorators or institutional art purchasers. The promoters may also make arrangements with a gallery. The commissions may then be split with the gallery, and while that is not of direct importance to the artist, the artist must still decide and fix the price on the sale of the work. If an artist has an exclusive arrangement with a promoter, and then the artist makes a subsequent arrangement with a different promoter, there is a risk that the artist may incur double commissions. To avoid this problem, it would be desirable that the promoter specify in writing what happens in such situations.

One way of dealing with the problem is for the artist, when signing such an agreement, to attempt to include some statements about allowing him or her to terminate the agreement on specific reasonable conditions. For example, the time for the relationship to continue may be based on objective criteria such as the success of the promoter in selling a certain number of works for a minimum dollar sum. There must be an agreement on the pricing of the artist's work prohibiting the promoter from going below such valuation unless the promoter is willing to reduce his or her commission. It could require that the promoter carry insurance for all work in his or her possession. The promoter must pass on to purchasers notice of any applicable laws regarding the artwork, such as, in California, the Resale Royalty Act and the Fine Arts Preservation Act. The agreement could be limited to only specific types of works selected by the artist, to works in particular media or to those works prepared for particular purposes.

Other areas which should be carefully considered before actually signing or entering into any such agreement include the following: How will the agreement operate for works prepared by the artist prior to entering into the agreement? And what system does the artist have to determine at what point the artwork was completed? Does a work which was started prior to the agreement fall within those works which are to be promoted? What about works which were started during the term of the agreement but were not completed until after the agreement was terminated? Is the promoter entitled to commissions on any of these?

INDEPENDENT CONTRACTOR OR EMPLOYEE

When you are commissioned or engaged to use your creative skills, you may be called an employee or an independent contractor. Sometimes, the commissioning party may ask if you would prefer to work as an independent contractor or as an employee. What are some of the differences? If you are an employee, the employer has the right to determine and control the manner, place and time of your work. If an independent contractor, you have that right.

If you are an employee, the employer will maintain worker's compensation insurance. That is required by law and it is a misdemeanor for an employer not to carry this insurance for you. Should you be injured in the scope or in the course of work, you can file claims for medical costs and disabilities. However, you will not be able to recover for what is called "pain and suffering" as a result of any such injury. Should you be injured in the scope of your employment and the employer did not carry worker's compensation insurance, you may have a greater legal claim against the employer. But if the employer is not financially responsible, the claim may be worthless. Even if you are called an independent contractor, if you are acting as an employee (i.e., the employer has the right to control the manner in which you work), the employer may still be required to carry worker's compensation insurance.

An employer will deduct from your pay disability insurance premiums. In the event that you are disabled in the course of your employment, you could obtain disability benefits.

If you are an employee, the employer is required to make deductions and withhold state and federal income taxes. That can amount to a sizable chunk of your paycheck. In addition, the employer will usually deduct a percentage (currently 6.65%) from your earnings for social security. The employer matches this amount as well and deposits those sums on a regular basis.

Although employee deductions may seem rather large, the independent contractor must take it upon himself or herself to make certain deductions as well. More information about this can be obtained from the article on taxes for the artist in this Manual. Although the visual artist is relieved of state and federal income tax withholding, he or she usually must make estimated tax deposits on a quarterly basis and may have to make larger tax payments if insufficient amounts have been deducted. While the independent contractor does not have to have social security benefit payments deducted from amounts earned at the end of the year, the independent contractor will have to pay a self-employment tax of approximately 9% of the artist's independent contractor earnings.

As an employee, you will probably also be subject to the protections provided by the Labor Code for employers, relating to prompt payment of wages and other matters. But you may also be subject to Labor Code Section 2870, which provides that everything you acquire in the course of employment belongs to the employer.

SOME PRACTICAL SUGGESTIONS

1. Read all agreements before signing.
2. If you have any bargaining power, consider asking for limitations on the number and nature of rights granted in your works. Keep as much of the copyright as you can. Specify limits as to time, manner of use and media.
3. Do not rely on the law to help you out of contracts you have no intention of upholding.
4. Watch for the magic words "work made for hire." They can appear anywhere.
5. Do not rely on statements made to you which do not appear in a written agreement.
6. Know the reputation of the person or of the company before entering into any agreements.
7. Request, obtain and keep copies of contracts.
8. Review what is stated in the contracts from time to time.
9. Seek legal counsel when in doubt.

A WORK-FOR-HIRE WARNING: The following memorandum, agreement, and check endorsement illustrate how and where you may expect to find work-for-hire provisions which, when signed or acted upon by you, give the other party the copyright in the work you have created.

SAMPLE NEWSPAPER/MAGAZINE/PUBLISHER WORK-FOR-HIRE NOTICE

MEMORANDUM TO OUR CONTRIBUTORS

The copyright law requires that we explain in writing the basis for transactions with you. This memorandum shall apply to all assignments whether made by us over the telephone or in writing. This is necessarily an all-inclusive statement and covers those who create work for our publication (magazine, daily paper, the Sunday magazine, the Book Review, etc.).

Our standard agreement with contributors is that all their material accepted by us is considered "work made for hire". This gives us all rights in the material throughout the world for which they are paid the regular fee, per diem page rate or whatever is agreed at the time of the assignment.

This does not change the fact that when you write for us you do so as an independent freelance contributor, not as our employee. Acceptance of your next check constitutes acceptance of this policy.

Please refer any questions to the editor with whom you regularly deal.

NOTE: This type of notification indicates that *all* assignments will be considered works made for hire and that acceptance of payment after receiving the notice means the artist has agreed to the terms in it.

SAMPLE AGREEMENT CONTAINING WORK-FOR-HIRE PROVISIONS

AGREEMENT made this ____ day of _____, 198_ , between XYZ COMPANY (hereinafter "XYZ") and VISUAL ARTIST (hereinafter "ARTIST") for the prepara- tion of three artworks for the "VISIONS" project.

W I T N E S S E T H:

NOW, WHEREFORE, in consideration of the mutual covenants and promises set forth herein, the parties agree as follows:

1. ARTIST will create three artworks for the forthcoming XYZ project entitled "VISIONS."

2. ARTIST shall submit the artworks in finished form no later than January 26, 1982.

3. XYZ will pay ARTIST the sum of $1,500.00 for each artwork, to be paid one half upon delivery of preliminary studies and one half upon delivery of the finished artwork.

4. Any and all artwork created pursuant to this agreement shall be consider- ed a work made for hire and XYZ shall be the sole owner of the original artwork and all rights, including copyright in and to the work, for any and all purposes throughout the world.

5. ARTIST represents and warrants that he/she is the creator of the art- work specified herein, that the work has not been published previously, that it does not infringe on any rights of copyright or personal rights and rights of privacy of any person or entity and that any necessary permissions have been obtained.

6. ARTIST agrees that in all respects other than the new copyright law, he/she is working as an independent, free-lance contractor and will be responsible for payment of all expenses incurred in his/her preparation of the artwork.

IN WITNESS WHEREOF, the parties hereto have duly executed the agreement the day and year first above written.

```
                              "XYZ"
                              XYZ COMPANY

                              By_____

                              "ARTIST"

                              _____

                              VISUAL ARTIST
```

Signature required. Check void if this endorsement altered. This check accepted as full payment for all rights in material described on face of check as work-made- for-hire. Signed _____ .

NOTE: If you cash the check you have agreed to a work-for-hire situation.

MUSEUM EXHIBITION AGREEMENT
Comments and annotations by Eileen L. Selsky, Esq.

The impact of museum exhibition on the artist's career should not be under-estimated. Showing one's work in a museum setting often yields the rewards of critical notice and acclaim, an increase in market value of the artist's work, greater exposure to international markets and exhibitors and a wider audience for the artist's work in the future. Any artist who "exhibits" publicly under an agreement with others who control and administer the space (whether a museum or the increasingly popular non-museum "alternative" space) should understand the "mechanics" of such agreements. *Whose responsibilities:* artwork must be collected and organized, transported and insured, displayed and properly lighted. *Who pays:* costs of the above, publicity and advertising. *Who controls:* admission, hours of exhibition, reproduction rights on posters and cards, design and installation. The agreement reproduced here is one example of how one artist and one museum decided these questions.

This Exhibition Agreement is made between Museum and Artist effective as of this _____ day of _____, 198__, in (city and state).

WHEREAS, Artist intends to assemble works of textile design ("Art Works") for the purpose of displaying said Art Works in an exhibition tentatively entitled ("Exhibition"); and

Comment: In this exhibition agreement, the artist appears to be undertaking as well the role of a curator or coordinator, who will assemble his/her works for his/her exhibition; it should be clearly stated whether the works of other creators as well as the artist/coordinator will be included in the exhibition.

WHEREAS, Museum desires to display the Exhibition;

NOW, THEREFORE, in consideration of the conditions, mutual covenants and promises hereinafter set forth, Museum and Artist agree as follows:

1. Location and Term of Exhibition

1.1 The Exhibition shall be displayed on the Museum premises at _____ _____ ("Premises") from _____ ("Opening Date") through _____, 1981 ("Closing Date") (collectively, "Exhibition Term"), such Exhibition Term subject to modification as hereinafter provided.

Comment: The description of the premises should be specific. Are there several buildings located on the premises? Several rooms or gallery spaces? Where will this Exhibition be located?

2. *Preparation of Exhibition*

2.1   Artist shall assemble for the Exhibition approximately 20 Art Works, as are consistent with and appropriate to the Exhibition. Museum shall in no event be responsible for locating or procuring the Art Works for the Exhibition or bear any expense incurred by Artist in connection therewith.

Comment: The museum should be responsible for insurance coverage, and this "expense" should be excluded (see paragraph 6).

2.2   Artist shall assist Museum in all phases of planning and installation of the Exhibition.

Comment: The artist agrees to assemble "consistent" and "appropriate" artworks. Textile design is a broad field. Will the designs be "consistent" with weavings, painted fabrics or printed materials? A reference to a certain period of the artist's work, particular materials or a limited subject matter might avoid misunderstanding after all the work has been shipped to the museum.

2.3   Should Museum determine that the quality of Art Works in the Exhibition fails to meet standard of quality, as reasonably determined by Museum, or that Artist has failed to adhere strictly to Museum guidelines, Museum may cancel the Exhibition by giving written notice to Artist as hereinafter provided in Paragraph 11.B. Cancellation, if any, shall be effective upon dispatch of written notice. Upon cancellation, Museum shall be liable for no expenses incurred to date of cancellation other than those incurred by Artist in the good faith preparation of the Exhibition, and Museum shall incur no additional obligation or liability whatsoever to Artist in connection with the Exhibition.

Comment: The museum is given the right to cancel the exhibition for failure to meet a "standard of quality." Rather than cancellation the artist might be given a reasonable amount of time to propose alternative sections; the museum's approval of such works will not unreasonably be withheld. The "standard" should be explained in sufficient detail so that the artist understands exactly what is expected.

2.4   It is expressly understood that certain details of the Exhibition, including, without limitation, catalogue budget, preparation and publication; exhibition budget; display design, floor plan and installation; educational information; publicity; inventory list; invitation and mailing; lecture and workshops; Travel of Exhibition and final title for the Exhibition are not provided herein. Prior to Opening Date, Artist and Museum shall enter into a supplemental agreement hereto setting forth such certain details of the Exhibition ("Supplemental Agreement"). Said Supplemental Agreement shall be in a form similar to Exhibit A attached hereto. Failure to enter into the Supplemental Agreement shall entitle Museum, at its option, to cancel the Exhibition.

Comment: The working details of the exhibition are relegated to a supplemental agreement. Again, the failure to enter the supplemental agreement should not necessarily result in cancellation of the exhibition. An arbitrator, such as an academic representative or an artist or an exhibitor agreed upon by the parties, might be called upon to resolve an impasse.

2.5 Artist shall provide Museum with an accurate and complete written inventory list of Art Works to be included in the Exhibition and the estimated value thereof, as determined by Artist prior to Opening Date, including a written description of and the mathematical dimensions of each Art Work included therein.

> *Comment:* The description of artworks included in the inventory should include the title of each work, the dimensions of the piece (as stated in the agreement) and the estimated value of the piece.

2.6 Artist shall cause all lenders of Art Works for the Exhibition to execute a separate loan agreement directly with Museum, in the form dictated by Museum.

3. Design and Installation

3.1 The design and subsequent installation of the Exhibition shall be undertaken by Artist following consultation with and approval by Museum.

A Display Design shall be submitted to Museum for approval pursuant to the schedule set forth in the Supplemental Agreement. Artist shall cooperate with reasonable requests of Museum in connection therewith. Museum shall retain supervisory control over all aspects of the Exhibition, including final determination with respect to Display Design and installation.

3.2 Should Museum reject the Display Design submitted by Artist, Museum may, at its option, either (i) undertake to design and install the Exhibition at Museum (ii) cancel the Exhibition.

> *Comment:* The design and installation of the exhibition is supervised by the artist with the approval of the museum. The amount of control by the artist depends, of course, on his/her bargaining power—how much the museum wants to show his/her artwork. However, the museum has retained the right to reject the artist's display design and handle the installation itself or, again, to cancel the exhibition. Reasonable cooperation of both parties should be specified; costs incurred in connection with the installation should be allocated in the agreement, but the artist should attempt to have the museum bear most expenses.

3.3 Artist shall be physically present at Museum Premises on such dates prior to Opening Date as Museum may reasonably request in order to assist in the installation of the Exhibition. Artist shall be present at the opening of the Exhibition and shall arrange his/her schedule in order to be available to fulfill all obligations in connection with the Exhibition which shall be set forth in this Agreement and in the Supplemental Agreement.

> *Comment:* The artist agrees to appear at the premises to assist with the installation and at the opening of the exhibition. It is always preferable that the artist be on hand to ensure that the works are displayed properly and illuminated properly. The artist's presence at the opening is good publicity as well as affording critics and reviewers a chance to meet him.

3.4 Artist shall provide to such persons as Museum directs at least one orientation lecture, including, without limitation, one during the term of the Exhibition.

Comment: The artist also agrees to provide an orientation lecture during the term of the exhibition. This should be subject to the artist's prior commitments. Scheduling conflicts for lectures or interviews may be avoided by a reference to alternate dates and reasonable cooperation by the artist in meeting such dates.

3.5 Artist shall cooperate with Museum in providing interviews with media and press.

4. *Finance*

4.1 Museum and Artist shall confer and Museum shall prepare a complete and detailed budget for the Exhibition. In addition, Museum shall retain the right to allocate the manner in which all sums shall be disbursed in connection with the Exhibition. Museum shall inform Artist both of the total sum committed by Museum for the Exhibition and the detailed breakdown thereof.

4.2 Compensation, if any, to be paid Artist shall be set forth in the budget in the manner as agreed to by the parties hereto. Museum shall set forth, in writing, pursuant to Paragraph 2.4 above, any and all agreements to reimburse Artist for expenses incurred by Artist in connection with the Exhibition.

Such sums, if any, to be paid Artist shall be the sole and only sums payable to Artist for performance of all obligations required of Artist herein and for all expenses of Artist incurred in connection with the Exhibition. It is expressly understood that Artist is an independent contractor and not an employee of Museum. In no event shall Artist have the right to bind Museum to an undertaking to any third party nor represent that Artist is an agent, employee or representative of Museum.

Comment: This provision grants the museum the right to allocate funds in connection with the exhibition. The artist receives a budget breakdown which sets forth his/her compensation. The source and amount of compensation, if any, is not stated and should be spelled out in the agreement. Is compensation dependent upon a grant? Upon paid admissions? The artist does have the right to consult on the exhibition budget and, depending again on bargaining power, can attempt to influence the museum on certain allocations. For example: (1) the cost of keeping the museum open one night each week so that more working people can attend; (2) the cost of publishing an extensive catalogue of the exhibition. Note that recent funding cutbacks may cause the museum to be very reluctant to commit itself to any budget.

4.3 Artist agrees to accept and abide by the Exhibition Budget established by Museum as provided pursuant to Paragraph 4.1 above. Museum shall not be responsible for any expenses incurred by Artist in excess of budgetary limits unless prior written approval is obtained from Museum.

Failure of Artist to adhere to budgetary limits established for the Exhibition shall be sufficient grounds for cancellation of the Exhibition by Museum as provided in Paragraph 2.3.

Comment: The artist must obtain prior written approval if budgetary limits will be exceeded. The exhibitor again has the option to cancel for budget overages.

4.4   Artist acknowledges and agrees that additional funds by way of grant, corporate sponsorship or otherwise may be solicited and accepted by Museum and applied to the funding of the Exhibition, all in the sole discretion of Museum.

5.   Transportation

5.1   In the case of a traveling Exhibition, Artist shall arrange transportation of the Exhibition to Museum Premises by shipper and mode of transport designated by Artist. In such cases, Museum shall be responsible only for certain costs of insurance and redelivery, as may be agreed to by the parties.

> *Comment:*   The artist agrees to arrange for transportation of the artworks to the premises, with the exhibitor bearing responsibility only for certain costs of insurance and redelivery. It should be determined whether the exhibitor is in a position to secure more favorable insurance terms to cover the transportation of pieces from the time they leave the artist's home or warehouse until arrival at the premises. Will all the pieces be assembled by the artist and then shipped to the premises or will they originate from various locations?

5.2   The parties hereto shall cooperate in order to arrange an Arrival Date at Museum mutually acceptable both to Artist and Museum. Artist acknowledges that Arrival Date shall in no event be later than 10 days prior to Opening Date. Museum shall incur no liability whatsoever to Artist for delay in Opening Date due to late arrival of Exhibition at Museum Premises.

Museum shall pay transportation and insurance costs for redelivery (as defined hereinbelow). The cost of such transportation and insurance shall be included in the total sum committed for the Exhibition by Museum.

> *Comment:*   The artist bears any costs resulting from a delay in the opening date caused by the late arrival of the exhibition at the premises. A provision should be negotiated that if the arrival has been delayed due to natural forces beyond the artist's control, such as weather disturbances, the artist and museum will allocate such costs between them. Obviously, the artist will attempt to have the museum bear the lion's share.

5.3   Within ten days after Closing Date, Museum shall arrange transportation of the Exhibition to the destination designated by Artist by carrier and mode of transport selected by Museum ("Redelivery"). All packing and shipping instructions of Artist, if any, shall be delivered to Museum no later than Closing Date. The date determined by Museum to be final date for Travel of Exhibition, pursuant to Paragraph 9 below, shall in all appropriate cases be the Closing Date.

> *Comment:*   The mode of transport for redelivery of the exhibition is left to the museum. If the artist wishes to specify a mode of transport, he/she may be responsible for any additional costs. These points must be discussed well in advance and included in the agreement. The artist should come to these discussions with an awareness of the problems and needs for shipping his artwork.

6. *Insurance*

6.1   Upon condition that Artist provide Museum with a complete and accurate written inventory list of Art Works pursuant to Paragraph 2.5, Museum shall obtain insurance on each Art Work for the value provided by Artist or Lender in the aforementioned inventory list while the Exhibition is at Museum Premises. Museum shall provide said insurance under its present (or replacement) all-risk blanket insurance policy. In no event shall Museum liability, if any, exceed the amount of insurance to be obtained pursuant to this Paragraph.

6.2   The cost of insurance of Art Works while at Museum Premises shall be the sole obligation of Museum. The cost of all said insurance shall be included in the total sum committed to the Exhibition by Museum pursuant to Paragraph 4.1.

> *Comment:*   The museum has the responsibility of insuring all works in the exhibition while at the museum. The artist should take care in preparing an accurate valuation of all works so that there will be adequate protection if they are lost or damaged.

7. *Poster*

7.1   Museum agrees to prepare a Poster for use in the Exhibition, the contents of which shall be agreed upon at a future date pursuant to Paragraph 2.4 above.

> *Comment:*   The museum agrees to prepare an exhibition poster, the contents of which will be agreed upon by the parties. The exhibitor is designated as the copyright owner of the poster, but the artist should insist that copyright be in his name if the image used on the poster is the artist's. The artist should be entitled to a share of any proceeds from the sale or reproduction of the poster, particularly if the artist's image is used and he/she participated in the design of the poster. The artist should also have some creative control and approval of the poster.

7.2   All sums received from sales of the Poster shall be applied to expenses incurred in connection with the preparation thereof.

7.3   The copyright in the Poster shall be registered in the name of Museum.

8. *Care*

8.1   Museum shall observe the same standard of care with respect to Art Works in the Exhibition as it exercises in the safekeeping of comparable property of its own.

> *Comment:*   The museum agrees to observe a standard of care similar to that exercised toward its own comparable property. The highest standard of care observed among exhibitors probably would be more reassuring to lenders of artwork. And the agreement should state that works will be returned in their pre-exhibition condition.

9. Travel of Exhibition

9.1 Museum will attempt to cause Travel of Exhibition for a period of up to 24 months following Closing Date. Artist shall cooperate with Museum in this connection. Such costs and expenses to be provided for the Exhibition by Museum pursuant to Paragraph 4.1 above.

Museum may determine to cease such Travel of Exhibition and return Art Works to Artist at any time as provided in Paragraph 5.3 herein.

Comment: The museum undertakes to promote future exhibitions at other premises. The artist should carefully consider granting this right. Does the museum have the ability to raise sufficient money to do so and can it get commitments from reputable museums? Presumably costs and expenses will be agreed upon in the supplemental agreement. The artworks may be returned to the artist at any time; the artist should receive prior notice of the return of any piece with an option to continue the traveling exhibition at his/her expense.

9.2 Museum undertakes to assure itself that the host museum(s) will follow normally accepted standards of conservation and security for the Exhibition and that all other procedures followed by said host museum(s) meet standards that are acceptable to Museum.

Comment: If particular standards of conservation, handling, display, packing and shipping are required for certain or all pieces, those standards should be specified and the museum should be required to exact promises of such responsibility from subsequent host museums. Host museums also are required to provide security for the artworks. Will security be provided at the initial museum's premises? What are normally accepted standards of conservation and security? Do these include: guards, alarm systems, temperature controls, particular lighting systems, crowd control procedures? Responsibility for customs duties also should be specified.

10. Other Provisions

10.1 All publicity and educational materials created or manufactured for or used in connection with the Exhibition, including, without limitation, posters, photographs, motion picture films, slides and textural materials, shall become the property of Museum and remain so upon termination of the Exhibition. Museum reserves the right to make use of said materials in any manner which it deems appropriate, including, without limitation, reproduction, reduplication, sale and transfer to another medium. Proceeds from the sale of any and all materials herein described shall remain the property of Museum.

Comment: Rights to publicity and educational materials created for the exhibition are granted to the museum for its further use without limitation, including all the income from those materials. The artist should seek to restrict such use to furthering the exhibition or require that he/she be consulted upon, or receive a royalty for, any additional use of these materials. The museum should also ensure that such uses do not interfere with the copyrights in the artworks being exhibited. The artist must require that the museum place the artist's copyright notice on all such materials if they use the artist's images.

11. Other Provisions

11.A.   Museum agrees that it shall instruct its representatives that Art Works provided by Artist for the Exhibition shall not be available for sale unless Artist shall instruct otherwise and Museum shall agree thereto.

It is the policy of Museum not to participate in arranging or effecting purchases of Art Works exhibited at Museum. In the event Artist desires the sale of Art Works in connection with the Exhibition, the Museum agrees thereto separately and in writing pursuant to Paragraph 2.4 above, Museum shall refer any and all inquiries pertaining to the sale of Art Works to Artist or any duly authorized representative thereof whom Artist may designate.

Comment: These paragraphs clearly state that the museum is not acting as an agent for the artist and is therefore not entitled to any commission should any of the works be sold. Museums rarely function as agents for the sale of artwork.

11.B.   Any notices required hereby or desired to be given by either party to the other hereunder, shall be given in writing and personally delivered or mailed by first-class mail, certified, to the addresses set forth below.

To Artist:

copy to

_____

_____

_____

To Museum:

copy to

_____

_____

_____

11.C.   This Exhibition Agreement shall not be assignable by either Museum or Artist without prior written consent of the other.

11.D.   This Exhibition Agreement may be amended only by an instrument in writing by Artist and Museum.

Comment: These are standard provisions covering the giving of notice, non-assignability and amendment of the agreement.

11.E.   It is mutually acknowledged that the State of California has the most significant contacts with this Exhibition Agreement and with the relationship between Museum and the parties of any particular state. It is therefore agreed that this Exhibition Agreement shall be construed and the legal relationship between the parties hereto shall be determined in accordance with the laws of the State of California applicable to contracts wholly executed and wholly to be performed within the State of California.

All actions or proceedings arising directly or indirectly from the Exhibition Agreement shall be litigated in a Court having a situs within Los Angeles, California, and the parties hereto agree and hereby consent to the jurisdiction of any local, state or federal court in which such an action is commenced that is located in Los Angeles.

> *Comment:* This sample agreement is taking place in California and the parties agree to litigate disputes under California law and, specifically, in a Los Angeles-based court. Nevertheless, if a dispute arises regarding an incident that occurs when the exhibition is in transit or when a particular work is displayed by a museum outside California, the parties may be litigating at the site of the artwork, or where the host museum or the shipper is located, and should be aware of the possibility of jurisdiction being asserted by a non-California court.

11.F.   This Exhibition Agreement, the Exhibits to be attached hereto and the Supplemental Agreement(s) herein contemplated shall constitute the entire agreement between the parties hereto.

11.G.   Artist shall not cause Art Works or similar type display to be displayed within a 60-mile radius of Museum without the prior written consent of Museum for a period of two (2) years from Opening Date.

> *Comment:* This provision should be eliminated. It appears to be a broad restriction on the artist's ability to have other exhibitions of his/her artwork, and specifically the ones shown in this exhibition. The geographic limitation, the two-year term and the restriction on exhibiting a "similar type display" are overly restrictive and burdensome. An artist's work, to be reviewed and sold, must be seen and this paragraph is a restraint on that professional process.

11.H.   Museum may include mention of Artist's identity in such announcements, invitations, press releases and other publicity or publications as Museum shall deem to be appropriate.

> *Comment:* The artist agrees to be mentioned in publicity materials and may wish to obtain such materials for his own reasonable use. The artist should attempt to have approval of publicity materials and should hold the museum to a standard of good taste.
>
> The parties should consider the possibility that ownership of an artwork may change during the exhibition or its travels. The artist may wish to substitute, within a reasonable time, an appropriate and "consistent" piece if a work is withdrawn for any reason.

11.I.   In the event that any provision of the Exhibition Agreement is deemed to be invalid for any reason whatsoever, the remainder of the Exhibition Agreement shall remain in full force and effect.

11.J.   Time is of the essence in this Exhibition Agreement.

IN WITNESS WHEREOF, Museum and Artist have executed this Exhibition Agreement on the date first herein set forth at Los Angeles, California.

_____
Museum

_____
Artist

SUPPLEMENTAL AGREEMENT TO MUSEUM EXHIBITION AGREEMENT

Re: _____

Dear Mr. Artist:

Pursuant to Paragraphs 2.4, 4.2, 7.1, 9.3 and 11.A of that certain "Exhibition Agreement" dated _____, between the Museum and you, as "Artist," we, as the parties thereto, have undertaken to provide additional details concerning certain aspects of the Exhibition which details are to be consistent with the Exhibition Guidelines attached as Exhibit B to the Exhibition Agreement. This letter memorializes our agreement with respect to the subjects set forth below and constitutes, upon signature of both parties hereto, a binding supplement to the Exhibition Agreement, as aforementioned.

1.   Except as herein supplemented or amended, the Exhibition Agreement shall continue in full force and effect.

2.   Budget

Pursuant to Paragraph 4.1 of the Exhibition Agreement, the total sum committed by Museum for support of the Exhibition is $_____. Consistent therewith, Museum shall commit the following sums to be spent in connection with certain components of the Exhibition, as hereinafter set forth:

For preparation and printing of a
Poster pursuant to Paragraphs 7.1,
7.2 and 7.3 of the Exhibition
Agreement $_____

For preparation and installation
of the Exhibition pursuant to
Paragraphs 3.1, 3.2 and 3.3 of the
Exhibition Agreement $_____

For transportation of the Exhibition
pursuant to Paragraphs 5.1, 5.2 and
5.3 of the Exhibition Agreement, the
total sum of $_____ to be prorated
among museum(s) receiving the Exhibition

For Insurance of the Exhibition pursuant
to Paragraph[s]_____of the Exhibition
Agreement $_____

For Opening Reception for Museum
members $_____

NOTE: Due to the recent cutbacks in funding it may no longer
        be possible to receive a budget commitment from a museum
        or exhibitor.

3.   Poster

        The Poster shall contain a full-color repro-
duction of one artwork to be selected by Artist and Museum,
the title of the Exhibition, the name of the museum and the
dates of exhibition on one side. The back side will contain
a short essay about the Artist and his work, and the Artist's
biography.

4.   Publicity

        Museum shall undertake the normal efforts to
publicize the Exhibition to news media and the public.

5.   Educational Information

        Artist shall provide one tour of the Exhibition
for Museum staff and volunteers shortly after the Opening Date
at a time mutually acceptable to both parties.

        Artist shall provide adequate information for
proper labeling of the Artworks.

        8.   It is understood that certain matters pertain-
ing to the sale of Artworks, installation, design, and travel
of Exhibition are to be determined in writing at a later date.

        If you are in agreement as to the foregoing, please
indicate your acceptance thereof by signing the duplicate original of this letter where indicated and returning the same
to us.

                        Sincerely,

                        _____
                                Museum Director

Receipt of the within letter is acknowledged and the terms
thereof accepted and agreed to.

_____
        Artist

Date_____   45

SAMPLE ARTIST'S RESERVED RIGHTS TRANSFER AND SALE AGREEMENT

AGREEMENT OF ORIGINAL TRANSFER OF WORK OF ART

fill in names, addresses of parties

Artist:_____ Address:_____

Purchaser:_____ Address:_____

WHEREAS Artist has created that certain Work of Art ("the Work"):

fill in data identifying the Work

Title:_____ Dimensions:_____

Media:_____ Year:_____

WHEREAS the parties want the Artist to have certain rights in the future economics and integrity of the Work, the parties mutually agree as follows:

fill in agreed value

1. SALE: Artist hereby sells the Work to Purchaser at the agreed value of $_____.

2. RETRANSFER: If Purchaser in any way whatsoever sells, gives or trades the Work, or if it is inherited from Purchaser, or if a third party pays compensation for its destruction, Purchaser (or the representative of his estate) must within 30 days:

(a) Pay Artist 15% of the "gross art profit," if any, on the transfer; and

(b) Get the new owner to ratify this contract by signing a properly filled-out "Transfer Agreement and Record" (TAR); and

(c) Deliver the signed TAR to the Artist.

(d) "Gross art profit" for this contract means only: "agreed value" on a TAR less the "agreed value" on the last prior TAR, or (if there hasn't been a prior resale) less the agreed value in Paragraph 1 of this contract.

(e) "Agreed value" to be filled in on each TAR shall be the actual sale price if the Work is sold for money or the fair market value at the time if transferred any other way.

3. NONDELIVERY: If the TAR isn't delivered in 30 days, Artist may compute "gross art profit" and Artist's 15% as if it had, using the fair market value at the time of the transfer or at the time Artist discovers the transfer.

4. NOTICE OF EXHIBITION: Before committing the Work to a show, Purchaser must give Artist notice of intent to do so, telling Artist all the details of the show that Purchaser then knows.

5. PROVENANCE: Upon request Artist will furnish Purchaser and his successors a written history and provenance of the Work based on TAR's and Artist's best information as to shows.

6. ARTIST'S EXHIBITION: Artist may show the Work for up to 60 days once every 5 years at a nonprofit institution at no expense to Purchaser, upon written notice no later than 120 days before opening and upon satisfactory proof of insurance and prepaid transportation.

7. NONDESTRUCTION: Purchaser will not permit any intentional destruction, damage or modification of the Work.

8. RESTORATION: If the Work is damaged, Purchaser will consult Artist before any restoration and must give Artist first opportunity to restore it, if practicable.

9. RENTS: If the Work is rented, Purchaser must pay Artist 50% of the rents within 30 days of receipt.

10. REPRODUCTION: Artist reserves all rights to reproduce the Work.

11. NOTICE: A Notice, in the form below, must be permanently affixed to the Work, warning that ownership, etc., are subject to this contract. If, however, a document represents the Work or is part of the Work, the Notice must instead be a permanent part of that document.

12. TRANSFEREES BOUND: If anyone becomes the owner of the Work with notice of this contract, that person shall be bound to all its terms as if he had signed a TAR when he acquired the Work.

13. EXPIRATION: This contract binds the parties, their heirs and all their successors in interest, and all Purchaser's obligations are attached to the Work and go with ownership of the Work, all for the life of the Artist and Artist's surviving spouse plus 21 years, except that the obligations of Paragraphs 4, 6 and 8 shall last only for Artist's lifetime.

14. ATTORNEYS' FEES: In any proceeding to enforce any part of this contract, the aggrieved party shall be entitled to reasonable attorneys' fees in addition to any available remedy.

15. MORAL RIGHT: The Purchaser will not permit any use of the Artist's name or misuse of the Work which would reflect discredit on his or her reputation as an artist or which would violate the spirit of the Work.

fill in date both sign

Dated:_____   _____
                                   Artist

Dated:_____   _____
                                   Purchaser

TRANSFER AGREEMENT AND RECORD

fill in data identifying the Work

Title:_____ Dimensions:_____

Media:_____ Year:_____

Ownership of the above Work of Art has been transferred between the undersigned persons, and the new owner hereby expressly ratifies, assumes and agrees to be bound by the terms of the Contract dated _____ between:

fill in date

fill in names, addresses of parties

Artist:_____ Address:_____

Purchaser:_____ Address:_____

Agreed value (as defined in said contract) at the time of this transfer: $_____

DO NOT fill in anythihg between these lines

Old Owner:_____ Address:_____

New Owner:_____ Address:_____

Date of this transfer:_____

---

cut out, affix to Work

fill in date, names of parties and Artist's address on both Notices

SPECIMEN NOTICE

Ownership, transfer, exhibition and reproduction of this Work of Art are subject to a certain Contract dated _____ between:

Artist:_____

Address:_____

Purchaser:_____
Artist has a copy.

NOTICE

Ownership, transfer, exhibition and reproduction of this Work of Art are subject to a certain Contract dated _____ between:

Artist:_____

Address:_____

Purchaser:_____
Artist has a copy.

COMMENTS ON THE ARTIST'S RESERVED RIGHTS
TRANSFER AND SALE AGREEMENT[2]

What the Contract Does

The contract is designed to give the artist:

15% of any increase in the value of each work each time it is transferred (California law requires a royalty of 5% of the *gross sale price*)

a record of who owns each work at any given time

the right to have the work remain unaltered by the owner

the right to be notified if the work is to be exhibited

the right to show the work for 2 months every 5 years (at no cost to the owner)

the right to be consulted if restoration becomes necessary

half of any rental income paid for the work, if there ever is any

all reproduction rights

The economic benefits would last for the artist's lifetime, plus the lifetime of a surviving spouse, plus 21 years, so as to benefit the artist's children while they are growing up. The aesthetic controls would last for the artist's lifetime.

When to Use the Contract

The contract form is to be used when the artist parts with each work FOR KEEPS:

whether by sale, gift or trade for things or services

whether it's a painting, a sculpture, a drawing, a non-object
    piece or any other fine art

whether to a friend, a collector, another artist, a museum, a
    corporation, a dentist, a lawyer—anyone

It's NOT for use when you *lend* your work or *consign* it to your dealer for sale; it IS for use when your dealer sells your work (or if he buys it himself).

How to Use the Contract

1. Photocopy the contract form. You'll need two copies for each transfer. Save the original to make future copies and for reference.

2. Fill out both copies, using the checklist instructions in the margin.

You may want to enter "artist's address" as c/o your dealer.

Note that the contract speaks in terms of a "sale"; the word "sell" is used for the sake of simplicity (likewise we use the word "purchaser" because it's the most all-inclusive word for this

[2] The Reserved Rights Transfer and Sale Agreement was originally conceived by Seth Siegelaub and drafted by Roger Projansky and subsequently revised in its present form by Mr. Projansky.

purpose). In a sense, even if you are giving or trading your work you are "selling" it for the promises in the contract plus anything else you get.

In Paragraph 1 enter the price OR the value of the work. You can enter any value that you and the new owner agree upon. If he sells it later for more he will have to pay you 15% of the increase, so the higher the number you put in originally, the better break the purchaser is getting. If you are giving a friend a work or exchanging with another artist (be sure to use two separate contracts for the latter situation) you might want to enter a very low value so you would get some money even if he/she resells it at a bargain price.

If there are things you wish to delete or modify, cross out what you don't want and make any small changes directly on the form, *making sure that both parties initial all such strikeouts and changes.* If you don't have room on the form for the changes you want, add them on separate sheets entitled "Rider to Contract" and be sure both are signed by the parties and dated. You should consult an attorney for extensive changes.

3. You and the purchaser sign both copies so each will have a legal original.

4. Before the work is delivered be sure to cut out the "Notice" from the lower right corner of one copy and affix it to the work. Put it on a stretcher bar or under a sculpture base or wherever it will be aesthetically invisible yet findable. Protect it with a coat of clear polyurethane or the like.

Your work may simply have no place on it for the "Notice" or your signature. In this case you should always use an ancillary document which describes the work, which bears your signature and which is transferred as a (legal) part of the work and you should glue or copy the "Notice" on that document.

Resale Procedure

When a work is resold the seller makes three copies of the "Transfer Agreement and Record" (TAR) from the original contract, fills them out entering the value that he and the next owner have agreed on, and both of them sign all three copies. The seller keeps one, sends one to the artist with the 15% payment (if required) and gives one to the new owner along with a copy of the original agreement, so he will know his responsibilities to the artist and have the TAR form if the work is resold again.

Remember, your dealer knows all the ins and outs of the art world; he knows the ways to get the few reluctant buyers to sign the contract—the better the dealer, the more ways he knows. He can do what he does now when he wants something for one of his artists—give the collector favors, exchange privileges, discounts, hot tips, advice, time and all the other things buyers expect and appreciate. It even gives him an opportunity to raise the subject of prospective increase in the value of your work without seeming crass.

The contract helps dealers do what they try to do now anyway. Dealers try to keep track of the work they have sold, but now they can only rely on hit-or-miss intelligence and publicity. The contract creates a simple record system which will automatically maintain a biography of each work and a chronological record of ownership. It makes giving a *provenance* no trouble at all. And it's almost costless to administer, only another few minutes of typing for each sale.

Using the contract is mostly a state of mind. If your dealer doesn't think the benefits of the contract are important he will have dozens of reasons why he can't get the buyers to sign it; if he cares and wants those benefits for you he'll use it every time and he won't lose a sale.

The Facts of Life: You, the Art World and the Contract

The vast majority of people in the art world feel that this idea is fair, reasonable and practical. Reservations about using the contract can be summed up in two basic statements:

"The economics of buying and selling art is so fragile that if you place one more burden on the collectors of art, they will simply stop buying art."

"I will certainly use the agreement, but only if everyone else uses it."

The first statement is nonsense. Clearly the *art* will be just as desirable with as without the contract, and there's no reason why the value of any work should be affected, especially if this contract is standard for the sale of art, which brings us to the second statement. If there's a problem here, it's the concern of artists or dealers that the insistence on use of this contract will jeopardize their sales in a competitive market. Under careful scrutiny this proves to be mostly illusory.

All artists sell, trade and give their work to only two kinds of people: those who are their friends; those who are not their friends.

Obviously, your friends won't give you a hard time. The only trouble will come with someone who isn't your friend. Since surely 75% of all serious art that's sold is bought by people who are friends of the artist or dealer—friends who drink together, weekend together, etc.—resistance will come only in some of those 25% of your sales to strangers. Of those people, most will wish to be friendly with you and won't hesitate to sign the contract to show their respect for your ongoing relationship with your work. This leaves perhaps 5% of your sales which encounter serious resistance over the contract, and even this should decrease toward zero as the contract comes into widespread use.

In short, this contract will help you discover who your friends are.

If a buyer wants to buy but doesn't want to sign, tell him that all your work is sold under the contract, that it's standard for your work.

You can point out to the reluctant buyer:

The contract doesn't cost anything unless your work appreciates in value; most art doesn't. If he makes a profit on your work you get only a small percentage of it—about the equivalent of a waitress's tip.

If you like you can offer to take your prospective 15% payment in something other than money, or to give him a partial credit against a new work.

Or you can offer to put in an original value that's more than what he's paying, giving him a free ride on part of any prospective profit.

Of course, if a collector buys a work refusing to sign the contract he will have to rely on good will when he wants you or your dealer to appraise, restore or authenticate it. Why he should expect to find good will there is anybody's guess.

Is the buyer really going to pass up your work because you ask him to sign this contract? Work that he likes and thinks is worth having? If the answer is yes, given the fact that it doesn't cost him a thing to give you, the artist, the respect that you as the creator of the work deserve—if that will keep him from buying, he is too stubborn and foolish for anyone to tell you how to illuminate him. Non-use of this contract is a dumb criterion for selecting art.

Enforcement

First, let's put this in perspective: Most people will honor the contract because most people honor contracts. Those who are likely to cheat you are likely to be the same ones who gave you a hard time about signing the contract in the first place. Later owners will be more likely to cheat you than the first owner, but there are strong reasons why both first and future owners of your work should fulfill the contract's terms.

What happens if owner #1 sells your work to owner #2 and doesn't send you the transfer form? (He's not sending your money, either.)

Nothing happens. (You don't know about it yet.)

Sooner or later you do find out about it because the grapevine will get the news to you (or your dealer) anyway. Then, if owner #1 doesn't come across you can sue him. He will be stuck for 15% of the profit he made OR 15% of the increase in value to the time you heard about it, which may be much more. Also, note that if you have to sue to enforce any right under the contract, Paragraph 14 gives you the right to recover reasonable attorney's fees in addition to any other remedy to which you may be entitled. Clearly, owner #1 would be foolish to take the chance.

As to falsifying values, there will be as much pressure from new owners to put in high values as there is from old owners to put in low values. In 95% of the cases the amount of money to be paid the artist won't be enough to make them lie to you (in unison).

We realize this contract, like its predecessor, will disturb some dealers, museums and high-powered collectors, but the ills it remedies are universally acknowledged to exist and no other practical way has ever been devised to cure them.

Its purpose is to put you—the artist—in the same position as the man behind the rent-a-car counter. He didn't write his contract, either, but he says: if you want it, sign here. You do the same.

Using this contract doesn't mean all your art world relationships will be strictly business hereafter or that you have to enforce every right down to the last penny. Friends will still be friends and if you want to waive your rights you can, but they will be YOUR rights and the choice will be YOURS.

The contract in its prior form has been used by many artists—known, well-known and unknown. Use it. It's enforceable. The more artists and dealers who use it, the better and easier it will be for everybody to use it. It requires no organization, dues, meetings, registration or government agency—just your desire to protect the integrity of your art.

What it gives you, the artist, is a legal tool you can use to establish continuing rights in your work at the time you transfer it, but whether or not you use the contract is up to you. Consider the contract as a substitute for what is available otherwise: nothing.

This has been created for no recompense to the author for just the pleasure of attacking a challenging problem, and it is based on the feeling that should there ever be a question about artists' rights in reference to their art, the artist is more right than anyone else.

SAMPLE BASIC DESIGN AGREEMENT
FOR DESIGN OF ARTWORK BY DESIGNER OR ILLUSTRATOR

This agreement, entered into on __(date)__ establishes the nature and extent of services __(Artist or Designer)__ will provide __(Client or Company)__ and sets forth the fee and payment schedule.

1. <u>SERVICES</u>

Project Title: _____

Project Description: (Fully describe all elements of the project, such as size, materials, method of construction, color, intended use, designated user and quantity of final product -- attach copies of any specifications and/or materials provided by Company)

Date(s) Roughs Due: _____   Date Final Project Due: _____

2. <u>COSTS</u>

__(Company)__ agrees to pay all costs incurred specifically for the project (including photostats, typography, film and processing). These costs shall be billed to and paid by __(Company)__ in addition to the design fee and are subject to __(Artist's)__ usual handling charge of __(designate percent)__.

Out-of-pocket and miscellaneous expenses, such as phone calls and travel related costs will be separately invoiced as incurred at __(Artist's)__ net cost.

3. <u>FEES AND PAYMENT SCHEDULE</u>

FEES:	Description of Services or Artwork	Fee in Dollars
	(Poster design, camera-ready art	$700.00)
(Sample)-	(or photography, per day	$600.00)
	(or illustration	$500.00)
	(or 4-color package design	$650.00)

(If more than one service is to be performed or more than one artwork created, list the fee for each service/artwork separately.)

<u>PAYMENT SCHEDULE:</u>

(Sample)- (One-third total design fee due on approval of this agreement.)
(One-third total design fee due on approval of comps.)
(One-third total design fee due on completion of camera-ready copy.)

    or

(Sample)- (One-half total design fee due on approval of agreement.)
(One-half total design fee due on approval of comps.)

All accounts are due within ten (10) days of billing and will be subject to a two percent (2%) monthly service charge if the balance is not received within thirty (30) days of billing. In the event the account is turned over for collection, __(Company)__ agrees to pay all costs and attorneys' fees.

The fees described above do not include sales tax, if applicable, and do not include fees for revisions requested by __(Company)__ after approval of comps. (Optional: insert an hourly rate for all requested revisions.)

4. <u>RETURN OF ORIGINAL ARTWORK</u>

Unless otherwise agreed in writing, all artwork prepared for __(Project Title)__ will be returned to __(Artist or Designer)__ within __(number)__ of days of its submission.

5. <u>REPRODUCTION RIGHTS</u>: COMPLETE BUY-OUT OF THE WORK OR LIMITED USE

(Select A or B)

A.   This agreement grants one-time nonexclusive/exclusive (choose one) use of <u>(Project Title)</u> for purposes of (Example: reproduction on calendars, album covers, book illustration) for a period of _____ months/years (choose one) (can also add a limitation on whether use shall be domestic or foreign). Any other use of the artwork shall be separately negotiated and invoiced.

B.   (Complete buy-out of the work)   In the event <u>(Company)</u> desires to purchase all the rights to the project, <u>(Company)</u> shall pay a sale price of $_____.   (Note: This price should take into account all the uses that can be made and the price Artist would charge for each. Also include, if Company requests, a cost for the original artwork. If not, specify that the sale price does not include the original artwork.)

6. <u>COPYRIGHT</u>

<u>(Artist or Designer)</u> reserves the copyright to <u>(artwork)</u> and has the sole and exclusive right to use or exploit it in any manner, or to authorize others to use or exploit it. <u>(Company)</u> shall not make any unauthorized use or display of <u>(artwork)</u>, or copy it or make or commission any form of replica or likeness of it without the prior written consent of <u>(Artist)</u>.

7. <u>KILL FEE</u>

In the event the artwork prepared under the terms of this agreement is rejected by <u>(Company)</u> within <u>(number of days)</u> of its submission, <u>(Artist)</u> shall receive <u>(percent)</u> of the agreed-on design fee as compensation for time and effort devoted to the project. In the event the artwork is rejected after <u>(number of days)</u> of its submission, <u>(Artist)</u> will receive one hundred percent (100%) of the agreed-on design fee as compensation for time and effort devoted to the project. All artwork shall be returned to <u>(Artist)</u> immediately or within <u>(number of days)</u> of its rejection by <u>(Company)</u>.

8. <u>MODIFICATION</u>

All modifications of this agreement must be mutual and in writing.

9. <u>BINDING ARBITRATION</u>

In the event of a breach of any of the terms of this agreement, the parties shall submit the dispute to binding arbitration. The prevailing party shall be entitled to reasonable costs and attorneys' fees.

Dated:_____   (Client or Company)_____

                                              By_____

Dated:_____   _____

                                              (Artist or Designer)

SAMPLE LETTER OF CONFIRMATION

(Artist's Letterhead)   November 14, 1981

Mr./Ms. Gallery Owner/Art Director/Publisher
1234 Picture Lane
Artville, California 90000

Dear Mr./Ms. Owner/Director/Publisher:

   This letter will confirm the terms of the agreement we discussed in your office (or on the phone) on November 10, 1981.

   I agree to (specify time, place, payments, services and any rights, obligations, prohibitions, etc.).

   You agree to (specify time, place, payments, services and any rights, obligations, prohibitions, etc.).

   Please sign and date both copies of this letter in the designated space below and return one fully executed copy to me in the envelope provided, keeping one fully executed copy for your files.

                              Yours sincerely,

                              V. Artist

AGREED TO AND ACCEPTED:

_____
(Gallery Owner/Art Director/Publisher)

Dated: _____

SAMPLE EXHIBITION CONFIRMATION LETTER

(Artist's Letterhead)

                              November 14, 1981

Mr. O. K. Exhibitor
Showplace, California

Dear Mr. Exhibitor:

   I am pleased that you will be showing 22 of my sculptural compositions in a five-week one-person show in February of 1982.

   As we discussed when we met at your office, each work will be lit directly from above in high-intensity light and no work will be less than eight feet from the next. I will supply four-foot-high bases and will ship the work to the gallery on February 8, 1982.

   I am delighted that you will have an opening celebration for critics and invited patrons. As requested, I am enclosing a mailing list for you to incorporate into your existing list of 2,000.

   I will be responsible for insuring the works up to the time they arrive at the exhibition space and you will insure them (at the amounts we discussed on the price list) from that point, during the exhibition and through shipping back to my studio.

   Pursuant to our agreement, you will receive a forty percent (40%) commission on all works sold during the exhibition.

                              Yours sincerely,

                              V. Artist

SAMPLE DEMAND LETTER

(Artist's Letterhead)

November 14, 1981

Mr. Deal Breaker
1234 Benefitter Lane
Artville, California 90000

Re: Photographs of Exterior of Breaker Office Building

Dear Mr. Breaker:

On August 1, 1981, we signed a written agreement in your office. Under the terms of that agreement, I agreed to photograph the exterior of your office building and furnish you on September 15 with an 8" x 10" glossy color print pursuant to your selection from fifteen proofs submitted to you. The fee we agreed upon for my services (including supplies and printing costs) was $175.00, to be paid on delivery of the photograph.

On September 1, 1981, I delivered the 8" x 10" glossy color print described above. When I requested the payment of my fee, you asked that I allow you to send me a check within five days, since your bookkeeper would return from vacation at that time. I agreed to that arrangement.

I have been unsuccessful in attempts to contact you personally and by phone regarding the lengthy delay in tendering payment. To date, you have received two invoices and one letter, dated October 1, 1981, requesting payment of my fee. I would appreciate your attention to this matter immediately. If, within five days of your receipt of this letter, you have not made the $175.00 past due payment, I will be forced to take legal action.

I look forward to the prompt and harmonious resolution of this matter.

Sincerely,

V. Artist

(NOTE: SEND THIS LETTER BY REGISTERED OR CERTIFIED MAIL, RETURN RECEIPT REQUESTED. RETAIN A COPY OF THE LETTER AND THE SIGNED RECEIPT FOR YOUR RECORDS.)

SAMPLE LETTER FOR THE SALE OF A WORK OF ART

(Artist's Letterhead)

November 14, 1981

Ms. Wise Buyer
1234 Collector Drive
Artville, California 90000

Dear Ms. Buyer:

At our meeting on November 2, 1981, at my studio, you agreed to purchase my original oil painting entitled "Masterpiece," which measures 3' x 2', with brass metal frame included, for the sum of $2,000.00.

As agreed, I shall hold the painting at my studio until November 28, 1981 (the date agreed upon for complete payment and transfer of the painting to you). At that time, we shall execute a complete bill of sale.

Please be advised that if the sale is not consummated on or before November 28, 1981, I shall be under no further obligation to sell the painting to you.

I look forward to our next meeting.

Sincerely yours,

V. Artist

SAMPLE LETTER OF TERMINATION

```
                              (Artist's Letterhead)
                                              November 14, 1981

Mr. B. Rep
Graphic House
Los Angeles, California

Dear Mr. Rep:

        Please be advised that I am giving you notice of termination of our agree-
ment of February 13, 1981, for purposes (insert nature of agreement) and that
thirty days after you have received this notice, our agreement is terminated.

        Pursuant to Paragraph ____ of our agreement, any payments due to you or
me (depending on who is to receive payments) will be made at the end of each
month (or however payment provision reads).

        Within thirty days, please return to me at my studio (or home or office)
all artwork by me which is presently in your possession on consignment or other-
wise.  At that time please forward to me copies of all records and accounts
(add invoices, purchase orders, if applicable) relating to me and my work.

                              Sincerely yours,


                              V. Artist
```

THE USE OF STANDARD FORMS

The decision to create and use a preprinted or standard form in lieu of a specifically drafted agreement should be made with care. Forms are convenient and efficient, but their benefits are not without risks.

A standard form, by its very nature, cannot be designed to address every contingency. When it does not deal precisely with a particular facet of your agreement, the form should be altered or augmented.

Deficiencies in standard forms range from inaccurately describing or omitting any part of your agreement to creating obligations and rights that neither party intended in a specific case. Be aware of basic areas of concern for your particular situation, which may include: responsibility for damage or loss at any given time, assignability of the agreement, settling disputes about the agreement through arbitration or other means, moral rights, copyright ownership, reproduction, licensing and merchandising, royalties, penalties, federal or state law affecting the agreement and so on.

These examples are but a few of the modifications you might consider. Approach the use of standard forms with an awareness that the form, as is, may not be a complete expression of the terms of your agreement.

BILL OF SALE FOR A WORK OF ART

The Bill of Sale is the document you should use in conjunction with the sale of a work of art. It should include the basic information that appears in the example shown.

The Bill of Sale satisfies at least three important needs:

1. A record of total art sales for purposes of computing taxable income.

2. An accurate inventory of the owners of your work, facilitating provenance and tracing of subsequent purchasers.

3. Additional protection for the artist and the artwork contained in the terms and conditions of the sale. This portion of the Bill of Sale may specify assumption of certain rights by the buyer, restoration rights for the artist, installment payment procedures, artist exhibition rights, reservation of copyright and reproduction rights to the artist, a notice of applicable state law (for example, in California, the Resale Royalty Act and Fine Arts Preservation Act), a requirement that if the work is donated, the donee will be obligated to notify the artist of its intention to sell the work.

In the absence of a more formal Reserved Rights Transfer Agreement (see example in this section), the Bill of Sale can be tailored to protect the artist.

SAMPLE BILL OF SALE

```
(NOTE:  FILL OUT AND SIGN IN DUPLICATE)

Artist:_____

Purchaser:_____(Name)_____

_____(Address)_____

Date of Sale:_____ Place of Sale:_____

Title of Work:_____

Description of Work: (Size, medium, etc.)_____

Price: _____ Sales Tax:_____

Terms of Payment:_____

_____

Terms of Sale:_____

_____

_____

© 19__. (Name of Artist). All reproduction rights reserved.

(Signature of Purchaser)_____      Dated:_____
Name of Purchaser

(Signature of Artist)_____      Dated:_____
Name of Artist
```

SAMPLE SHORT FORM
ARTIST/GALLERY RECEIPT OF CONSIGNED ARTWORK

Received from_____

             Name of Artist

Address_____ Phone_____

the following:

Title	Medium	Size	Selling Price	Percent Commission
1.				
2.				
3.				

etc. (Use additional sheets if necessary.)

for __(purpose: e.g., sale, exhibition, inspection, etc.)__ to be held from __(date)__ to __(date)__ .

Until the works listed above are returned to the possession of the Artist, each will be fully insured against the loss or damage for the benefit of the Artist in an amount not less than the selling price less commission. None may be consigned, sent out on approval or removed during the period of the exhibition except as agreed in writing. All of the above works are to be returned to the Artist on demand. Reproduction rights reserved by Artist.

The Gallery shall provide the Artist with a Statement of Account within fifteen days of the end of each calendar quarter commencing with __(date)__ . The accounting will state for each work, the title, its sale or rental status, the date, price and terms of any sales or rental, the gallery commission, the amount due to the artist, the name and address of each purchaser or renter and the location of all consigned works not sold or rented.

Dated:_____   (Gallery)_____

                            By (Signature of Dealer/Agent of Gallery)_____

Dated:_____   (Signature of Artist)_____

                            Name of Artist

(Based on the Artists Equity Standard Receipt form, reproduced by permission of Artists Equity.)

SAMPLE SHORT FORM STATEMENT OF ACCOUNT

Name of Artist:_____ Date:_____

Address:_____ Quarter:_____

Title	Status (Sold/ Rented/Other)	Date	Price	Gallery Commission	Amount Due Artist	Purchaser/ Renter & Address	Location, If Not Sold/Rented
1.							
2.							
3.							

Terms:

Net Due Artist:_____

                            (Gallery)_____

                            By (Signature of Dealer/Agent of Gallery)

ASSIGNMENT CONFIRMATION

DATE:

PHOTOGRAPHER:

CLIENT:

ADDRESS:

COMMISSIONED BY:

ACCOUNT:

JOB #:

CLIENT'S P.O. #:

EXPENSES TO BE PAID BY CLIENT:

FEE:

TERMS OF PAYMENT:

RIGHTS PURCHASED:

USAGE PURCHASED:

DATE TO BEGIN:

JOB DESCRIPTION AND ADDITIONAL INFORMATION:

This assignment is subject to the terms which appear on the back of this form. All terms apply unless objected to in writing within ten (10) days.

ACCEPTED BY:

Photographer Representative Signature Date _____

Authorized Client Signature Date _____

IT IS ALSO AGREED THAT:

1. All transparencies and photographs remain the property of the photographer and rights and usage are reserved by the photographer except as stated herein.

2. Any changes or requests for additional usage or reproduction rights will require further negotiation, a determination of additional fees, and another Assignment Confirmation form completed and signed.

3. There will be a charge for assignment interruptions based on a percentage of the photographer's total fee. Cancellations will cost 50% of the fee, and postponements will cost 25%.

4. If a re-shoot becomes necessary because the photographer or his representative has broken a written agreement that is contained herein, no additional photographer's fee will be charged the client.

5. An additional fee will be charged for a re-shoot that is not due to the fault of the photographer or his representative. The fee will not be more than 75% of the original photographer's fee for the same assignment.

6. The photographer does not render free services on speculation, or on an "approval" basis.

7. If requested, the photographer will provide model releases for photographs providing they are warranted.

8. Transparencies are to be promptly returned to the photographer after reproduction has been completed unless unlimited rights and usage have been purchased.

9. The client and his agents are solely responsible for the safekeeping of the transparencies while they are in the client's possession until their return to the photographer and will indemnify him for any loss or damage.

10. Grant of rights and usage are conditional and contingent upon receipt of full payment to the photographer.

11. If payment to the photographer is not made when due and the account is placed in the hands of an attorney for collection, the client agrees to pay the additional court costs and reasonable attorney's fees of not less than $250.00.

12. The photographer and his authorized representative will be bound only by the terms contained in this Assignment Confirmation and no waiver of any of these agreements will be binding on them unless subscribed to by them in writing.

Reproduced with permission from Jae Wagoner.

CONFIRMATION OF ENGAGEMENT

Illustrator's
Letterhead

Date:

Client:

Authorized Art Buyer:

Illustrator's Job Number:

Client's Job Number:

JOB DESCRIPTION:

DELIVERY SCHEDULE:

FEE (payment schedule):

ADDITIONAL ESTIMATED EXPENSES:

CANCELLATION FEE:

Before sketches: _____ % of Fee

After sketches: _____ % of Fee

After finish: _____ % of Fee

RIGHTS TRANSFERRED: (All other rights reserved by the illustrator)

For use in magazines and newspapers. First North American reproduction rights, unless specified otherwise here:

For all other uses, client acquires only the following rights: *(Specify number of uses, duration of use, geographical extent of use, etc.)*

Title or product: *(Specify name)*

Category of use: *(Specify advertising, corporate, promotional, editorial, etc.)*

Medium of use: *(Specify consumer or trade magazine, brochure, annual report, TV, book, etc.)*

Original artwork, including sketches and any other preliminary materials, remain the property of the illustrator unless purchased by a payment of a separate fee.

TERMS:

1. Payment is due within 30 days of receipt of invoice. A 1½% monthly service charge will be billed for late payment. Any advances or partial payments shall be indicated under "payment schedule" on front.

2. The client shall assume responsibility for all collection and legal fees necessitated by default in payment.

3. The grant of reproduction rights is conditioned on receipt of payment.

4. The client shall reimburse the illustrator for all expenses arising from the assignment.

5. The client shall be responsible for the payment of sales tax, if any such tax is due.

6. In the event of cancellation or breach by the client, the illustrator shall retain ownership of all rights of copyright and the original artwork, including sketches and any other preliminary materials.

7. Revisions not due to the fault of the illustrator shall be billed separately.

8. On any contribution for magazine or book use, the illustrator shall receive name credit in print. If name credit is to be given with other types of use, it must be specified here:

_____
_____
_____

9. ☐ If this box is checked by the illustrator, he or she shall receive copyright notice adjacent to his or her work in the form
©_____198

10. Client assumes responsibility for the return of the artwork in undamaged condition within 30 days of first reproduction.

11. Client will indemnify illustrator against all claims and expenses, including reasonable attorney's fees, arising from uses for which no release was requested in writing or for uses which exceed the authority granted by a release.

12. Both parties agree to submit any disputes hereunder involving more than _____* to arbitration under the rules of the American Arbitration Association. An award therefrom may be entered for judgment in any court having jurisdiction thereof.

13. If the terms of this confirmation are not objected to within 10 days of receipt, the terms shall be deemed accepted.

*Insert maximum limit for small claims court.

MEMBER

ILLUSTRATOR'S SIGNATURE
_____

CLIENT: NAME
_____

By: _____
AUTHORIZED SIGNATURE AND TITLE

Reproduced with permission from Graphic Artists Guild.

STOCK PICTURE DELIVERY/INVOICE

FROM: **TO:**

Date:
Subject:
Purchase Order No:
Client:
A.D./Editor
Shooting Date(s)
Our Job No:
☐ Assignment Confirmation
☐ Job Estimate
☐ Invoice

RIGHTS GRANTED

One-time, non exclusive reproduction rights to the photographs listed below, solely for the uses and specifications indicated, and limited to the individual edition, volume series, show, event or the like contemplated for this specific transaction (unless otherwise indicated in writing).

SPECIFICATIONS (if applicable)

PLACEMENT (cover, inside etc.) _____
SIZE (½ pg. 1 pg., double pg., etc.) _____
TIME LIMIT ON USE _____
USE OUTSIDE U.S. (specify, if any) _____
COPYRIGHT CREDIT: © 19____ _____
                                         (name)

MEDIA USAGE

ADVERTISING		EDITORIAL/JOURNALISM	
Animatic	☐	Book Jacket	☐
Billboard	☐	Consumer Magazine	☐
Brochure	☐	Encyclopedia	☐
Catalog	☐	Film Strip	☐
Consumer Magazine	☐	Newspaper	☐
Newspaper	☐	Sunday Supplement	☐
Packaging	☐	Television	☐
Point of purchase	☐	Text Book	☐
Television	☐	Trade Book	☐
Trade Magazine	☐	Trade Magazine	☐
Other	☐	Other	☐

CORPORATE/INDUSTRIAL		PROMOTION & MISC.	
Album Cover	☐	Booklet	☐
Annual Report	☐	Brochure	☐
Brochure	☐	Calendar	☐
Film Strip	☐	Card	☐
House Organ	☐	Poster	☐
Trade Slide Show	☐	Press Kit	☐
Other	☐	Other	☐

DESCRIPTION OF PHOTOGRAPHS	Format:	2¼	4×5	5×7	8×10	11×14	Other	USE FEES ($)
Total Black & White	Total Color							

If this is a delivery kindly check count and acknowledge by signing and returning one copy. Count shall be considered accurate and quality deemed satisfactory for reproduction if said copy is not immediately received by return mail with all exceptions duly noted.

TOTAL USE FEES: _____
MISCELLANEOUS: _____
Service Fee: _____
Research Fee: _____
Other: _____
TOTAL: _____
DEPOSIT: _____
BALANCE DUE: _____

SUBJECT TO TERMS ON REVERSE SIDE PURSUANT TO ARTICLE 2, UNIFORM COMMERCIAL CODE
ACKNOWLEDGED AND ACCEPTED

Terms and Conditions

(a) "Photographer" hereafter refers to (insert name   ). Except where outright purchase is specified, all photographs and rights not expressly granted on reverse side remain the exclusive property of Photographer. All editorial use limited to one time in the edition and volume contemplated for this assignment. In all cases additional usage by client requires additional compensation and permission for use to be negotiated with Photographer.

(b) Absent outright purchase, client assumes insurer's liability to (1) indemnify Photographer for loss, damage, or misuse of any photograph(s) and (2) return all photographs prepaid and fully insured, safe and undamaged by bonded messenger, air freight or registered mail, within 30 days of publication. In any event, client agrees to return all unpublished material to Photographer in the above manner, and supply Photographer with two free copies of uses appearing in print.

(c) Reimbursement for loss or damage shall be determined by a photograph's market value or, in the absence of that due to lack of prior use, then its intrinsic value.

(d) Adjacent credit line for Photographer must accompany editorial use, or invoice fee shall be doubled. Absent outright purchase, client will provide copyright protection on any use and assign same to Photographer immediately upon request, without charge.

(e) Photographer has supplied or will supply specifically requested releases on photographs requiring same for use. Client will indemnify Photographer against all claims and expenses due to uses for which no release was requested in writing. Photographer's liability for all claims shall not, in any event, exceed the fee paid under this invoice.

(f) Time is of the essence for receipt of payment and return of photographs. Grant of right of usage is conditioned on payment. Payment required within 30 days of invoice; 1½% per month service charge on unpaid balance is applied thereafter. Adjustment of amount, or terms, must be requested within 10 days of invoice receipt. All expense estimates subject to normal trade variance of 10%.

(g) Client may not assign or transfer this agreement. Only the specified terms, hereby incorporating Article 2 of the Uniform Commercial Code, are binding. No waiver is binding unless set forth in writing. Nonetheless, invoice may reflect, and client is bounded by, oral authorizations for fees or expenses which could not be confirmed in writing due to immediate proximity of shooting.

(h) Any dispute regarding this agreement, including its validity, interpretation, performance, or breach, shall be arbitrated in (Photographer's City and State) under rules of the American Arbitration Association and the laws of (State of Arbitration). Judgment on the Arbitration award may be entered in the highest Federal or State Court having jurisdiction. Any dispute involving $1000 or less may be submitted, without arbitration, to any Court having jurisdiction thereof. Client shall pay all arbitration and court costs, reasonable Attorneys' fees plus legal interest on any award or judgement.

(i) Additional Specifications: (to be filled in as applicable)
Placement (cover, inside, etc. _____).
Size (½ page, 1 page double page, etc. _____).
Time limit on use _____ Use outside U.S. (if any) _____.
Copyright Credit Line is required in the following form: © 19____ (insert photographer's name).

(j) Client agrees that the above terms are made pursuant to Article 2 of the Uniform Commercial Code and agrees to be bound by same, including specifically clause (h) above to arbitrate disputes.

SAMPLE FORM GRANTING PERMISSION
TO REPRODUCE A WORK OF ART IN A PUBLICATION

<u>PERMISSION AGREEMENT</u>

_____(Name of Artist)_____ grants you permission to reproduce the work:

Title of Work:_____ Dimensions:_____

Date:_____ One Time Only In/For:_____

Publisher/Producer:_____

Proposed Publication/Use:_____ Date of Publication/Use:_____

under the following terms and conditions:

1. Permission is granted for one-time use of the specified work, only in the publication or for the use designated in this agreement.

2. The following copyright notice must appear adjacent to the work in all copies of the publication:
   "© 19___ _(Name of Artist)_ . All Rights Reserved."
   "Photograph by ___(Name of Photographer)_____."

3. Nothing may be superimposed on the photograph. No deletions from, additions to, or changes in the photograph may be made without the written approval of _(Name of Artist)_ .

4. The reproduction of the work must bear the complete title as specified above.

5. The rights hereby granted may not be assigned or transferred and shall terminate in the event publication or use does not occur within two years from the date of this agreement or if the publication remains out of print for six months.

6. This permission confers non-exclusive rights in the English language and use or distribution in the United States, its dependencies and Canada.

7. _(Name of Artist)___ will receive a complimentary copy of the publication in which the work appears.

8. The permission fee for use of the work is _____, payable _____.

This is not an authorization until signed below and payment has been received.

Kindly return one signed copy of this letter for our files.

_____
(Name of Artist)

AGREED TO AND ACCEPTED:

_____
(Name of Grantee)

Dated:_____

THE USE OF BINDING ARBITRATION CLAUSES IN VISUAL ARTISTS' CONTRACTS

A binding arbitration clause is often employed in contracts to avoid the time and financial burdens of extended legal action when disputes arise about the contract. Frequently, artists find themselves in the following situation: The artist has performed all or part of the obligations under the contract and a controversy arises over payments, abuse or misuse of the artwork, poor or lack of performance by the other party. If the money to be gained from the contract is a modest sum, the artist will probably elect to retain what he/she already has rather than expend it on what could be time-consuming and/or costly legal action. Arbitration affords a relatively speedy and economical means of settling such disputes.

When a controversy is submitted for arbitration, the arbitrator will hear both sides and render a decision to resolve the dispute. Since the arbitrator's award is final and binding, neither side will be able to seek further legal action on the matter.

SAMPLE BINDING ARBITRATION CLAUSE

The parties agree that any controversy arising out of this agreement shall be submitted to binding arbitration and that a final decision or award by the arbitrator shall be final. The arbitration procedure, including the selection of an arbitrator, shall be in accordance with the rules of (name of selected arbitration association) in force at the time the arbitration proceeding is initiated. The decision or award of the arbitrator shall be the complete and final settlement of the arbitrated controversy and the parties agree to be bound by and comply with all the terms of the decision or award. The parties specifically understand that any further proceedings in a court of law regarding an arbitrated controversy are limited to enforcement of the arbitrator's decision or award.

SAMPLE NOTICE TO PURCHASER OF RESALE ROYALTIES AND MORAL RIGHTS (ART PRESERVATION)

Pursuant to the laws of the State of California, the sale of this work is subject to the provisions of the California Resale Royalty Act (California Civil Code Section 986) and the California Fine Arts Preservation Act (California Civil Code Section 987).

Under the Resale Royalty Act, you are responsible, when the work is sold or transferred in any form, to pay to the artist 5% of the gross sales price received by you for the work providing that amount is $1,000 or more (in the event other artworks or property are part of the sales price, the 5% royalty will be calculated from the fair market value of such goods). This provision shall not apply if the gross sales price for the work is less than the purchase price paid by you to the artist.

Pursuant to the California Fine Arts Preservation Act, you may not intentionally deface, mutilate, alter or destroy the work or authorize another to do so.

NOTE TO ARTIST USING THIS NOTICE: This notice may be used only with regard to original painting, sculpture and drawing.

It should be given to a purchaser accompanying a Bill of Sale when the purchaser has refused or is not likely to sign a more formal Resale Royalty Agreement which would encompass as well the preservation of the work of art. (See Sample Artist's Reserved Rights Transfer and Sale Agreement.)

It can also be used, at your request, by your gallery or representative and in conjunction with other contracts for the sale of your work.

Similar notices may be drafted to reflect the laws of other states.

CHAPTER THREE
THE VISUAL ARTIST AND THE MOVIES

Hope London, Esq.

Fifty years ago, artists played an integral role in the development of animated films as they gave life to imaginary characters and settings. Today, as moviemakers attempt to realize increasingly fantastic visions, artists are faced with new challenges to their skills. Yet the visual artist has often been treated as a marginal, supporting player in the movie industry rather than as an essential creative force.

Traditionally, the visual artist in the film industry has had little bargaining power. Artists are often willing to accept poor compensation and working conditions in order to obtain any kind of employment which will enable them to exercise their professional abilities. The possibility of retaining any rights in their work has, until recently, received little contemplation. Formal negotiations and contracts are the exception, not the rule. Conditions for the artist in the movie industry seem to be improving, due to the increased business sophistication of some artists and, to a certain extent, union activities. There are promising opportunities in the areas of animation and special effects, but the future role of the artist is far from clear.

This article will explore the relationship of the artist to the film industry, through interviews with two people whose work the industry uses. Art Babbitt is a pioneer in the art of animation, popularly known as the creator of the Disney character Goofy and as choreographer of the dance of the Chinese mushrooms in *Fantasia*. He is currently working on a feature-length film in production at Richard Williams Animation, as well as a multimedia animation "bible."

Syd Mead is an illustrator and industrial designer who originally specialized in architectural rendering. Several years ago, he was asked to participate in the design of the "V'ger" vehicle for the *Star Trek* motion picture. Since then, he has continued to apply his skills to the creation of what he terms "alternate realities" in film, and is now working on Filmways' *Bladerunner*.

The perspectives of these two artists differ vastly in terms of the time and conditions under which they entered the industry and the ways in which their talents are employed. Each has unique insights and experiences to share with other artists, especially those who either are now or wish to become involved in the movie industry.

THE ARTIST IN AN EMERGING INDUSTRY: ART BABBITT

When Art Babbitt began working as an animator in the 1920s, negotiated contracts between artist and studio were practically unheard of. In his first job, at Terrytoons in New York, he had no contract of any kind. In his next job, at Walt Disney Studios, the situation was quite different. All the animators and assistants were obliged to sign contracts if they wished to work. According to Mr. Babbitt, these were "very bad, yellow dog contracts" completely in favor of the studio. "They [the studio] could do anything they pleased, and everything you did belonged to them. You had no rights whatsoever, and they could cut you off in a minute if they wanted to, or they could hang on to you." Apparently even animators who remained at the Disney studio for years were constantly in fear of losing their jobs. The small size of the animation industry and the economic depression of the time contributed to these fears. Artists who simply were glad to be working gave little thought to asking for copyrights, residuals or improved compensation and working conditions. This was true despite the fact that, as "actors with a pencil," the animators were the real stars of the Disney films.

Mr. Babbitt's assessment of working conditions at Disney is incisively illustrated by this recollection: "One of the elements of your social status at Disney was determined by the kind of covering you had on your floor. If you were an assistant or an in-betweener, you just had linoleum on the floor. If you were an animator just starting to animate with an uncertain future, you had carpeting, but it never got closer than a foot from the walls of your room. If you had it made, if you were a recognized animator, and I was one of them, you had wall-to-wall carpeting . . . it was absolutely insane." Mr. Babbitt tempered this view, however, noting that the artistic compensation at Disney was unparalleled. There was room for individual development and expression, and the artists were proud of their product. "I must say that animation would never have reached the epitome that it did if it hadn't been for his [Disney's] drive. He couldn't even begin to draw as well as the people around him, but he was astute enough to surround himself with the best."

To Mr. Babbitt's knowledge, the one-sided Disney contracts were not challenged until Disney personnel went on strike in 1941. He played an important part in organizing that strike, which resulted in the formation of the Motion Picture Screen Cartoonists union. "We did, through our strike, get a number of benefits that we didn't have before. A contract was a contract that was meaningful; wages jumped astronomically. People like inkers and painters, who were earning $18.00 a week, got the munificent minimum of $35.00 a week. The minimum for animators went up to $85.00 a week." Some health and pension benefits also were obtained. Although Mr. Babbitt was much better paid than most of his colleagues prior to the strike, he believed strongly that artists must unite in order to increase their bargaining power, and risked his career for this belief. He was fired from Disney four times for being a "labor agitator." That led to an extended court battle which he ultimately won, but the experience left both sides very bitter.

Although the animators have a union today, Mr. Babbitt feels that it is essentially powerless. He sees one reason as the nondemanding level of animation work required for the Saturday-morning type of children's cartoons which comprises most of the work done by union members. The work can often be done more cheaply outside the United States without an appreciable difference in quality. Job security is as nonexistent as ever. In Babbitt's terms, "When the season is over, out you go." He feels that the situation for today's animators is better only in the financial aspect, and worse in that there is little chance to improve one's abilities or to participate in productions of high quality. The union has not enabled the artist to retain any rights in his work, and Mr. Babbitt is still irked when he sees work that he did as far back as the 1920s being used again and again while he receives no additional compensation. He believes that artists should fight for some sort of residual payment in the future. When he was elected president of the cartoonists' union in 1946, Mr. Babbitt unsuccessfully urged fellow members to demand such payments. He recalls how at that time "nobody knew what residuals were, but it seemed to me that it was only fair that those people who had made major contributions to pictures like *Snow White* or *Dumbo* or *Fantasia* or *Pinocchio* should get some sort of repayment or additional payment when the pictures were released again."

Mr. Babbitt cited the lack of unity between artists in the technical and creative branches of animation as a reason for the failure of his proposal. The union is vertical, and includes "everybody from the janitor to the Pope." Mr. Babbitt believes that this detracts from the bargaining power of the union members at the top of the profession. "All the janitors get together and the poor Pope is left out in the cold." It is interesting to note that the polarization of "technical" and "creative" personnel parallels the division of labor in the animation industry according to sex. Women have traditionally been relegated to the tedious tasks of inking and painting animation cels, while animation was a male preserve. While this attitude is becoming somewhat less prevalent today, it was voiced in Mr. Babbitt's comment that when he proposed the idea of residuals, "some little girl in the ink and paint department stood up and said, 'But we've been paid for it once.'"

Still another, more basic cause may account for the weak bargaining position of the artist. In Mr. Babbitt's view, the artist "has yet to make himself indispensable. He is not that good yet, and that's a prerequisite. You cannot demand a certain salary from an orchestra if you can't play the goddamned fiddle." He favors splitting the union into technical and creative branches, so that those people who make significantly greater creative contributions will be in a position to demand more protection and participation in their artwork in return. Another method of improving conditions might be to use an attorney or business manager to negotiate contracts, but Mr. Babbitt has never done this. Even today, his business arrangements are relatively informal. At one point in his career, he directed animated and live-action commercials, and it was all done "on a handshake." His present work for Richard Williams Animation has been partially documented through a letter of intent which discusses basic terms such as compensation, but is very flexible. Mr. Babbitt prefers the informality in this case, apparently because he has a great deal of faith and a close working relationship with his employer, and believes in the artistic merit of the work he is doing. Ordinarily, however, he would advise an artist who is in a position to do so to request not only substantial periodic payments, but benefits such as health insurance and contributions to a pension plan, as well as a guarantee of a certain term of employment. As far as control of the artwork is concerned, Mr. Babbitt finds it reasonable that the employer retain original artwork as well as copyright when work is done on a work-for-hire basis. He suggests, however, that artists might consider some unorthodox approaches, such as developing their own characters and licensing them to a studio. In addition, he would strongly recommend that artists attempt to structure some type of residual compensation into their employment agreements.

In the end, the treatment the artist receives is determined by his individual abilities and standing in the profession. Under the best of circumstances, an established animator may achieve a certain level of creative control, similar to that which an actor whose opinions are respected would have. More often, taking too much artistic control is a risky business. Mr. Babbitt relates how he once "padded" a scene (something which is strictly taboo), increasing it from seven feet to fifty-six feet of film. That, however, was the scene that established Goofy as a major Disney character. A caveat from Mr. Babbitt: "You'd better not take that chance if you want to keep your job!"

How can an artist attain respect as an animator and the bargaining leverage that would come with that respect? Mr. Babbitt states that "you can't command anything unless you have something that is irreplaceable to offer." His advice to aspiring animators would be first to "know how to draw, because that is [the animator's] vocabulary . . . I'm stodgy and I believe that if you can draw the human figure from the skeleton out, then you can probably draw a motorcycle or a house or what have you." Then, the animator must constantly observe and analyze the movement of each person and thing he sees, "from a piece of grass waving as the result of some invisible force, to some peculiar walk that is due to the fact that one shoulder is lower than the other. . . . People say they always look at eyes first. I don't. I look at hands and feet." Nor is Mr. Babbitt threatened by the emerging use of computer animation in film. He sees it as a useful tool that might streamline the animation process, but not capable of replacing the unique perceptions of the animator. "It still comes back to the human being, the artist, to handle it."

A NEW ROLE FOR THE ARTIST: SYD MEAD

Syd Mead is a knowledgeable artist/businessperson who is concerned about his legal rights and obligations. Like Mr. Babbitt, he has conducted most of his business on the "honor system" rather than through formal contracts. As an independent illustrator and designer, his usual practice is to send clients proposal letters specifying their requirements and outlining the degree and nature of artistic control which he will have in preparing the work. He often inserts special provisions for items such as additional compensation for later modification of the work at the client's request, in order to avoid subsequent foreseeable problems. He did not routinely use an attorney to negotiate or draft agreements until after his involvement in motion pictures began.

Mr. Mead is unusual in that he did not intentionally seek to enter the movie business. On the contrary, he had been an extremely successful artist for years when he was approached by the manager for special effects expert John Dykstra. Dykstra was designing sets and vehicles for the *Star Trek* movie, and desired assistance with concept drawings. Syd Mead was "discovered" because some of the corporate brochures he had designed were being used by a local university as design and rendering reference materials. *Star Trek* designers who were former students remembered his work and recommended him for the job. Mr. Mead worked on the design of the "V'ger" spacecraft for the film, which brought his work to the attention of the producers of *Bladerunner,* who required precisely the kind of science fiction, "high tech" illustration and design in which Mead excels. Unlike most artists, he was in an excellent bargaining position because he did not need the work. Ironically, his most difficult problem in entering the movie industry has been that his daily rates are often more than producers can afford.

It was at this point in his career that Mr. Mead decided to use an attorney to negotiate for him. In his words, he needed someone who was removed from the artwork to do the infighting. He likens the function of attorneys to that of "seconds at a duel." It is important to him to have someone to discuss business so that he can concentrate on the personal and artistic aspects of his relationship with the filmmakers. He commented that "in Hollywood, it's almost considered indecent if you discuss your own price." Mead's current agreement for work on the film *Bladerunner* contains a number of provisions which were important to him on a personal level. For example, he insisted upon working at home rather than at the studio, in order not to be isolated from his other clients. He makes his services available to the studio on an "on call" basis rather than giving them the exclusive use of his time while the film is being made, and is paid a per diem rate at least equivalent to what he would receive for his corporate design work. This is a significant benefit, because the single daily rate relieves the artist from the pressure of having to accept step payments or penalties for lateness. In pre-production, concept drawings are needed early so that sets and props can be constructed. In special effects, which are usually done post-production, pressure is intense to finish the film.

Mr. Mead's attorney stressed other points as well. One is the importance of the artist's retaining original artwork, although the studio generally retains the copyright. Occasionally, the artist may be able to negotiate for the right to reproduce the work, but that would be possible only with exceptional bargaining strength. Another provision insisted upon is the automatic reversion of copyright to the artist if uses are made of the artwork which were not contemplated at the time of the agreement. Specifically, this is aimed at the situation in which a prospective producer asks the artist to prepare concept drawings of things such as buildings, vehicles and costumes for use in presentation to potential backers of the film. If the film is actually made, the producer will then be forced to renegotiate with the artist for the use of the artist's work. This avoids a potential "rip-off" of the artist if payment for the initial work was low.

Mr. Mead's attorney was able to obtain another provision for his client which is innovative and unique for a visual artist: he will receive a point distribution on the merchandising of any items which incorporate his concepts. Mr. Mead attributes his success in bargaining with the producers to the fact that his particular skills as an artist and designer have set him apart and put him in demand: "One of the reasons I was selected to do *Bladerunner* specifically is because the fact that I paint is sort of beside the point. I'm usually hired for my ideas. The fact that I'm an artist is an added convenience to myself, because I can interpret my own ideas . . . and it's a convenience to the client because in that case you have a one-source idea and presentation person. The idea doesn't have to go through a second stage and it comes out more accurate. It's irritating a little bit to a very structured industry like the movie industry because I don't fit into a convenient category."

At the present time, Syd Mead is in the process of working out an arrangement with M-G-M to create the "visual tone" of an upcoming film. He states: "I can do that, being a designer, because you can synthesize any degree of reality or technological accomplishment that you think is going to be appropriate; whereas an artist per se or an illustrator can do beautiful illustrations, but not having a design sense would not be able to invent a kind of a mechanical or a design integrity and then illustrate that. They have to take somebody else's accomplished idea and then make a picture out of it." He also pointed out that most of the people who worked with George Lucas on the effects and designs for *Star Wars* and *The Empire Strikes Back* had backgrounds in design as well as sketch and illustration technique. In fact, Mr. Mead approaches his work in films as he would an industrial design project. "There's a problem, and you figure out what the problem is and how somebody wants to solve it." With the current popularity of films that take place in extraterrestrial environments, his ability to invent an alternate reality and then illustrate it photographically has put him in great demand.

The film industry has utilized Syd Mead's creative imagination and conceptual abilities as an artist in addition to his skills as a renderer. This is significant for all artists. His experience illustrates the elevation of the visual artist from technician status to that of a person with more fundamental input into the structure and mood of a film, and a corresponding increase in bargaining power and remuneration.

These interviews document two distinct approaches to the relationship between the artist and the film industry. Mr. Babbitt's contractual arrangements have been either informal or structured by a studio or union. His status as one of the top animators working today now allows him to make very satisfactory deals with a minimum of negotiation. However, he still laments the fact that he never obtained residuals or other proprietary interests in the movies and characters to which he so significantly contributed. His original artwork remains the property of the studios that employed him. Syd Mead has approached the situation differently from the outset. By employing an attorney who is an advocate of artist rights, he has entered into agreements that permit him to retain original artwork and even receive a portion of profits that will accrue from the use of the work. Mr. Mead's attorney advises artists to seek legal assistance as soon as they "separate themselves from the pack," by doing more than straight union work. The proverbial "bottom line" is bargaining power—if the artist can offer something the moviemaker needs, the opportunities for creative work and fair compensation are as unlimited as the artist's imagination.

PART TWO

LEGAL PROTECTION FOR THE CREATOR AND THE CREATION

CHAPTER FOUR

WHAT TO DO UNTIL THE LAWYER ARRIVES

Jerald Ordover, Esq.

This article will touch upon the kinds of problems which the artist may expect to encounter in the course of his or her career. I will draw upon my own experiences and will describe some of the cases I have handled for artists to illustrate these problems and how they may be solved.

The first artist I was ever called upon to help was being harassed by his landlady. This was in 1958. It was not until 1964 that I was again called upon to assist an artist, but starting in that year, a growing number of artists and art world people began to retain me and, within several years, my law practice was almost totally given over to their problems.

The main thrust of this article is the point that most of the problems that the artist may encounter will not be related to his profession, but are the sort of problems that could befall any small businessperson or professional. At the same time, whether as an aspect of the typical "artist personality" or the societal and peer pressures on the artist to deny any knowledge or awareness of business practices, those routine problems are often laden with odd details and twists when the client is an artist.

For example, in that 1958 case, the artist came to me after having been charged in criminal court by the landlady-complainant with having stolen the furniture with which his sublet apartment had been furnished. The furniture turned out to be so decrepit and worn that the artist and his roommate had bought usable secondhand furniture, throwing away the old material after the Salvation Army refused to take it. The landlady, who occupied a second apartment elsewhere in the building, had kept a key to my client's apartment and would march through the place frequently and at all hours, asserting this to be her right. He put up with this for several months before he made an inquiry and learned that he did not have to put up with these intrusions and changed the lock. She thereupon filed the theft complaint. The matter was later resolved and the complaint withdrawn after my client signed over the replacement furniture to the landlady. Several months later, I came across her name in the New York *Daily News;* she had been arrested for attacking a Central Park Zoo employee with her umbrella after he told her that she was not allowed to feed the zoo's gorilla. She resented this interference, contending that she and the gorilla were friends.

In 1964, I was retained to get an artist out of jail and defend him against charges of disorderly conduct and assaulting a police officer. Six months later, I was again called upon to spring an artist and his wife from jail; I obtained the wife's release in night court and returned the following morning to secure his release on bail. The charges again involved an alleged assault on a police officer.

Please don't assume that I had become involved with the Hell's Angels of the art world. The first client, while intoxicated, had allegedly assaulted the club of a mounted policeman with his head and back; the second altercation developed in a Central Park playground early one summer evening when a policeman mistakenly tried to order the young couple out, not having noticed their three-year-old daughter playing in the sandbox. This expanded into a dispute over whether the wife was violating a park ordinance against placing one's feet on park benches when she tucked one foot beneath her as she sat beside her husband.

Over the years since then, I have rendered other services to these artists, both of whom achieved national recognition early in the 1960s, so that they have been able to devote their full time to art. As an example of the kinds of problems that could send an artist running for a lawyer, the following are among the twenty-odd matters I have handled or reviewed for the first artist since 1964:

He returned to see me in mid-1965, after the assault charges were dismissed, for help in getting him out of his loft lease. The rent for the 5,000-square-foot studio was $250 per month; he was moving to Santa Fe and none of the artists he knew who needed space could afford a rent that high. We worked out a settlement with his landlord and, before he left for New Mexico, I did his first will. Thereafter, with the artist back in New York, I helped him close the purchase of a house in Santa Fe for his family. In 1966, I assisted him in the preparation of a successful application for a Guggenheim Foundation fellowship by editing his statements, helping to collect references, photos and requested information and reviewing the finished application.

In 1967, I first advised him on an art-related matter. Another sculptor had made a piece which involved my client making one of his metal sculptures, so that the finished piece contained equal contributions by both men. My client learned that the other sculptor had sold the piece to a collector and that his part of the sculpture had been repainted. This did not result in a landmark decision defining the right of an artist to keep his work intact and in its original form, as against the wishes of the work's owner to improve, restore or change it, because, like so many art world problems, it was settled. The first sculptor remitted a share of his profit and my client was invited by the collector to inspect the work. The repainting turned out to be a restoration of damaged portions.

Thereafter, I collected payment from an insurance carrier for damage to a sculpture while on loan to a Pittsburgh museum, then went on to assist him in matters involving the long-term loan of his truck to a colleague and the subletting of his Fourteenth Street studio to an eccentric performance artist. I reviewed or negotiated several other leases and lease assignments for him during the next ten years and, in 1968, I represented him in his divorce.

Then, during the 1970s, I collected the balance due him for the sale of a sculpture made directly to a collector and halted the attempted sale of metallic debris salvaged from a former studio, which was being passed off as the artist's sculpture. In 1976, I was called upon to settle an old judgment obtained against him in Los Angeles County years before, after the judgment creditor attached sculptures being exhibited in Los Angeles. He consulted me about forming a company to market sculptural furniture he had designed. Following the death of his first wife, I handled his appointment as guardian of the property of his infant children.

Note that none of these matters involved disputes with his own dealers. During the twenty-five years that he has been exhibiting work, he has never had a written contract with the two dealers who have represented him for most of that time. This is typical of relations between major galleries and the artists they care about.

Copyright problems may also arise. Commercial artists may find their work or concepts readapted to advertising uses without their consent; photographers face the problem of unauthorized reproduction of their work without credit or payment. As fine art prints and multiples find a growing public, unauthorized reproductions become a greater problem, and the artist must become acquainted with methods of copyright protection and enforcement. The artist and the photographer must be aware of libel laws and of civil rights laws that protect against having one's likeness ridiculed or utilized for commercial purposes without permission. Thus one may reproduce a news photograph of a topless performance artist or musician in a news publication, but may not produce and market an edition of posters of the photograph. A money judgment was obtained against a New York artist by two of his colleagues after he painted them, in a clearly identifiable way, as muggers attacking the helpless Muse.

In collaborating with or employing other artists, it is important to be very clear about roles and rights in the finished product. If an artist hires another to fabricate his sculpture, or to re-create a geometric wall drawing, or to mount a work of conceptual art consisting of letters and words, the relationship is generally rather clear and understood. But when an artist enlists friends in a work of performance art, or collaborates with a photographer or a sound engineer in creating a work, the question of credits and share of profits, if the work is sold, should be discussed and agreed upon before the work is performed or exhibited. If a photographer's slides are to be an integral part of an artist's work, credits and reproduction rights should be discussed and agreement reached in advance. When a photographer takes pictures of an artist's work, it is generally understood that the artist will pay for the copies he wants and the photographer owns the photograph. But what if the photograph is of a work of temporary art or an earthwork, where the work will be known only through the photograph? Again, prior agreement generally provides the solution to any possible problems for both parties.

Just as this article was being written, I learned of a new claim. A temporary artwork consisting of a prearranged layout of lights in a group of Manhattan office towers was photographed at the request of a nonprofit organization which had sponsored and helped to arrange the project for the artist. The organization had purchased a quantity of the photographs. Thereafter, the photographer sold several copies to others and has now been presented with a claim by the artist, who wants a share of the sale proceeds on the grounds that his work provided the subject matter for the photographs. I am not involved in the matter and do not represent any of the parties. In my opinion, the artist cannot recover; if his argument is that photographs are the only way in which he can benefit from his artwork, this should have motivated him to make special arrangements before the event took place. It does not constitute a good legal argument after the fact.

Examples of outright stealing by a dealer or representative are rare. Most of the disputes between artists and dealers that have come to my attention relate to the dealer's loss of faith or interest in the artist's work, his failure to press for sales or to carry on the various activities that will advance the artist's career or the demand for his work—or to the artist's perception that this is the case. All of this is ordinarily beyond the power of the lawyer to correct or recover damages for, except where the perception is incorrect or the dealer wishes to correct the situation. At times, the lawyer, as a third party, can discuss these complaints with the dealer or representative, clear the air and bring about an improvement in the handling of the artist. But specific and real problems do arise where the artist is not being paid his share of sales in a timely manner, where he is not receiving the correct amounts, where inventory is sloppily handled and work is lost, mislaid or damaged, where reports of sales and payments are not sent on a regular and timely basis.

When a dispute arises between artist and dealer, I am generally unconcerned about whether or not a written agreement exists unless, of course, the dispute relates to any contract terms. If the parties are no longer getting along, for whatever reason and no matter who is to blame, and if *my* client would be better off leaving the gallery—or the dealer no longer wants to represent him—then the written contract becomes irrelevant. The artist gains nothing from remaining with a dealer who dislikes him or his work and won't do an effective job of promoting it. Nor can the dealer force an angry artist to produce work for his gallery. To try to bind the artist to the contract and keep him from selling to others is bad business for the dealer; it can only hurt the prices of the works he already owns, besides being difficult to enforce.

In one case, I guided and advised an artist who wished to withdraw from his gallery and feared economic reprisals. Remaining in the background, I helped him to extract most of the money owed to him by the gallery and most of his works in its inventory. When he finally broke the news to his dealer, his accounts were even and there was little the dealer could do except to accept the artist's decision with an outwardly amicable attitude. In another case, I had the artist collate his various lists of works produced and consigned to the dealer during the preceding ten years. The dealer's annual statements fortunately listed the titles of the works which had been sold. The artist then requested an inventory of unsold works from the dealer, which was forthcoming several weeks later. The report listed some older works which were not on my client's tally. And the dealer turned up two sales for which he had failed to account to the artist. We were satisfied that this was a matter of faulty bookkeeping rather than chicanery, but it did net the artist an additional $3,000. Following my advice, the artist had the dealer return any of the older works which the dealer did not think were salable. As for the works he retained, having thus been reminded of their existence, the dealer managed to sell a number of them during the next two years. The dealer also agreed to update and to report the inventory annually. The artist began keeping an accurate list of the works he produced in a bound notebook rather than on scraps of paper.

The establishment by the artist of his own inventory and sales records and the general tightening up of the business relationship between artist and gallery eased much of the tension between them and worked a great improvement in their personal relationship, so that it continued for another six or seven years. At that point, for other reasons, the artist shifted to a smaller but more prestigious gallery. His reputation had meanwhile increased to match his talent, so that he is now recognized as one of the masters of American sculpture. And those early works, returned to him by the dealer as unsalable, have increased sharply in value.

In representing artists I have had to learn two key maxims. The first is that they usually have little or no experience in business and often demonstrate a lack of awareness of those basic protective procedures which most people have learned to apply in money matters as a matter of common sense. Thus, we come across artists who obtain no receipts for works consigned to a dealer, who leave work with an out-of-town dealer for one or more years and never inquire about it (often out of a feeling that if one doesn't nag the dealer, perhaps the fellow, moved by the good taste this reticence displays, will someday sell it). The other side of this naiveté is the occasional display of unethical conduct. I have listened to artists describe their relations with a dealer and tell me, with not a trace of self-consciousness, of secret sales from the studio directly to collectors at prices below those set by the gallery, of the refusal to deliver work knowing that the dealer has a buyer because the artist has found a new gallery and has then instructed his new dealer to make the sale to the same collector, or of changing galleries and canceling a scheduled show a short time before the opening. Such ignorance or naiveté often enables the lawyer to emerge as a hero with very little effort.

The second maxim is that achieving a successful result for an artist often requires that we aim for less than a total victory. Even if the dealer or publisher is not "the only wheel in town," it may be more important for the parties to continue working together than for the artist to recover a full measure of damages for the past wrong. Even if the artist and the dealer have no interest in a future association, care must be taken that the artist not acquire a reputation for being "difficult" which might discourage other dealers from taking him on.

This may be unnecessary in the world of advertising, but the artist or photographer interested in editorial work for the major magazines of his area of specialization should heed these factors. But whether in an ad agency or an art gallery, money and power govern.

During the mid-sixties, I came across a New York dealer who regularly employed a written contract, the only dealer I then knew of who did so. He also enjoyed a singular reputation for petulance, a nasty temper and broken promises. Since his contract did not require him to do much more than remit the artist's share of any sales within a reasonable time, I never heard him accused of a direct breach of contract. An artist newly arrived from Washington brought me one of this man's contracts to read. I told him some horror stories and pointed out how little the proposed agreement gave him. His reply was that he knew all this, but that he had been promised a one-person show and this was the only offer he had had to exhibit in New York. He had his show, and, predictably, within two years they broke up in anger.

In another case, three artists, each with written agreements calling for monthly stipends from their newly established gallery, came to me complaining that the dealer had, without prior notice, suspended the stipends and announced that he would pay no more. My inquiry revealed that these artists had been signed up by a director who had been discharged just before the gallery opened. The gallery had been in operation for three or four months at the time of the breach. The dealer's defense was that he had failed to sell any of their works during that time and just could not afford to continue the stipends. The contracts were clear and enforceable and each ran for three years. In return for exclusivity, each contract obliged the gallery to pay the artist a fixed monthly advance, to be covered by the artist's share of the proceeds of any sales and, if sales were insufficient, the gallery was to select work from the artist at the end of each year to settle the account.

I pointed out to my clients that the contracts could be enforced, but it meant that they could then deal only with this gallery for the contract term, so that for the next three years the bulk of their output would disappear into this dealer's storage rooms, with no guarantee of exhibitions beyond the single show that each was guaranteed during the first year. The dealer offered to continue showing their work if they gave up the stipend, although he expressed little confidence in his ability to sell their work. He made it quite clear that if they insisted on enforcement of the contracts, he would make no effort to deal the work. The settlements I negotiated reflected the different attitude of each artist. The first artist, who had been given the inaugural exhibition and who had been receiving the largest stipend, $1,500 a month, decided that he could part with a year's output. He was paid the balance of the year's stipend and delivered additional works to the gallery at the then agreed-upon price, to cover the payment. The second artist wanted nothing further to do with this gallery and settled for five months of payments, or $2,500, and gave the gallery no work at all. The third artist, new to New York and looking forward to his first exhibition, agreed to settle for nine monthly payments and was given his one-man show. None of his works sold and he turned over most of the works in the show to cover the payments to him. These had been the only contracts which called for monthly stipends. In this case the artists were fortunate in that the dealer possessed sufficient assets, an unusual situation in that most newly formed art galleries are undercapitalized.

Often the dealer fails to meet his obligations to the artist because he just does not have the money. There is no general advice that can cover all such situations except that artists should stay on top of their dealings with the gallery. One need not become an accountant or a pest. (1) If the gallery does not furnish the artist with immediate memos of sales, loans or consignments to other dealers, the artist should visit or call the gallery at regular intervals, monthly or more frequently if past activity warrants, have friendly talks with the gallery assistant and bookkeeper about the artist's work and sales, (2) should keep tabs on the physical location of his work at the gallery and (3) when sales are made, find out when the money is coming, let the dealer know how badly the money is needed and come by for the check on the promised day. It may not be there or the dealer may put the artist off, but he is more likely to pay that artist than the one who shows up only when the dealer calls him.

A written contract need not be a formal document. If the artist has any uncertainty about his gallery arrangements, a letter to the dealer, setting forth his understanding of the terms mentioned in their talk, is strongly recommended. If the dealer disagrees with certain points, he is likely to reply in writing. If he does not, send a second letter summarizing the details corrected by the dealer's call. Not only does the letter or exchange of letters provide a reference to settle future disputes, but they are valid evidence of the contract, should the dispute move to court. More often, the existence of the writing leads to a resolution before litigation becomes necessary. (See the Contracts section of this Manual.)

Litigation is often the last resort, but in the art world, in many instances, it must be ruled out, not only because it may be counterproductive to the artist's future career, but for the simple reason that the artist does not have the money to sustain a court action or that the amounts involved do not justify suit. Regardless of whether the amounts are too low or the value of the art is high, this value is meaningless unless the work is sold. However, the option to sue should always be kept alive and in mind. Just as I suggested letters and memos to keep oral agreements straight, hold on to all the papers that come your way as you sell or try to sell your art: receipts, consignment memos, letters received and copies of letters sent. Make memos of important conversations relating to all business transactions and certainly do so if disputes occur. If money is due, do not rely solely on the telephone, but send letters periodically asking for payment and referring to prior demands for payment and promises to pay. Keep a log of the dates of your phone calls and visits. Do all this so that when you visit the lawyer you will have a case backed by solid facts and details. It will increase the chances of effecting a good recovery by settlement or of winning if litigation is resorted to. Moreover, if you and the lawyer agree that litigation is out of the question, he/she will be more likely to take on the matter for collection without litigation if there is strong supporting material with which to convince the adversary to settle.

In the 1978 trial of the suit by Lynn Factor against Frank Stella in Los Angeles, which the artist won, the complicated facts involved the existence of three separate versions of an abstract painting of the same geometric shape, each done in a different year in a different paint.

Around 1961, the artist began a new series of eight paintings to be done in aluminum paint. He painted the first three works using aluminum house paint, then switched to alumichrome, a different kind of oil paint, for the last five. Compulsive about such things, he redid the first three paintings in the second paint and this was the series exhibited. One was later bought by Mr. and Mrs. Factor from a Los Angeles dealer.

The artist eventually traded the original three paintings to artist friends for works of theirs. The Factors lent their painting to the Los Angeles County Museum, where it was badly damaged. Without seeing this painting (it did not leave the museum for another five years) and basing his opinion on the earlier restoration of another work from the series, the artist advised that the work could not be totally restored with no blemishes. The Factors then asked the artist to paint them a new version in exchange for the insurance proceeds. He agreed and did one, this time in acrylic paint, with the Factors' approval.

Several years later, that painting was put up at auction at Parke-Bernet in New York City in 1970. Meanwhile, the artist who owned the first version had sold it in 1968 to a New York collector who then lent it to a retrospective exhibition of Stella's work mounted in 1970 by the Museum of Modern Art.

The auction results disappointed Mrs. Factor. The painting brought "only" $17,000, below the optimistic estimate. She and her former husband had paid $1,800 for it eight years earlier. On the day of the auction, she and her attorney father learned of the existence of the other version in the museum show and immediately concluded that this was their original damaged work, secretly restored by the artist and then resold by him. They charged fraud, repeated this charge at annual intervals for several years despite my letters explaining the facts, after I pieced them together, and then brought suit shortly before the statute of limitations would have expired. Several years of expensive discovery proceedings, pleadings and counterpleadings elapsed before the three-day trial took place. At its end, the judge found in favor of the artist, based on testimony and proof of all of the facts which had been set forth in my letters to the plaintiff's father years before. But the artist's legal fees exceeded $35,000. At today's prices, his costs would probably be twice that.

What made it impossible for me to convince my adversary of the facts before suit was the absence of any written records or letter exchanges relating to the first version's creation, its trade, the agreement between the Factors and the artist to create the replacement version, the later disposition of the damaged painting and the failure of the artist to document the exhibited version as "Version I" and to describe the different versions for the catalogue text. I was able to turn up the sales invoices from the dealer's records, one dealer letter relating to the creation of the new painting for the Factors, shipping documents showing how late in time the damaged painting left the Los Angeles County Museum and, most importantly, the records of the New York art restorer who had treated all three versions at one time or another. All of the claims of fraud (which shifted as we eventually convinced our adversary of key facts) were afterthoughts. None of the alleged actions of the artist, which affected the value of each work not at all, would have distressed the collectors had they been described at the time.

CHAPTER FIVE
COPYRIGHT: AN ARTIST'S TOOL

Stephen F. Rohde, Esq.

What do a photograph of Oscar Wilde, a balsawood model of the steamship *Queen Mary,* the Zapruder film of the assassination of John F. Kennedy and a miniature sculptured reproduction of Rodin's "Hand of God" have in common?

Answer: They have each been found to be entitled to federal copyright protection.

Visual artists are quite comfortable with the tools of their trade: brush, palette, canvas, clay, knife, camera, ink, paints, etc. But all too often and, frankly, in the ordinary course of events artists rarely use a tool just as valuable and certainly as useful in the creation and perpetuation of their works; namely, copyright protection.

If you retain nothing else from this brief review of our copyright laws, the effort will have been justified if you learn once and for all that your artistic creations may be protected from plagiarism, infringement and unauthorized exploitation by simply taking advantage of one of the most important self-help statutes ever enacted. Without hiring a lawyer, without dealing with a bureaucratic labyrinth, without waiting months or years and (perhaps most importantly) without paying more than $10.00 for each work, you can enjoy sweeping rights and remedies which not only will protect your work for your own sense of security and control, but will significantly enhance the commercial value of your works, leading to widespread dissemination in a variety of media, all under your control and all for your financial benefit.

Forget all of the rumors and half-baked stories you may have heard from other artists or semi-professional suggesting that your painting, graphic, sculpture, design, photograph or other work of visual art is, for some esoteric reason, not entitled to copyright protection. Begin with the positive assertion that your work *is* entitled to copyright protection and that you intend to take advantage of all of the legal protection that is rightfully yours by following the simple and inexpensive steps described below and more elaborately set forth in numerous circulars available free from the Copyright Office.

What Is the Copyright Office?

The United States Copyright Office is a division of the Library of Congress. It is part of the federal government and, among other things, is empowered to administer the Copyright Act. All communications can be simply addressed to the Register of Copyrights, Library of Congress, Washington, DC 20559. The Copyright Office is not permitted to give legal advice but will provide, *free of charge,* a wide variety of circulars, all of which are listed in "Publications of the Copyright Office."

In simple, nontechnical language, these materials explain all of the provisions of the Copyright Act. Certainly, the best place to start is Circular R1, entitled "Copyright Basics," which in twelve pages provides a useful overview of the copyright law.

Although the Copyright Office is delighted to provide this information without charge, it hastens to point out that if you need information or guidance on matters such as disputes over the ownership of a copyright, suits against possible infringers, the procedure for getting a work published or the method of obtaining royalty payments, it may be necessary to consult an attorney.

One widespread misconception is that the Copyright Office "grants" copyrights to particular "applicants." This is inaccurate. Without ever contacting the Copyright Office, one obtains copyright protection merely by creating a work and upon publication affixing a proper copyright notice to the work. These steps themselves, without more, create copyright protection. If, however, it becomes necessary to bring a lawsuit for copyright infringement and, in addition, in order to enjoy *all* of the remedies available under the Copyright Act, it is necessary to file an application, pay a fee of $10.00 and deposit one or more copies of the work. (More about these procedures later.) The Copyright Office routinely reviews these applications to make certain that minimal statutory requirements have been met, and issues a Certificate of Registration of Copyright. Except in rare instances, there are no hearings, there are no further requirements and there is no additional expense. Indeed, obtaining a copyright registration is certainly easier than obtaining a driver's license (and it doesn't have to be renewed every few years).

What Is the "New Copyright Act"?

After years of debate and lobbying, Congress passed the Copyright Act of 1976 (Title 17 of the United States Code), which became effective on January 1, 1978. This was the first general revision of the United States copyright law since 1909. For certain limited purposes, the 1909 law is still applicable but has generally been superseded by the Copyright Act of 1976. The comments in this article deal, for the most part, with the law as it presently exists under the Copyright Act of 1976.

What Is Copyright?

Copyright is a form of legal protection provided under federal law to the authors of "original works of authorship," including literary, dramatic, musical, artistic and certain other intellectual works. It is not necessary for a work to be published or generally distributed to the public for it to be entitled to copyright protection.

The owner of a copyright has the *exclusive right* to do and to authorize others to do each of the following:

To reproduce the copyrighted work.

To prepare derivative works based upon the copyrighted work.

To distribute copies of the copyrighted work to the public by sale or other transfer of ownership, or by rental, lease or lending.

To perform the copyrighted work publicly, in the case of literary, musical, dramatic and choreographic works, pantomimes, and motion pictures and other audiovisual works.

To display the copyrighted work publicly in the case of literary, musical, dramatic and choreographic, and sculptural works, including the individual images of a motion picture or other audiovisual work.

It is a violation of law for anyone to exercise these rights without the permission of the copyright owner, subjecting the infringer to civil and criminal penalties (although criminal prosecutions are rare, except in the highly publicized cases of motion picture piracy).

The rights enjoyed by a copyright owner are not, however, unlimited in scope. In some cases, the copyright statute provides specific exemptions from copyright liability. In addition, the Copyright Act recognizes the doctrine of "fair use," treated separately below.

One of the fundamental limitations on copyright protection is the First Amendment to the United States Constitution. Copyright protects the form of expression of an idea, but not the idea itself. No artist can claim exclusive ownership over the idea of a winter glade, a sunset or a child's smile. An artist can most definitely claim copyright protection in his original painting, photography or sculpture of these public domain ideas.

What Works Are Protected by Copyright?

Copyright protection exists for "original works of authorship" when they become fixed in a tangible form of expression. The fixation does not need to be perceptible by the human eye so long as it may be communicated with the aid of a machine or device. The Copyright Act recognizes seven different categories of copyrightable works, of which the category "pictorial, graphic and sculptural works" is most important for our purposes here.

This list is illustrative and is not intended to exhaustively set forth the wide variety of artistic works entitled to copyright protection. Accordingly, provided the requirements of "creativity" and "originality" (discussed below) are met, the following are examples of copyrightable works: two-dimensional and three-dimensional works of fine, graphic and applied art, photographs, prints and art reproductions, maps, charts, globes, technical drawings, diagrams, models, artistic jewelry, enamel, glassware, tapestries, designs printed upon scarves and dress fabrics, dinnerware patterns, dolls, Christmas decorations, cemetery monuments, letterheads, bookends, clocks, lamps, door knockers, candlesticks, inkstands, chandeliers, piggy banks, sundials, salt and pepper shakers, fishbowls, casseroles, ashtrays, prints, lithographs, photoengravings, and labels.

The law requires a minimal element of *creativity*. The courts have continuously grappled with drawing a discernible line between that which contain some creativity and that which does not. One court put forth the following definition: "A thing is a work of art if it appears to be within the historical and ordinary conception of the term 'art.' " But Mr. Justice Holmes detected the cultural bias implicit in such a definition when he wrote that "it may be more than doubted, for instance, whether the etchings of Goya or the paintings of Manet would have been sure of protection when seen for the first time." Most artists need not be troubled by the requirement of creativity so long as they contribute an ounce of creative authorship.

Separate from creativity, a copyrightable work must be *original*. It cannot merely be a copy of another copyrighted work or even work in the public domain. But any distinguishable variation created by the artist in an otherwise unoriginal work of art will constitute sufficient originality to support a copyright. Likewise, an original reproduction of a work of art can itself be subject to copyright protection. For example, a miniature sculptured reproduction of Rodin's "Hand of God" was found to be protected because of the "complexity and exactitude" of the miniaturization, although a mere scale reduction would not itself be sufficiently original. Here again, most artists pride themselves on their originality and so long as they avoid the slavish copying of existing works, the requirements of originality will be met.

What Is Not Protected by Copyright?

Statutory copyright protection is generally not available for certain material, including:

Titles, names, short phrases and slogans; familiar symbols or designs which have not been originated by the author; mere variations of typographic ornamentation, lettering or coloring; mere listings of ingredients or contents.

Ideas, procedures, methods, systems, processes, concepts, principles, discoveries or devices, as distinguished from a description, explanation or illustration of such matters.

Works that have not been fixed in a tangible form of expression, such as choreographic works which have not been notated or recorded or improvisational performances or multimedia shows that have not been written or recorded.

Works consisting *entirely* of information that is common property and contains no original authorship, such as standard calendars, height and weight charts, tape measures and rules, and lists or tables taken from public documents or other common sources.

Can the Right of a Copyright Owner Be Divided and Separately Licensed?

One of the significant changes contained in the Copyright Act of 1976 is the abolition of the concept of the "indivisibility of copyright." Under the 1909 law there was a single "copyright" and the "bundle of rights" belonging to a copyright owner were "indivisible," making it impossible to "assign" anything less than all of the rights encompassed by the copyright.

The Copyright Act of 1976 explicitly recognizes the *divisibility* of copyright and provides that any of the exclusive rights comprised in a copyright may be transferred and owned separately. Moreover, so long as the assignment of a particular right is exclusive it may be limited in time or place of effect. Thus, for example, an artist who creates a distinctive design, let's say the caricature of a famous movie star, can enter into a series of separate exclusive licenses granting the copyright in the work for the jacket of a hardcover biography; a full-size poster; sheets and pillowcases; wallpaper; school book covers; and on and on. In addition, each of these exclusive licenses can be limited to a specific number of years or to a specific geographical market. (See Licensing and Merchandising section in this Manual.)

Divisibility benefits both the artist and the licensee. The artist is able to deliberately and, hopefully, with great care and foresight subdivide each of the separate rights he enjoys as copyright owner without the compulsion which previously existed under the 1909 law to assign his entire copyright to the first gallery or patron willing to pay enough to cover the overdue rent bill. Today, the artist, whether well established or unknown, can retain to himself certain rights or certain markets or certain time periods, thereby hedging his bets in hopes of increased popularity and commercial success.

By the same token, one who acquires a copyright by exclusive license of some but not all of the rights comprised in a copyright, is himself a "copyright owner" of those particular rights and is entitled to all of the protection and remedies accorded to a copyright owner, including the right to register his copyright and sue for infringement without joining the original copyright owner of the entire work.

Given the divisibility of copyright, great care must be taken in writing agreements by which certain rights in a work of art are transferred. An artist must make certain that the piece of paper he signs accurately describes exactly what it is he is disposing of, with any limitations as to time, territory or specific rights clearly expressed. In addition, if separate compensation is to be paid for separate rights (hopefully on the theory that the sum of the parts may be greater than the whole) similar care should be used in allocating the compensation, including any cash payments or royalties, as well as stating whether compensation for one exclusive right may be cross-collateralized against the compensation for another exclusive right. Depending upon the importance of the work and the money at stake, such negotiations and the drafting of agreements may require an attorney.

Who Can Claim Copyright?

Copyright protection arises upon the moment of creation. As soon as a work of authorship is created in fixed form, the copyright in that work immediately becomes the property of the author who created it. Thus the moment brush touches canvas or ink touches paper, a copyright comes into existence and is owned by the artist or author.

The only exception to this magnificent notion is that in the case of a "work made for hire" the employer and *not* the employee is presumptively considered the "author." (See Contracts for Employment section in this Manual.)

The authors of a joint work who have collaborated together are co-owners of the copyright in the work, unless there is a written agreement altering this relationship.

Copyright in each separate contribution to a periodical or other collective work is distinct from the copyright in the collective work as a whole and vests initially in the author of the separate contribution.

It is particularly important for artists to understand that mere ownership through purchase, gift or other transfer of a painting, photograph, sculpture or other work of visual art (or for that matter any copyrightable work) does not give the purchaser or possessor the copyright to the work itself. The law provides that transfer of ownership of any material object that embodies a protected work does not in and of itself convey any rights in the copyright. Thus, unless the artist and purchaser have a *written agreement* giving the purchaser some or all of the rights in the copyright, the purchaser of an artist's work is not entitled to reproduce that work, prepare derivative works, distribute copies of the work or license others to do so. Each of those rights comprised in the copyright are retained by the artist himself to do with as he sees fit, so long as he does not breach any agreement he has with the purchaser.

How Is a Copyright Secured?

As noted at the outset, no publication or registration or other action in the Copyright Office or elsewhere is required to secure copyright under the Copyright Act of 1976, unlike the 1909 law, which required either publication with copyright notice or registration in the Copyright Office. To repeat, copyright protection attaches to a work immediately upon its creation in fixed form. If work is prepared over a period of time, the part of the work existing in fixed form on a particular date constitutes the created work as of that date, giving rise to the peculiar notion that the upper portion of a painting, if completed first, is protected by copyright even before the lower portion is finished.

Although publication is no longer a crucial step in obtaining statutory copyright, publication remains important to copyright owners. The Copyright Act of 1976 defines "publication" as the distribution of copies of a work to the public by sale or other transfer of ownership or by rental, lease or lending and notes that the offering to distribute copies to a group of persons for purposes of further distribution, public performance or public display constitutes publication but a public performance or display or a work does not in and of itself constitute publication.

Publication remains an important concept because of several significant consequences which follow from publication, including:

When a work is published, published copies should bear a copyright notice.

Works that are published with notice of copyright in the United States are subject to mandatory deposit with the Library of Congress.

Publication of a work can affect the limitations on the exclusive rights of the copyright owner set forth in the Copyright Act of 1976.

The year of publication is used in determining the duration of publication for anonymous and pseudonymous works and for works made for hire.

Deposit requirements for registration of unpublished works differ from those for registration of published works.

A recurring question is whether the public display of a work of art constitutes "publication." Under the 1909 law, the answer to this question was highly disputable and the consequences drastic for the artist. Under the old law, several courts had decided that the mere public exhibition of a work constituted a publication thereof and that without a proper copyright notice, the work had been injected into the public domain and all copyright protection had been lost. The United States

Supreme Court softened this position by ruling that a general publication of a painting does *not* occur although it is publicly exhibited if the public is admitted to view the painting on the express or implied understanding that no copying shall take place, provided further that measures are taken to enforce this restriction.

Fortunately, the new Copyright Act makes clear that a display of a work of art does not in and of itself constitute publication. The only remaining quandary for the artist is presented by the principle that *public display combined with public sale or public offer of sale* can constitute a publication of the work. Once again, great care must be taken to ensure that if a public exhibition is not intended to constitute a sale or offer of sale, this is made apparent to the exhibitor or gallery and to the public. Of course, the safest route is to affix a proper copyright notice to the work in order to avoid any question or unintended publication.

What Is the Proper Copyright Notice?

When a work is published under the authority of the copyright owner, a notice of copyright should be placed on all publicly distributed copies, whether published inside or outside the United States. Failure to comply with the notice requirements can result in the loss of certain additional rights otherwise available to a copyright owner. As noted, the Copyright Office is not involved in the affixation of the copyright notice and the copyright owner need not obtain prior permission from the Copyright Office.

A proper copyright notice should contain three elements:

1. The symbol © or the word "copyright" or the abbreviation "copr." It is generally recommended that the symbol © be used since it (and only it) complies with the Universal Copyright Convention entitling the artist to certain international protection.

2. The year of first publication of the work. In the case of compilations or derivative works incorporating previously published material, the year date of first publication of the compilation or derivative work is sufficient. Of particular importance to visual artists is the rule that the year date may be *omitted* where a pictorial, graphic or sculptural work, with accompanying textual matter, if any, is reproduced in or on greeting cards, postcards, stationery, jewelry, dolls, toys or any "useful article."

3. The name of the owner of copyright in the work, or an abbreviation by which the name can be recognized, or a generally known alternative designation of the owner. Under most circumstances, a trade name, nickname or other generally known assumed name will suffice.

There is a special short-form notice applicable to pictorial, graphic and sculptural works published prior to January 1, 1978, and to later publications of works first published prior to January 1, 1978. Not only does the special short-form notice dispense with the requirement of the year of the first publication, but instead of the copyright owner's name, the notice can simply contain the initials, monogram, mark or symbol of the copyright owner, accompanied by the symbol ©. In such circumstances the name of the copyright owner must appear if not in the notice then on some accessible portion of the work, or on the margin, back, permanent base or pedestal, or on the substance on which the work was mounted. This special short-form notice does *not* apply to works first published after January 1, 1978.

Given the importance of a proper copyright notice, the Copyright Office warns: "Because of problems that might result in some cases from the use of variant forms of the notice, any form of the notice other than those given here [in Circular R1] should not be used without first seeking legal advice."

Where Should the Copyright Notice Be Placed?

The copyright notice should be "affixed" to copies of the work in such a manner and location as to "give reasonable notice of the claim of copyright." The three elements of the notice should ordinarily appear together on each copy. Whether "reasonable" notice has been given is a question of fact depending upon the circumstances of each case, and the artist should make a genuine effort to give "reasonable" notice notwithstanding his or her artistic concern about the disfigurement of the work.

A notice need not appear in the most prominent place on the work so long as it is legible to the naked eye (except where the work itself requires magnification, such as motion pictures, microfilms or filmstrips). Courts have upheld notices placed on the back or underside of a work. But no matter how prominent or legible, the notice must be "affixed" to the work. Copyright notices on tags, wrappers, containers or the wall of a room in which a work was displayed have been held by the courts *not* to constitute proper notice. On the other hand, a copyright notice on a gummed label intended to be pasted on the work and a copyright notice on cardboard display package with a plastic window containing a doll and used as a "keeping place" of the doll, have been upheld as sufficiently "affixed" to the work.

The Copyright Office has promulgated Regulations under the Copyright Act of 1976 specifying examples of acceptable methods of affixation and positions of the copyright notice for various works, including pictorial, graphic and sculptural works. Because of the importance of this issue and the uncertainties it presents for an artist genuinely interested in obtaining copyright protection, the five guidelines of the Copyright Office are set forth in full below:

> (1) where a work is reproduced in two-dimensional copies, a notice affixed directly or by means of a label cemented, sewn, or otherwise permanently secured to the front or back of the copies, or to any backing, mounting, matting, framing, or other material to which the copies are permanently attached in which they are permanently housed, is acceptable;
>
> (2) where a work is reproduced in three-dimensional copies, a notice affixed, sewn, or otherwise permanently secured to any visible portion of the work, or to any base, mounting, framing, or other material on which the copies are permanently attached or in which they are permanently housed, is acceptable;
>
> (3) where, because of the size or physical characteristics of the material in which the copies are reproduced, it is impossible or extremely impractical to affix a notice to the copies directly or by means of a permanent label, a notice is acceptable if it appears on a tag that is of durable material and that is attached to the copy with sufficient permanency that it will remain with the copy during the entire time it is passing through the normal channels of commerce;
>
> (4) where a work is reproduced in copies consisting of sheet-like or strip material bearing multiple or continuous reproductions of the work, the notice may be applied:
>
> (i) to the reproduction itself;
>
> (ii) to the margin, selvage, or reverse side of the copies at frequent and regular intervals; or

(iii) if the material contains neither a selvage nor a reverse side, to tags or labels attached to the copies, and to any spools, reels, or containers housing them in such a manner that a notice is visible during the entire time the copies are passing through their normal channels of commerce;

(5) If the work is permanently housed in a container, such as a game or puzzle box, a notice reproduced on the permanent container is acceptable.

While the Copyright Office's valiant effort at anticipating questions concerning the proper placement of the copyright notice is most laudable, it should be apparent that this issue, like so many others in the copyright law, is destined for judicial review.

Fortunately, unlike the law in effect before 1978, the new Copyright Act provides procedures for correcting errors and omissions of the copyright notice on works published on or after January 1, 1978. Generally, the omission or error does not *automatically* invalidate the copyright in a work if registration for the work has been made before or is made within five (5) years after the publication without notice, and a reasonable effort is made to add the notice to all copies that are distributed to the public in the United States after the omission has been discovered. If copyright protection was lost prior to 1978 through the use of an improper copyright notice, copyright protection cannot be recaptured under the more lenient provisions of the new law.

Finally, although a copyright notice is not required on unpublished works, it is prudent for the artist to affix a proper copyright notice to any copies which leave his or her control.

What Is the Procedure to Register a Copyright?

As noted, copyright registration is not a condition of obtaining copyright protection but is a legal formality intended to make a public record of the basic facts relating to a particular copyrighted work. Copyright registration is only required to preserve a copyright that would otherwise be invalidated because of the omission of the copyright notice or the omission of the name or date or a certain error in the year date. Nevertheless, the copyright law provides several attractive benefits which make registration highly recommended. These benefits include:

1. Registration establishes a public record of the copyright claim and provides the copyright owner with an official document which can prove useful in persuading potential infringers from risking liability.

2. Registration is ordinarily necessary before a copyright infringement lawsuit may be filed in court.

3. Registration establishes prima facie evidence in court of the validity of the copyright and of the facts stated in the copyright registration certificate, if made before or within five (5) years of publication.

4. If registration is made within three (3) months after publication or prior to an infringement of the copyrighted work, statutory damages and attorneys' fees will be available to the copyright owner in court actions, whereas otherwise only an award of actual damages and profits is available to the copyright owner.

In order to register a work for copyright, three items must be sent to the Copyright Office *in the same envelope or package:*

1. A properly completed application form. The proper form for a Work of the Visual Arts is form VA, a copy of which, together with the very useful instructions prepared by the Copyright Office, is reproduced at the end of this article.

2. A fee of $10.00 for each application. Artists working on a tight budget (are there any who aren't?) may be able to register a group of works for a single $10.00 fee if they can properly be considered a collective work or a series.

3. A deposit of the work being registered. The deposit requirements vary depending on the circumstances and the general guidelines are as follows:

(a) If the work is unpublished, one complete copy.

(b) If the work was first published in the United States on or after January 1, 1978, two complete copies of the "best edition."

(c) If the work was first published in the United States before January 1, 1978, two complete copies of the work as first published.

(d) If the work was first published outside the United States, whenever published, one complete copy of the work as first published.

(e) If the work is a contribution to a collective work (a magazine, book, etc.), and published after January 1, 1978, one complete copy of the "best edition" of the collective work.

Given the unusual size, shape and bulk of some visual arts, the Copyright Office regulations may allow the deposit of "identifying material" instead of copies. Such material should consist of photographic prints, transparencies, photostats, drawings or similar two-dimensional reproductions or renderings of the work, in a form visually perceptible without the aid of a machine or device. If the work is a pictorial or graphic work, the material should reproduce the actual colors employed in the work and in all other cases the material may be in black and white or may consist of a reproduction of the actual colors. As many pieces of identifying material should be submitted as are necessary to show clearly the entire copyrightable content of the work for which registration is being sought. Only one set of complete identifying material is required. Additional technical requirements regarding the size and dimension of the identifying material can be obtained by requesting Circular R40a from the Copyright Office.

Likewise, the Copyright Office has established detailed regulations concerning the determination of the "best edition" of a work. These technicalities are beyond the scope of this article, but are clearly and concisely set forth in Circular R7b, which may be obtained free of charge from the Copyright Office.

Although a copyright registration is not required, the Copyright Act establishes a mandatory deposit requirement for works published with notice of copyright in the United States. Such a deposit must be made within three (3) months of publication in the United States for the use of the Library of Congress. Failure to make the deposit can give rise to fines and other penalties but does not affect copyright protection.

How Long Does Copyright Protection Last?

For Works Originally Copyrighted on or after January 1, 1978 As noted, a work that is created and fixed in tangible form for the first time on or after January 1, 1978, is automatically protected from the *moment of its creation.* Ordinarily, it enjoys copyright protection for the duration of the life of the author plus an additional 50 years after the author's death. In the case of a joint work prepared by two or more authors who did not work for hire, the term lasts for 50 years after the last-surviving author's death (resulting in the possibility of increasing collaborations with very young joint authors). For works made for hire or where the copyright owner is a corporation and for anonymous and pseudonymous works (unless the author's identity is revealed in Copyright Office records), the duration of copyright will be 75 years from publication or 100 years from creation, whichever is shorter.

Works that are created before January 1, 1978, but had been neither published nor registered for copyright by that date, have been automatically brought under the new statute and are now given federal copyright protection generally computed in the same way as for new works. However, all works in this category are guaranteed at least 25 years of statutory protection.

For Works Copyrighted before January 1, 1978   Under the 1909 law, copyright was secured either on the date a work was published or, for unpublished works, on the date of registration, if any. In both cases, the copyright lasted for a first term of 28 years and, if renewed, for a renewal term of 28 years.

The new copyright law has extended the renewal term from 28 years to 47 years for copyrights that were valid on January 1, 1978. However, the copyright *must* be timely renewed to receive the 47-year period of additional protection. The complexities of renewal under the old and new copyright laws are beyond the scope of this article and more detailed information can be obtained by requesting Circulars 15A and R1 from the Copyright Office or by consulting a copyright attorney.

How Can a Copyright Be Transferred?

As noted, given the doctrine of "divisibility of copyright" any or all of the exclusive rights, or any subdivision of those rights, of a copyright owner may be transferred to a third party, but the transfer of *exclusive rights* is not valid unless the transfer is (a) in writing and (b) signed by the owner of the rights conveyed or his or her duly authorized agent. Transfer of a right on a non-exclusive basis need not be in writing.

A copyright may also be conveyed by operation of law and may be bequeathed by will or passed as personal property under the applicable laws of interstate succession. Copyright is a personal property right, and it is subject to the various state laws and regulations that govern the ownership, inheritance or transfer of personal property as well as terms of contracts or conduct of business, the details of which are, of course, beyond the scope of this article and require consultation with an attorney.

Transfers of copyright are usually made in a written document, which may be recorded in the Copyright Office, although the Copyright Office does not provide any particular forms for such purposes. Recordation of a transfer is not required to make it valid between the parties, but it may provide certain legal advantages and does serve to put third parties on notice for a variety of purposes.

Under the 1909 law, if an artist had assigned his copyright, it reverted to him or her, if living, or, if not living, to other specified beneficiaries, provided a renewal claim was registered in the 28th year of the original term, unless the renewal rights had been expressly assigned and the author survived to the commencement of the renewal term. The new Copyright Act has eliminated the renewal feature, except for works already in their first term of statutory protection as of January 1, 1978. In place of the renewal, the new law generally permits any transfer of the copyright or any part thereof to be terminated within a 5-year period commencing 35 years after the grant of rights under certain conditions by serving a written notice on the transferee. Artists who wish to reacquire their rights should make a note in their calendar 35 years from the transfer so they won't miss this opportunity.

Of more immediate concern, for works already under statutory copyright protection, the new law provides a similar right of termination covering the newly added years that extended the former maximum term of copyright from 56 to 75 years.

It is worth noting that these beneficial termination provisions do *not* apply to works made for hire, since in such cases the employer or person who commissioned the work is the "author," not by reason of any transfer of copyright, but by operation of the Copyright Act itself.

Although the termination of transfers may appear to be something not to be concerned with in the short run, it is sure to be a valuable right for an author or his heirs, particularly where a work of art has appreciated in value beyond the artist's original expectations at the time he relinquished his rights.

How Can International Copyright Protection Be Obtained?

Although a detailed examination of international copyright law is not possible here, particularly since such protection varies from country to country, some general observations may prove useful.

The United States is a member of the Universal Copyright Convention (the UCC), which came into effect on September 16, 1966, and by reason of other treaties and conventions, enjoys reciprocal copyright protection with other countries which are not members of the UCC. A work by a national or domiciliary of a country that is a member of the UCC or a work first published in a UCC country may claim protection under the UCC, if it bears the notice of copyright in the form and position specified by the UCC. This notice will satisfy and substitute for certain other formal conditions which a UCC member country would otherwise require to secure copyright protection.

An author who wishes protection for his or her work in a particular foreign country should first find out the extent of protection available in such country. If possible, this should be done before the work is published anywhere, since protection may often depend on the facts existing at the time of *first* publication anywhere.

What Remedies Are Available in Case of Infringement?

A copyright owner or the owner of any exclusive rights in a copyright may recover "the actual damages suffered by him or her as a result of the infringement, and any profits of the infringer that are attributable to the infringement and are not taken into account in computing the actual damages." The Copyright Act provides for injunctions, impounding and disposition of infringing articles, increased damages in lieu of actual damages and reasonable attorneys' fees and court costs, as well as (rarely enforced) criminal penalties.

The plaintiff in a copyright infringement action must prove that the infringer had *access to the copyrighted work* and that the *infringing work is substantially similar to the original work.* Various defenses are available, including "fair use," discussed below. While most aspects of copyright law can be mastered by laymen without the expense of engaging an attorney, the prosecution or defense of a copyright infringement action can rarely be successfully mounted without using an attorney experienced in both copyright law and litigation.

In many circumstances, a copyright infringement action can be combined with an action for unfair competition, violation of various state and federal trademark laws and breach of express or implied contractual agreements. Federal courts have primary jurisdiction over copyright infringement cases and can exercise jurisdiction over related state law claims.

What Is the "Fair Use" Doctrine?

Some artists and others who are not particularly conversant in copyright law often bandy about the doctrine of "fair use" to justify infringement of copyright. The doctrine of "fair use," which was recognized by the courts under the 1909 law and has now received specific statutory recognition in the Copyright Act of 1976, allows the limited use of a copyrighted work for certain prescribed purposes and under certain restricted circumstances.

The new law provides that for purposes "such as criticism, comment, news reporting, teaching (including multiple copies for classroom use), scholarship or research" the "fair use" of a copyrighted work is not an infringement of copyright. In determining whether the use made of a work in any particular case is a fair use, the factors to be considered, as identified in the statute, shall include:

(1) the purpose and character of the use, including whether such use is of a commercial nature or is for nonprofit educational purposes;
(2) the nature of the copyrighted work;
(3) the amount and substantiality of the portion used in relation to the copyrighted work as a whole; and
(4) the effect of the use upon the potential market for or value of the copyrighted work.

While these factors are relatively self-explanatory, it is immediately apparent that each case depends upon its own particular facts. In order to avoid a controversy over whether a particular use is "fair" or not, it is prudent to seek permission for the use of a copyrighted work or any portion thereof. Handy rules gratuitously offered by friends and colleagues suggesting that an artist can always make "fair use" of a certain amount of copyrighted work without fear of infringement usually lead one astray.

This article has attempted to highlight the fundamental aspects of copyright law as it relates to the visual artist. It is hoped that it has raised questions and will trigger further inquiry in the daily application of this important field of law to the day-to-day labors of the visual artist.

HOW TO FILL OUT FORM VA

Specific Instructions for Spaces 1-4

> • The line-by-line instructions on this page are keyed to the spaces on the first page of Form VA, printed opposite.
>
> • Please read through these instructions before you start filling out your application, and refer to the specific instructions for each space as you go along.

SPACE 1: TITLE

• **Title of this Work:** Every work submitted for copyright registration must be given a title that is capable of identifying that particular work. If the copies of the work bear a title (or an identifying phrase that could serve as a title), transcribe its wording completely and exactly on the application; otherwise give the work a short descriptive title, making it as explicit as possible. Remember that indexing of the registration and future identification of the work will depend on the information you give here.

• **Previous or Alternative Titles:** Complete this line if there are any additional titles for this work under which someone searching for the registration might be likely to look, or under which a document pertaining to the work might be recorded.

• **Publication as a Contribution:** If the work being registered has been published as a contribution to a periodical, serial, or collection, give the title of the contribution in the space headed "Title of this Work." Then, in the line headed "Publication as a Contribution," give information about the larger work in which the contribution appeared.

• **Nature of this Work:** Briefly describe the nature or character of the pictorial, graphic, or sculptural work being registered for copyright. Examples: "Oil Painting"; "Charcoal Drawing"; "Etching"; "Sculpture"; "Map"; "Photograph"; "Scale Model"; "Lithographic Print"; "Jewelry Design"; "Fabric Design".

SPACE 2: AUTHORS

• **General Instructions:** First decide, after reading these instructions, who are the "authors" of this work for copyright purposes. Then, unless the work is a "collective work" (see below), give the requested information about every "author" who contributed any appreciable amount of copyrightable matter to this version of the work. If you need further space, use the attached Continuation Sheet and, if necessary, request additional Continuation Sheets (Form VA/CON).

• **Who is the "Author"?** Unless the work was "made for hire," the individual who actually created the work is its "author." In the case of works of the visual arts, "authors" include artists, cartographers, sculptors, painters, photographers, printmakers, and all others who create pictorial, graphic, or sculptural material. Where a work is made for hire, the statute provides that "the employer or other person for whom the work was prepared is considered the author."

• **What is a "Work Made for Hire"?** A "work made for hire" is defined as: (1) "a work prepared by an employee within the scope of his or her employment," or (2) "a work specially ordered or commissioned" for certain uses specified in the statute, but only if there is a written agreement to consider it a "work made for hire."

• **Collective Work:** In the case of a collective work, such as a catalog of paintings or a collection of cartoons by various artists, it is sufficient to give information about the author of the collective work as a whole.

• **Author's Identity Not Revealed:** If an author's contribution is "anonymous" or "pseudonymous," it is not necessary to give the name and dates for that author. However, the citizenship or domicile of the author **must** be given in all cases, and information about the nature of that author's contribution to the work should be included.

• **Name of Author:** The fullest form of the author's name should be given. If you have checked "Yes" to indicate that the work was "made for hire," give the full legal name of the employer (or other person for whom the work was prepared). You may also include the name of the employee (for example: "Fremont Enterprises, Inc., employer for hire of L.B. Jeffries"). If the work is "anonymous" you may: (1) leave the line blank, or (2) state "Anonymous" in the line, or (3) reveal the author's identity. If the work is "pseudonymous" you may (1) leave the line blank, or (2) give the pseudonym and identify it as such (for example: "Richard Heldar, pseudonym"), or (3) reveal the author's name, making clear which is the real name and which is the pseudonym (for example: "Henry Leek, whose pseudonym is Priam Farrel").

• **Dates of Birth and Death:** If the author is dead, the statute requires that the year of death be included in the application unless the work is anonymous or pseudonymous. The author's birth date is optional, but is useful as a form of identification. Leave this space blank if the author's contribution was a "work made for hire."

• **"Anonymous" or "Pseudonymous" Work:** An author's contribution to a work is "anonymous" if that author is not identified on the copies of the work. An author's contribution to a work is "pseudonymous" if that author is identified on the copies under a fictitious name.

• **Author's Nationality or Domicile:** Give the country of which the author is a citizen, or the country in which the author is domiciled. The statute requires that either nationality or domicile be given in all cases.

• **Nature of Authorship:** After the words "Author of" give a brief general statement of the nature of this particular author's contribution to the work. Examples: "Painting"; "Photograph"; "Silk Screen Reproduction"; "Co-author of Cartographic Material"; "Technical Drawing"; "Text and Artwork".

SPACE 3: CREATION AND PUBLICATION

• **General Instructions:** Do not confuse "creation" with "publication." Every application for copyright registration must state "the year in which creation of the work was completed." Give the date and nation of first publication only if the work has been published.

• **Creation:** Under the statute, a work of the visual arts is "created" when it is fixed in a copy for the first time. A work is "fixed" in a copy when its embodiment "is sufficiently permanent or stable to permit it to be perceived, reproduced, or otherwise communicated for a period of more than transitory duration." Where a work has been prepared over a period of time, the part of the work existing in fixed form on a particular date constitutes the created work on that date. The date you give here should be the year in which the author completed the particular version for which registration is now being sought, even if other versions exist or if further changes or additions are planned.

• **Publication:** "Publication" is defined as "the distribution of copies or phonorecords of a work to the public by sale or other transfer of ownership, or by rental, lease, or lending"; a work is also "published" if there has been an "offering to distribute copies or phonorecords to a group of persons for purposes of further distribution, public performance, or public display." The statute makes clear that public display of a work "does not of itself constitute publication." Give the full date (month, day, year) when, and the country where, publication first occurred. If first publication took place simultaneously in the United States and other countries, it is sufficient to state "U.S.A."

SPACE 4: CLAIMANT(S)

• **Name(s) and Address(es) of Copyright Claimant(s):** Give the name(s) and address(es) of the copyright claimant(s) in this work. The statute provides that copyright in a work belongs initially to the author of the work (including, in the case of a work made for hire, the employer or other person for whom the work was prepared). The copyright claimant is either the author of the work or a person or organization that has obtained ownership of the copyright initially belonging to the author.

• **Transfer:** The statute provides that, if the copyright claimant is not the author, the application for registration must contain "a brief statement of how the claimant obtained ownership of the copyright." If any copyright claimant named in space 4 is not an author named in space 2, give a brief, general statement summarizing the means by which that claimant obtained ownership of the copyright.

INSTRUCTIONS FOR SPACES 5-9

SPACE 5: PREVIOUS REGISTRATION

• **General Instructions:** The questions in space 5 are intended to find out whether an earlier registration has been made for this work and, if so, whether there is any basis for a new registration. As a general rule, only one basic copyright registration can be made for the same version of a particular work.

• **Same Version:** If this version is substantially the same as the work covered by a previous registration, a second registration is not generally possible unless: (1) the work has been registered in unpublished form and a second registration is now being sought to cover the first published edition, or (2) someone other than the author is identified as copyright claimant in the earlier registration, and the author is now seeking registration in his or her own name. If either of these two exceptions apply, check the appropriate box and give the earlier registration number and date. Otherwise, do not submit Form VA: instead, write the Copyright Office for information about supplementary registration or recordation of transfer of copyright ownership.

• **Changed Version:** If the work has been changed, and you are now seeking registration to cover the additions or revisions, check the third box in space 5, give the earlier registration number and date, and complete both parts of space 6.

• **Previous Registration Number and Date:** If more than one previous registration has been made for the work, give the number and date of the latest registration.

SPACE 6: COMPILATION OR DERIVATIVE WORK

• **General Instructions:** Complete both parts of space 6 if this work is a "compilation," or "derivative work," or both, and if it is based on or incorporates one or more "preexisting works" that are not eligible for registration for one reason or another: works that have already been published or registered, or works that have fallen into the public domain. A "compilation" is defined as "a work formed by the collection and assembling of preexisting materials or of data that are selected, coordinated, or arranged in such a way that the resulting work as a whole constitutes an original work of authorship." A "derivative work" is "a work based on one or more preexisting works." In addition to various forms in which works may be "recast, transformed, or adapted," derivative works include works "consisting of editorial revisions, annotations, elaborations, or other modifications" if these changes, as a whole, represent an original work of authorship.

• **Preexisting Material:** If the work is a compilation, give a brief, general statement describing the nature of the material that has been compiled. Example: "Compilation of 19th Century political cartoons." In the case of a derivative work, identify the preexisting work that has been recast, transformed, or adapted. Examples: "Grünewald Altarpiece"; "19th Century quilt design."

• **Material Added to this Work:** The statute requires a "brief, general statement of the additional material covered by the copyright claim being registered." This statement should describe all of the material in this particular version of the work that (1) represents an original work of authorship; (2) has not fallen into public domain; (3) has not been previously published; and (4) has not been previously registered for copyright in unpublished form. Examples: "Adaptation of design and additional artistic work"; "Reproduction of painting by photolithography"; "Additional cartographic material"; "Compilation of photographs."

SPACES 7, 8, 9: FEE, CORRESPONDENCE, CERTIFICATION, RETURN ADDRESS

• **Deposit Account and Mailing Instructions (Space 7):** If you maintain a Deposit Account in the Copyright Office, identify it in space 7. Otherwise you will need to send the registration fee of $10 with your application. The space headed "Correspondence" should contain the name and address of the person to be consulted if correspondence about this application becomes necessary.

• **Certification (Space 8):** The application is not acceptable unless it bears the handwritten signature of the author or other copyright claimant, or of the owner of exclusive right(s), or of the duly authorized agent of such author, claimant, or owner.

• **Address for Return of Certificate (Space 9):** The address box must be completed legibly, since the certificate will be returned in a window envelope.

MORE INFORMATION

THE COPYRIGHT NOTICE: For published works, the law provides that a copyright notice in a specified form "shall be placed on all publicly distributed copies from which the work can be visually perceived." Use of the copyright notice is the responsibility of the copyright owner, and does not require advance permission from the Copyright Office.

• **Form of the Notice:** The required form of the notice for copies generally consists of three elements: (1) the symbol "©", or the word "Copyright", or the abbreviation "Copr."; (2) the year of first publication; and (3) the name of the owner of copyright in the work, or an abbreviation by which the name can be recognized, or a generally known alternative designation of the owner. Example: "© 1978 Samuel Marlove." Under the statute, the year date may be omitted from the notice in cases "where a pictorial, graphic, or sculptural work, with accompanying text matter, if any, is reproduced in or on greeting cards, postcards, stationery, jewelry, dolls, toys, or any useful articles."

• **Position of the Notice:** The notice is to be affixed to the copies "in such manner and location as to give reasonable notice of the claim of copyright."

• **Errors or Omissions:** Unlike the law in effect before 1978, the new copyright statute provides procedures for correcting errors in the copyright notice, and even for curing the omission of the notice. However, a failure to comply with the notice requirements may still result in the loss of some copyright protection and, unless corrected within five years, in the complete loss of copyright. For further information about the copyright notice and the procedures for correcting errors or omissions, write to the Copyright Office.

FORM OF DEPOSIT FOR WORKS OF THE VISUAL ARTS

Exceptions to General Deposit Requirements: As explained on the reverse side of this page, the statutory deposit requirements (generally one copy for unpublished works and two copies for published works) will vary for particular kinds of works of the visual arts. The copyright law authorizes the Register of Copyrights to issue regulations specifying "the administrative classes into which works are to be placed for purposes of deposit and registration, and the nature of the copies or phonorecords to be deposited in the various classes specified." For particular classes, the regulations may require or permit "the deposit of identifying material instead of copies or phonorecords," or "the deposit of only one copy or phonorecord where two would normally be required."

What Should You Deposit? The detailed requirements with respect to the kind of deposit to accompany an application on Form VA are contained in the Copyright Office Regulations. The following does not cover all of the deposit requirements, but is intended to give you some general guidance.

• For an unpublished work, the material deposited should represent the entire copyrightable content of the work for which registration is being sought;

• For a published work, the material deposited should generally consist of two complete copies of the best edition. Exceptions:

—For certain types of works, one complete copy may be deposited instead of two. These include greeting cards, postcards, stationery, labels, advertisements, scientific drawings, and globes.

—For most three-dimensional sculptural works, and for certain two-dimensional works, the Copyright Office Regulations require the deposit of identifying material (photographs or drawings in a specified form) rather than copies.

—Under certain circumstances, for works published in five copies or less or in limited, numbered editions, the deposit may consist of one copy or of identifying reproductions.

SAMPLE APPLICATION FOR COPYRIGHT REGISTRATION

FORM VA
UNITED STATES COPYRIGHT OFFICE

REGISTRATION NUMBER
VA   VAU
EFFECTIVE DATE OF REGISTRATION
(Month)   (Day)   (Year)

DO NOT WRITE ABOVE THIS LINE. IF YOU NEED MORE SPACE, USE CONTINUATION SHEET (FORM VA/CON)

(1) Title

TITLE OF THIS WORK: *NOVEMBER SUNSET*

NATURE OF THIS WORK: (See instructions) *GRAPHIC DESIGN*

Previous or Alternative Titles

PUBLICATION AS A CONTRIBUTION: (If this work was published as a contribution to a periodical, serial, or collection, give information about the collective work in which the contribution appeared.)

Title of Collective Work   Vol   No   Date   Pages

(2) Author(s)

IMPORTANT: Under the law, the "author" of a "work made for hire" is generally the employer, not the employee (see instructions). If any part of this work was "made for hire," check "Yes" in the space provided, give the employer (or other person for whom the work was prepared) as "Author" of that part, and leave the space for dates blank.

1
NAME OF AUTHOR: *ARLEN V. ARTIST*
Was this author's contribution to the work a "work made for hire"?   Yes   No ✓
DATES OF BIRTH AND DEATH: Born *1948* (Year) Died ___ (Year)

AUTHOR'S NATIONALITY OR DOMICILE: Citizen of *U.S.A.* (Name of Country) or Domiciled in (Name of Country)
WAS THIS AUTHOR'S CONTRIBUTION TO THE WORK: Anonymous? Yes No ✓ Pseudonymous? Yes No ✓
If the answer to either of these questions is "Yes," see detailed instructions attached

AUTHOR OF: (Briefly describe nature of this author's contribution) *4-COLOR GRAPHIC DESIGN with Scroll Border*

2
NAME OF AUTHOR:
Was this author's contribution to the work a "work made for hire"?   Yes   No
DATES OF BIRTH AND DEATH: Born (Year) Died (Year)

AUTHOR'S NATIONALITY OR DOMICILE: Citizen of (Name of Country) or Domiciled in (Name of Country)
WAS THIS AUTHOR'S CONTRIBUTION TO THE WORK: Anonymous? Yes No Pseudonymous? Yes No
If the answer to either of these questions is "Yes," see detailed instructions attached

AUTHOR OF: (Briefly describe nature of this author's contribution)

3
NAME OF AUTHOR:
Was this author's contribution to the work a "work made for hire"?   Yes   No
DATES OF BIRTH AND DEATH: Born (Year) Died (Year)

AUTHOR'S NATIONALITY OR DOMICILE: Citizen of (Name of Country) or Domiciled in (Name of Country)
WAS THIS AUTHOR'S CONTRIBUTION TO THE WORK: Anonymous? Yes No Pseudonymous? Yes No
If the answer to either of these questions is "Yes," see detailed instructions attached

AUTHOR OF: (Briefly describe nature of this author's contribution)

(3) Creation and Publication

YEAR IN WHICH CREATION OF THIS WORK WAS COMPLETED: Year *1981*
(This information must be given in all cases.)

DATE AND NATION OF FIRST PUBLICATION:
Date   (Month)   (Day)   (Year)
Nation   (Name of Country)
(Complete this block ONLY if this work has been published.)

(4) Claimant(s)

NAME(S) AND ADDRESS(ES) OF COPYRIGHT CLAIMANT(S):
ARLEN V. ARTIST
2 VISUAL WAY
SCENIC, CALIFORNIA 90001

TRANSFER: (If the copyright claimant(s) named here in space 4 is different from the author(s) named in space 2, give a brief statement of how the claimant(s) obtained ownership of the copyright.)

- Complete all applicable spaces (numbers 5-9) on the reverse side of this page
- Follow detailed instructions attached   • Sign the form at line 8

DO NOT WRITE HERE
Page 1 of .... pages

	EXAMINED BY	APPLICATION RECEIVED:	
	CHECKED BY		
	CORRESPONDENCE ☐ Yes	DEPOSIT RECEIVED:	FOR COPYRIGHT OFFICE USE ONLY
	DEPOSIT ACCOUNT FUNDS USED ☐	REMITTANCE NUMBER AND DATE:	

DO NOT WRITE ABOVE THIS LINE. IF YOU NEED ADDITIONAL SPACE, USE CONTINUATION SHEET (FORM VA/CON)

PREVIOUS REGISTRATION:

- Has registration for this work, or for an earlier version of this work, already been made in the Copyright Office? Yes .... No ..✓....

- If your answer is "Yes," why is another registration being sought? (Check appropriate box)
  ☐ This is the first published edition of a work previously registered in unpublished form.
  ☐ This is the first application submitted by this author as copyright claimant.
  ☐ This is a changed version of the work, as shown by line 6 of the application.

- If your answer is "Yes," give: Previous Registration Number.................... Year of Registration...........

(5) Previous Registration

COMPILATION OR DERIVATIVE WORK: (See instructions)

PREEXISTING MATERIAL: (Identify any preexisting work or works that this work is based on or incorporates.)

....

....

....

MATERIAL ADDED TO THIS WORK: (Give a brief, general statement of the material that has been added to this work and in which copyright is claimed.)

....

....

....

(6) Compilation or Derivative Work

DEPOSIT ACCOUNT: (If the registration fee is to be charged to a Deposit Account established in the Copyright Office, give name and number of Account.)

Name ....

Account Number...

CORRESPONDENCE: (Give name and address to which correspondence about this application should be sent.)

Name *ARLEN V. ARTIST*

Address *2 VISUAL WAY* (Apt.)

SCENIC   CALIFORNIA   90001
(City)   (State)   (ZIP)

(7) Fee and Correspondence

CERTIFICATION: # I, the undersigned, hereby certify that I am the: (Check one)
☑ author ☐ other copyright claimant ☐ owner of exclusive right(s) ☐ authorized agent of ....
(Name of author or other copyright claimant or owner of exclusive right(s))

of the work identified in this application and that the statements made by me in this application are correct to the best of my knowledge

Handwritten signature: (X) *Arlen V. artist*

Typed or printed name *ARLEN V. ARTIST* Date *Nov. 14, 1981*

(8) Certification (Application must be signed)

ARLEN V. ARTIST
(Name)

2 VISUAL WAY
(Number Street and Apartment Number)

SCENIC   CALIFORNIA   90001
(City)   (State)   (ZIP code)

MAIL CERTIFICATE TO

(Certificate will be mailed in window envelope)

(9) Address for Return of Certificate

17 U.S.C. § 506(e) FALSE REPRESENTATION – Any person who knowingly makes a false representation of a material fact in the application for copyright registration provided for by section 409, or in any written statement filed in connection with the application, shall be fined not more than $2,500.

☆ U.S. GOVERNMENT PRINTING OFFICE: 1979-281-421/5

March 1979—100,000

CHAPTER SIX
DESIGN PATENTS AND TRADEMARKS

Paul D. Supnik, Esq.

DESIGN PATENTS

One area of protection for the artist that is often overlooked is that of design patent protection. A design patent gives the designer the right to exclude others from making, using or selling an ornamental design for a utilitarian article of manufacture. Typical subject matter covered by design patents have included textile patterns, jewelry, furniture and ceramic goods. While copyright generally provides protection for works of art, sometimes copyright protection may not be available if it is determined that the work of art, no matter how aesthetically attractive, cannot stand apart from the work as a utilitarian article.

Design Patent Applications

Design patent protection is more difficult to obtain than copyright protection. To obtain design patent protection, an application (which includes a designation of the article to which the design is applied, a brief description of the views of the design shown in accompanying drawings and a sworn statement by the creator to the effect that he or she is the originator and first known creator of the design), drawings and a fee are submitted to the U.S. Patent and Trademark Office in the Washington, D.C., area. An examination of the application is made to determine, among other matters, if the design is new, ornamental and "non-obvious" in view of all other pre-existing designs.

There are time limits for filing an application. Assuming that only protection in the United States is desired, the application must be filed within one year of first offering the design for sale or using the design in the United States or elsewhere, and within one year of its first appearance in a printed publication. There are certain other restrictions as well. In the event you are interested in protection in countries in addition to the United States, an application should usually be filed prior to any public disclosure, use, sale or publication, as other countries often do not have the same one-year grace period that exists in the United States.

**DECLARATION
AND POWER OF ATTORNEY
Design Application**

ATTORNEY'S DOCKET NO. (IF ANY)

. . . .

As a below named inventor, I declare that the information given herein is true, that I believe that I am the original, first and sole inventor if only one name is listed at 201 below, or a joint inventor if plural inventors are named below at 201 et seq., of the design entitled:

. . . .

. . . .

which is described and claimed in:
☐ the attached specification or ☐ the specification in application Serial No. . . . . .filed . . . .
(for declaration not accompanying application)

that I do not know and do not believe that the same was ever known or used in the United States of America before my or our invention thereof or patented or described in any printed publication in any country before my or our invention thereof, or more than one year prior to this application, or in public use or on sale in the United States of America more than one year prior to this application, that said design has not been patented or made the subject of an inventor's certificate issued before the date of this application in any country foreign to the United States of America on an application filed by me or my legal representatives or assigns more than six months prior to this application and that no application for patent or inventor's certificate on this design has been filed by me or my legal representatives or assigns in any country foreign to the United States of America except as identified below.

FOREIGN APPLICATION(S), IF ANY, FILED **WITHIN** 6 MONTHS PRIOR TO THE FILING DATE OF THIS APPLICATION			
COUNTRY	APPLICATION NUMBER	DATE OF FILING (day, month, year)	PRIORITY CLAIMED UNDER 35 U.S.C. 119
			YES ___ NO___
			YES ___ NO___
ALL FOREIGN APPLICATIONS, IF ANY, FILED **MORE** THAN 6 MONTHS PRIOR TO THE FILING DATE OF THIS APPLICATION			

POWER OF ATTORNEY: As a named inventor, I hereby appoint the following attorney(s) and/or agent(s) to prosecute this application and transact all business in the Patent and Trademark Office connected therewith. *(list name and registration number)*

SEND CORRESPONDENCE TO:	DIRECT TELEPHONE CALLS TO: (name and telephone number)

201	**FULL NAME OF INVENTOR**	LAST NAME	FIRST NAME		MIDDLE NAME	
	RESIDENCE & CITIZENSHIP	CITY OR OTHER LOCATION	STATE OR FOREIGN COUNTRY		COUNTRY OF CITIZENSHIP	
	POST OFFICE ADDRESS	POST OFFICE ADDRESS	CITY	STATE OR COUNTRY		ZIP CODE
202	**FULL NAME OF INVENTOR**	LAST NAME	FIRST NAME		MIDDLE NAME	
	RESIDENCE & CITIZENSHIP	CITY OR OTHER LOCATION	STATE OR FOREIGN COUNTRY		COUNTRY OF CITIZENSHIP	
	POST OFFICE ADDRESS	POST OFFICE ADDRESS	CITY	STATE OR COUNTRY		ZIP CODE
203	**FULL NAME OF INVENTOR**	LAST NAME	FIRST NAME		MIDDLE NAME	
	RESIDENCE & CITIZENSHIP	CITY OR OTHER LOCATION	STATE OR FOREIGN COUNTRY		COUNTRY OF CITIZENSHIP	
	POST OFFICE ADDRESS	POST OFFICE ADDRESS	CITY	STATE OR COUNTRY		ZIP CODE

☐ Additional matter on page 2 (Form PTO-1298). (When page 2 is used, all signatures should be placed on page 2.)

I further declare that all statements made herein of my own knowledge are true and that all statements made on information and belief are believed to be true; and further that these statements were made with the knowledge that willful false statements and the like so made are punishable by fine or imprisonment, or both, under section 1001 of Title 18 of the United States Code, and that such willful false statements may jeopardize the validity of the application or any patent issuing thereon.

SIGNATURE OF INVENTOR 201	SIGNATURE OF INVENTOR 202	SIGNATURE OF INVENTOR 203
DATE	DATE	DATE

FORM PTO-1296 (1-76)
USCOMM-DC 32267-P76

U.S. DEPARTMENT OF COMMERCE
PATENT AND TRADEMARK OFFICE

Patent Attorneys

Because of the complicated and technical aspects of the patent laws, it is recommended that a patent attorney be consulted at an early date if you wish to seek this type of protection. A patent attorney is an attorney that is registered to practice before the U.S. Patent and Trademark Office. They may be found through word of mouth, through many lawyer referral services of various bar associations, and they generally have listings under "Patent Lawyers" or "Patent Attorneys" sections of telephone directories.

Protection Provided by Design Patents

After the application is on file in the U.S. Patent and Trademark Office, the designation "patent pending" or "design patent pending" may be used on the products embodying the design. After a design patent is obtained (perhaps one to two years after filing) the patent number is to be marked on the products which are covered by the design. The design patent protects against infringement after its issuance (often a year or two after filing) for a period of 3½, 7 or 14 years, depending on the term selected by the designer. Anyone who thereafter applies the design or any colorable imitation of the design to any article of manufacture for the purpose of sale, or sells or exposes for sale any article of manufacture to which the design or colorable imitation has been applied, is liable for infringement. The law provides for recovery of the infringer's profits from sale of the products having the design.

One limitation of design patents is that frequently they are held invalid by courts, usually if the design is "functional" rather than "ornamental" or if prior relevant designs were not considered during the examination process in the Patent and Trademark Office.

A new type of protection for designs may be available in the next few years in the United States that has similarities to both the protection provided by the copyright law and the design patent law. Several bills have been introduced in Congress relating to special design protection, and if granted would probably be of interest to visual artists.

United States Patent [19]

Diskin

[11] **Des. 258,808**

[45] ** **Apr. 7, 1981**

[54] **CLOCK**

[76] Inventor: **Stephen P. Diskin,** 613 S. Ridgeley Dr., Los Angeles, Calif. 90036

[**] Term: **14 Years**

[21] Appl. No.: **938,528**

[22] Filed: **Aug. 31, 1978**

[51] **Int. Cl.** .... **D10—01**
[52] **U.S. Cl.** **D10/15;** D10/22
[58] **Field of Search** .... D10/1, 2, 15, 21, 22, D10/23, 24, 25, 26; 58/53, 57, 58, 2, 152 R, 127 R, 4 R, 4 A, 6 R, 6 A, 50 R, 23 R, 144, 125 C

[56] **References Cited**

U.S. PATENT DOCUMENTS

D. 234,149	1/1975	Rowman	D10/15 X
2,757,508	8/1956	Zanetti	58/2
3,849,978	11/1974	Davis	58/2 X
3,875,736	4/1975	Gulko	58/125 C X

OTHER PUBLICATIONS

Gifts & Dec. Access., 2/71, p. 68, Clock at bottom left.
Jeweler's Circular–Keystone, 3/5/74, p. 26, Clock 2nd from top.

Primary Examiner—Nelson C. Holtje
Attorney, Agent, or Firm—Paul D. Supnik

[57] **CLAIM**

The ornamental design for a clock, substantially as shown and described.

DESCRIPTION

FIG. **1** is a front elevational view of a clock showing my new design;
FIG. **2** is a top plan view thereof;
FIG. **3** is a bottom plan view thereof;
FIG. **4** is a rear elevational view thereof;
FIG. **5** is a left side elevational view thereof;
FIG. **6** is a right side elevational view thereof; and
FIG. **7** is a top and front perspective view thereof.

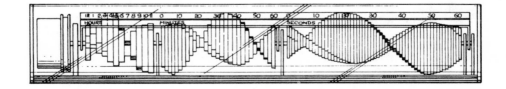

FIG. 1

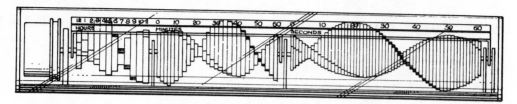

FIG. 2.

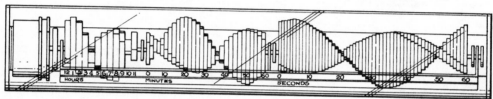

FIG. 3.

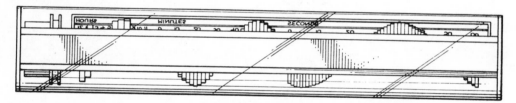

FIG. 4.

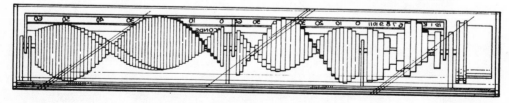

FIG. 5.

FIG. 6.

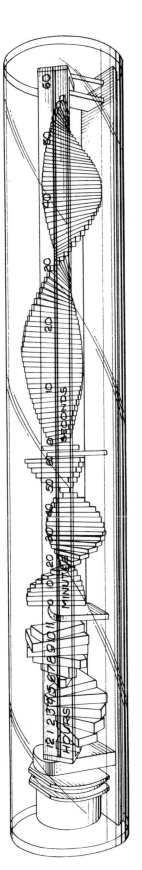

FIG. 7.

TRADEMARKS AND SERVICE MARKS

What are trademarks and service marks? And why would trademarks be of interest to visual artists? A trademark is a symbol, a word, a group of words, a slogan, insignia, indicia or a variety of different elements which designate the origin of goods or services. Those goods may be paintings, prints, lithographs, photographs, and the services may be artistic services. The public may find it easier to recognize some artists' goods by symbols than by full name. Trademarks become important in the area of mass merchandising of artworks in various media.

Some examples of artist's and designer's use of trademarks are the stylistic signature of scarves by Vera, the well-known signature of Picasso, the lion of Anne Klein and the polo insignia associated with Ralph Lauren. Only limited use of trademark rights has been made in the past by artists. But it is suggested that the artist become more aware of such trademark potential, as the concept of merchandising of artwork continues to grow.

The purpose of a trademark is to assure the public that goods bearing the mark come from a single or unique source, such as you the artist. Once proper trademark protection has been established, it may be possible for you to prevent others from using not only the same marks but other marks which are "confusingly similar" to your mark. Confusing similarity is determined by considering a number of factors, such as the visual impact that the mark has on the public, the sound of the mark, the meaning of the mark, the nature and similarity of goods to which the mark is applied and the channels of commerce in which the mark is used.

The best trademarks tend to be arbitrary, fanciful and unrelated to the goods or services in connection with which the goods are used. For example, "Kodak" is a coined word having no meaning. And "Camel" really doesn't have anything meaningful to do with cigarettes.

If the mark selected is descriptive (rather than arbitrary or fanciful), it can acquire trademark rights, but only after it is sufficiently known by the public as to have acquired a "secondary meaning." By secondary meaning it is meant that the public readily thinks of the mark as designating origin of the goods, rather than looking first to its descriptive meaning. For this reason, marks primarily merely descriptive of the goods or services in connection with which the mark is used are *not* recommended. For similar reasons, avoid using the title of a *single* work of art as a trademark, as the title will be treated as being descriptive of that particular work. However, if that mark is used for a substantial series of different works, the title of the series may be used. It is noted that some marks probably can never acquire secondary meaning so as to designate origin and be protectable as a trademark, if they are highly descriptive or generic (e.g., "Color Portraits" for artist painting services).

How Do I Establish Rights in a Mark?

In the United States, rights in a trademark are established primarily by *use* of the mark. In the absence of other factors, the first person to *use* the mark in a geographic territory acquires rights to use the mark in that territory. That date of first use must be a bona fide actual sale of a product bearing the trademark. Thus the sale of a painting having a special inscription or designation to a dealer may be the date of first use. Or the sale of one of your paintings in a gallery may establish that date of first use. But the mark has to be affixed to the goods which are sold in commerce. The cost of the sale should be for the regular market value of the artwork. Do not attempt to give the work away for next to nothing in order to establish trademark rights. It probably won't work. It is very desirable to retain proof of the date of first use. Documentation such as invoices or bills of sale and photocopies of the check which you received *before* you cash it may be useful later on in establishing that the sale took place on the date when you said it did. In addition, there should be some way of identifying the nature of the artwork which was sold (such as on the invoice) to establish that first sale.

(FORM FOR USE OF INDIVIDUAL)
(Instructions on reverse side)

U.S. DEPARTMENT OF COMMERCE
PATENT AND TRADEMARK OFFICE

APPLICATION FOR TRADEMARK/SERVICE MARK REGISTRATION
(DECLARATION)

Mark _____
(Identify Mark)

Class No. _____
(Insert number, if known)

TO THE COMMISSIONER OF PATENTS AND TRADEMARKS:

1

2

3

[4] a citizen of

The above identified applicant has adopted and is using the mark shown in the accompanying drawing for[5]

and requests that said mark be registered in the United States Patent and Trademark Office on the Principal Register established by the Act of July 5, 1946.

The mark was first used on[6]   , 19   ; was first used in[7]   commerce on[8]   , 19   ; and is now in use in such commerce.

The mark is used by applying it[9]

and five specimens showing the mark as actually used are presented herewith.

The undersigned applicant [10] _____ declares: That he believes himself to be the owner of the mark sought to be registered; that to the best of his knowledge and belief no other person, firm, corporation, or association has the right to use said mark in commerce, either in the identical form or in such near resemblance thereto as may be likely, when applied to the goods of such other person, to cause confusion, or to cause mistake, or to deceive; that all statements made herein of his own knowledge are true and that all statements made on information and belief are believed to be true; and further that these statements were made with the knowledge that willful false statements and the like so made are punishable by fine or imprisonment, or both, under section 1001 of Title 18 of the United States Code and that such willful false statements may jeopardize the validity of the application or document or any registration resulting therefrom.

[11]

_____
(Date)

_____
(Signature of applicant)

[Enclose Filing Fee of Thirty-Five Dollars]

INSTRUCTIONS

1. Insert name of partnership or firm, followed by "a partnership composed of (naming the members)," or "a firm composed of (naming the members)," as the case may be.

2. Insert the business address: street, city, State, and ZIP Code.

3. Insert State of domicile of partnership or firm.

4. Insert country of citizenship of partners or firm members.

5. Name by their common, usual, or ordinary commercial name (e.g., canned fruit and vegetables) the products or goods on which the mark has actually been used.

6. Insert the date of first use anywhere on *any of the goods* recited in the application.

7. Insert the kind of commerce, i.e., "interstate" or "Territorial" (District of Columbia, Virgin Islands, Puerto Rico), or such other specified type of commerce as may be regulated by Congress. Foreign applicants must specify: "commerce with the United States."

8. Insert the date of first use on any of the goods in interstate or foreign or Territorial commerce, as the case may be.

9. Insert the method of using the mark on the goods, i.e., "to containers," "to labels applied to containers," "to tags or labels affixed to the goods," "to name plates attached to the goods," "by stamping it on the goods," or other appropriate method, and send specimen labels, or containers, or name plates, etc., showing such use. If the specimens are third dimensional, photographs should be supplied in lieu of the article itself, except if the specimen is a carton or box which can be folded to a size not exceeding 8½ by 13 inches.

10. Insert name of individual executing declaration.

11. Individual's signature.

NOTE

If an attorney at law, or other person who is recognized by the Patent and Trademark Office in trademark matters, is to file and prosecute this application, a *signed* power or authorization in substantially the following form should accompany the application:

Please recognize _____ , *

_____ , †

with offices at _____ ,
to prosecute this application, to transact all business in connection therewith, and to receive the certicicate.

---

*Insert the name of the individual attorney at law or the law firm, or other recognized individual or firm, as the case may be.

† If an individual attorney at law, insert "a member of the bar of the State of" and name the State of admission to the bar.

If a law firm, insert "a firm composed of" and list the names of the members of the firm and their States of admission.

If a recognized individual other than an attorney at law, insert Patent and Trademark Office Registration number.

If a firm of nonlawyers, insert "a firm composed of" and list the members of the firm and the Patent and Trademark Office Registration number of each. Names of firms of nonlawyers may not be used unless all members of such firm are recognized under Rule 2.12(b) of the Rules effective August 15, 1955.

NOTE

The drawing must be made upon pure white durable paper, the surface of which must be calendered and smooth. India ink alone must be used for pen drawings to secure perfectly black solid lines.

The size of the sheet on which a drawing is made must be 8 to 8½ inches wide and 11 inches long.

A heading should be placed on the left-hand side at the top of the drawing. This heading consists of the applicant's name, his post office address, the first dates of use, and the goods.

If the application is for registration only of a word, letter, or numeral, or any combination thereof, not depicted in special form, the drawing may be the mark typed in capital letters on paper, otherwise complying with the requirements.

(FORM FOR USE OF PARTNERSHIP OR FIRM)
(Instructions on reverse side)

U.S. DEPARTMENT OF COMMERCE
PATENT AND TRADEMARK OFFICE

APPLICATION FOR TRADEMARK/SERVICE MARK REGISTRATION
(DECLARATION)

Mark _____
(Identify Mark)

Class No. _____
(Insert number, if known)

TO THE COMMISSIONER OF PATENTS AND TRADEMARKS:

[1]

[2]

[3] domiciled in the State of

[4] citizens of

The above identified applicant has adopted and is using the mark shown in the accompanying drawing for[5]

and requests that said mark be registered in the United States Patent and Trademark Office on the Principal Register established by the Act of July 5, 1946.

The mark was first used on[6]   , 19   ; was first used in[7]   commerce on[8]   , 19   ; and is now in use in such commerce.

The mark is used by applying it[9]

and five specimens showing the mark as actually used are presented herewith.

[10] _____ declares that he is a member of the applicant firm, he believes said firm to be the owner of the mark sought to be registered; to the best of his knowledge and belief no other person, firm, corporation, or association has the right to use said mark in commerce, either in the identical form or in such near resemblance thereto as may be likely, when applied to the goods of such other person to cause confusion, or to cause mistake, or to deceive; that all statements made herein of his own knowledge are true and that all statements made on information and belief are believed to be true; and further, that these statements were made with the knowledge that willful false statements and the like so made are punishable by fine or imprisonment, or both, under Section 1001 of the United States Code and that such willful false statements may jeopardize the validity of the application or document or any registration resulting therefrom.

[11]

_____
(Date)

_____
(Signature)

108

[Enclose Filing Fee of Thirty-Five Dollars]

INSTRUCTIONS

1. Insert name of applicant and if applicant has a trade style or name, insert "doing business as _____" following the name.

2. Insert the business address: street, city, State, and ZIP Code.

3. Insert residence address: street, city, State, and ZIP Code.

4. Insert country of citizenship.

5. Name by their common, usual, or ordinary commercial name (e.g., canned fruit and vegetables) the products or goods on which the mark has actually been used.

6. Insert the date of first use anywhere on *any of the goods* recited in the application.

7. Insert the kind of commerce, i.e., "interstate" or "Territorial" (District of Columbia, Virgin Islands, Puerto Rico), or such other specified type of commerce as may be regulated by Congress. Foreign applicants must specify: "commerce with the United States."

8. Insert the date of first use on any of the goods in interstate or foreign or Territorial commerce, as the case may be.

9. Insert the method of using the mark on the goods, i.e., "to containers," "to labels applied to containers," "to tags or labels affixed to the goods," "to name plates attached to the goods," "by stamping it on the goods," or other appropriate method, and send specimen labels, or containers, or name plates, etc., showing such use. If the specimens are third dimensional, photographs should be supplied in lieu of the article itself, except if the specimen is a carton or box which can be folded to a size not exceeding 8½ by 13 inches.

10. Insert name of individual executing declaration.

11. Individual's signature.

NOTE

If an attorney at law, or other person who is recognized by the Patent and Trademark Office in trademark matters, is to file and prosecute this application, a *signed* power or authorization in substantially the following form should accompany the application:

Please recognize _____ , *

_____ , †

with offices at _____ ,
to prosecute this application, to transact all
business in connection therewith, and to receive
the certicicate.

---

*Insert the name of the individual attorney at law or the law firm, or other recognized individual or firm, as the case may be.

†If an individual attorney at law, insert "a member of the bar of the State of" and name the State of admission to the bar.

If a law firm, insert "a firm composed of" and list the names of the members of the firm and their States of admission.

If a recognized individual other than an attorney at law, insert Patent and Trademark Office Registration number.

If a firm of nonlawyers, insert "a firm composed of" and list the members of the firm and the Patent and Trademark Office Registration number of each. Names of firms of nonlawyers may not be used unless all members of such firm are recognized under Rule 2.12(b) of the Rules effective August 15, 1955.

NOTE

The drawing must be made upon pure white durable paper, the surface of which must be calendered and smooth. India ink alone must be used for pen drawings to secure perfectly black solid lines.

The size of the sheet on which a drawing is made must be 8 to 8½ inches wide and 11 inches long.

A heading should be placed on the left-hand side at the top of the drawing. This heading consists of the applicant's name, his post office address, the first dates of use, and the goods.

If the application is for registration only of a word, letter, or numeral, or any combination thereof, not depicted in special form, the drawing may be the mark typed in capital letters on paper, otherwise complying with the requirements.

Trademark Registration

You may apply for registration of your trademark in any state in which you have used the mark. But registration may not be obtained or applied for prior to your actual first use, as was discussed above. In states such as California and New York, trademark registration requires the filling out of an application specifying the date of first use anywhere of the mark and the first use in the state for which registration is applied for. The application is typically accompanied by five identical specimens showing the mark as it is actually used. If the mark is used by affixing it to a work of art, it is often best to take a photograph of the artwork with sufficient clarity to show the mark as it is used, and submit five identical photographs (not photocopies) showing the mark as it is used in your artwork.

Federal trademark registration may not be obtained until such time as the mark has actually been used in interstate commerce. Use in interstate commerce generally means (at least in connection with artworks rather than art services) the sale of the artwork in more than one state. To establish the date of usage interstate, again it is advisable to maintain such documents as photocopies of checks before cashing and invoices and bills of sale.

Why Trademark Registration?

Federal trademark registration when finally obtained gives what is known as "constructive notice" to the public that you contend you own the trademark which is registered. The importance of registration is that once your mark has been federally registered, there can be no good faith adoption of the same mark by anyone anywhere in the United States without their risking a lawsuit at such time as you are in competition with them in connection with the same type of goods. Federal trademark registration supersedes all state trademark registration.

The federal trademark registration process can easily become complex. The time that it takes to register a mark is typically a few years or more. It is generally advisable to consult with an attorney familiar with trademark matters before filing the application. Should you be tempted to file a trademark registration application yourself, there is a substantial risk that it will be done incorrectly and that the time delay before you find out errors will be at least a year. It is strongly recommended that if you are serious about trademark rights and about registration that you do actually consult a trademark attorney at an early date prior even to use and selection of a mark. An example of a federal trademark application is presented. The form is deceptively simple. Knowing the right information to put in the blanks and the legal effect of that information generally takes considerable experience. Knowing the nature of the information required to apply for registration when you consult a trademark attorney is likely to make it easier for you and the attorney to properly prepare the trademark application.

You can also apply for state trademark registration. The concern over time delay is nowhere near as critical as with federal registration and if you take the time and have limited means, you have a better chance of completing an application by yourself without significant adverse consequences (though there always may be some problems which you will not be aware of which will probably readily be spotted by an attorney experienced in trademark matters). California registration typically will take approximately one month, so if you have gone wrong, you may be informed at an early point in time. State registration, unlike federal registration, gives you more limited rights. The effect of state registration may be simply to increase your bargaining power a bit with any potential infringers. The registration certificate gives rise to a presumption that the information which is stated in the application is correct. As with federal registration, it does not guarantee your ownership of the mark and it creates generally little if any additional substantive rights in the mark.

Do I Have the Right to Use the Mark?

Just because you have used a mark and have applied for registration or even registered it does not necessarily mean that you have the right to use the mark. There is always a possibility that other persons may have used the mark prior to your first usage and may have created a superior right. Because of this, it is often advisable to have a trademark search run to determine whether your mark is confusingly similar to any other marks or trademark or trade name usages. A trademark search and search interpretation is best done through an attorney having familiarity with trademark matters. The attorney will generally contact a searching firm which has access to patent and trademark office files, state trademark registers, company names and other information. The trademark search will attempt to uncover situations where possibly confusingly similar prior use may have existed. Not only do prior trademark usages present a problem but even a prior trade name use which might create a likelihood of confusion could expose you to liability from someone else who has used the mark. A search should be made if the proposed mark is important to you, if you intend to use it over a significant portion of your career and if you do not want to be in a position to be forced to change the mark. As a practical matter, however, you may find out that the cost of the search compared to the usage that you intend to make of the mark is more than would be beneficial to you and you may in this situation prefer to risk using the mark without a search.

Sources of Information

Most patent lawyers have a familiarity with trademark law. They may be found preferably through referrals through someone you know and trust or from the lawyer referral services of a number of bar associations. In addition, patent lawyers are also listed in the yellow pages of telephone directories and if you have no other source, that is a place where you could look.

Further information on trademarks may readily be obtained by telephoning the U.S. Government Printing Office bookstore in your area and asking how to obtain a copy of "General Information Concerning Trademarks." For state trademark information and applications, contact the Secretary of State's office in the state where you reside or do business.

Trademark Parody

Over the past few decades, the appearance of trademarks in works of art has become fairly common (e.g., Warhol depicting Campbell's soup can labels). There have also been a number of lawsuits in various situations by owners of trademarks for parodying their marks. For example, lawsuits were filed by Coca-Cola against a poster manufacturer for publishing a poster in which the familiar white-on-red script of Coca-Cola appeared in a poster stating "Enjoy Cocaine." Coca-Cola won.

Another lawsuit in recent years was by the Girl Scouts of America against the manufacturer of a poster which said "Be Prepared" and showed a girl in a Girl Scout uniform. The girl appeared to be pregnant. The poster manufacturer won because the court thought it obvious to the public that the poster was not sponsored by the Girl Scouts of America.

Walt Disney Productions was able to stop "Air Pirates" from publishing underground comics depicting characters recognizable as Disney characters but in X-rated situations, on the basis of copyright infringement, though, not trademark infringement.

The conclusion that can be drawn from these cases is that if you choose to use designations of others in your artwork, whether by way of parody or not, you may expose yourself to litigation. If the manner of use tends to be more humorous rather than defamatory, you could stand a better chance of prevailing. If the manner of use is political rather than commercial, you have a better chance of prevailing. The decision of course is yours, but it is probably better to be aware of the risks.

CHAPTER SEVEN
CREATIVE LEGISLATION FOR THE VISUAL ARTIST

Susan A. Grode, Esq.

For the first time in the history of the United States Congress, an arts caucus has been organized by representatives from *both* parties. Its purpose is to become familiar with and analyze issues affecting the arts and artists, to ensure the steady growth of arts support in the Congress and to focus on arts legislation. But it is at the state level, most notably in California, where legislative history for the visual arts is being made. Each year, in a growing number of states, bills are being proposed to invest visual artists with rights that are enjoyed by artists in other countries and by Americans in other professions.

French artists enjoy the benefits of the *droit de suite,* or resale royalty, a statutory right now shared by California artists. In 1981 this law survived a constitutional challenge in the United States Supreme Court and similar legislation has been proposed in other states. Throughout the country anyone owning a work of art may donate that work for charitable purposes and receive a deduction based upon the fair market value of the work at the time of the donation—anyone, that is, except the person who created the work of art. This, too, is being legislated at the state level and artists in California, Kansas, Maryland, Michigan, Oregon, North Carolina and Wisconsin now have the ability, for state tax purposes, to receive the same deduction as other donors of art.

Obviously, there is some legislation that is best accomplished on the national/federal level, especially where the problems being addressed require uniform national control (labeling and packaging requirements to warn artists of potential health hazards of the materials they use) or where substantial benefits are realized at the federal level (income and estate tax regulations affecting the value of the artist's work during his/her life and after death). To date, the federal legislation with the most substantial and long-range impact for the visual artist is the revised copyright law (see the Copyright section of this Manual.)

To be effective, any legislation must be used and tested by the group for which it was intended. To be used, laws must first be understood. The use of the laws or even the awareness that one has the potential to exercise rights and receive benefits from such laws is a foundation for professional power and security for the visual artist.

ARTIST-DEALER CONSIGNMENT RELATIONS LAW

In effect in California (since 1976, Civil Code Section 1738), Connecticut, Massachusetts, New York (since 1966), Minnesota, Texas and Wisconsin. Under consideration in Washington and Oregon.

Three sculptures are placed with a dealer for exhibition and sale. The dealer lends them to a movie producer for use in a film, thinking it will be excellent publicity for the artist. Two of the works are severely damaged en route to the film studio. The artist and dealer have no written contract.

A gallery buys a suite of silk screens from the artist and pays the artist half the price on account. In the meantime the gallery has sold the prints to a collector—and at a profit. The gallery tells the artist to wait until the next accounting period for her money.

How the Law Works

This law protects the artist when work is placed with a gallery/dealer. Laws of this type state that as soon as the artist leaves works of art with a gallery or dealer for sale and/or exhibition, the gallery/dealer has an obligation to safeguard the work from damage or loss of value and ensure that the artist receives the proceeds from any sales.

Under the California law, unless an artist is delivering artwork to a dealer or gallery as an outright sale and receives full payment at the time that delivery is made, the delivery of the work to the dealer or gallery and the acceptance of the work automatically creates a "consignment." In such a consignment situation, the gallery/dealer becomes a *trustee* of both the artist's work and the money from the sale of the work: First, the gallery/dealer is made responsible for any damage to or loss of the artwork during the entire time it is at the gallery or in the dealer's possession; then, after a work is sold, the amount paid by a purchaser (less any commission to the gallery/dealer) must be held for and paid to the artist and not used for any other purpose by the gallery/dealer. The work is further protected in that no creditor of the gallery/dealer can take the artist's work as payment for any debts owed by the gallery/dealer. The artist is also entitled to receive his/her agreed-upon percentage of the sale price of each work *first,* unless he/she agrees otherwise in writing. (If the gallery/dealer sells a work on an installment basis, the gallery/dealer must pay the artist the full amount of each installment until the artist's share of the sale price has been completely paid. Only then can the gallery/dealer begin to take its share of the sale price.) Finally, if the artist has not been paid in full after the gallery/dealer purchases an artwork itself and then sells it to an ordinary buyer, the money received from that buyer must first go to pay any amount that is still owing to the artist.

Types of Work Protected

The types of art included under this law are: painting, sculpture, drawing, works of graphic art (etchings, lithographs, offset prints, silk screen and other printing processes, calligraphic work, mixed-media works such as collage, assemblage and other combination art forms).

Penalties

If the gallery/dealer fails to perform the obligations imposed by this law, the artist can sue the gallery/dealer for breach of those responsibilities, in addition to suing for breach of contract, if there is one. (Since artist-gallery agreements are often verbal, it might be difficult to prove that the gallery/dealer has broken a specific point of agreement.) In addition, the gallery/dealer is also subject to criminal liability under Section 506 of the California Penal Code if it violates its obligation to hold the property of the artist for the artist until it is sold. Any contract or provision the artist and gallery/dealer may agree to which tries to avoid the obligations set up by the law will not be valid. For example, if the gallery/dealer presents a contract which states that the gallery/dealer shall not be responsible for any damage to the artwork whether negligent or accidental, that provision is automatically invalid since under the law the gallery/dealer has complete responsibility for the work while it is in its possession.

THE FINE PRINT DISCLOSURE LAW

In effect in California (since 1971, Civil Code Section 1740) and thereafter in Illinois, Maryland and Hawaii; most recently in New York in 1981 (General Business Law Article 12-H, Section 220).

These laws attempt to remedy many deceptive practices in the selling of prints and thereby protect both the artist and the buyers of such prints. Fakes, forgeries, unlimited editions (unsigned and unnumbered), color photographs and photomechanical reproductions, prints made from canceled plates when marketed as originals personally created and authorized by the artist, not only mislead a buyer as to the value of the work being purchased but can damage the reputation and value of the artist's work if these uncontrolled multiples or fakes are flooding the market. Since original artworks produced in multiples are more moderately priced than unique, one-of-a-kind works, they have become very attractive to collectors and a substantial source of income for artists.

How the Law Works

This legislation requires that anyone selling "fine prints" to the public must disclose the basic facts about the prints. The seller must give the name of the artist; state whether the artist's signature appears on the print and how many are signed; identify the medium and whether it is a photomechanical reproduction (as opposed to a hand-made, artist-supervised print); provide information as to when and how the "master" was used; and specify how many prints were produced if the edition was a "limited" one. A seller may not advertise, promote or distribute written materials about prints being sold unless this information is provided, and if any required facts are not available, the seller must clearly state what is not known. All known and unknown required information must be clearly stated on the invoice or sales receipt. It should be noted that an artist who sells directly to consumers may have the same responsibility as any other person selling fine prints.

Types of Work Protected

In California: fine prints, including engravings, etchings, woodcuts, lithographs, serigraph or silk screen prints. In New York: visual art multiples, including prints (same as California) *and* "photographs (positive or negative) and similar art objects . . . pages or sheets taken from books and magazines and offered for sale or sold as visual art objects . . ."

Comparison of California and New York Legislation

The required information in California is compared to New York's legislation as follows:[1]

(a) *Name of artist.* Also required in New York.

(b) *Whether the edition is a "limited edition" and if so an exact statement of the numbers involved, i.e., how many signed, unsigned, numbered and unnumbered are in the edition and how many proofs.* This is also required in New York, but New York does not require an exact statement of the number of proofs as to prints in existence, or the number of proofs as to prints made after the laws' effective date if they do not exceed the limited edition by 10 or 10%.

(c) *Whether the plate has been destroyed or canceled.* This is not required in New York.

(d) *A description of prior "states," if any, and which "state" is being sold.*

(e) *Information as to the existence and numbers involved in other editions from the same plate.* This is also required in New York when an edition is put forward as a "limited edition."

(f) *Whether the edition is a posthumous edition or restrike and if so whether the plate has been reworked.* New York requires information, when applicable, as to "posthumous" prints, and whether a plate or its derivative is used to produce additional prints after a limited edition has been produced.

(g) *The name of the workshop where the prints were made.* This is not required in New York.

(h) California's law covers all prints sold for $25 or more without a frame and $40 when framed. The New York law only covers prints sold in excess of $100 exclusive of any frame. (In Illinois $50 or more unframed, $60 or more framed.)

(i) Items of information included in the New York law but not in California pertain to: signature; medium, whether a multiple is a photomechanical reproduction; and the approximate time produced.

Penalties

California and New York provide for refunds when the information accompanying a print proves to be false and consumers are entitled to three times the price of the print if the gallery/dealer knowingly defrauded them.

[1] Reproduced with permission from a memorandum, "New York Disclosure Legislation as to the Sale of Visual Art Multiples" by Gustave Harrow, Assistant Attorney General of the State of New York.

The obvious side benefits to the artist from these disclosure laws are that they discourage unauthorized copies, encourage restoring control of the quality and production of the print to the artist, keep the size of the edition as the artist originally specified, thereby maintaining the value of the print in the marketplace, not only for that print but for the artist's other graphic output as well, reinforce the artist's right to license the making of photomechanical copies and receive the financial rewards from the granting of such rights or withholding them.

THE ART PRESERVATION ACT

In effect in California (since 1979, Civil Code Section 987); proposed in New York.

A black-and-white mobile entitled "Pittsburgh" by Alexander Calder is donated by a private collector for installation in the Pittsburgh International Airport. Without Calder's consent or knowledge, the mobile is repainted in the official county colors of green and gold. The artist's protests are ignored and it is not until twenty years later, after his death, that public pressure brings about its return to the original form and color.

The executor of sculptor David Smith's estate deliberately orders that the paint be stripped from several of Smith's sculptures in the belief that this improves their aesthetic quality and appeal.

A collector purchases a painting and trims inches off the top and sides in order to make it fit an antique frame.

A muralist creates paintings on the walls of a much-traveled building which is later refurbished. The painter discovers that the murals are being painted over and, without a contract stating to the contrary, is unable to stop the obliteration of her paintings.

This law prohibits any person, except the artist, from intentionally defacing, mutilating, altering or destroying a work of fine art in his possession and also allows the artist to claim or disclaim authorship of the artwork. The California law is the first of its kind in this country to establish the moral right, or *droit moral.* The moral rights of the artist have been recognized by statute in sixty-three nations. In France, such moral rights are perpetual, whereas in Germany and other countries, they expire simultaneously with the expiration of copyright. Prior to the advancement of this type of legislation in the United States, American courts have enforced the moral right under the doctrines of privacy, defamation and unfair competition. The rationale here is that the artist's name is being associated with work that no longer represents him or that the altered work is being represented to the public as the artist's product and it is wrong to hold out the artist as the creator of a version or work which substantially departs from the original creation. The California law serves two interests: the reputation of the artist and the public concern in protecting artistic creations for the benefit of society in generations to come.

How the Act Works

Anyone but the artist who owns and possesses a work of art may not *intentionally* alter or mutilate, deface or destroy the work and may not authorize anyone else to do so. Included in this prohibition are framers, conservators and restorers, but they are held responsible only in the case where the damage to the work results from so negligent a treatment of the artwork that it amounts to "indifference" toward it (this allows museums and others interested in serving and conserving art to use their best efforts at preservation and restoration without being held responsible for "altering" the work).

As with copyright law, the rights given the artist under this act last until 50 years after his/her death. Therefore, the law can be enforced by the artist during his/her lifetime and for a period of 50 years after the death of the artist, by the artist's heirs.

The act is designed to apply to all works of fine art regardless of when they were created as long as the prohibited act occurred after the effective date of the law, January 1, 1980.

The rights of the artist under this law cannot be waived unless the artist specifically agrees to forgo each or all of them in a signed agreement. There is no requirement that the artist reside in California, simply that the work itself be physically located in the state. The act *does not* deal with the question of the right to control how, where and under what conditions a work is displayed or pictured, although an artist might have other means of preventing a museum or owner from exhibiting his/her work upside down or in a demeaning fashion. It is questionable that the artist will be able to use the Preservation Act in such a battle.

Negligent behavior with regard to works of fine art do not fall under the scope of the act except in regard to the possible gross negligence of restorers, framers or conservators. Therefore, a collector whose painting has been damaged by a moving company would not have the additional grief of the artist bringing suit under the act.

Artworks Attached to a Building

If the work of art is so integral to a building that it cannot be removed without actually mutilating, altering, defacing or completely destroying the work and the owner of the building and the artist do not have a signed agreement giving the artist the right to preserve the work (if this agreement is properly recorded, it would mean that even subsequent owners of the building would not have the right to destroy the artwork), then the artist will have no protection under this legislation. If, on the other hand, the artwork can be removed without such damage, the owner's only obligation is to make a diligent effort to find and notify the artist in writing of the coming fate of the building. Once the artist has been notified, he/she has the choice of paying for the expense of removing the artwork within 90 days or abandoning it. If, however, the work is removed at the artist's expense, the ownership of the art passes back to the artist.

The Right of Paternity

The artist has the right to claim authorship in his/her artwork. When a work has been altered or changed in such substantial fashion that it cannot be restored to its original form, the artist has the right to have his/her name disassociated from the work.

Types of Work Protected

The law explicitly covers original paintings, sculptures and drawings and implicitly excludes prints, collages, photographs and crafts. Other explicit exclusions are: (i) works of art created under a "contract for commercial use," (ii) works of art by an artist who has been dead 50 years or longer, (iii) works so integral to a building that they cannot be removed without being damaged or destroyed and (iv) any work of art that is not of "recognized quality." This latter requirement that a work be of recognized quality to be protected by the law will, no doubt, cause some controversy in the years to come. To establish whether or not a work is of "recognized quality," experts, art dealers, collectors of fine art, curators of art museums and other persons involved with the creation and marketing of art shall be heard by the court.

Penalties and Remedies

An artist may bring an action for the following:

1. Injunctive relief. If the damage being done to the artwork can be halted, reversed or corrected, the court can order that it be done.

2. Actual damages. If the damage cannot be reversed or if the work has been totally destroyed, the artist may be awarded compensation for loss to his/her reputation. Since the injury to an artwork that is owned by somebody else does not cause any immediate out-of-pocket loss to the artist, the artist's actual damages could possibly be of some future economic loss the artist will suffer because of the injury to his/her work or reputation.

3. Attorneys' fees and expert-witness fees will be awarded to the artist, who should not have to bear these costs in the cause of protecting his/her work.

4. Punitive damages. These damages are awarded to punish the wrongdoer whose behavior has been willful or intentional. But to cool the temptation for speculative lawsuits, any such awards made by the court are given not to the artist but to art-related California charitable or educational activities and organizations in the fine arts.

Federal legislation which would add a moral rights provision to Section 113 of the revised Copyright Act has been proposed in the past. It would give the artist less of an ability to pursue specific legal remedies than the California legislation. Although arts of earlier centuries as well as contemporary reproduction, photography and other types of art not "recognized" by the California legislation do not yet have the benefit of preservation by statute, it appears that there is at least in this country a movement toward protection of the artist's personality through the assurance of respect for the work of art, a respect that enhances the quality of life through preserving our cultural heritage.

HOUSING LAWS FOR JOINT LIVING AND WORK SPACE

Such legislation allows local governments to establish zones where artists may live and work in buildings in urban areas previously zoned for commercial and/or industrial use and to authorize alternative building code requirements in those areas. This could also be accomplished in overall state zoning statutes establishing live/work zones. (See Chapter 20 of this Manual.)

STATE TAX INCENTIVES FOR ARTISTS

For federal tax purposes, an artist donating work to a museum or other charity can claim only the cost of materials used in the work as a deduction, although a collector donating the same work could claim a deduction of the fair market value of the work (what the work would bring if sold in the normal art market). For example: An artist buys paint and canvas at a cost of $50 and over a period of four weeks creates two similar paintings. The artist donates one work to a hospital and is entitled to a federal income tax deduction of $25. The artist sells the other painting at a gallery exhibition for $2,500. The purchaser of the painting donates it to the same hospital and is entitled to a deduction of $2,500.

Most states simply follow federal rules on income tax. However, five states so far have passed legislation which rectifies this situation for purposes of state income tax.

CALIFORNIA. Passed 1979. Allows deduction of fair market value for work donated by the artist to a museum, charity or government agency. The law applies to any professional artists deriving a "significant" portion of their income from sale of their work (at least 20% of gross income for the year or at least 50% of gross income for the three prior years). The donated art can be visual art, musical compositions or literary works. The artist must have been a resident of California for the entire year and the value of the donated work must be established by an independent appraisal.

KANSAS. Passed 1980. This legislation is not limited to professional artists and applies to any work of art created by a taxpayer. The law applies only to visual art and must be donated to a nonprofit museum or gallery receiving public funds. The work must also be appraised, but in this case by the recipient. (All other states require an independent appraisal.)

MARYLAND. Passed 1980. This law is limited to professional artists, who are defined as persons receiving half of their current or previous year's income from the sale of their artwork. Work must be donated to a museum in Maryland open to the public and deductions for such donations are limited to 50% of the artist's gross income for that year.

MICHIGAN. This legislation does not provide for a deduction, but rather a direct tax credit of 50% of the fair market value of the work donated, up to the lesser of 20% of total tax or $100.

OREGON. This legislation is not limited to professional artists but is confined to works of visual art. Work may be donated to a museum or any charity.

WISCONSIN. Legislation has been introduced which would provide fair market value deductions of up to three works per year. The deduction would apply to visual art as well as calligraphy and crafts.

NORTH CAROLINA. Such legislation has not been introduced, as the state simply does not follow the federal tax instructions in this respect. The North Carolina Department of Revenue has always held that fair market value is the proper basis for a deductible gift.

ESTATE TAX BENEFITS FOR VISUAL ARTISTS

For federal estate tax purposes, the unsold works left by an artist at the time of his/her death are valued at their fair market value for purposes of computing estate taxes. Example: Prior to his death, an artist has been selling his graphic works at $1,000 apiece. At his death, he has 150 unsold works in his studio. Under the present federal law, these works would be valued at fair market value ($150,000) and this amount would be added to the other assets in the artist's estate, thereby raising the amount of estate taxes. Some states have begun to deal with this problem on behalf of the visual artist.

MAINE. A 1980 statute allows a credit against an artist's estate taxes for works of art which the Maine State Museum Commission agrees to accept for display in a public institution, after determining that the acquisition would be advantageous to the state. It is advantageous if such an acquisition would: (a) encourage the preservation of original or noteworthy works of art; (b) further the preservation and understanding of fine arts traditions which have existed in Maine; (c) further the understanding of the fine arts by the people of Maine; or (d) aid in the establishment of important state collections of works of art.

CALIFORNIA. A proposed statute would allow the heirs of an artist who inherit the art to defer payment of state inheritance taxes on the art for 5 years and then pay 10% of the tax due each year for the next 10 years at 7% interest. Similar legislation would allow the death tax to be paid with the artwork left by the artist. The artwork would be valued by the state death tax appraiser and then delivered to an appropriate institution or museum.

OTHER. Other proposed state legislation would value the artwork in the artist's estate at death at the cost of materials in each work until such time as the works are sold.

PROPOSED FEDERAL LEGISLATION

Although much can be achieved through state legislatures, federal support and legislation for the visual artist is desirable, especially as it relates to the tax and estate tax benefits for the artist and support by the community at large for the artist.

In 1981 a sample of proposed arts legislation included moral rights, 0.5% to 1% of the cost of public buildings allocated for artworks for those buildings, a National Historic Preservation Act, standards for toxic artist's supplies, tax credit for contribution of artwork by artists, estate tax rectified for artists, taxpayers' contributions to the arts by designating contributions on their tax returns.

"An important index of the moral and cultural strength of a people is their official attitude towards, and nurturing of, a free and vital community of artists." (Judge Robert M. Takasugi in a

District Court decision upholding the California Resale Royalties Act.) This "official attitude" has been expressed in California through innovative and creative legislation which recognizes the rewards to society when artists and their works are protected and allowed to flourish.

A SURVEY OF STATE ARTS LEGISLATION

(NOTE: The bills are listed numerically according to frequency of introduction and/or passage by the greatest number of states.)

1. *Percentage for Arts.* Appropriates a specific percentage of the annual construction budget for state buildings to commission and/or purchase art to be placed in such buildings or in existing state buildings.

2. *Sales and Use Tax Exemption.* Exempts from state sales and use taxes purchases of art by nonprofit or municipal art museums and art purchased for donation to such museums (and, in at least one state, art purchased for donation to *any* nonprofit organization).

3. *Artist-Art Dealer Relations.* Provides protection to an artist who gives a work of art to an art dealer to sell or exhibit. The dealer in that situation acts as a trustee in holding the artist's works and funds from the sale of the art. The artist is also protected against loss or damage to the artwork while in the dealer's possession and against claims by the dealer's creditors.

4. *Informational Disclosure for Limited Edition Prints.* Protects consumers of fine art prints issued in limited editions by requiring art dealers to disclose specific information regarding each print sold. Other proposals declare specific warranties by art dealers with respect to the sale of limited edition prints.

5. *Artists' Tax Deductions.* Enables professional artists to deduct for state income tax purposes the fair market value of artworks donated to charitable organizations. Current law limits the artist's tax deduction to the cost of materials only.

6. *Resale Royalties.* Provides artists with a percentage of the resale price of their artworks, provided that the resale is profitable to the seller and the resale price is in excess of a specific minimum amount.

7. *Artists' Live-Work Space.* Allows local government to establish artists' zones where artists may live and work in buildings in urban areas previously zoned for commercial use (or enacts state zoning statute in states where zoning is a function of the legislature). Also provides rent control and other protection for artists occupying such dwellings.

8. *Appropriation for Arts Institutions.* Provides direct state appropriation for one or more major public arts institutions.

9. *Art Preservation.* Provides the artist, and in some cases the public, the right to bring legal action to protect artworks against intentional physical defacement, alteration or destruction by government agencies or others. Both injunctive relief and an action for damages are authorized.

CHAPTER EIGHT
THE CALIFORNIA RESALE ROYALTIES ACT

Mark E. Halloran, Esq.

In 1973, Robert Scull, a well-known collector of American modern art, decided to auction part of his collection. The auction was conducted by Sotheby Parke-Bernet and brought Scull $2.2 million. Among those present was Robert Rauschenberg, whose painting entitled "Thou" had been purchased by Scull in the early 1960s for $960. It sold for $85,000. Afterwards, Rauschenberg confronted Scull and loudly remarked: "I've been working my ass off just for you to make that profit . . ." Still, Rauschenberg had no legal claim to Scull's incredible profit; he had only his rage.

After the experience of Rauschenberg and many other artists, California has legally recognized that it is inherently unjust for an artist not to share in the increased value of his or her work when it is resold.

On January 1, 1977, the California Resale Royalties Act went into effect. Fundamentally, the Resale Royalties Act provides that living creators of fine art (defined as an original painting, sculpture or drawing) are legally entitled to 5% of the gross sale price when their artwork is resold for more than $1,000. The theory is that the original creator should continue to share in the proceeds of the sale of his or her work after the initial sale. The act recognized that the creator of fine art, unlike book authors and songwriters, creates a single work that is normally not reproduced. Unlike book authors and songwriters, who derive economic benefit from multiple reproduction, the visual artist typically relies exclusively on the initial sale of a work. After this sale it is the galleries, collectors and museums who trade in the profitable art market.

California is the first state in the United States to enact a resale royalties law, but the concept is not new. The act is a legal recognition of the "umbilical cord" between the artist and his or her work. This concept is known in Europe as *droit de suite* (literally: "follow-up right"). Resale royalties laws exist in many European countries, notably France, West Germany, Italy and Switzerland. The California law is the first and only one of its kind in the United States. At this time no other states have passed similar legislation, although resale royalties legislation has been introduced in at least eight other states, including New York. Federal legislation was introduced by Henry Waxman, representative from California, in 1977, but passage seems far off.

For your reference the Resale Royalties Act is reprinted in its entirety at the end of this article.

HOW THE LAW WORKS

Under the act, when there is a resale of a work of fine art for a price of more than $1,000, the seller must withhold 5% of the resale price, locate the artist and pay the artist.

If the seller cannot locate and pay the artist within 90 days, the seller must pay the 5% royalty to the California Arts Council.

The California Arts Council then attempts to locate and pay the artist. If the artist can't be found and if the original artist does not file a written claim for the money within seven years, the money goes to the operating fund of the Council, which it applies to its programs.

The following will guide you concerning the situations where the Resale Royalties Act does *not* apply.

1. *Resale.* The Resale Royalties Act does *not* apply to the initial sale of a work of fine art between the artist and original buyer, but only *resales.*

2. *Less than $1,000.* The act does not apply if the resale is for a gross sales price of less than $1,000 or an exchange when the property transferred has a fair market value of less than $1,000.

3. *Death of Artist.* The act does not apply to resale after the death of the artist—the artist must be living.

4. *Sales Price Less than Purchase Price.* The act does not apply to resales when the gross sales price is less than the purchase price paid by the seller.

5. *Fine Prints, Tapestries and Books.* Since the act defines "fine art" as "original paintings, sculpture or drawings," fine prints, tapestries and books do not fall within the scope of the law.

Let's take a simple example. You create a sculpture and sell it to a local gallery for $500. The gallery, in turn, sells the sculpture for $2,000. If you are living the gallery is obligated, under the Resale Royalties Act, to retain 5% ($100) of the sales price and give it to you.

In this simple example, the gallery shouldn't have much trouble finding you, since you were the original seller. Still, suppose they don't pay. What can you do?

Your sole "remedy" under the Resale Royalties Act is to bring a lawsuit against the gallery for damages (i.e., money). There are no criminal penalties for violation of the act. Your damages are what the gallery should have paid you, $100. Unfortunately, you can't recover for your aggravation, lost time or hurt feelings.

You must also bring your suit within three years from the date of the resale or one year after discovery of the resale, whichever is longer. The legislature inserted the "discovery" provision to protect artists who do not discover resales within the three-year period.

Fortunately, an increasing number of galleries and collectors are now complying with the Resale Royalties Act. The act would be even more effective if it provided artists with more clout (such as a multiple of damages) to force compliance.

CONSTITUTIONAL ATTACK

Until recently the constitutionality of the Resale Royalties Act was in jeopardy. The test case *Morseburg* v. *Baylon* was brought by a Los Angeles art dealer, Howard Morseburg. Shortly after the Resale Royalties Act went into effect (January 1, 1977), Morseburg sold two paintings under circumstances requiring him to pay resale royalties.

Morseburg filed an action in federal court in Los Angeles seeking to have the Resale Royalties Act struck down as unconstitutional. The lawsuit pitted Morseburg and his sponsoring group of art dealers and collectors, Concerned Artists and Dealers for Responsible Equity (CADRE), against Bay Area Lawyers for the Arts (BALA) and the Artist Equity Association, Northern California Chapter. The act, however, was upheld by the District Court, the 9th Circuit Court of Appeals and, most recently, the United States Supreme Court, which refused to hear Morseburg's appeal.

Morseburg's main argument was that the Resale Royalties Act was "pre-empted" (superseded) by the Copyright Act of 1909. United States District Court Judge Takasugi held that the Resale Royalties Act did not conflict with but was consistent with federal copyright law, because it would encourage the production and distribution of works of fine art.

ADDITIONAL CONTRACT PROTECTION

The Resale Royalties Act does not preclude you from protecting yourself in a written contract with buyers of your art. Your contract will protect you even if the Resale Royalties Act is struck down or changed. Even though anyone who sells your art is required by law to pay you the 5% resale royalty, it cannot hurt to insert a clause requiring such 5% payment in a sale agreement or signed bill of sale. You should also note that you can negotiate a *higher* resale royalty percentage, and that your right to receive the 5% royalty cannot be transferred or "waived" (given up) unless the contract provides for a royalty of more than 5%. Also, the buyer should inform you of the name and address of any subsequent buyer. There are also certain rights (e.g., the right to borrow a work and prohibition against the collector's altering the work) that you might want to include. (See the Artist's Reserved Rights Transfer and Sale Agreement section in this Manual.)

California is the first state to recognize an artist's right to retain financial interest in resales of original works of fine art. The Resale Royalties Act has survived a constitutional challenge, and is a symbol of this state's commitment to visual artists.

As an artist you can take the following steps to increase the likelihood of your receiving your royalty:

1. Include a provision in your contracts with dealers providing the minimum royalty of 5% on resale.

2. Keep records of all your sales.

3. Require the buyer of your art to notify you upon any resale, and not only pay you the 5% royalty but also provide the name and address of the new buyer.

4. Attach a notice to your artwork or to the bill of sale stating that the work is subject to the California Resale Royalties Act. (See sample notice in the Contracts section of this Manual.)

THE RESALE ROYALTIES ACT

§ 986. [Sale of fine art]

(a) Whenever a work of fine art is sold and the seller resides in California or the sale takes place in California, the seller or his agent shall pay to the artist of such work of fine art or to such artist's agent 5 percent of the amount of such sale. The right of the artist to receive an amount equal to 5 percent of the amount of such sale is not transferable and may be waived only by a contract in writing providing for an amount in excess of 5 percent of the amount of such sale.

(1) When a work of art is sold at an auction or by a gallery, dealer, broker, museum, or other person acting as the agent for the seller the agent shall withhold 5 percent of the amount of the sale, locate the artist, and pay the artist.

(2) If the seller or agent is unable to locate and pay the artist within 90 days, an amount equal to 5 percent of the amount of the sale shall be transferred to the Arts Council.

(3) If a seller or his agent fails to pay an artist the amount equal to 5 percent of the sale of a work of fine art by the artist, or fails to transfer such amount to the Arts Council, the artist may bring an action for damages within three years after the date of sale or one year after the discovery of the sale, whichever is longer.

(4) Moneys received by the council pursuant to this section shall be deposited in an account in the Special Deposit Fund in the State Treasury.

(5) The Arts Council shall attempt to locate any artist for whom money is received pursuant to this section. If the council is unable to locate the artist and the artist does not file a written claim for the money received by the council within seven years of the date of sale of the work of fine art, the right of the artist terminates and such money shall be transferred to the operating fund of the council as reimbursement to fund programs of the council.

(6) Any amounts of money held by any seller or agent for the payment of artists pursuant to this section shall be exempt from attachment or execution of judgment by the creditors of such seller or agent.

(b) Subdivision (a) shall not apply to any of the following:

(1) To the initial sale of a work of fine art where legal title to such work at the time of such initial sale is vested in the artist thereof.

(2) To the resale of a work of fine art for a gross sales price of less than one thousand dollars ($1,000).

(3) To a resale after the death of such artist.

(4) To the resale of the work of fine art for a gross sales price less than the purchase price paid by the seller.

(5) To a transfer of a work of fine art which is exchanged for one or more works of fine art or for a

combination of cash, other property, and one or more works of fine art where the fair market value of the property exchanged is less than one thousand dollars ($1,000).

(c) For purposes of this section, the following terms have the following meanings:

(1) "Artist" means the person who creates a work of fine art.

(2) "Fine art" means an original painting, sculpture or drawing.

(d) This section shall become operative on January 1, 1977, and shall apply to works of fine art created before and after its operative date.

(e) If any provision of this section or the application thereof to any person or circumstance is held invalid for any reason, such invalidity shall not affect any other provisions or applications of this section which can be effected, without the invalid provision or application, and to this end the provisions of this section are severable.

EDITOR'S NOTE: Senate Bill No. 1759 has amended the California Resale Royalties Act to create enforceable rights in artists to assign their right to collect royalty payments, and in artists' heirs to royalty payments for twenty years after the artist's death, provided that (1) the artist died after January 1, 1983, as a U.S. citizen and resident of California and (2) all sales within ten years of the initial sale by the artist to a dealer were only between dealers, not between a dealer and a third person. The amendment further allows a successful artist-litigant in an action to collect royalty payments to recover reasonable attorney's fees.

PART THREE

LICENSING, MERCHANDISING AND PUBLISHING VISUAL ART

CHAPTER NINE
LICENSING AND MERCHANDISING A WORK OF VISUAL ART

Susan A. Grode, Esq.

In today's climate of commercial marketing and reproduction, artwork is duplicated and replicated, transferred into other media and onto objects, enlarged or miniaturized. Charlie Brown, the original artwork of Charles Schultz, appears on book covers, posters, tableware and dolls. Robert Indiana's LOVE painting has been transmuted into brass paperweights, greeting cards and beach towels; scarves, bathroom tissue and linens bear the logo of Vera. What's in demand? A particular artwork so distinctive in and of itself that it can be associated with a type or line of products, or an artist whose reputation, identified in his/her logo, is sufficient to promote sales.

One need not have worldwide notoriety to engage in some form of licensing arrangement. The copyright law (see Copyright section of this Manual) provides that an artist retains all rights to the artwork which are not specifically granted in writing. Therefore, a painter can sell the original painting to a collector and license one publisher to reproduce it on posters, another on greeting cards. A photographer can sell one-time reproduction rights for use of his/her image in a magazine and license a different use of it on lunch boxes.

Each time an artist receives an offer for the use of his/her work, some form of license (and not outright sale of all rights or work-for-hire agreement) should be considered. The ability to negotiate terms favorable to the artist (maximizing the number of different uses to which the work can be applied, approval of each use, a substantial advance and royalties based on retail sales, to name but a few) depends largely on the bargaining power of the artist. If the artist or the particular work is in great demand—when either the art or the artist has achieved sufficient recognition in the minds of consumers that it is able to generate sales of products which would be less salable without it—it should be possible to obtain many of the advantages and protections articulated in the merchandising and licensing agreements reproduced here.

In licensing your work for fine art print publication, commercial or merchandising use or other purposes, remember that you need not grant all the rights in the work to the licensee/reproducing entity and the rights need not be granted forever (although for business reasons and to avoid competition by the work in another form, most licensees will ask for the right to reproduce in any and all forms for the term of the copyright, which is your life plus 50 years). An example of a negotiated solution might be to grant the right to reproduce the work for purposes of a poster only for a period of five years with the possibility of renewing the right to reproduce if your royalties on poster sales exceed a certain amount by the fifth year.

Other considerations to note:

1. That the work as reproduced must bear your copyright notice.

2. That the original artwork be returned to you or negotiated for separately as a sale with a separate purchase price.

3. Payment of a reproduction fee upon signing the licensing agreement, which fee shall not be treated as an advance against your future royalties.

4. The right to approve the final product (important in the case of a fine art reproduction) and the right to a specified number of prints or licensed articles without charge.

5. Where your royalty is based on net sums, make sure that there is a definition of what expenses will be subtracted from the gross selling price to arrive at such net amounts (actual costs of producing the print are acceptable expenses, wages paid to secretaries of the publisher are not). Naturally, if possible, attempt to negotiate a royalty on the gross selling price or on the gross amount received by the publisher/licensee.

AGREEMENT TO PUBLISH LIMITED EDITION ARTWORKS
Comments and annotations by Susan A. Grode, Esq.

THIS AGREEMENT is made and entered into this _____ day of _____, 198__, by and between _____ of _____, (hereinafter referred to as "Artist") and _____, (hereinafter referred to as "Publisher").

WHEREAS, Publisher is in the business of publishing and distributing limited edition posters and graphics; and

WHEREAS, Artist is an artist in the business of producing artwork (hereinafter referred to as "images") for the purposes of having same published and distributed as limited edition posters and graphics; and

WHEREAS, Publisher desires the sole and exclusive right to produce, publish and distribute limited edition posters and graphics of images produced by Artist, within the United States and the World; and

WHEREAS, Artist desires to grant Publisher the exclusive right to produce, publish and distribute limited edition posters and graphics of images produced by Artist, within the United States and the World; and

NOW, THEREFORE, in consideration of promises and the mutual covenants herein contained, Artist and Publisher do hereby agree as follows:

1. Publisher shall be the sole and exclusive producer, publisher and distributor for the United States and the World of limited edition posters and graphics both signed and unsigned, produced by any printing process, including, without limitation, etching, lithography, serigraphy and aquatint, of images produced by Artist. Artist shall personally sign and number as many editions as Publisher shall request.

Comment: The intent of this paragraph should reflect that this agreement will apply to only those limited edition posters and graphics that the artist and publisher agree shall be produced, published and distributed by the publisher. If this is the first time the artist and publisher are working together the artist should be reluctant to limit his/her production to one outlet. All other graphic production by the artist should not be subject to the agreement. This does not preclude the artist from allowing the publisher to distribute other of the artist's work on a non-exclusive basis.

2. The term of this Agreement shall be _____ years from the date first written above; provided, however, that Publisher shall have the right to terminate this Agreement upon ten (10) days' prior notice to Artist if Artist's images do not, in Publisher's reasonable discretion, meet Publisher's aesthetic standards. Artist shall provide Publisher with at least 10 original images each year and shall produce a particular image or theme if so requested by Publisher. From such images, Publisher shall publish a minimum of 4 editions per year during the term of this Agreement, and Publisher shall have the sole right to determine the number of editions to be published in excess of the stated minimum.

Comment: The term of the agreement should be for one or two years, renewable at the mutual option of the publisher and the artist and should be mutually terminable on thirty days' notice if either the artist or the publisher does not meet the other's aesthetic standards. With regard to the original images to be provided by the artist, the number to be provided per year should be reasonable (possibly six, with the publisher being required to publish a minimum of four editions from these original images per year). In addition, the publisher and the artist should mutually decide how many prints comprise each edition, how many will be signed and how many will be unsigned, with the addition of twenty-five artist's proofs and the first ten numbers of each edition going to the artist and two extra prints to go to the artist for purposes of copyright registration. In addition, any images not selected for publication by the publisher should, upon notice from the publisher at the expiration of each year, revert to the artist's control and the artist should be free to use these images for any purposes whatsoever thereafter.

The artist should have the right to approve the final printing of the edition with regard to color separation, fidelity to the original and the artist's satisfaction that the finished printed product is an aesthetically acceptable reproduction of the original image. The artist should not sign the edition until he/she so approves. The artist should have the right to make changes to the print-in-progress.

The "technical" quality of the edition is generally the responsibility of the publisher. The publisher should bear the cost of reprinting, reproofing and changes to the print-in-progress.

3. Publisher may enter into agreements of joint venture or partnership with third parties for the purposes of publishing and/or distributing limited edition posters and graphics from the images, but in no event shall Publisher enter into any agreements which would result in Publisher receiving less than fifty percent (50%) of all net proceeds realized.

Comment: Any agreements of joint venture or partnership with third parties should be with the prior consent and approval of the artist, and there should be no assignment of this agreement without the artist's written consent. The rationale for these comments is that the artist, in making the agreement with the publisher, has accepted a working relationship where he/she has knowledge of the quality and reputation of the publisher's output and he/she would not have the same confidence or ability to work with a third party unknown to him/her.

4. Artist shall receive twenty-five percent (25%) of Publisher's net proceeds from the sale of all limited edition posters and graphics of images produced by Artist, after a deduction of $500 per edition for advertising and the greater of: (a) $_____ per poster or graphic; or (b) 15% of the wholesale selling price per poster or graphic, for administrative and distribution costs.

Comment: If the artist has enough bargaining power the participation of the artist could be raised to 50%. The net proceeds should be defined as proceeds from the sale of all posters and graphics from images produced by the artist after reimbursement to the publisher for *actual costs of production.* With regard to deduction for advertising fees, no more than $500 should be deducted for such advertising, but in the event the actual cost for advertising is less than $500, the lesser amount should be deducted (the amount suggested in this contract is not necessarily illustrative of average advertising costs). A suggested alternative to the above: that the artist receive 40% of the proceeds actually received until the publisher has recouped its cost of producing the works, with the publisher giving the artist a list of the production costs prior to commencement of publication, and after recoupment of these costs, the artist and publisher could share equally, 50%/50%, in all proceeds received. An advertising provision similar to the one listed above could also apply here. A second alternative: allow the artist to receive 35% of all proceeds actually received for the first year, thus allowing the publisher, out of its larger percentage, to recoup its production costs, and 50% in all years thereafter.

Insert some reference to an advance or, preferably, a non-recoupable, non-refundable creation fee to be paid to the artist for the first image, and specify that, thereafter, advances/fees for all future images to be published and distributed by the publisher will be negotiated in good faith as each image is approved by the publisher for production, publication and distribution.

5. Artist shall receive his/her share of net proceeds as stated above on a quarterly basis, based upon the actual receipts of Publisher in connection with Artist's images during said quarter, less returns. Artist shall receive payment due no later than twenty (20) days subsequent to the close of each fiscal quarter year and said payment shall be accompanied by a statement of sales.

Comment: This is the accounting paragraph. Add that the artist shall have the right on reasonable request and notice to examine the books as they pertain to the artist's images and to the production and distribution of those images. The statement of sales should be detailed and the artist should state in the agreement that the publisher shall not hold back a reserve to cover possible returns.

6. In the event that at the end of any fiscal year of this Agreement, Artist has not received aggregate payments of at least _____, Publisher agrees to pay Artist any deficiency, which shall be paid to Artist within thirty (30) days of the close of each fiscal year of the term of this Agreement.

> *Comment:* Here, the publisher is guaranteeing the artist a specific minimum yearly amount. The artist should consider the guaranteed amount: is it, along with the advance, sufficient to warrant committing his/her images to this publishing venture? The guaranteed amount to the artist for the second year of this agreement and thereafter should be negotiated in increasing amounts.

7. Artist represents and warrants that he/she is the sole and exclusive owner of the images, free and clear of all liens, claims and encumbrances, and that the images, if published, will not infringe on the copyright or rights of any other person or entity. Artist shall assign and transfer to Publisher all rights, title and interest of every kind whatsoever throughout the World in and to all original copyrights, renewal copyrights and the right to renew original copyrights and extensions thereof, together with the right to sue and recover for any past infringement thereof, to all images created by Artist under this Agreement. In no event shall Publisher retain the ownership of the original artwork, which shall be returned to Artist.

> *Comment:* In this paragraph the artist gives standard assurances that he/she has the right to contract for the artwork and that the publisher will not incur any legal harm as a result of publishing and distributing it. There should be no assignment of the artist's copyright of the images. All images should be copyrighted in the artist's name and the appropriate copyright notice should appear on each poster. There is no problem with the publisher's name also appearing on the poster and an agreement that the publisher may jointly with or independently of the artist pursue any legal remedy against any infringement of the image in the poster or graphic. The publisher would have this right during the agreement and after the term of the agreement as long as it continues to sell the graphics. As a result of the artist's maintaining the copyright ownership, the contract should also indicate that the exclusive right of reproduction is being granted to the publisher for the purposes of an edition of a particular number, to be stated after agreement by the parties on that number, and that any other right to the image shall be negotiated in good faith. The publisher is contracting for the right to reproduce the limited edition of the image and not for the ownership of the image. As a result, the artist can agree that once the publisher has performed its obligation of production, publication and distribution under this contract, the artist shall not sell, authorize or license any use of the particular image for any purposes which would specially conflict with or diminish the rights granted to the publisher. (This would also diminish the market value of the published images.)

8. Publisher shall have the right to use Artist's name and likeness in promoting the sale of the editions, and Artist shall provide reasonable assistance in that regard. Artist acknowledges that his/her services hereunder are of a special, unique, unusual and extraordinary character, which gives such services a particular value, the loss of which cannot be reasonably or adequately compensated

in damages or in an action of law. Accordingly, in addition to any other remedy Publisher may have at law or in equity, an injunction may be granted to prevent the breach of this Agreement.

> *Comment:* With regard to the publisher's use of the artist's name and likeness in promoting the sale of the editions, the artist should have the right to approve such promotion and to require that all sales of the artist's work be conducted according to the highest standards, in a dignified manner and consistent with the artist's reputation and professional standing. With regard to the rest of this paragraph, beginning "Artist acknowledges that his/her services hereunder . . . ," this language is burdensome and restrictive and must be deleted. An injunction could prevent the artist from publishing art for other purposes and with other publishers. In light of the fact that the publisher does not have the exclusive right to publish all of the artist's output, such a remedy is unreasonable. Replace this language with an arbitration clause.

9. This Agreement shall be deemed fully executed in _____, and shall be governed and construed in accordance with the internal laws of the State of _____. No provision of this Agreement is to be interpreted for or against any party because that party or such party's legal representative drafted such provision.

10. This Agreement contains the sole and entire agreement and understanding of the parties with respect to the entire subject matter hereof, and any and all prior discussions, negotiations, comments and understandings related hereto are hereby merged in this Agreement. No representations, oral or otherwise, express or implied, other than those contained herein have been made by any party.

> *Comment:* Further additions to this agreement should include: that the parties recognize that the various federal and state statutes presently in effect, which apply to the subject matter of this agreement, shall apply; that any rights not specifically granted in this agreement are reserved to the artist; that this agreement should not prevent the artist from granting others the rights to publish images which are not subject to this agreement or from engaging in artistic services to others; and that the artist shall have the right to exhibit the images for his/her own professional purposes.

IN WITNESS WHEREOF, the parties hereto have executed this Agreement as of the date first above set forth.

By _____   By _____

  PUBLISHER   ARTIST

CHAPTER TEN
MERCHANDISING LICENSE AGREEMENT

Comments and annotations by Lawrence J. Blake, Esq.

The agreement reprinted and annotated below is an example of the type of agreement which might be entered into when the creator or owner of a logo, painting, graphic design, cartoon character, sculpture or photograph enters into an agreement with a manufacturer for the use of that logo or other artwork on merchandise manufactured by the manufacturer. This particular form of agreement seems to have been designed initially to cover merchandising rights to the name of a popular motion picture or television series and was subsequently revised to cover merchandising rights to the name and logo of a popular rock music group. This form of agreement could easily be adapted, with only minor revisions required, to cover merchandising rights to any other logo, design or other artwork (for convenience referred to in the agreement as the "Mark") created by an artist. There are countless items that you see every day which are sold primarily on the basis of the name, trademark or artwork associated with them rather than on the intrinsic merits of the item itself. Accordingly, many merchandising agreements are extremely lucrative to the owners of the rights in the Mark.

When an artist creates a logo or design or other artwork for use by an entertainer, motion picture company, record company or other corporation or business entity, the artist should think about the potential value of the Mark in derivative uses, such as merchandising.

This annotation is designed to give the artist an understanding of the framework of merchandising agreements. The particular form of agreement reprinted below is somewhat unusual in that it is, from a legal point of view, very detailed. Most merchandising agreements are very sketchy and not precisely drafted. Accordingly, this form could prove very helpful as a model against which to compare a different form of merchandising agreement which might be submitted to the artist.

This particular form is very favorable to the artist/owner (licensor). This is due to the strong bargaining power of the particular licensor who was a party to the actual agreement from which this form has been derived and because that licensor's attorneys were very diligent in negotiating changes favorable to the licensor. An artist should not expect to receive from a manufacturer a form of agreement which is as detailed, clear and favorable as this one.

AGREEMENT made this _____ day of _____, 19____, between _____
_____ (hereinafter called "Licensor") and _____
_____ (hereinafter referred to as "Licensee").

WITNESSETH:

WHEREAS, Licensor has rights to the name, character, symbol, logo, design, likeness and visual representation of _____ (which name, character, symbol, logo, design, likeness and visual representation and/or each of the individual components thereof shall hereinafter be called the "Mark"), and

WHEREAS, Licensee desires to utilize the Mark upon and in connection with the manufacture, sale and distribution of articles hereinafter described;

NOW, THEREFORE, in consideration of the mutual promises herein contained, it is hereby agreed:

1. GRANT OF LICENSE:

(a) *Articles.* Upon the terms and conditions hereinafter set forth, Licensor hereby grants to Licensee and Licensee hereby accepts the non-exclusive right (as more particularly set forth in paragraph 3 hereof), license and privilege of using the Mark in connection with the manufacture, sale and distribution of these articles: School supplies, specifically wirebound and tapebound notebooks,* steno books, memo books, tablets, binder paper, binders* and paper portfolios* with or without bound paper.

Comment: Obviously, the particular articles to be manufactured pursuant to the agreement will depend on what has been negotiated in the particular circumstances. Each different type of item should be clearly specified.

(b) *Territory.* The license hereby granted extends only to the territory specified in Schedule A attached hereto and made a part hereof. Licensee agrees that it will not make or authorize to be made any use, direct or indirect, of the Mark in any other area, and that it will not knowingly sell articles covered by this license agreement to persons who intend or are likely to sell them in any other area.

Comment: The territory in which the licensee may sell the articles should be specifically negotiated. The territory should be limited to those areas where the licensee has demonstrated an ability to adequately distribute the articles. Some companies which may be outstanding in one country or in one region of the United States, for example, may have no market penetration in another country or another region of the United States. The licensor wants to be with the company in each particular territory which is best equipped to handle the sale of the articles in that territory.

(c) *Initial Term.* The initial term of this license hereby granted shall be effective on the date specified in Schedule B, attached hereto and made part hereof, and shall continue until the date specified in Schedule B, unless sooner terminated in accordance with the provisions of this license agreement.

(d) *Option Terms.* Upon condition that Licensee has performed all of its obligations hereunder and shall have paid to Licensor no less than $_____ during the initial term hereof,

Licensee shall have the option by written notice to Licensor, no later than one hundred twenty (120) days prior to the expiration of the initial term hereof, to extend said term for a one-year period. In the event Licensee exercises such option, Licensee agrees to pay to Licensor, upon exercise of said option, an advance of $_____ against royalties due during the option year. This license shall be automatically renewed thereafter from year to year, upon all the terms and conditions contained herein, including advances and guarantees, with the final renewal to expire on _____, 19____, unless either party hereto shall have given notice in writing to the contrary at least one hundred twenty (120) days prior to the expiration date of the then current option year.

Comment: The term of the agreement must also be specifically negotiated. It is in the licensor's best interest to keep the term as short as possible, without depriving the licensee of the time it needs to manufacture and market the product successfully. Normally in merchandising agreements the licensee will have an initial term of one to two years, with an option or options for one or two additional years. Very rarely do merchandising agreements last longer than that, because the Mark will only very rarely have popularity for a period longer than a few years. Accordingly, it is crucial that the licensor place performance criteria on the licensee, so that if the licensee is not doing an adequate job of selling the merchandise, the licensor will have the right to terminate the agreement and make a new agreement with a different licensee. It is important that the licensee be required to pay an advance upon the exercise of the option for each option term, so that the licensee has additional economic incentive to aggressively market the merchandise.

2. TERMS OF PAYMENT:

(a) *Royalty Rate.* Licensee agrees to pay Licensor as fees for the use of the Mark a sum or sums of money as specified in Schedule C attached hereto and made a part hereof.

Comment: Obviously, the royalty rate must be specifically and carefully negotiated in each agreement. It is not sufficient simply to say, for example, 10%. 10% of what? Is it of the retail selling price to the ultimate consumer or 10% of the wholesale price at which the manufacturer sells to its various accounts? There may be more than one wholesale price as well, depending on the volume of merchandise purchased by a particular account. Although the licensee may not desire to negotiate and may insist on paying the same royalty rate which it customarily pays in deals of this type, nonetheless it is important for this to be negotiated so that the licensor knows exactly what it is entitled to receive. This may entail taking the time to become familiar with the licensee's marketing strategies and sales incentive plans. Obviously, the more the licensor knows about how the licensee conducts its business, the more secure the licensor will feel in entering into the agreement.

In many merchandising agreements the royalty paid by the licensee is not stated as a percentage but as a flat cent rate, e.g., 10 cents per unit sold. In such cases, the cent rate should be tied to a particular wholesale or retail selling price, so that if the selling price subsequently increases, the agreement should provide for a proportionate increase in the royalty payable to the licensor.

(b) *Advance Fees.* Licensee agrees to pay to Licensor simultaneously with the execution of this license agreement and upon the commencement of each option term the sum specified in Schedule D attached hereto and made part hereof as an advance guarantee against fees to be paid to Licensor during the applicable term of this license agreement and as a further inducement and additional and material consideration for the granting of this license. No part of such advance guarantee shall in any event be repayable to Licensee.

> *Comment:* Obviously, advances must be specifically negotiated. Advances (including any minimum guaranteed payments), royalties, term, territory, exclusivity and articles to be manufactured should all be agreed upon before a formal contract is presented for consideration, since these are the most important deal points. The amount of the advance is based upon the volume of sales anticipated and the cash resources of the licensee. It is generally in the best interest of the licensor to get as much money up front as possible, for three basic reasons: (1) that money can be used to earn more money, (2) it gives the licensee an incentive to push the merchandise and earn back the advance, and (3) licensees sometimes disappear, go bankrupt, decide that other debts are more important to pay than the licensor's royalties or are simply happy to be able to hold the licensor's money for as long as possible. Advances are by definition prepayment of royalties anticipated to be earned. They should always be stated to be non-returnable in the event that sales prove insufficient to earn the total amount of the advance at the royalty rate specified.

(c) *Minimum Fees.* Licensee agrees to pay to Licensor during the initial term and each option term of this license agreement for and as a guarantee of the minimum amount of fees to be paid to Licensor during such term and as a material and additional consideration and inducement to Licensor to execute this license agreement, the sum or sums specified in Schedule E attached hereto and made a part hereof. It is understood and agreed that there shall be credited against the foregoing guaranteed minimum such fees as Licensee shall pay to Licensor hereunder. No part of such guaranteed minimum sum or sums shall in any event be repayable to Licensee. Upon the termination or expiration of the initial term and any option term hereof, any advance guarantee or guaranteed minimum provided for herein and not then paid shall be immediately due and payable in full.

> *Comment:* Guaranteed minimum payments are similar to advances to the extent that they place incentives upon the licensee and give assurance to the licensor, but they are not always paid up front. In this agreement the licensee is agreeing that if the advances and royalties (fees) paid by the licensee do not equal or exceed the amount of the minimum guaranteed payment, the licensee will pay the difference at the end of the applicable term, whether it be the initial term or an option term.

(d) *Periodic Statements.* Within one hundred thirty-five (135) days after the initial shipment of the articles covered by this agreement, and promptly on or before the forty-fifth (45th) day after the end of each calendar quarter thereafter, Licensee shall furnish to Licensor complete and accurate statements certified to be accurate by Licensee showing the number, description and gross sales price, itemized deductions from gross sales price of the articles covered by this agreement distributed and/or sold by Licensee during the preceding calendar quarter, together with any returns made during the preceding calendar quarter. Such statements shall be furnished to Licensor whether or not any of the articles have been sold during the preceding calendar quarter.

(e) *Royalty Payments.* Royalties in excess of the aforementioned advance shall be due on the forty-fifth (45th) day after the end of the calendar quarter in which earned, and payment shall accompany the statements furnished as required above. The receipt or acceptance by Licensor of any of the statements furnished pursuant to this agreement or of any royalties paid hereunder (or the cashing of any royalty checks paid hereunder) shall not preclude Licensor from questioning the correctness thereof at any time, and in the event that any inconsistencies or mistakes are discovered in such statements or payments, they shall immediately be rectified and the appropriate payment made by Licensee.

(f) All payments shall be made payable to Licensor. All such payments and all statements hereunder shall be mailed to:

_____

_____

_____

Comment: This agreement provides for quarterly accounting. Many agreements will provide for only semiannual accounting. Obviously, quarterly accounting is preferable to the licensor, since the money will come in faster and the licensor will be able to tell more quickly whether the licensee is doing its job in a satisfactory manner and complying with its contractual obligations. The accounting should be required to be sufficiently detailed so that the licensor can get a clear picture of the transactions that occurred during the prior period. The licensor must be given rights to inspect the books and records of the licensee. These are set forth in paragraph 11 below.

3. LIMITED EXCLUSIVITY:

(a) Nothing in this agreement shall be construed to prevent Licensor from granting other licenses for the use of the Mark or from utilizing the Mark in any manner whatsoever, except that Licensor agrees that except as provided herein, it will grant no other licenses for the territory to which this license extends effective during the term of this agreement, for the use of this Mark in connection with the retail sale of school supply articles listed in subparagraph 1(a) hereof. Notwithstanding the foregoing, Licensor shall have the right to license any such articles for sale through mail order merchandising.

Comment: It is a matter of negotiation whether the rights conveyed to the licensee are exclusive or non-exclusive. Normally the licensee will require exclusivity in order to protect his investment. Obviously the exclusivity should be limited to the term of the agreement, the territory covered thereby and the particular articles agreed to be manufactured. The licensee should lose exclusivity with respect to articles it has ceased to manufacture. Sometimes the licensee may require exclusivity to extend to articles which, although not identical to the articles agreed to be manufactured under the agreement, are perceived to be similar enough as to be competitive, for example, articles of apparel. This may be acceptable only if the licensee agrees to manufacture substantially all of the articles which the licensor believes to be marketable.

In the sample agreement there is an exception to exclusivity which allows the licensor to sell the same types of articles through mail order merchandising; this is unusual, but apparently in this case the licensee did not perceive this as interfering with its marketing strategy.

(b) It is agreed that if Licensor should convey an offer to Licensee to purchase any of the articles specified in subparagraph 1(a), in connection with a premium, giveaway, mail order offer, or for concert tour sales, Licensee shall provide those articles to Licensor in the quantities ordered within sixty (60) days from the date ordered. Licensee agrees to charge Licensor the lowest wholesale selling price that Licensee offers to the general trade for the respective articles, said price being further reduced by the royalty which would accrue to Licensor if Licensee sold those respective articles to the general trade. Licensor will not receive a royalty on any articles sold to Licensor by Licensee pursuant to this subparagraph 3(b). Licensor agrees that if product so ordered is not in stock upon receipt of order, Licensee shall be given a reasonable amount of time, as specified by Licensee, to fill the order.

> *Comment:* This is one of the provisions of the agreement which are very favorable to the licensor. Although it is customary for the licensor to be able to purchase small quantities of the articles at the licensee's cost, it is unusual for the licensor to have such a broad right to resell these articles.

4. GOOD WILL, LICENSOR'S TITLE AND PROTECTION OF LICENSOR'S RIGHTS:

(a) Licensee recognizes the great value of good will associated with the Mark, and the identification of the licensed articles with the Mark, and acknowledges that the Mark and all rights therein and good will pertaining thereto belong exclusively to Licensor, and have a secondary meaning in the mind of the public.

> *Comment:* This is a recitation for the benefit of the licensor which is intended to prevent any future claims by the licensee that it acquired any continuing rights in or to the Mark or that it created the value of the Mark.

(b) Licensee agrees that it will not, during the term of the agreement, or thereafter, attack the title or any rights of Licensor in and to the Mark or attack the validity of this license.

> *Comment:* This is another valuable recitation for the benefit of the licensor. There have been countless lawsuits in which a licensee has claimed that its licensor did not own the exclusive rights to a Mark that was covered by a license agreement in an effort by the licensee to avoid paying the license fees. In many cases, the suits were filed because a third party was using the Mark or a similar Mark without having to make any payments. The courts have generally ruled that the licensee cannot avoid paying the licensor by attacking his title to the Mark. However, it is always preferable to have the contract recite this.

(c) Licensee agrees to assist Licensor at Licensor's expense to the extent necessary in the procurement of any protection or to protect any of Licensor's rights to the Mark, and Licensor, if it so desires, may commence or prosecute any claims or suits in its own name or in the name of Licensee or join Licensee as a party thereto. Licensee shall notify Licensor in writing of any infringements or imitations by others of the Mark on articles similar to those covered in this agreement which may come to the Licensee's attention, and Licensor shall have the sole right to determine whether or not any action shall be taken on account of any such infringements or imitations. Licensee shall not institute any suit or take any action on account of any such infringement or imitations without first obtaining the written consent of the Licensor to do so.

> *Comment:* This paragraph provides that it is the licensor, as the owner of the Mark, who has the right to control the institution or disposition of lawsuits involving the Mark. It is very important that the licensee not be given this control, since the decision in any one lawsuit may affect the use of the Mark in many areas outside that covered by the particular license agreement.

(d) To preserve Licensor's identification with the Mark and to avoid confusion of the public, Licensee agrees not to associate other characters and/or personalities with the Mark hereunder in connection with the articles or the advertising or display thereof on which the Mark is used, except that Licensee shall have the right to advertise or display the articles in connection with any other articles sold by Licensee.

> *Comment:* This is another very important provision for the benefit of the licensor. To maintain rights in the Mark it is necessary that it not become associated in the mind of the public with other marks, logos, symbols, etc. If it does, the Mark may no longer be protectable and will lose its value for merchandising. All of the provisions of this paragraph 4 are somewhat unusual in merchandising agreements, which generally tend to cover only the most important points and to handle the important legal issues only in a cursory fashion. They should be added to agreements which do not include them, wherever possible.

5. INDEMNIFICATION BY LICENSOR:

Licensor hereby indemnifies Licensee and undertakes to hold it harmless against all liability, damages, penalties, losses or expense awarded in any final judgment which may be suffered by or obtained against Licensee arising solely out of the use by Licensee of the Mark as authorized in this agreement. Licensee shall notify Licensor promptly of any such claim or action. Licensor shall have the option to undertake and conduct the defense of any such claim or action so brought, in which event Licensee will cooperate with and assist Licensor, at Licensor's expense, to the extent Licensor deems it necessary, in the defense of any such claim or action. It is expressly agreed that Licensee shall not settle or compromise any such claim or action without the prior written consent of Licensor.

> *Comment:* This is a provision which you will find in every agreement of this type. It is there to protect the licensee from claims by third parties that its use of the Mark violates rights they have. It is necessary because the licensee is entitled to rely upon the licensor's express or implied representation that it owns all rights in and to the Mark for purposes of the agreement. It is important, however, that the licensee not be able to settle any claim made by a third party without the consent of the licensor and that the licensor's indemnity extend only to claims so settled and judgments awarded by the court. An indemnity essentially means that one party (here the licensor) will prevent the other party from suffering any damage or incurring any expense by reason of the first party's breach of the

agreement. That means the licensor would pay for or reimburse the licensee for any damages or expenses suffered.

6. INDEMNIFICATION BY LICENSEE AND PRODUCT LIABILITY INSURANCE:

Licensee hereby indemnifies Licensor and undertakes to defend Licensor against and hold Licensor harmless from any claims, suits, loss, liability expense (including costs of suit or attorney's fees) and damage arising out of any allegedly or in fact unauthorized use of any patent, process, idea, method or device by Licensee in connection with the articles covered by this agreement or any other alleged or other action by Licensee and also from any claims, suits, loss, liability expense (including costs of suit and attorney's fees) and damage arising out of alleged or actual defects in the articles. Licensee agrees that it will obtain, at its own expense, product liability insurance from a recognized insurance company providing adequate protection (at least in the amount of $100,000/$300,000) for Licensor (as well as for Licensee) against any claims, suits, loss or damage arising out of any alleged defects in the articles. As proof of such insurance, a fully paid certificate of insurance will be submitted to Licensor by Licensee for Licensor's prior approval before any article is distributed or sold, and at the latest within thirty (30) days after the date first written above; any proposed change in certificates of insurance shall be submitted to Licensor for its prior approval. Licensor shall be entitled to a copy of the then prevailing certificate of insurance, which shall be furnished Licensor by Licensee. As used in the first 2 sentences of this paragraph 6, "Licensor" shall also include the officers, directors, agents and employees of the Licensor, or any of its subsidiaries or affiliates, any person(s) the use of whose name may be licensed hereunder, the package producer and the cast of the radio and/or television program whose name may be licensed hereunder, the stations over which the programs are transmitted, any sponsor of said programs and its advertising agency, and their respective officers, directors, agents and employees (but such inclusion shall not be required for the named insured parties). In the event of any claims, suits, loss, liability expense and damage as defined in this paragraph, Licensee shall have the sole right to control all litigation in connection therewith.

Comment: This provision is the reciprocal provision to paragraph 5 above. It protects the licensor from adverse consequences of things which are in the licensee's control, such as damages or losses arising from features or elements of the articles other than the Mark. It is very helpful that this provision also requires the licensee to carry certain product liability insurance. This is particularly important if the articles to be manufactured are toys, food or drugs which could lead to injury to persons. This provision is very favorable to the licensor because it covers alleged unauthorized uses and alleged defects, regardless of whether the third party claiming such unauthorized use or defects actually prevails in a trial or a settlement.

7. QUALITY OF MERCHANDISE:

Licensee agrees that the articles covered by this agreement shall be of high standard and of such style, appearance and quality as to be adequate and suited to their exploitation to the best advantage and to the protection and enhancement of the Mark and the good will pertaining thereto, that such articles will be manufactured, sold and distributed in accordance with all applicable Federal,

State and local laws, and that the policy of sale, distribution and/or exploitation by Licensee shall be of high standard and to the best advantage and that the same shall in no manner reflect adversely upon the good name of Licensor or any of its programs or the Mark. To this end, Licensee shall, before selling or distributing any of the articles, furnish to Licensor free of cost, for its approval, a reasonable number of samples of each article, its cartons, containers and packing and wrapping material. The quality and style of such articles, as well as any carton, container or packing or wrapping material shall be subject to the approval of Licensor. Any item submitted to Licensor shall be deemed approved unless the same shall be disapproved by Licensor in writing within twenty (20) days. Any disapproval notice shall specify all objections and modifications required to earn approval, and approval shall not be unreasonably withheld. After samples have been approved pursuant to this paragraph, Licensee shall not depart therefrom in any material respect without Licensor's prior written consent, and Licensor shall not withdraw its approval of the approved samples.

Comment: This is another provision which is favorable to the licensor since it specifically requires the articles manufactured to be of a high quality. Very often there are no such warranties made by the licensee. Thus, if the quality of the goods manufactured was below average, the licensor would arguably have grounds for terminating the contract on account of a material breach. What is more typical is the provision for approval of samples of the articles to be manufactured. This is very important, since it allows both parties to agree in advance as to what will be an acceptable product in terms of quality and appearance.

8. LABELING:

(a) Licensee agrees that it will cause to appear on or within each article sold by it under this license and on or within all advertising, promotional or display material bearing the Mark the copyright notice © (year) and any other notice desired by Licensor and, where such article or advertising, promotional or display material bears a trademark or service mark, appropriate statutory notice of registration thereof. Such legal notices are specified in Schedule F attached hereto and made a part hereof. In the event that any article is marketed in a carton, container and/or packing or wrapping bearing the Mark, such notice shall also appear upon the said carton, container and/or packing or wrapping material. Each and every tag, label, imprint or other device containing any such notice and all advertising, promotional or display material bearing the Mark shall be submitted by Licensee to Licensor for its written approval prior to use by Licensee. Approval or disapproval shall be subject to the terms specified in paragraph 7. Approval by Licensor shall not constitute waiver of Licensor's rights or Licensee's duties under any provision of this agreement.

Comment: This requires the licensee to place the necessary and appropriate copyright or trademark notices on the articles so that the licensor's rights in the Mark will not fall into the public domain and be lost for failure to comply with the laws requiring notice. A copyright can be claimed in any design or other work of visual art. A claim to copyright should be filed with the United States Copyright Office. Even if a claim has not been filed, if the design is original and bears a modicum of novelty, it will be copyrightable, and a copyright notice should be placed on all articles sold or offered for sale to the public.

The encircled TM trademark notice may be placed on articles for which a trademark registration application is pending. The encircled R notice may be placed only on articles for which federal trademark protection has actually been secured. An attorney should be consulted with regard to securing statutory trademark protection.

(b) Licensee agrees to cooperate fully and in good faith with Licensor for the purpose of securing and preserving Licensor's (or any grantor of Licensor's) rights in and to the Mark. In the event there has been no previous registration of the Mark and/or any material relating thereto, Licensee shall, at Licensor's request and expense, register such as a copyright, trademark and/or service mark in the appropriate class, in the name of Licensor or, if Licensor so requests, in Licensee's own name. However, it is agreed that nothing contained in this agreement shall be construed as an assignment or grant to the Licensee of any right, title or interest in or to the Mark, it being understood that all rights relating thereto are reserved by Licensor, except for the license hereunder to Licensee of the right to use and utilize the Mark only as specifically and expressly provided in this agreement. Licensee hereby agrees that at the termination or expiration of this agreement Licensee will be deemed to have assigned, transferred and conveyed to Licensor any trade rights, equities, good will, titles or other rights in and to the Mark which may have been obtained by Licensee or which may have vested in Licensee in pursuance of any endeavors covered hereby, and that Licensee will execute any instruments requested by Licensor to accomplish or confirm the foregoing. Any such assignment, transfer or conveyance shall be without other consideration than the mutual covenants and considerations of this agreement.

Comment: This provision is also favorable to the licensor in that the licensee is agreeing to cooperate with the licensor to obtain and maintain protection of the Mark, for the licensor's sole benefit. Of course, anything done by the licensee will be at the licensor's expense. This is appropriate. Once again, the licensee agrees that any use it makes of the Mark is for the sole benefit of the licensor.

(c) Licensee hereby agrees that its every use of such Mark shall inure to the benefit of Licensor and that Licensee shall not at any time acquire any rights in such Mark by virtue of any use it may make of such Mark.

9. PROMOTIONAL MATERIAL:

(a) In all cases where Licensee desires artwork involving articles which are the subject of this license to be prepared, the cost of such artwork and the time for the production thereof shall be borne by Licensee. All artwork and designs involving the Mark, or any reproduction thereof, shall, notwithstanding their invention or use by Licensee, be and remain the property of Licensor and Licensor shall be entitled to use the same and to license the use of the same by others upon termination of this agreement. Licensee shall not be obligated to turn over color separations or artwork prepared at its expense for such a purpose. Licensee may agree to provide such material, but only at the expense of Licensor.

Comment: This provision is also favorable to the licensor in that the licensee not only bears the entire cost of any artwork the licensee desires to prepare, which is customary, but it also agrees that the licensor may use any such artwork after the term of the agreement expires, for the licensor's sole benefit.

(b) Licensor shall have the right, but shall not be under any obligation, to use the Mark and/or the name of Licensee so as to give the Mark, Licensee, Licensor and/or Licensor's programs full and favorable prominence and publicity. Licensor shall not be under any obligation whatsoever to continue broadcasting any radio or television program or use the Mark or any person, character, symbol, design or likeness or visual representation thereof in any radio or television program or on records or tapes or otherwise.

> *Comment:*   This provision is unusual and, again, is favorable to the licensor in that it does not obligate the licensor to continue to use the Mark in its own business endeavors. This provision often arises in the context of the license of the name of a television program or series, which is subject to cancellation.

10. DISTRIBUTION:

(a) Licensee agrees that during the term of this license it will diligently and continuously manufacture, distribute and sell the articles covered by this agreement and that it will make and maintain adequate arrangement for the distribution of the articles.

> *Comment:*   This is also a provision favorable to the licensor and is somewhat unusual because it allows the licensor, if it is unhappy with the volume of sales under the agreement, to claim that there was not an adequate arrangement for distribution of the articles and thereby to claim a material breach relieving it of its obligations under the contract.

(b) Licensee agrees that it will sell and distribute the articles covered by this agreement outright at a competitive price and not on an approval, consignment or sale or return basis and only to jobbers, wholesalers, distributors and manufacturers for sale and distribution to retail stores and merchants, and to retail stores and merchants for sale and distribution direct to the public. Licensee shall not without prior written consent of Licensor, knowingly sell or distribute such articles to jobbers, wholesalers, distributors, manufacturers, retail stores or merchants whose sales or distribution are or will be made for publicity or promotional tie-in purposes, combination sales, premiums, giveaways or similar methods of merchandising, or whose business methods are questionable. In the event any sale is made at a special price to any of Licensee's subsidiaries or to any other person, firm or corporation related in any manner to Licensee or its officers, directors or major stockholders, there shall be a royalty paid on such sales based upon the price generally charged the trade by Licensee.

> *Comment:*   This is a more standard provision requiring the licensee not to sell the articles in any manner which would tend to make them appear to be of inferior quality, since this might adversely impact upon the value and good will associated with the Mark. This provision, however, restricts the licensee much more than the ordinary provision of this kind does, and such a restrictive provision is not generally found in agreements of this type.

11. RECORDS:

Licensee agrees to keep accurate books of account and records covering all transactions relating to the license hereby granted, and Licensor and its duly authorized representatives shall have the right at all reasonable hours of the day to an examination of said books of account and records and of all other documents and materials in the possession or under the control of Licensee with respect to the subject matter and terms of this agreement, and shall have free and full access thereto for said purposes and for the purpose of making extracts therefrom for the sole purpose of verifying the statements and payments made hereunder. Licensor agrees that Licensee's customer lists constitute proprietary information, and that any examination involving these lists shall be conducted only through an independent certified public accountant, and not through Licensor's own auditors or other employees. All books of account and records shall be kept available for at least two (2) years after the termination of this license.

> *Comment:* This provision giving the licensor the right to audit the books and records of the licensee is very important. It is favorable to the licensor in that it allows the licensor at least two years after the termination of the license to conduct the audit. Very often contracts of this type will provide a much shorter period of time in which to conduct audits. It is customary that the licensee will require the licensor to agree that its customer lists are confidential information.

12. BANKRUPTCY, VIOLATION, ETC.:

(a) If Licensee shall not have commenced in good faith to manufacture and distribute in substantial quantities the articles listed and starred in subparagraph 1(a) within six (6) months after the date of this agreement or if at any time thereafter in any two consecutive calendar months Licensee fails to sell any of the articles (or any class or category of the articles), Licensor, in addition to all other remedies available to it hereunder, may terminate this license with respect to any articles or class or category thereof which have not been manufactured and distributed during such month, by giving written notice of termination to Licensee. Such notice shall be effective when mailed to Licensee.

> *Comment:* This is a very helpful provision for the licensor. Obviously, this provision was specifically negotiated by the parties. This is not a standard clause by any means, but should be considered.

(b) If Licensee files a petition in bankruptcy or is adjudicated a bankrupt or if a petition in bankruptcy is filed against Licensee or if it becomes insolvent, or makes an assignment for the benefit of its creditors or an arrangement pursuant to any bankruptcy law, or if Licensee discontinues its business or if a receiver is appointed for it or its business, the license hereby granted shall automatically terminate forthwith without any notice whatsoever being necessary. In the event this license is so terminated, Licensee, its receivers, representatives, trustees, agents, administrators, successors and/or assigns shall have no right to sell, exploit or in any way deal with or in any articles covered by this agreement or any carton, container, packing or wrapping material, advertising, promotional or display material pertaining thereto, except with and under the special consent and instructions of Licensor in writing, which they shall be obligated to follow.

> *Comment:* This is a very helpful and important provision for the licensor. First, the licensor does not wish its articles to be sold by a bankrupt entity, since the proceeds may very well go to other creditors who are entitled to a higher priority, e.g., secured creditors. Second, the licensor does not wish his articles to be sold by a receiver or trustee in bankruptcy, since this would result in their being sold in bulk at an auction or other forced

sale, thereby diminishing the value of the merchandise and possibly adversely affecting the good will associated with the Mark, and again the licensor would not receive the royalties it is entitled to under the agreement.

(c) If Licensee shall violate any of its obligations under the terms of this agreement, Licensor shall have the right to terminate the license hereby granted upon ten (10) days' notice in writing, and such notice of termination shall become effective unless Licensee shall completely remedy the violation within the ten-day period and satisfy Licensor that such violation has been remedied.

Comment: It is normal for agreements of this type to contain a provision giving the licensee the opportunity to cure any breach. However, the licensee is normally given thirty days to effect the cure.

(d) Termination of the license under the provisions of this paragraph 12 shall be without prejudice to any rights which Licensor may otherwise have against Licensee. Upon the termination of this license, notwithstanding anything to the contrary herein, all royalties on sales theretofore made shall become immediately due and payable and no minimum royalties shall be repayable.

Comment: This is also a helpful provision, the purpose being to accelerate the licensee's obligations to pay royalties in the event that the licensee breaches the contract.

13. FINAL STATEMENT UPON TERMINATION OR EXPIRATION:

Sixty (60) days before the scheduled expiration of this license or, in the event of its termination, thirty (30) days after receipt of notice of termination or the happening of the event which terminates this agreement where no notice is required, a statement showing the number and description of articles covered by this agreement on hand or in process shall be furnished to take a physical inventory to ascertain or verify such inventory and statement, and refusal by Licensee to submit to such physical inventory by Licensor shall forfeit Licensee's right to dispose of such inventory, Licensor retaining all other legal and equitable rights Licensor may have in the circumstances.

Comment: This is another helpful provision which is often not contained in contracts of this type.

14. DISPOSAL OF STOCK UPON TERMINATION OR EXPIRATION:

After termination of the license under the provision of paragraph 12, or upon expiration, Licensee, except as otherwise provided in this agreement, may dispose of articles covered by this agreement which are on hand or in process upon expiration or at the time notice of termination is received for a period of one hundred eighty (180) days after notice of termination, provided advances and royalties with respect to that period are paid and statements are furnished for that period in accordance with paragraph 2. Notwithstanding anything to the contrary herein, Licensee shall not manufacture, sell or dispose of any articles covered by this license after its expiration or its termination based on the failure of Licensee to affix notice of copyright, trademark or service mark registration or any other notice required by Licensor to the articles, cartons, containers, or packing or wrapping materials or advertising, promotional or display material, or because of the departure by Licensee from the quality and style approved by Licensor pursuant to paragraph 7.

Comment: It is customary for the licensee to have a six-month sell-off period in which to dispose of excess inventory. This should be non-exclusive, so that the licensor will be able to enter into a new exclusive agreement with a different licensee. This provision is favorable to the licensor in that it specifically takes away the licensee's sell-off rights if the licensee has breached the contract in a way that sales could be detrimental to the licensor.

15. EFFECT OF TERMINATION OR EXPIRATION:

Upon and after the expiration or termination of this license, all rights granted to Licensee hereunder shall forthwith revert to Licensor, who shall be free to license others to use the Mark in connection with the manufacture, sale and distribution of the articles covered hereby and Licensee will refrain from further use of the Mark or any further reference to it, direct or indirect, or anything deemed by Licensor to be similar to the Mark in connection with the manufacture, sale or distribution of Licensee's products, except as provided in paragraph 14.

Comment: The first part of this paragraph is a simple recitation of the legal consequences of a license. The second part is helpful in that it prohibits the licensee from using anything similar to the Mark in connection with the manufacture of the licensee's own products, thereby preventing confusion and dilution of the Mark.

16. LICENSOR'S REMEDIES:

(a) Licensee acknowledges that its failure (except as otherwise provided herein) to commence in good faith to manufacture and distribute in substantial quantities any one or more of the articles listed and starred in subparagraph 1(a) within six (6) months after the date of this agreement and to continue during the term hereof to diligently and continuously manufacture, distribute and sell the articles covered by this agreement or any class or category thereof will result in immediate damages to Licensor and will constitute a material breach hereof.

(b) Licensee acknowledges that its failure (except as otherwise provided herein) to cease the manufacture, sale or distribution of the articles covered by this agreement or any class or category thereof at the termination or expiration of this agreement will result in immediate irreparable and irremediable damage to Licensor and to the rights of any subsequent Licensee. Licensee acknowledges and admits that there is no adequate remedy at law for such failure to cease manufacture, sale or distribution, and Licensee agrees that in the event of such failure Licensor shall be entitled to equitable relief by way of temporary and permanent injunctions and such other further relief as any court with jurisdiction may deem just and proper.

(c) Resort to any remedies referred to herein shall not be construed as a waiver of any other rights and remedies to which Licensor is entitled under this agreement or otherwise.

Comment: The provisions of paragraph 16 are recitations that certain provisions contained in this agreement are important and that their breach by the licensee will entitle the licensor to "damages" and/or "injunctive relief." In any action brought to remedy a claim to breach by the licensee, the licensor would still be obligated to prove that the licensee in fact did breach the agreement and that the licensor is entitled to damages and/or equitable relief thereby.

In legal parlance "damages" is the name for the monetary loss alleged to have been suffered by the plaintiff (the person suing) in a lawsuit; it also refers to the amount of money awarded by a court or a jury as compensation to a victorious plaintiff. In actions for breach of contract, it is most commonly measured by the direct out-of-pocket losses of the plaintiff or by the lost profits from transactions that would have been made except for the defendant's breach. A breach of contract means an unexcused violation of or a failure to comply with a material (i.e., important) provision of the contract.

Although the awarding of damages is by far the most common remedy for a breach of contract, in many cases money alone cannot adequately compensate the plaintiff. This occurs most often where a "unique" product or service is involved. Although there is really no such thing as a "priceless" work of art—in the sense that expert appraisers can always be found to testify as to what a willing buyer would pay to a willing seller for that work of art, based on the selling prices of other works by the same artist or artists of comparable stature, among other factors—in many cases it is impossible to accurately measure the damages which a plaintiff has suffered or will suffer from the defendant's breach.

The example referred to in subparagraph (b) above is where the licensor has made an agreement with a different licensee to acquire some or all of the rights granted to the present licensee, which agreement is to commence on the expiration of this one. If the licensee continues to act as if this agreement had not terminated, the new licensee will be damaged to an extent that is impossible to predict with any degree of certainty, and the new licensee may seek to hold the licensor liable, in which case the licensor will have to seek "injunctive" or "equitable" relief to prevent or restrain the current licensee from breaching this agreement. Another example of a breach for which the licensor would want equitable relief (i.e., an order of the court requiring the defendant to do or cease doing a specific thing) is where the licensee's conduct threatens to destroy the value of the Mark, for example by distributing items for sale without the necessary copyright notices.

The plaintiff must prove several elements to a court's satisfaction (e.g., irreparable damage, inability to compensate for such damage by a monetary award, among other things) in order to obtain equitable or injunctive relief. This contractual provision is intended as an acknowledgment by the defendant licensee that those elements mentioned are met, although if an injunction should be sought, the defendant licensee would almost certainly deny that, and the plaintiff licensor would be required by the court to prove those elements based on the actual facts and circumstances of the case.

17. EXCUSE FOR NONPERFORMANCE:

Licensee shall be released from its obligations hereunder and this license shall terminate in the event that governmental regulations or other causes arising out of a state of national emergency or war or causes beyond the control of the parties render performance impossible and one party so informs the other in writing of such causes and its desire to be so released. In such events, all royalties on sales theretofore made shall become immediately due and payable but no advance royalties shall be repayable; but no minimum fees shall be payable.

Comment: This is a typical "force majeure" clause which excuses the licensee for nonperformance due to an act of God or other event which is beyond the control of the licensee. It should always be expressly stated that the licensee is liable to pay royalties on sales already made and that advances previously paid to the licensor shall not be repayable.

18. NOTICES:

All notices and statements to be given, and all payments to be made hereunder, shall be given or made at the respective addresses of the parties as set forth above unless notification of a change of address is given in writing, and the date of mailing shall be deemed the date the notice or statement is given.

19. NO JOINT VENTURE:

Nothing herein contained shall be construed to place the parties in the relationship of partners or joint venturers, and Licensee shall have no power to obligate or bind Licensor in any manner whatsoever.

Comment: This paragraph attempts to characterize the legal relationship between the parties. It states they are not "partners" or "joint venturers." A joint venture is a partnership limited to a particular activity or group of activities where one or both of the joint venturers also engage in other activities outside the scope of the joint venture. Joint venturers are treated, under the law, as partners.

Partners are "jointly and severally" liable for obligations of the partnership; that means, for example, that if a partnership of two persons owes a third party $10,000, the third party could sue either or both of the partners for the $10,000, and if one had no money and the other did, the other would be liable for the full $10,000.

Partners can legally bind each other by their dealings with third parties. For example, if one partner signs a lease of space for the partnership, the other partner will be liable for the full amount of the rent on that space, even if he did not authorize the other partner to enter into that lease and in fact may have been unaware of it or even have told the other partner not to enter into it. The law is primarily concerned with protecting the innocent third party who is relying on the ability of the partnership to perform its obligations. Of course, the partner who enters into the lease in violation of an agreement with his partner would be liable to his partner for the damages suffered due to his breach.

You never want to be deemed to be a partner or joint venturer without your consent and a knowledge of the consequences. If you do intend to become a partner or joint venturer, it is important to enter into a written partnership agreement stating your respective rights and obligations to each other. A lawyer should be consulted to draft such an agreement and to explain to you the legal consequences, both with respect to the rights and obligations of the partners to each other and with respect to obligations to third parties.

By implication, the parties to this agreement are what are legally characterized as "independent contractors." This is distinguished also from "employees." With very rare exceptions a visual artist should never be characterized as an "employee." The most dangerous consequence is that your works may be legally deemed to be "works made for hire," the copyrights to which are owned from inception by the employer. Works made for hire are excluded from the application of the termination provisions of the U.S. Copyright Act (see the Copyright section of this Manual), so that they will never revert to the artist or his estate. A less dangerous, but normally undesirable consequence is that withholding taxes must be deducted from the compensation payable to an employee.

"Independent contractors" means that neither party is the partner, employee or agent of the other. They are, aside from the contract, unrelated, and neither one can obligate the other to pay debts incurred by him, except as specifically provided to the contrary in an agreement. If there is any doubt, your agreements should specify that you are acting as an "independent contractor."

20. NO ASSIGNMENT OR SUBLICENSE BY LICENSEE:

This agreement and all rights and duties hereunder are personal to Licensee and shall not, without the written consent of Licensor, be assigned, mortgaged, sublicensed or otherwise encumbered by Licensee or by operation of law; provided, however, that Licensee shall have the right, without written consent, to grant sublicenses to _____ _____ which such licenses shall provide for payment to Licensor on no less favorable terms than contained herein. Licensee agrees to bear all responsibility for the fulfillment of this agreement on behalf of these sublicensees.

Licensor may assign but shall furnish written notice of assignment.

Comment: It is customary for the licensee to be able to assign the agreement to an affiliate or a corporation which is acquiring its stock or assets. Normally the licensee may not assign or sublicense the agreement to an unrelated third party. This is because the licensor is bargaining for this particular licensee to perform the contract; he is looking to the expertise and reputation of this particular licensee. This can be extremely important.

However, where the licensee is a corporation which has established a relationship over the years with various sublicensees, it may be perfectly acceptable to the licensor for the sublicensees to fulfill the licensee's obligations under the agreement. It is important that the licensor know which sublicensees, if any, will be handling the articles and that the licensee be liable for their nonperformance.

21. NO WAIVER, ETC.:

None of the terms of this agreement can be waived or modified except by an express agreement in writing signed by both parties. There are no representations, promises, warranties, covenants or undertakings other than those contained in this agreement, which represents the entire understanding of the parties. The failure of either party hereto to enforce, or the delay by either party in enforcing, any of its rights under this agreement shall not be deemed a continuing waiver or a modification thereof and either party may, within the time provided by applicable law, commence appropriate legal proceeding to enforce any or all of such rights. No person, firm, group or corporation (whether included in the Mark or otherwise) other than Licensee and Licensor shall be deemed to have acquired any rights by reason of anything contained in this agreement, except as provided in paragraphs 6 and 20.

22. ATTORNEYS' FEES:

If any legal action or other proceeding is brought for the enforcement of this agreement or as a result of a breach, default or misrepresentation in connection with any of the provisions of this agreement, the successful or prevailing party shall be entitled to recover reasonable attorneys' fees and other costs incurred in that action or proceeding, in addition to any other relief to which that party may be entitled.

> *Comment:* Paragraphs 21 and 22 contain legal boiler plate, customarily found in agreements of this type. Paragraph 22 is helpful to the licensor, since almost all of the obligations contained in this agreement are obligations of the licensee, and therefore it is most likely that if the agreement were breached, the breach would be by the licensee.

23. RESERVED RIGHTS:

Rights not herein specifically granted to Licensee are reserved by Licensor and may be used by Licensor without limitation. Any use by Licensor of such reserved rights, including but not limited to the use or authorization of the use of the Mark in any manner whatsoever shall, notwithstanding anything to the contrary herein contained, not be deemed unfair competition with or interference with or infringement of any of Licensee's rights hereunder.

> *Comment:* Above is another recitation of the fact that all rights not granted to the licensee remain with the licensor. This is a simple, but essential clause for every licensing agreement of any type entered into by a visual artist because there is an unlimited array of derivative rights in copyrighted artistic works. The artist's objective is to be able to parcel those rights out for as many different uses as possible, many of which may be unknown at the time a particular license is granted. You never want to give away anything for free, without your express consent, and the easiest way for this to happen is to have generalistic and overbroad language in a contract, particularly in the grant-of-rights provisions. Be as specific as possible as to what rights you are granting and state expressly that all other rights are reserved to you.
>
> Paragraph 24 below contains additional standard boiler plate. The law selected by the parties to govern the agreement should, if possible, be that of the state of the artist's residence. Beware of clauses which obligate you to bring suit against the licensee in a state in which you do not reside, unless your lawyer is in that state.

24. CONSTRUCTION:

This agreement shall be construed in accordance with the laws of (state of execution) applicable to contracts fully executed and performed herein. The headings of paragraphs, subparagraphs and other divisions of this license agreement are for convenient reference only and shall not be given any weight in interpreting the meaning of any provisions hereof. In the event that a number of copies of this license agreement shall be executed by all of the parties, each of such executed copies shall be deemed to be an original. In the event that the Licensee consists of two (2) or more persons, each of the persons comprising Licensee shall be jointly and severally liable for all the obligations of Licensee. The term "person" hereinabove used in this license agreement shall be deemed to mean and include person, firm, corporation, governmental authority or body, and/or any other entity.

IN WITNESS WHEREOF, the parties hereto have caused this instrument to be duly executed as of the day and year first above written.

"Licensor"

By _____

Its _____

"Licensee"

By _____

Its _____

SCHEDULE A

TERRITORY:

The United States and Canada.

SCHEDULE B

TERM:

From _____ through _____ .

SCHEDULE C

ROYALTY RATE:

Ten percent (10%) of all net sales by Licensee or any of its affiliated or subsidiary companies.

The term "net sales" shall mean gross sales less quantity discounts and returns, but no deductions shall be allowed for cash, freight or advertising allowances, or other discounts or uncollectible accounts. No costs of manufacture, sale, distribution or exploitation of the articles shall be deducted.

SCHEDULE D

ADVANCE FEES:

The sum of _____ dollars.

SCHEDULE E

MINIMUM FEES:

The sum of _____ dollars, per term, to be paid during the initial term and each renewal term.

SCHEDULE F

LEGAL NOTICES:

Initial here

_____   Licensor
_____   Licensee

CHAPTER ELEVEN
VAGA—"AN IDEA WHOSE TIME HAS COME"

Martin Bressler, Esq., and Dorothy M. Weber

In 1914, as the story goes, Victor Herbert, the famous composer, was sitting in a nightclub of the day and heard one of his compositions being performed by the band. While Mr. Herbert may very well have been pleased that his music was being performed, word has it that he was dismayed that he was not being paid for the performance. Although the copyright law which had been enacted in 1909 had provided for compensation to authors and composers for the public performance of music, there simply was no mechanism for policing the public renditions of music and collecting fees for such use. Mr. Herbert's anger was channeled positively and ASCAP (American Society of Composers, Authors and Publishers) was born. Now, over sixty years later, ASCAP is flourishing as a collection agency and trade association of the creators and publishers of much of the music we hear on radio and television.

Victor Herbert's dismay in 1914 can be multiplied manyfold in the world of visual arts. As with the public performance of music, one of the rights given the creator of a work of visual art under the 1909 copyright law (and the new copyright law, effective January 1, 1978, as well) is the right to reproduce his or her creation in a different medium. Under the law, an artist who paints a picture has the right to determine who is to reproduce the work, under what circumstances, and to negotiate the quality of the reproduction and the fee to be paid.[1]

As with composers and authors before 1914 who did not benefit from their rights in the public performance of their music, the rights to benefit from the reproduction of works of art are seldom exercised by visual artists. Most artists either are unaware of the rights they have in the reproduction of their works (in the event they have not waived these rights) or find the cost of enforcement of those rights prohibitive. The artist must first discover the unauthorized use and if necessary hire an attorney to assert a claim against the use. Not all unauthorized reproductions of art are predatory. Frequently, the user (typically a magazine or other periodical) may wish to seek permission from the artist and to pay for the use, but may not know where to find the artist.

The authors firmly believe that the formation of VAGA (Visual Artists' and Galleries' Association) has finally brought visual artists to the point where they will be able in a systematic way to benefit financially from the reproductions of their works of art and to maintain the integrity of their work.

VAGA, formed in early 1977 in New York City, is modeled after both ASCAP and the equally successful French visual artists' rights society (SPADEM). VAGA's members consist of artists

[1] This statement is an oversimplification of the law in that the artist's right may very well depend upon whether a copyright notice was placed on the work and whether the work was done on commission or the like.

and galleries—the creators and vendors of visual art, respectively. For a small annual membership fee ($10 for artists and $50 for galleries) and a portion of the licensing fees, the artists and galleries authorize VAGA to act as the agent to license the reproduction of the artist's works in different media.

VAGA has established a minimum fee schedule depending upon the type of use (e.g., full-page black-and-white or one-half page in color, postcards, posters, etc.). An artist member may, if he or she wishes, increase the fees beyond the minimum schedule; refuse to grant a particular license at all; insist upon approving the reproduction before publication and the like.

The organization will also police the reproduction of its members' works to determine whether arrangements that have been made are adhered to and in those cases where there is an unauthorized reproduction, VAGA will prosecute the infringer, with the proceeds—after expenses—going to the member.

VAGA's services will benefit the user as well as its members. For the first time users will know where they have to go to obtain permission to reproduce a work. In addition, VAGA is developing a program by which it will rent the user a photograph and color separation if it is available in its files. The artist will benefit from this rental because a portion of the proceeds will be paid over to the artist. This will in effect create a new residual right for the artist. The user in turn will benefit in that it will for the first time be able "in one stop" to obtain the wherewithal to reproduce the work. This will save it time and money.

VAGA members are offered benefits in addition to the licensing function. A health insurance plan is offered, for example, to members who otherwise may not have a group to join. Committees of artists and dealers are being established to create a dialogue between groups who have far too often become adversaries.

The board of directors of VAGA consists of artists and gallery owners in the main (six of each) and three who are neither.

A typical example of pre-VAGA practices and how VAGA will operate demonstrates the role it plays in the publication of art reproductions.

Artist X has become a member of VAGA. Since she has kept good records, she gives VAGA a list of works created by her over the years and, where available, either photographs of the work or the names of the owners. The member has examined the schedule of fees and finds them satisfactory.

VAGA receives an inquiry from a manufacturer of soap saying that it wishes to produce one of X's illustrations in connection with its national advertising campaign. A half-page color reproduction is contemplated. The manufacturer is advised by VAGA that the fee is $350.[2] Since VAGA has a transparency available, an additional rental fee of $75 is imposed. If VAGA does not have the transparency in its files, but knows where one is located, then VAGA attempts to arrange the rental of the transparency, with the owner receiving a fee which is shared with VAGA (and thus the artist) for the rental.

The transaction is then completed.

At the end of the quarter, X is paid her fee for the reproduction, as well as for any other licenses that may have been granted during the quarter, after VAGA deducts a predetermined percentage for administrative costs.

[2] The fees are illustrative only.

The example given is typical but by no means exclusive. For example, a publisher may wish to produce a poster edition of a member's work; a television station may seek permission to display the work on a TV program. The uses are myriad. Not only is there a new source of revenue for the artist, but the quality of the permitted reproductions is now controlled.

An additional benefit flowing from VAGA is that VAGA attempts to reduce the unauthorized reproductions of its members' works. This is done by close policing of publications and commencing litigations where appropriate. A small portion of fees received by VAGA will be reserved to pay the cost of litigation. The aggrieved artist would not be required to pay the large fees often involved in litigation.

Members are also being protected abroad in the same manner as in the United States and arrangements have been made with foreign rights societies to act as collecting agents for reproduction of the members' works in countries other than the United States.

While this brief description deals largely with the licensing activities of VAGA, the founders are convinced that its other purposes will also be of benefit to the art community. The dialogue between artists and galleries may hopefully set forth standard practices in the art industry.

Artists have historically had a "handshake" relationship with their galleries. The problem with this kind of relationship, no matter how well the two parties get along, is readily apparent—it leaves too many issues open. Who pays for the reproduction costs of the catalogue for the show, what guarantees are given to the artist, and what rights the artist is giving the gallery are illustrative of the many questions. Unilaterally drafted form contracts such as the famous Projansky contract have to date not taken hold, in large measure because they are not reflective of the needs of all parties. It is the authors' view that input from both the galleries and the artists can produce a form contract acceptable to both sides which will touch on the points which the individual artist and gallery must negotiate between themselves.

The reaction from the art community has thus far been very encouraging and it is believed that VAGA is "an idea whose time has come."

If further information is desired, please contact VAGA in care of its executive director:

Ms. Dorothy M. Weber
One World Trade Center
Suite 1535
New York, NY 10048
(212) 466-1390

SAMPLE VAGA SUGGESTED PRICE LISTS

ADVERTISING	Color	B & W
Consumer Magazine		
National	$1,500	$1,000
Regional/Local	750	600
Trade Magazine	750	500
Newspaper		
National Advertising Campaign		$1,000
Local Advertising Campaign		500
Brochure		
Above 500,000 Printed	$ 650 per reproduction	$ 400 per reproduction
Below 500,000 Printed	400 per reproduction	200 per reproduction
Catalogue or Brochure Cover	$1,000	$ 600

Other advertising uses - subject to negotiation.

CORPORATE/INDUSTRIAL		
Annual Reports		
Cover	$ 900	$ 600
Inside (per page)	500	400
House Organs		
Cover	$ 600	$ 350
Outside	200	150
Record-Album Covers		
Cover	$ 700	$ 400
Inside	350	200

MISCELLANEOUS MEDIA

Posters, calendars, greeting cards - usually on a percentage of receipts - subject to negotiation.

VISUAL ARTISTS AND GALLERIES ASSOCIATION (VAGA) SUGGESTED PRICE LIST

B O O K S

			PAGE RATES					
		1/4	1/2	3/4	Full	Front Cover or Dust Jacket	Frontis-piece	Double Page
Trade Books, Art Books, Encyclopedias:	Color	$125	$150	$175	$200	$400	$225	$500
	B&W	75	100	125	150	250	175	300

School Texts, and Children's Books: 75% of above rates

Monographs: Use of substantial number of works of art created by member -- subject to negotiation.

M A G A Z I N E S

Including SUNDAY SUPPLEMENTS

(In accordance with circulation)

	Below 100,000		100,000 to 500,000		500,000 to 1,000,000		1,000,000 to 3,000,000		Above 3,000,000	
	B & W	Color	B & W	Color	B & W	Color	B & W	Color	B & W	Color
Cover	$300	$400	$400	$500	$600	$750	$750	$1,000	$1,000	$1,500
Full Page	150	200	250	300	300	400	250	600	300	750
3/4 Page	100	150	150	200	175	225	200	400	350	550
1/2 Page	75	125	100	150	150	200	150	300	250	350
1/4 Page & Under	50	100	75	125	100	150	125	170	150	200

N E W S P A P E R S*

(In accordance with circulation)

	Circulation Under 250,000			Circulation 250,000 and Over		
	Up to 1 Column	1 to 3 Columns	Over 3 Columns	Up to 1 Column	1 to 3 Columns	Over 3 Columns
Color	$ 25	$ 50	$ 100	$ 50	$ 75	$ 125
B & W	25	25	50	25	50	75

* No fee required for reproductions relating to current exhibitions.

CHAPTER TWELVE
PUBLISHING BOOKS ON VISUAL ARTISTS AND THEIR ART

Margaret L. Kaplan, Vice President and Executive Editor, Harry N. Abrams Publishers, Inc.

Creating an art book is a time-consuming, intricate, fascinating business. It requires the skills of many people and a steady supply of patience. When the result is a beautiful and useful volume, everyone involved feels a special joy.

The complexities of the process and their endless variations make the publishing of illustrated books an ever-changing set of challenges. It helps to know as much as possible about what each member of the group contributes and what each member needs from the others.

I'll use Harry N. Abrams, Inc., as my example, since that is the publishing house I know best. Also, it publishes the greatest number and variety of art and illustrated books.

In a typical year, we publish 50 titles. Of these we bring out 15 to 20—heavily weighted toward serious works on the visual arts—in the spring. (Normally, spring means March to May.) The rest are completed in late July–early August and are shipped to the bookstores until mid-November. These titles rely more heavily on the Christmas gift-giving season and tend to have larger print runs and a greater mix of subject matter.

The Abrams list has shifted in emphasis over the last several years. At one time it was almost exclusively limited to books about the fine arts. Today these books remain an important part of the list, but added to them are extensively illustrated books of more general interest—in particular, books on nature subjects and the performing arts. Crafts, decorative arts movements and architecture are also well represented.

Abrams has traditionally done best in the marketplace with big books on big subjects. *The History of Art* or *The Italian Renaissance* or *The Complete Works of . . .* or *Picture History of Photography.* We also publish and distribute—through Prentice-Hall's College Division in most cases —a complete list of art history textbooks, which we are constantly revising, updating and increasing. This element adds financial stability to a business that is basically full of guesswork—about what will be popular, and how popular—and therefore full of risks. Textbooks also keep us solidly anchored in the academic community.

Another important element in our list is the series of monographs on contemporary artists. These, begun by Mr. Abrams twenty years ago, are large and lavish books, printed in small editions. To them we have just recently added *Artbooks by Artists,* a smaller-format series which also gives exposure to individual artists, but often does so by documenting a particular work or aspect of their work. These books and the *Contemporary Artists* series are not normally self-supporting, because of their small print runs and large amounts of color. Both series are, however, by far the best-loved books in the house—the most design care is lavished on them, the most meticulous color correction, the finest ingredients.

Museums are wonderful partners in the creation of fine art books at reasonable prices. First of all, their aims are the same as ours—they want to get the best and best-looking book for the money available. For a major popular traveling exhibition, museum participation can raise the print run to the point where a book can sell for half what it would cost otherwise. This is an area where good things continue to happen. The drawback is that schedules tend to be very tight.

How does an art book come into being? There are so many variations on this theme that it is only possible to provide some general guidelines and then indicate alternative methods. The thing to remember is that book publishing, lacking a standardized product and sophisticated means of market testing and distribution, does have one invaluable advantage: flexibility. Things can be done in many different ways. Special needs can be accommodated. Terms can be tailored to fit circumstances.

From the time a manuscript and illustration material are accepted for publication until finished books reach the stores, something between a year and a half and two years will elapse. And this schedule, which may sound long to you, is not the result of manuscripts waiting their turn like shoes in a shoe repair shop, but the time it takes to edit and design, to make the color reproductions as accurate as possible, to check and recheck facts. Occasionally we can "crash" through a book more quickly by assigning more people to it, but we have to save that exceptional capacity for important museum catalogue/books that have inflexible delivery dates tied to exhibition schedules and for top commercial titles.

Add to a typical production schedule of eight months: four or five months for editing and picture acquisition, two for design and another two for cartoning and shipment to stores across the country and you see how quickly the time is compounded.

Who Originates the Idea? The Book Proposal

It may be the publisher, the artist, the photographer, the museum, a foreign publisher looking for an English-language edition, a textbook house with a new course it sees coming up strong (nineteenth-century art is the current example of a subject on which the colleges are several years ahead of the general public). It may be a packager—someone who provides all the elements for a book up to the actual production stage or even delivers finished books. What the packager does *not* do is distribute the books to bookstores.

If you are offering an idea to a publisher of art books, here is what is useful:

(a) A clear and concise proposal, no more than three double-spaced pages long. It should include:

      (1) a description of the book

      (2) an outline

      (3) the composition and size of its potential audience

      (4) what already exists in the marketplace that might compete with it or show the

strength of interest in the subject. Remember that if there is no other book on the subject, this may indicate lack of general interest. The twentieth book on a popular subject may well succeed (see the number of diet books on the best-seller lists)

(5) any special sales you can arrange or envisage, such as textbooks, sales to trade organizations, commercial sponsors of exhibitions, etc.

(b) A sample of the author's writing and/or some examples of the artist's work. This can be in the form of previously published work, some slides, a sample chapter (a sample chapter of the proposed book is not essential at this point).

(c) Any visual material that will make the project appealing and understandable. Remember that art book people are visual people—they respond to high quality in presentation and material. At the same time, they can imagine the rest from a small sampling of good material.

(d) Possible additional uses of material in the project for the following:

(1) calendars, wall or engagement style
(2) oversize reproductions
(3) trade paperbacks
(4) video cassettes or video disks
(5) limited editions with special bindings, original graphics, signed bookplates
(6) product licensing (for example, on greeting cards).

How the Project Begins—Compiling the Facts and Figures

Regardless of who originates the idea, certain people will be involved at the beginning. They include the sponsoring editor, picture editor, heads of the design and production departments. The sales manager will be consulted on general marketability and will be asked to estimate sales on a one-, two- and three-year basis. The promotion and publicity director will be asked if this is a particularly promotable title. The head of the special sales department will assess the project from the point of view of possible sales to book clubs, catalogue companies, corporate customers, foreign sales. At Abrams the editorial department discusses each project before it reaches the publication group, but, formally or informally, all the elements listed above must be taken into account at every publishing house.

If everyone is enthusiastic about a project in principle, the next step is to see whether and in what format it is financially feasible. At this point it is necessary to have in hand some firm specifications, which have probably been arrived at in consultation with whoever originated the idea. The basics are:

Trim size (width by height of the book's page size, not counting the binding)
Number of pages
Number and placement of color illustrations—whether color will run in groups of pages, be distributed according to a precise formula or be scattered throughout (last is by far the most expensive)
Number and placement of halftones (black-and-whites)—similar questions as for color, but must also specify either gravure printing or one-color or two-color (duotone) offset printing
Number of line drawings

Size of printing

    (a) hardcover

    (b) paperback

    (c) for special sales (English-language and foreign-language sales)

Kind of binding

    (a) sewn

    (b) notch

    (c) perfect bound

Endpapers—will they be white or colored?

Where will delivery be made?

Will the book be individually cartoned or shrink-wrapped?

Armed with these specifications, the production manager will provide prices for a basic print run and for additional copies.

Using these figures, a profit-and-loss statement is prepared. To the figures from the production department will be added the proposed advance or fee to the writer, the royalty on the entire printing envisaged, the estimated costs of picture acquisition, editorial work (including proofreading and indexing if the house undertakes these tasks), cost of design work, any special fees for consultants or honorariums for prefaces, etc., and costs for special promotions. Then an overhead figure is added as a percentage of the gross revenue. The gross revenue is calculated at an average 55% of the suggested retail price when considering sales through typical trade channels (sales through other means generally produce different—mostly lower—margins). Part of this overhead goes to pay costs of sales, warehousing, delivering the books to the stores and handling returned books. The rest pays the rent, phone bill, etc., not to mention that alarmingly significant factor, interest on capital employed. What is left is called profit before taxes.

In general terms, for trade sales, it is necessary to have the retail price of a book be at least 4 times the cost of production. To reach that figure realistically, with all the slippage (extra costs that creep in—four more pages added here, two new color plates added there), it is sensible to figure 4.5 at the start. Thus, on a $45 book we hope that at the end of the day we will have spent no more than $10 on paper, printing, binding, typesetting, halftone and color separations, freight, royalties, editorial and design costs and picture fees. Another $9.90 will go to the cost of sales, warehousing, fulfillment. That is $19.90. At an average of 55% of list as income, we hope to receive $24.75 per book. That leaves $4.85 to pay the rent and run the office, pay general salaries and taxes and generate some profit.

From Contract to Production—Creating the Art Book

When the decision is made that the house would like to publish a book, final negotiations take place and, if all goes well, a contract is signed. When both an artist and a writer are involved, there are usually separate contracts. If a museum is involved, the museum usually stands in the place of the author, but occasionally the author may also receive an agreement from the publisher covering subsidiary rights. Contracts with museums, packagers or foreign publishers tend to be tailored to the special circumstances involved. Photographers may also have written agreements.

At Abrams, once the contract is signed a project director is designated, and an editor may also be assigned to the project. The project director and editor may be the same person, or may be a house editor or editorial executive if the project has a free-lance editor. Thus, the author and/or artist always have a house person to talk to about questions that may come up regarding deadlines, problems, interim evaluations and just plain human communication. Whenever it seems feasible, meetings are arranged with the design department, which takes on more responsibility after the manuscript and pictures are turned over for design.

In most cases, the picture acquisitions department is one of the keys to a successful art book. Even if the author or artist provides all the illustration material, the picture department will check it for quality, put it in well-marked envelopes, trace its movements through the publishing process, make sure it comes back and is returned to its owner(s) in good order. The amount of detail work involved in dealing with thousands upon thousands of pictures every year is staggering. And then, of course, there are the projects for which the author or artist supplies lists of the pictures needed and where they are located. In this situation the picture department writes endless letters, tracks down pictures that have changed hands six times since last heard of, cajoles private owners into allowing photographers to drag their equipment over valuable carpets to photograph the subject. The picture department also has to deal with increasingly complicated and conflicting demands—fees for the photos themselves plus reproduction fees for the artist perhaps (or an organization that represents artists), plus the museum that owns the work, plus the fees for photographers, plus appropriate and correct credit for such use where required. There is a desperate need to clarify who is entitled to reproduction fees, and a rational scale of fees for heavy users. Increasingly, we find that interesting projects are becoming marginal or impossible to create because the picture costs are prohibitive or impossible to ascertain.

Once the manuscript is edited and the pictures are all in and captioned and labeled, the package moves to the design department. Abrams has traditionally welcomed the artist and the author to join in the design process (artists are the true superstars to the design department), and the chance to work on a *Contemporary Artists* or *Artbook by Artists* volume is considered a great plum. When the design is finished the package moves to production. In most cases at Abrams the book will be produced in Japan, where large sizes and beautiful workmanship are still economically feasible.

The author will see first proofs but is not responsible for finding typographical errors. Abrams employs two proofreaders, each reading a fresh set of proofs independently against a copy of the manuscript. The editor usually also reads either first or second proofs. So a number of eyes and minds see the various stages and try to eliminate errors. The design is subjected to the same rigorous checks, and there is a nine-member team in Japan to oversee the production work there.

Just the same, there *is* a difference between the printing of ink on paper and the printing of oil on canvas that cannot be totally bridged. The amount of effort expended in compensating for reduction in size and the flat page is enormous, and as technology advances we see greater quality, especially in the printing of black-and-whites.

Well before the book arrives, promotion plans are made. A picture of the book and a description of it are published in the catalogue, which is itself perhaps the one most important book we publish each year, since it is our principal selling device. General ads featuring several books or the whole season's list are prepared for newspaper and magazine use. Then, about fifteen hardbound advance copies are flown in—arriving about a month before the rest of the shipment. One goes to the author and one to the artist. One is for making the book's carton, which is individually tailored to each book. The rest go to the departments that really need them and to the main book reviewers. At this point books are really not available for general purposes. The mere cost of flying them in can be two or three times the manufacturing cost!

For those books that will benefit from special promotion—and that is by far not the case with every book—author tours, individual ads and special events are arranged. For many art books this is only a waste of time, and money is better spent on the production itself, for in the long run it is the care and talent lavished on them that results in publications people buy and treasure for a lifetime.

PART FOUR
MONEY AND THE VISUAL ARTIST

CHAPTER THIRTEEN
A TAX AND BUSINESS PLANNING GUIDE FOR THE VISUAL ARTIST

Marc Darrow, Esq.

The focus of this article will be on the federal income tax and state and local taxes as they affect the visual artist. Estate and gift taxes are dealt with in another article, as are the tax provisions for charitable organizations and private donors who contribute to the arts.

Basic to an understanding of the income tax and tax immunization is an understanding of what constitutes income. For tax purposes, there are two basic types of income: "ordinary income" and "capital gains." Ordinary income is taxed under a regular progressive rate schedule, while the maximum on long-term capital gains is being reduced as of January 1, 1982, from 28% to 20%. As the name implies, ordinary income encompasses the ordinary earnings of an artist, such as income from the sale of works in the form of fees, salaries or commissions, and income from copyright of other royalties from the use or reproduction of an artist's work. Income does not need to be received as cash: if artists exchange their works, or trade their works for goods or services, such as dental care or rent, the transaction is treated as a sale for tax purposes and ordinary income is recognized equal to the value of the goods or services received, less the cost of raw materials in work delivered.

Capital gains income is income from the sale of a capital asset, that is, property held for purposes of investment or property used over a period of time in a trade or business. To qualify for favorable tax treatment as a long-term capital gain, the property must have been held for more than a year before resale. A visual artist's own works or copyrights on his works are not capital assets. Sales of an artist's own works to customers result in ordinary income equal to the amount received less the cost of the raw materials in the work. If an artist gives his work away or sells it for less than "fair market value"—the amount that a willing buyer would pay a willing seller, neither being under constraint to enter into the transaction—the work does not become a capital asset in the hands of the recipient. However, if the artist leaves unsold works in his estate, they may be treated as capital assets by his heirs or legatees. (For fuller discussion, see Chapter 18 of this Manual.) Works of other artists held for sale to customers in the ordinary course of business are considered to be inventory, yielding ordinary income, not capital assets. If an artist is not a dealer but occasionally buys and sells the work of other artists for investment purposes, the income from these transactions may be considered capital gain. It will be necessary for the artist or his/her accountant to keep careful records of works bought and held for investment to establish the long-term capital gain qualifications of these transactions.

KEEPING RECORDS

Internal Revenue Code Section 6001 requires every self-employed individual to keep books of accounts or records sufficient to substantiate the information shown on his/her tax return. In this respect the self-employed visual artist is treated no differently than any other self-employed professional or businessman. The IRS in its *Audit Technique Handbook for Internal Revenue Agents* identifies two classes of tax records—primary and secondary. Primary or "informal" records are documents such as invoices paid, bills, receipts, canceled checks, bank statements, etc., upon which are recorded individual business transactions of the taxpayer. Secondary or "formal" records are the permanent books, work sheets, etc., that summarize the individual transactions in a manner designed to aid the taxpayer in determining his financial status or profit or loss for any given period. The secondary record-keeping system need not be complex. A single-entry bookkeeping system recording only the flow of cash and amounts receivable and amounts payable by the artist is sufficient. But the records must be kept in a businesslike orderly fashion and all primary documents that substantiate the record entries kept in a safe place. Sketchy memoranda approximations of income or expenses will not do if the IRS decides to audit the artist's return, and there are penalties imposed for negligent underpayment of taxes.

There are two basic methods of accounting, the "cash method" and the "accrual method." The cash method, which depends on the receipt and payment of cash, is the easiest to understand and use. It is the method usually adopted by most individuals, unless the artist is one required to keep inventories. Under the cash method, the taxpayer includes in gross income all items of income actually or constructively received during the year. Constructive receipt of income occurs when an amount is set aside for the artist or credited to his account without any substantial restriction as to time and manner of payment even though the artist may not yet have the sum actually in his possession. For instance, a check received at the end of one year is income for that year even though it may not be cashed until the following year. Expenses are treated similarly. Expenses for carrying on business are usually deducted in the tax year in which they are paid. Expenses paid in advance that relate to several years are not deducted all in one year but are deducted proportionately in each year to which they apply.

In the accrual method of accounting all items are included in the taxable year in which they are actually "earned." An item of income is "earned" when all events required to establish the right to receive the income have occurred, and the amount of income involved can be determined with reasonable accuracy. For instance, if a portrait commissioned for an agreed-upon sum is completed in December, the amount to be paid is income for that year even though it is not actually paid until the following year. Similarly, the expenses of carrying on a business are deductible in the year actually incurred even though they are not paid until the following year.

An artist who produces works for eventual sale to customers may be obliged to maintain inventories at the beginning and end of each taxable year. The purpose of keeping inventories is to prevent the distortion of income that could result if the costs of production were deducted in one year and the income from sales reported in another year. If required to keep inventories, you as an artist must use the accrual method of tax accounting at least for sales from inventory and cost of goods sold.

If sales from inventory only account for a small part of your total business activity, other business expenses may be recorded using the cash method, if you prefer.

The visual artist, like any taxpayer, must take care to separate business from personal items. He or she should have separate checking accounts for business and personal expenses and not confuse the two. Business expenses are reported on Schedule C of Form 1040 and personal expenses on Form A. Sometimes, however, it may be necessary to apportion an expense between the two, such as interest on a credit account that is used for both business and personal purchases.

ARTISTIC ACTIVITIES FOR PROFIT VERSUS HOBBY LOSSES

Like any other entrepreneur, you as a visual artist can deduct from gross income ordinary and necessary expenses incurred during the taxable year while carrying on your work or business. However, you can deduct your expenses as an artist from other income sources other than your artistic activity only if you are considered to be actively engaged in the business of being an artist for a profit. One who is not actively engaged in the business of art for a profit is considered a hobbyist, and may deduct the expenses of his hobby only up to the amount of income generated by the hobby. It is obviously important for an artist who is forced to take another job to make ends meet, to establish himself or herself as an artist for profit in order to recoup all the expenses involved. If you can show a profit from your artistic activities in two of the previous five years, the presumption is that you are an artist for profit. The test is not conclusive, however, and an artist who cannot show a profit still may be able to establish that he/she is in the business of being an artist rather than using his/her other source of income to support a hobby. The IRS has developed nine factors which it considers in determining whether an activity in question is pursued for a profit motive (Treasury Regulation 183.2). The list includes:

(1) Manner in which the taxpayer carries on the activity, especially with respect to maintenance of complete and accurate business records.

(2) The expertise of the taxpayer or his adviser. The artist's standing as a professional is enhanced by study, professional acceptance, exhibitions and prizes.

(3) Time and effort expended in carrying on the activity. No minimum time has been specified, but four hours a day has been considered sufficient.

(4) Expectation that assets used in the activity may appreciate in value.

(5) The success of the taxpayer in carrying on other similar or dissimilar activities.

(6) The taxpayer's history of income or losses with respect to the activity. Losses over a long period of time, with the artist sustained by income from non-art sources, may indicate an absence of a profit motive.

(7) The amount of occasional profits, if any, which are earned. Substantial profit though only occasional is considered indicative that the activity is engaged in for profit.

(8) Financial status of the taxpayer. Substantial income from sources other than the activity may indicate that the activity is not engaged in for profit. The wealthy artist is at a disadvantage under this standard.

(9) Elements of personal pleasure or recreation. The fact that the taxpayer derives personal pleasure from the activity is not sufficient to cause the activity to be classified as not for profit if the activity is in fact engaged in for profit as shown by other factors.

These nine factors are not the only ones the IRS will consider, nor is any one of them determinative. Since there are no hard and fast rules, you should be careful to develop and retain any indicia of a profit motive, including businesslike accounts, records of exhibitions, awards, favorable critical comments and other tokens of professional acceptance. In case you are challenged by the IRS as a hobbyist you should seek out competent tax counsel immediately so that the issue may be resolved inexpensively during the early stages of the audit procedure.

DEDUCTIONS, DEPRECIATION, INSTALLMENT SALES

All ordinary and necessary expenses paid or incurred during the taxable year in carrying on any trade or business are deductible. If the expense is "ordinary and necessary" and is not the purchase price of inventory or an asset to be used over a period of time in your business, the expense is deductible in the year paid for or incurred. Rental expense, however, may be a little more complicated. If you rent a studio that is used for business purposes only, that amount is clearly deductible. But if you live in the studio space as well, and you are a self-employed artist, you can get a deduction only for that portion of the studio space that is used exclusively and on a regular basis as your principal place of business or as a place used by customers in meeting with you. The portion of the living quarters for which a business deduction is taken must be used exclusively for this purpose.

In addition, studio expenses are deductible only to the extent of gross income from the artist's work less other deductions, so an artist with a small amount of art-related income for the year may not be able to take his/her full studio deduction even though he/she is considered to be in the business of being an artist. The cost of property used in the visual artist's business, such as building, machines, equipment fixtures and the like, that has useful life extending beyond the taxable year is ordinarily not deductible as an expense but is recoverable through depreciation over the expected useful life of the property involved. To calculate depreciation you or your accountant can use the useful life for an asset as established by the IRS under the asset depreciation range system, or ADR. The artist may lengthen or shorten the IRS estimates by up to 20%, but he/she must apply ADR to all depreciable property placed in service during the taxable year. He or she also must follow certain reporting and accounting rules established by the IRS. An artist considering election of the ADR system should consult an accountant about its use. A more common method of determining useful life is by estimating the period over which one expects the asset to be actually of use in one's business. This may be based on past experience with similar property, or the guidelines suggested by the ADR system. In addition, the estimate of useful life may be changed later if affected by unexpected conditions. Before calculating the annual depreciation deduction, the artist must reduce his or her cost "basis" in the item —usually the purchase price of the property—by the salvage value of the property at the end of its useful life. The artist does not need to estimate salvage value if it is personal property that will last at least three years and be worth no more than 10% of its original cost at the end of that time, if the item involved will have no value at the end of its use or if the artist elects the ADR method of establishing useful life. Otherwise salvage value must be estimated, but it may be reduced by 10% of the cost of the item before deducting it from basis. The simplest method of calculating depreciation is called straight-line depreciation. Under this method the cost of an asset less its salvage value is deducted evenly over the years of its expected life. If the depreciable personal property has a life of at least six years the taxpayer is entitled to an extra depreciation deduction in the year of purchase. This additional first-year depreciation is 20% of the entire cost of the property, not exclusive of salvage value, up to $2,000 on a separate return or $4,000 on a joint return. Regular depreciation is then calculated on the cost basis of the property less both salvage value and the first year's extra depreciation. Writing off the cost of business assets or methods of "accelerated depreciation" is also allowed by the IRS. Rather than deducting the same amount for depreciation each year, methods of accelerated depreciation allow the taxpayer to deduct more for depreciation in the item's early years and less in the later years. Those of you fortunates who acquire an expensive business asset at a time when your income is greater than you expect it to be in future years may want to consider one of the methods of accelerated depreciation. However, you should consult an accountant or tax attorney before adopting an accelerated method of depreciation, as there are limits on their use.

The Tax Act of 1981 permits substantially faster write-offs for new or used depreciable property placed in service after December 30, 1980. Depreciable property is now called "recovery property" and placed in one of five categories depending on expected life. Most personal property is considered "five-year" property. Under the new tables found in Internal Revenue Code Section 168, the deduction begins with an accelerated depreciation method. For example, for an item of five-year personal property placed in service this year, 15% of the cost may be recovered in 1981, 22% in 1982 and 21% in the next three years. The taxpayer may still elect to depreciate over longer useful lives using the straight-line method.

An "investment tax credit" is also available for tangible personal property purchased for use in a trade or business if the property is a depreciable asset with a useful life of at least three years from the time it is put into service. An investment tax credit is more valuable than a tax deduction of the same amount because a tax credit is a direct reduction of the amount of tax due rather than a mere reduction of the amount of income on which the tax is calculated. The tax credit on depreciable property is 10% of the cost if the property has a useful life of at least seven years. If the useful life is less than seven years only part is used in calculating the tax credit. If the useful life is less than seven but at least five years, the tax credit is 10% of two-thirds of the cost. And if the useful life is less than five but more than three years the tax credit is 10% of one-third of the cost.

The investment tax credit is limited to the amount of income tax liability or $25,000 plus 80% of tax liability over $25,000, whichever is less. However, unused credits for any tax year can be "carried back" or "carried forward" to reduce tax liabilities in other years.

Depreciable property used in one's trade or business is a capital asset. Special provisions of the Tax Code, however, require the taxpayer to report as ordinary income certain portions of any gain attributable to prior depreciation. For depreciable property other than a building, the taxpayer must report as ordinary income the amount of any depreciation taken on the items from 1963 to the date of sale. For a building held longer than one year the taxpayer must report as ordinary income any depreciation claimed over what would have been the straight-line rate. Similarly, with respect to the investment tax credit, if prior to the end of seven years or the property's useful life (whichever is shorter) the property is sold or otherwise disposed of, the taxpayer's tax liability for the year of sale will be increased by some or all of the tax credit previously taken.

If an artist's business involves the sale of products, he or she may have special options if the sales are made on any type of installment basis where one or more payments are due the year after sale. If the sale is a "casual" one as opposed to a sale by a "dealer" who regularly sells personal property on the installment plan, the visual artist as seller can choose to report the income under the installment method or can choose to "elect out" and report the income under the deferred payment method. Under the installment method income is reported from each payment only to the extent of profit included in such payment. The effect is to even out income over the course of the installment payments. Under the deferred payment method, the cost of the product is deducted from the initial payment and discount value of the note, if any, and subsequent payments are reported as all income. The deferred payment method is advantageous when the year of sale is one of unusually high income for the artist so that he/she may defer income to subsequent years.

A "dealer," someone who regularly sells personal property on the installment plan, can also choose to report his or her income on the installment method and may switch from the cash or accrual method of reporting to the installment method by simply indicating the change on his or her tax return. But a dealer who has once chosen the installment method of reporting cannot switch to another method without getting the permission of the IRS. A dealer calculates income on each installment by use of a "gross profit percentage" which reflects the percentage of gross profit included in the contract price. This can be done on a sale-by-sale basis or as a gross profit percentage of all installment collections received in the taxable year.

In any installment-type sale where the sales price is over $3,000 and one or more payments are due a year after the date of sale, interest at the rate of 6% will be imputed to the sale if no interest or interest at a rate of less than 6% is provided for. This is of significance if the property being sold is a capital asset because the imputed interest would turn part of the anticipated capital gain to ordinary income. If the return will be all ordinary income the seller is not obligated to calculate the amount of imputed interest.

BUSINESS STRUCTURE

A visual artist may want to consider the tax consequences when deciding how he or she wants to organize his business. The IRS recognizes three basic forms of business organization: sole proprietorships, partnerships and corporations. The best form for an artist to use in conducting his/her business will depend on the circumstances of his/her particular situation.

The majority of professional artists who are not employees conduct their businesses as sole proprietors, reporting income and deductions from their art business on Schedule C of Form 1040. Sole proprietorships require no formal documentation or written statements unless the business is conducted under an assumed name, in which case a certificate of doing business under an assumed name is required. Sole proprietorships also have the advantage over partnerships and corporations as they are easy to terminate without the risk of excessive legal entanglements or tax liability.

PARTNERSHIPS

The Uniform Partnership Act, adopted with some modifications in all states, defines a partnership as "an association of two or more persons to carry on as co-owners a business for profit." All four characteristics must be present or the association is not a partnership. A partnership does not pay federal income tax. Rather, it passes income or loss through to the individual partners in the proportions established by the partnership agreement. Income to the partners retains the same character that it had coming into the partnership: personal service income remains personal service income, capital gains remains capital gains. The partnership may agree to pay salaries to some or all partners. Losses incurred by the partnership generally may be used by the partners to offset income from other sources, as is the case of an artist in a sole proprietorship. Even though a partnership is not a taxable entity it must file an information return on Form 1065 with the IRS.

Like a sole proprietorship, a general partnership may be formed without formal documents or written agreements though a written agreement between the partners is certainly advisable. The death, retirement or resignation of a general partner dissolves the partnership. However, unlike a sole proprietorship, the winding up of a partnership may lead to disagreement about valuation of assets and liabilities, and may require legal advice and result in tax liabilities.

The chief non-tax disadvantage of a partnership is that all partners are personally liable, jointly and severally, for everything chargeable to the partnership. The personal liability of partners for losses chargeable to the partnership may be a matter of concern to potential business partners, particularly where one partner is wealthy and the other is not, or where one or two partners will take a more active part in the business than the others, who will nonetheless be personally liable for the outcome of their decisions. One way of insulating those partners who do not take an active part in the business is by formation of a "limited partnership." Unlike a corporation, which effectively protects all participants from personal liability to outside parties, a limited partnership must have at least one general partner who is personally liable for everything chargeable to the partnership, while the limited partners' liability is limited to the capital investment they have made or agreed to make in the partnership. However, one potential drawback is that a limited partner may not participate in the control of the business of the partnership. If he or she does participate in the control and decision making of the partnership, he or she will lose his immunity as a limited partner and be treated as a fully liable general partner.

A limited partnership is more complicated to establish than a sole proprietorship or general partnership. A certificate of limited partnership giving the name, address, amount invested and profit share of each general and limited partner must be filed with the county recorder in the state of organization and, generally, in any other state in which the limited partnership does business. Death, resignation or retirement of a general partner dissolves the limited partnership, although death of a limited partner does not. As is the case with a general partnership, unwinding the affairs of a limited partnership is apt to be more complicated and costly than establishing it in the first place.

Corporations

The major tax advantage of incorporation is the opportunity it offers to defer income. Qualified pension, profit-sharing and stock bonus plans can be established to provide for tax-deferred retirement benefits far more generous than those permitted the owners and employees of unincorporated businesses. Similarly, income can be deferred through stock options or restricted stock offerings. Income tax can be deferred at the shareholder level by deferring dividend distributions, within statutory limits. Finally, there are tax-free benefits available to employees, such as medical reimbursement plans, which are deductible as expenses by the employer.

The major tax disadvantage of a corporation is double taxation. A corporation is a separate taxable entity. It must file its own federal tax return, and in the absence of a "Subchapter S" election, must pay tax on its taxable income. Then, when a corporation makes a distribution to its shareholders from income upon which it has already paid a corporate income tax, its shareholders are taxed again on the dividend received. In actual practice, however, corporations often arrange to have little or no corporate income. It can be set aside in pension, annuity, insurance or medical plans, or it is distributed to shareholders in the form of salaries or rent of shareholder property. These latter expenditures are allowed as corporate deductions provided the amounts are "reasonable," and the use of the rented property is "ordinary and necessary" in the corporation's business. A second technique for avoiding the possibility of double taxation is the election of Subchapter S status by a qualifying corporation. Under Subchapter S a corporation is treated in effect as a partnership and not taxed on corporate income (see discussion below).

Additional disadvantages arise if the corporation suffers a loss. Absent Subchapter S election shareholders are not permitted to deduct losses suffered by a corporation from other sources of income. However, a corporation that incurs a net operating loss can carry the loss back three years or forward seven years and deduct it from past or future profits that might accrue. If the corporation is liquidated at a loss to the shareholders or if the stock becomes worthless, the shareholders will generally have capital losses, which can only be deducted from capital gains, not ordinary income, unless the corporation has made an election under IRS Code Section 1244.

If the stock of a new corporation is to be issued for money or property other than stock or securities, it is to the advantage of the shareholders if the incorporators elect to issue the stock under the Section 1244 plan. To qualify, the corporation must:

1. Adopt a formal plan to offer its stock for only a specified time, no longer than two years after the plan was adopted.
2. Qualify as a small business corporation, with a total capital of $1,000,000 or less.
3. Have no prior issue of stock outstanding.
4. Issue its stock for money or property other than stock or securities.

If the corporation electing the Section 1244 plan has during its last five years of existence (or during the period of its existence if less than five years) derived more than 50% of its aggregate gross receipts from sources other than passive investments or sales or exchanges of securities, and if during the same period the corporation's deductions did not exceed its gross income, the corporation is subsequently liquidated or its stock becomes worthless, an individual stockholder who received his or her stock from the corporation itself (and not from a former stockholder) is entitled to take as an ordinary loss up to $50,000 ($100,000 on a joint return) in any one taxable year. Losses over this amount will be treated as capital losses. Section 1244 has no disadvantages. If the corporate venture is successful, it will never come into operation or affect corporate income or taxation. (It could be malpractice for an attorney not to counsel his client on this election.)

Visual artists who incorporate need to be aware of the personal holding company provisions. A personal holding company is defined by the IRS Code as a corporation with more than 50% of its stock owned actually or constructively by five or fewer individuals, and more than 60% of its income derived from certain passive investments, including dividends, interest, royalties, copyright royalties, with certain exceptions, film rentals, with certain exceptions, and income received from the use of corporate property by a shareholder who owns 25% of the corporate stock.

The penalty for being declared a personal holding company is a maximum 70% tax on all retained personal holding company income. This will drop to 50% for the 1982 tax year. The tax may be avoided by paying out all income in dividends or salaries to the stockholders, but the personal holding company is denied the options available with respect to deferring income available to ordinary corporations. Code Section 547 provides for the payment of a deficiency dividend if a corporation is determined to be a personal holding company, so the 70% tax on income is *actually rarely* paid. The corporation will still be liable for penalties and interest, however. And the statute of limitations on assessments is six years rather than the normal three.

For purposes of determining personal holding company income, copyright royalties are defined by Code Section 543(a)(4) as:

> compensation; however designated, for the use of or right to use, copyrights in works protected by copyright issued under Title 17 of the United States Code and to which copyright protection is also extended by the laws of any country other than the United States of America by virtue of any international treaty, convention or agreement or interest in such copyrighted works, and includes payments from any person for performing rights in any copyrighted work and payments (other than produced film rents . . .) for the use of or right to use films.

An intricate exception to the inclusion of copyright royalties from personal holding company income provides a "safe haven" for publishing companies whose royalty income is not attributable to the work of 10% or more shareholders.

Produced film rents are:

> payments received with respect to an interest in a film for the use of or right to use, such film, but only to the extent that such interest was acquired before substantial completion of the production of such films.

The Code provides that film rental is not considered personal holding company income if film rents comprise 50% or more of the corporation's gross income, thus providing a "safe haven" for film production companies.

A special type of personal holding income may arise from certain personal service contracts. This occurs if a stockholder who owns 25% or more is designated or can be designated by a person other than the corporation as the person who is to furnish personal services in a contract with the corporation. The example in the Treasury Regulations concerns an actor under contract to his own wholly owned corporation, which corporation enters into a contract with a producer for his services. The money paid to the corporation by the producer is personal holding company income. The same problem arises for the visual artist, whether you be a painter, a photographer, a cartoonist or the like. Therefore, if you are an artist who predominantly provides services, you must be sure to get competent tax advice before deciding to incorporate.

Subchapter S Corporations

A qualifying corporation may make an election whereby it will be for the most part exempt from federal income tax. Under Subchapter S rules the corporation's taxable income or loss is taken into account pro rata by the shareholders on their individual returns and income is not taxed to the corporation.

To qualify to make a Subchapter S election a corporation must meet certain requirements:

1. It must have no more than fifteen shareholders. (The 1981 Tax Act raises this number to twenty-five beginning in 1982.)

2. Only individual estates and certain trusts may be stockholders. The permissible trusts are limited to grantor trusts with assets in the control of the grantor, voting trusts, each beneficiary consisting as one stockholder, and a trust that obtains stock under a will, but only for sixty days.

3. No shareholder may be a non-resident alien.

4. The corporation may not own more than 80% of the stock of a subsidiary corporation, unless the subsidiary has never begun business and has no taxable income.

An election may be made by a qualifying corporation any time within the first seventy-five days of the tax year to which it applies, or at any time during the preceding tax years. All stockholders must agree to the election. A shareholder's consent is binding and may not be withdrawn after the election, unless all stockholders agree to terminate.

A Subchapter S election can be terminated by the consent of all the shareholders or if a new shareholder affirmatively refuses to consent to the election. The election is automatically terminated if the corporation does not continue to meet the requirements outlined above, i.e., by acquiring an active subsidiary or issuing a second class of stock. It will also be terminated if the corporation receives more than 80% of its gross receipts from sources outside the United States, or 20% of its gross income from passive investments. Gross receipts refer to the amount received by the corporation before allowance for expenses and other deductions. However, with respect to passive income, gross receipts only comprise the gains from sales or exchanges of stock or other securities. Still, the limitation on passive income means a Subchapter S corporation will have to earn its income primarily from other than investment activities. A voluntary termination by all the stockholders is effective for a given tax year only if made in the first month of that year. Otherwise it applies to the subsequent year. An automatic termination or termination by a new stockholder is effective for the entire tax year in which it occurs. Once a valid election has been terminated, the corporation cannot re-elect Subchapter S status prior to the fifth tax year after the tax year in which the termination took place, unless the IRS consents to an earlier date.

As mentioned, if you are still with us, the primary effect of a Subchapter S election is that corporate income is divided pro rata among the shareholders and taxed directly to them whether distributed or not. Capital gains to the corporation are also treated as capital gains to the shareholders. However, there is a capital gains tax imposed on the corporation if the corporation's net capital gain is more than $25,000 and is also more than 50% of its taxable income, and the taxable income itself is more than $25,000.

Several deductions are disallowed in computing the corporation's net income. A Subchapter S corporation's pension donations are limited to the amounts allowed by the H.R. 10 or Keogh plans. Deductions for net operative losses are not allowed, and net capital losses may be carried forward for five years but may not be carried back. Since actual distributions of income to stockholders are taxed at dividend rate, a Subchapter S corporation may well elect to pay out income in salaries which will be taxed at the lower personal service income rate.

Stockholders in a Subchapter S corporation are also taxed for income they would have received had the corporation distributed all of its undistributed taxable income. Stockholders increase their basis in their stock to the extent of this constructive dividend. Once this income has been taxed it may under certain circumstances be distributed tax-free in subsequent years. A tax-free later distribution is limited to cash only in excess of that year's corporate income. The right to receive this tax-free distribution is personal and does not follow a transfer of stock. And it is terminated by a termination of the Subchapter S election.

One of the most important aspects of a Subchapter S corporation is the pass-through of corporate operating losses to the stockholders. Stockholders may use these losses as ordinary losses in computing their individual adjusted gross income. Unused losses may be carried back three years, then forward seven. A stockholder's share of operating losses is limited by the amount he has "at risk." Deduction of the operating losses reduces the basis he or she has in his/her stock, and then the basis he/she has in any corporate debts. Once the basis of both is used up, the stockholder can no longer deduct his/her share of the corporate losses unless he/she is willing to invest more money in the corporation before the corporate tax-year end.

Formation of a corporation requires more formality than the formation of other business entities and will involve more expense. Articles of Incorporation must be filed with a state official, and a lawyer should be consulted for their preparation. There will also be filing fees and taxes. In addition, a corporation has stockholders, directors and officers, and normally must arrange for stockholders' meetings, board of directors' meetings and other corporate formalities. The principal non-tax advantage of a corporation is the limitation of liability with respect to shareholders, officers and directors. This means that creditors of the corporation can in the normal course look only to the assets of the corporation to satisfy their claims. However, this limitation can be lost or at least challenged if the artist who has incorporated does not give formal recognition to the corporation by holding shareholders' and directors' meetings, keeping formal minutes, holding assets and conducting business in the corporation name. The IRS can also reallocate income between a corporation and its stockholders if it decides a controlling shareholder is only using the corporate shell for his or her own purposes.

Incorporation can be a tax-free transaction in that a shareholder can transfer appreciated property to the corporation in return for stock without a taxable gain if after the transfer he or she owns 80% of all the corporate stock. Two or more shareholders can escape taxable gains in this way if they act together in transferring property, and collectively own 80% of the stock. A problem can arise if the corporation assumes liabilities in excess of the transferor's basis in his or her property. For example, if you are an artist with outstanding liabilities who incorporates and who contributes paintings in which your only basis is the cost of paint and canvas in exchange for stock, it may be that the liabilities assumed by the corporation exceed your basis in your paintings, and the result will be a taxable gain to you for the amount of the difference.

Getting out of incorporation is apt to involve tricky tax questions, and an artist interested in selling his/her stock or liquidating the corporation is advised to seek competent legal advice.

OTHER TAXES

Social Security

Presently, an employer must withhold from each employee's paycheck social security contributions of 6.65% on all wages up to a maximum annual wage of $29,700. The employer must match these contributions.

A self-employed person whose self-employed activities yield a net income of $400 or more must contribute to social security 9.3% of their net earnings up to the same maximum income of $29,700 annually. Anyone who carries on a trade or business for profit is considered to be self-employed, so any artist who is in business for purposes of deducting his/her art-related losses from other income will be liable for self-employment social security when his/her artistic activities bring in net earnings over $400. A sole proprietor and an independent contractor are both considered self-employed. So is a member of a partnership that carries on a trade or business. An officer or employee of a corporation, even though a controlling shareholder, is not self-employed, but is an employee of the corporation, which must deduct and match the social security contributions like any other employer.

State Income Taxes

A visual artist, like anyone else, is liable for the personal income tax levied by the state of California. The state of California levies a graduated tax on net income up to a certain maximum, currently $30,000, plus a flat percentage rate on all net income above that amount. Employers are obliged to withhold state taxes as well as federal taxes from their employees' paychecks. Taxes are not withheld from wages paid to an independent contractor. In deciding whether someone is an independent contractor, the state looks to whether the employer has the right to "direct and control" the person that he or she has hired. If it is not absolutely clear, the state will look to other factors, such as whether the individual hired has his or her own place of business, owns and uses his or her own tools, is paid by the hour or the job, is licensed in his or her trade or business or holds himself/herself out as self-employed to make a determination.

The state of California does not tax sole proprietorships or unincorporated associations as such, but does tax corporations. A corporation presently must pay a $200 advance to the Franchise Tax Board upon incorporation in the state of California and also must pay a state corporate income tax. The corporate tax is 9.6% of net corporate income, with a minimum income tax of $200 due annually, whether or not the corporation has any actual net income.

State Unemployment and Disability Taxes

An employer in the state of California must contribute 3.2% of his employees' wages up to a maximum annual wage of $6,000 to the state unemployment compensation fund. The employee has withheld from his paycheck 0.6% of all wages up to $14,900 annually as a contribution for state disability insurance. These taxes are not levied on the self-employed or independent contractors, although they may contribute to the disability fund if they desire to.

State and Local Sales Taxes

A retailer of goods in Los Angeles is generally obliged to collect a sales tax of 6%, of which 4% is state sales tax, 1.75% local sales tax, and 0.25% county sales tax. The sales tax is to be submitted to the State Board of Equalization monthly, quarterly or annually depending on how frequently retail sales are made. An artist who sells his/her own work is obliged to collect and submit this tax. If he/she sells through a gallery, the gallery owner will collect and submit the tax. Artists who sell services rather than "goods" are not subject to sales tax. Therefore, a painter who sells a canvas must collect a sales tax on the transaction, whereas one who is hired as an independent contractor to paint a mural is not obliged to deal with the sales tax. An artist who sells items subject to a sales tax should consider obtaining a State Sales Permit, which exempts him/her from paying the sales tax on materials that are to be incorporated in other items offered for sale. Artists who offer services rather than goods do not qualify for a sales permit, and thus are obliged to pay sales tax on the materials they use.

The Tax Game

The real name of the tax game is to write off any possible deductions before the end of the fiscal year rather than waiting for the next tax year and to defer as much income as possible as far into the future as possible.

To further aid this endeavor, President Reagan on August 13, 1981, signed the Economic Tax Act of 1981. The new 1981 act makes many tax reductions. For example, the maximum tax on all income as of January 1, 1982, will drop from 70% to 50%. It is therefore especially useful if possible for the high income taxpayer to defer such income from 1981 into 1982.

One great method of deferring income is to incorporate and split this year's income into personal income prior to incorporation and corporate income thereafter. The amount attributable to corporate income would be deferred until the end of the corporate fiscal year, which would be beyond December 31, 1981, thereby deferring tax on income earned in the latter part of 1981 from the date of incorporation forward. This is a wise technique to use for any non-corporate artist in a year when a very large increase in income is expected. The corporation must, however, be formed prior to the receipt of income.

For those of you with your own business supplying products in the form of artwork, expensive photographs or other media, the corporation is set up in a normal fashion. For those of you who simply provide services, a "loan-out" corporation is suitable. A contract is entered into between the corporation and yourself whereby the corporation may loan out the services of you to the third party that hires the corporation to do the artwork. This is similar to and provides the advantages of the professional corporation used by doctors and lawyers.

With a corporation more income can also be sheltered and deferred by use of retirement plans. As of the 1982 tax year, 25% of income plus $2,000 through an individual retirement plan can be deducted from gross income. Income from the plan's investment is not fixed when incurred and the fund's cash can be loaned back to the taxpayer. Not a bad deal.

Other possibilities in deductions are to use investment tax credit property prior to year end, pay bonuses prior to year end, prepay state and local and personal and real property taxes prior to year end and enter leveraged tax shelters prior to year end so that the depreciation may be deducted.

And, of course, it is always wise to file tax returns if earnings are small so that the basis for income averaging can be established. Income averaging may be used if during the four preceding years one's income is less than 60% of this year's income and if the four-year average is substantially under the 50% rate for earned income.

One final word of advice is that the tax rules are not really made to be broken. Many people feel that their tax return is merely an offer to the IRS and that any battle will be well deserved. Many other people watch their friends slip by and hear stories that the tax revolt is at hand because taxes are unconstitutional. Be advised that the ones that slipped by did so because they were not audited. Many of the tax revolters you don't hear about are spending their vacations in federal prisons for the evasion.

Be watchful and be careful to keep records and cover your assets.

CHAPTER FOURTEEN

SALES TAXES—WHO, WHAT, WHEN, WHERE, WHY ME?

Melvin Nefsky, CPA

The sales and use tax regulations in the visual arts have been the subject of much confusion and misunderstanding, resulting in a great deal of consternation among persons associated with the arts.

As a CPA and business manager specializing in the visual arts and entertainment industries, I can testify that the problems attendant to sales taxes are numerous.

Clients often ask:	*Clients often state:*
Who is to pay?	I can't charge this!
How do I charge?	They won't pay me!
What if I don't collect?	No one else is doing this!
Can we do this on the side?	
How will they ever know?	
How do they apply to me?	

When artists open their businesses, they are confronted with the necessity of registration (i.e., business licenses, DBAs, identification numbers, payroll and sales taxes). For most, the fear of the unknown exists. They lack the familiarity of dealing with the maze of regulatory institutions, and thus many attempt to block out dealing with them until they receive that certain "telephone call."

Anyone, including an artist, who fails to register with the State Board of Equalization (the regulatory body) is often picked up through audits of a company he/she has dealt with when the company's invoices are examined and a determination is made that sales tax should have been charged. The artist is then contacted by the Board and asked to register and provide the supporting information as to why he/she didn't originally register or report. The Board will usually go back a period of time (up to eight years) and request documentation of all sales during that period. If the records are not available, an arbitrary assessment may be made by the audit staff. This usually takes the form of determining the amount of unreported tax for a test period and amortizing this amount for the entire period in question.

The above process can be quite costly, since you are subject to a 10% penalty, in addition to having interest computed at the rate of 1% per month until paid. Sales taxes are always assessed upon the seller. Therefore, the burden of proof is upon you to provide the information. The dilemma is further complicated since, in the most pragmatic sense, one cannot go back to his/her clients and try to collect a tax he/she failed to charge. The result: you wind up paying the tax, penalties and interest out of your own pocket. An expensive proposition, to say the least.

The California State Board of Equalization is the sixth-largest tax collecting agency in the world, yet one of the smaller agencies in the state. Since federal budget cutting is now a part of the eighties, allocations to state and local governments are certain to decrease. With this in mind, and with a decrease in property taxation (California's noted Proposition 13), the focus on sales tax will increase considerably. State congressional discussion has emphasized the need to provide the regulatory agencies with the proper staffing necessary to monitor the collection of tax. It is a certainty that this agency will grow and develop specialized audit staffs to focus on a specific industry. The visual arts are no exception and I cannot overemphasize the need for all persons involved to educate themselves about specific regulations as they apply to their area or business.

In the most general sense, the visual arts are categorized by the Board into: fine art painters and sculptors, commercial artists and designers, photographers, advertising agencies and motion picture production. Specific regulations exist for each category; however, it is not uncommon for there to be some overlapping. The regulations are often confusing, but certain general principles apply:

Whenever a sale involves tangible personal property, all of the costs associated with that sale are taxable. As an example: For commercial artists and ad agencies the cost of photostats, blueprints, supplies and copy are taxable; for fine artists the entire sale price of a painting or sculpture is taxable. Of course, exceptions apply, as in the case of "preliminary art" used as the model for the finished product. These costs must be separately stated and invoiced as such. If not, they are deemed to be part of the finished product and sales tax must be charged.

My clients have often argued that their clients are buying the artist's talents and services, not just a product, and that the majority of their billing results from ideas and concepts. They ask why they should be taxed for services when those in other service industries, such as doctors, attorneys and accountants, are exempt. I explain that under the regulations a fundamental distinction exists: whether the objective of the buyer is to purchase the service or the product provided by the service. In other words, whether the transfer of tangible personal property is incidental to the performance of the service or whether a particular transaction involves the actual sale of such property. If the former, then the tax would not apply; if the latter, the buyer receives the services in tangible physical form and tax will apply.

Another distinction is whether, in the course of business, you are deemed to be the consumer or the seller of goods. This is important because in the visual arts a variety of goods are consumed, not only in the production process but in the course of running the business. As a consumer you pay tax on all of your purchases, unless you submit a resale card indicating that these items are to be resold. If you have paid tax on an item that is incorporated into the final product and you charge your client, you may claim a credit on your sales tax return as a "tax paid purchase."

To conclude, there is a need for persons in the visual arts to acquaint themselves with all the aspects of the sales tax regulations as they may apply in each business. In my experience, clients involved in the creative process are often needlessly intimidated by tax law. Just as the once unwieldy tools of your trade are now familiar and useful, the various tax laws, once clarified, will facilitate the management of your profession, provide benefits and avoid problems.

CHAPTER FIFTEEN

VISUAL ART AND SALES TAX CONSEQUENCES

Richard Nevins, Member, State Board of Equalization

California Sales and Use Tax Law

The sales tax is imposed on the retailer for the privilege of selling tangible personal property at retail. The tax is paid to the state by the retailer, who ordinarily adds tax reimbursement to the sales price. The tax applies to retail sales of tangible personal property in California. The use tax is the companion tax to the sales tax and is imposed on the consumer of tangible personal property. It is collected and remitted to the state by the seller, if the seller is registered to collect use tax. Otherwise, the use tax is remitted to the state by the consumer. The use tax applies to the use in California of tangible personal property purchased from a retailer in another state or from a California retailer under a resale certificate. It applies only when the sales tax does not apply.

Sales of Works of Art in General

Under the California Sales and Use Tax Law, tax applies to the entire amount charged for sales of artistic expressions in the form of paintings, sculptures, ceramics, tapestries, photographs or any other products of the fine arts which are in the form of tangible personal property.

Materials Purchased by Artists

With regard to items purchased by an artist, Regulation 1540 Section (d) explains that the artist is the consumer of tangible personal property used in the operation of his business. Such property may include stationery, ink, paint, tools, drawing tables, T squares, pens, pencils and other office supplies. Tax applies to the sale of such property to the artist.

The artist is the seller of, and may purchase for resale, any tangible personal property that the artist resells before use, or that becomes physically an ingredient or component part of tangible personal property sold by the artist prior to use. Such property may include illustration board, paint, ink, rubber cement, flap paper and wrapping paper.

An artist is the consumer of property, such as photographs and art, which he uses in the preparation of tangible property, as to which he is acting as a seller unless, prior to any use having been made of the property, the property is sold or becomes an ingredient or component part of other tangible personal property sold. The artist may purchase for resale photographs and art which, prior to any use, are sold or become physically an ingredient or component part of other tangible personal property that is sold by the artist.

The term "ingredient or component part of other tangible personal property" includes only those items that become physically incorporated into the property sold and not those which are merely consumed or used in the production of the property sold. A photograph, for example, does not become an ingredient or component part of property sold merely because the image of the photograph is reproduced as part of the property sold. A photograph or art is regarded as having been used when a reproduction is made from the photograph or art.

Improvements to Real Property

It is possible that an artist might be performing a construction contract by making improvements to realty. Improvements to realty are those operations which involve the permanent attachment of "material" such as paint, tiles, glass, etc., to land or building. The tax consequences of making such improvements are different from regular sales and are rather complex, but basically the artists are the consumers. If an artist is in a situation where he is making improvements to realty and is in doubt about how the Sales and Use Tax Law applies, he should call or write the nearest office of the California State Board of Equalization.

Advertising Agencies, Commercial Artists and Designers

Sales and Use Tax Regulation 1540 implements the law with respect to advertising agencies, commercial artists and designers. The sale of artwork may or may not be taxable, depending on whether it is preliminary or finished art. Section (b)(4)(A) of Regulation 1540 provides that "preliminary art" means roughs, visualizations, layouts and comprehensives, title to which does not pass to the client, but which are prepared by an advertising agency, commercial artist or designer for the purpose of demonstrating an idea or message for acceptance by the client before a contract is entered into or before approval is given for the preparation of the finished art to be furnished by the agency. Tax does not apply to separately stated charges for preliminary art, except where the preliminary art becomes physically incorporated into finished art.

On the other hand, Section (b)(4)(B) of Regulation 1540 explains that finished art is the final art for actual reproduction by photomechanical or other processes or for display purposes. Generally, tax applies to the total charges for finished art. However, it is possible that the sale of finished art could be an exempt sale for resale.

Sales to Museums

Sales and Use Tax Regulation 1570 (Sales and Use Tax Law Sections 6365 and 6366.3) provides that sales or use tax does not apply to the gross receipts from the sale, storage, use or other consumption in this state of original works of art, if purchased under the following conditions: (1) if purchased by a governmental entity or nonprofit organization operating a museum for such entity; (2) if purchased by a nonprofit organization for a museum operated by it or by another nonprofit organization, under specified conditions; (3) if purchased for a donation to, and actually donated to, a governmental entity or nonprofit organization operating a museum; (4) if purchased under specified conditions to become part of the permanent collection of a nonprofit corporation which regularly loans its art collection to museums.

For purposes of this section a "museum" shall only include:

1. A museum which has a significant portion of its space open to the public without charge; or

2. A museum open to the public without charge for not less than six hours during any month the museum is open to the public; or

3. A museum which is open to a segment of the student or adult population without charge.

There is also an exemption available for items which have value as museum pieces purchased by certain nonprofit museums to replace property destroyed by fire, flood, earthquake or other calamity, under specified conditions.

Photographers

Sales and Use Tax Regulation 1528 implements the law with respect to photographers. Section (a)(1) of the regulation explains that tax applies to sales of photographs, whether or not produced to the special order of the customer, without any deduction for such expenses of the photographer as travel time, rental of equipment, salaries or wages paid to assistants or models, whether or not such expenses are itemized in billings to customers. Accordingly, sales tax applies to such itemized items as shooting fees and travel time in addition to the charge for the finished photographs.

Section (a)(1) of Regulation 1528 also provides that tax does not apply to sales to photographers of tangible personal property which becomes an ingredient or component part of photographs which are sold, such as mounts, frames and sensitized paper. Tax does apply to sales to the photographer or producer of materials used in the process of making the photographs which do not become an ingredient or component part thereof, such as chemicals, trays, films, plates, proof paper and cameras.

Section (d)(2) of Regulation 1660 exempts from tax the lease of photographs, whether or not produced to the special order of the consumer, when the possession, but not the title, of the photograph is transferred for the purpose of being reproduced one time only, in a newspaper regularly issued at average intervals not exceeding three months.

If possession and use of a photograph is temporarily transferred for a consideration, the transaction constitutes a lease within the meaning of Section 6006.3(a) regardless of whether reproduction rights are granted by the lessor.

Additional Information

The Board has Tax Tips to help taxpayers interpret the law. The following pamphlets are of special interest to artists: #35 for Interior Designers and Decorators, #37 for the Graphic Arts Industry and #38 for Advertising Agencies. Copies of these pamphlets can be obtained by writing Richard Nivens, Member, State Board of Equalization, Caller 16, Arcadia, CA 91006-0016.

CHAPTER SIXTEEN
ART VALUATIONS FOR ARTISTS

Martin Weber

When Are Valuations Necessary or Useful?

For Federal Taxes   Valuations must be included with tax returns for art as gifts worth over $3,000 (the amount to be raised to $10,000 on January 1, 1982) and for art as part of estates of deceased artists (when the total value of the estate is over $175,000; this threshold to be raised to $600,000 by 1987).[1] Valuations of works traded among artists are not generally useful.[2]

For California Taxes (also applicable in a few other states)   Valuations are becoming increasingly necessary for state income tax purposes in a growing number of states for artists donating their own work to charitable institutions.[3] In states having resale royalty legislation or where artist and purchaser have signed agreements requiring a royalty on gross sale price or appreciated value, the value of traded works (works traded by owners who are not the creators of the works) is important to the artist since his or her royalty is based on 5% of the gross sale or 5% of the fair market value of artwork and any other items traded for the artist's work. Obviously, valuations for royalties occur after works have left the possession of their creators.

For Insurance   Valuations of one's work are also important when insuring the work against loss and damage in the studio or when attempting, in contracts for the use and reproduction of originals (whether painting, sculpture, graphic designs, photographic negatives, etc.), to require the user to pay for the value of the originals if lost or damaged. Remember that graphic artists and photographers, as well as painters and sculptors, may have at any point in their career a formidable collection of original artworks which have a high sale value of their own precisely because they are

[1] This essay addresses valuations for artists (who generally desire low valuations) and not valuations for collectors (who often desire high valuations). Collectors seeking valuation information are referred to "The Favored Tax Treatment of Purchasers of Art," by William M. Speiller, *Columbia Law Review,* Vol. 80 (March 1980).

[2] Assuming the materials in the traded works to be of roughly equal value, each artist in a trade gets the same basis in the work he receives as he had in the work he traded—that basis is the cost of materials, not the retail value (which would require a valuation).

[3] This is because the basis of a work donated by its creator to a charitable organization has been changed, in California and other states, from the cost of materials to fair market value of the donated work (requiring a valuation).

originals. (Norman Rockwell's *Saturday Evening Post* covers are a notable example of work done for a commercial purpose having an independent value as an original.)

Who May Make a Valuation?

Although for some purposes a professional appraiser is not required,[4] for all tax purposes an artist should use an appraiser. For gift and estate tax returns the regulations require an appraisal by an "expert or experts." For insurance valuations, a professional appraisal is beneficial because it connotes competence and impartiality.

The appraiser should be one with documentable experience in the appraisal of artworks of the type and price range of that which is being appraised. Appraisals which rely heavily upon subjective judgments, such as those based upon the quality of the particular work rather than upon statistical data of comparable works (such as the artist, medium, size, period of the artist's development) should be made by the most credible appraisers obtainable. However, the IRS will not accept appraisals grounded merely upon the unsupported opinion of an expert.

Membership in professional appraisal organization gives credence to an appraiser, although membership does not automatically establish his or her competency. Dealers who traffic in work comparable to that being appraised are especially credible appraisers; but dealers' prices tend to be higher than auction prices. Artists planning to make non-deductible gifts of their works (usually for estate tax purposes) could benefit from placing a few of their works in auctions of major houses which publish prices, for if these works bring low prices, the artist profits from the ability to document low valuation on the gifts he intends to make. With regard to higher valuation for insurance and risk of loss or damage and traded works triggering royalty payments, the artist can use documented gallery sales, contracts and paid invoices where the price of the sale of an original is specified, lists of standard fees paid for originals by a particular agency or industry.

Museum personnel, especially curators, who are specialists in the kind of art being appraised are highly credible, especially if they are employed by federally maintained museums such as the Smithsonian or National Gallery. A few art museums prohibit their personnel from making appraisals; some museums monitor appraisals to ensure against abuses. The American Association of Museums' Code of Museum Ethics demands that "any appraisal or authentication must represent an honest and objective judgment, and must include an indication of how the determination was made" (p. 13). Museum personnel tend to rely heavily upon auction records for appraisals. So using museum personnel as appraisers doubles the credibility of the valuation by including as grounds for the appraisal both the auction records and the museum employee's expertise. In valuation contests, courts have been favorably influenced by the sheer number of experts testifying on behalf of a taxpayer, and the museum curator using auction records carries the weight of two.

What Is an Acceptable Tax Valuation?

For taxation purposes the test of a valid appraisal is "fair market value," which is defined as "the price at which the property would change hands between a willing buyer and a willing seller,

---

[4] An excellent source on do-it-yourself appraisals is "Commentary on Personal Property Appraisal," available through the American Society of Appraisers, P.O. Box 17265, Washington, DC 20041, for $2.50.

neither being under any compulsion to buy or sell and both having reasonable knowledge of relevant facts." IRS regulations further define "fair market value" as retail value (not wholesale value).[5]

The most widely published art sales prices are auction prices, which are often substantially lower than retail value because many art dealers acquire their merchandise at auctions, mark them up and sell them at "retail" prices. Today, the art being sold at auction houses includes paintings, sculptures, graphics, photographs, original illustrations, original cartoons, posters, designs, architectural renderings, etc. But fortunately and paradoxically for the artist, auction prices are accepted by the IRS as proof of retail value. Sources for auction prices include the *World Collectors' Annuary*, *International Auction Records* and the selling prices included in catalogues of major houses such as Sotheby's. These sources can be found in the Los Angeles area at the art library of UCLA and the library of the Los Angeles County Museum of Art.

What Information Should a Valuation Contain?

The minimum contents of an appraisal should include:[6]

(1) A summary of the appraiser's qualifications.

(2) A statement of the value and the appraiser's definition of the value he or she has obtained.

(3) The bases upon which the appraisal was made, including any restrictions, understandings or covenants limiting the use or disposition of the property.

(4) The date as of which the property was valued.

(5) The signature of the appraiser and the date the appraisal was made.

The IRS recommends that appraisals of art objects, particularly paintings, should include:[7]

(1) A complete description of the object, indicating the size, the subject matter, the medium, the name of the artist, approximate date created, the interest transferred, etc.

(2) The cost, date and manner of acquisition.

(3) A history of the item, including proof of authenticity such as a certificate of authentication if such exists.[8]

(4) A photograph of a size and quality fully identifying the subject matter, preferably a 10″ × 12″ or larger print.

(5) A statement of the factors upon which the appraisal was based, such as:

(a) Sales of other works by the same artist particularly on or around the valuation date.

(b) Quoted prices in dealers' catalogues of the artist's works or of other artists of comparable stature.

(c) The economic state of the art market at or around the time of valuation, particularly with respect to the specific property.

---

[5] Artists, compared to collectors, are grievously overtaxed by this provision, at least for federal tax purposes. Valuations for the artists are made in the context of paying gift and estate taxes; the high "retail" value assigned artworks at these times is a disadvantage to the artists. The collector, however, profits by the retail value standard; he can buy at low wholesale prices from artists or auctioneers and then donate the works to art museums, taking an income tax deduction predicated upon a high retail price.

[6] Revenue Procedure 66–49.

[7] Ibid.

[8] The requirement of a statement of authenticity applies more to old works of questionable authorship than to works given by the creating artist or inventoried in his estate.

(d) A record of any exhibitions at which the particular art object had been displayed.

(e) A statement as to the standing of the artist in his profession and in the particular school or time period.

For valuations of prints, information should include the number of prints in the edition, the number of the impression being appraised and a statement about the quality of the particular impression being appraised if quality within the edition varies (as with etchings).

The information included within the appraisal should be as complete as possible; well-documented comprehensive valuations by credible appraisers discourage expensive audits and valuation contests with the IRS. Remember: *The burden of supporting the fair market value listed on a return is the taxpayer's.*

Are There Any Differences Among Valuations Depending upon Whether They Are to Be Used for Gift, Estate or Insurance Purposes?

Gifts   The artist who wishes to make a gift of his/her work (usually as a device for reducing the size and tax burden on his/her estate) generally desires a low valuation. Since auction prices are usually more comparable to low wholesale prices, the valuation should usually be based upon the auction price paid for a comparable work.

Estate Tax   Likewise the artist will benefit from a low valuation on his/her work for estate purposes. Low auction prices are the most likely tool. In addition, under certain conditions estate tax return values may be based upon bona fide sale of artworks through newspaper classified ads or through public auction. While this device may be convenient, it offers no substantial tax advantages to the artist's heirs.[9]

The most useful valuation tool for artists' estates is "blockage." The effective valuation date for estate taxes is the date of death (or six months thereafter if the value of the *total* estate has decreased). If the deceased artist left a large number of works in his/her estate, the executor can argue that if all these works were sold at once on the date of death, the art market would be glutted with an excessive number of the artist's works, driving prices down; this is "blockage." The theory of blockage was effectively used in the estate of the sculptor David Smith, who left 425 works in his estate. The appraisers of Smith's estate argued that because of blockage of the art market, the 425 works would bring only one-sixth of their highest aggregate selling price. The government contested this valuation, and a settlement was made based on a valuation of about one-third of the highest possible aggregate selling price.

The persuasiveness of the blockage argument depends heavily upon the appraiser's credibility as an authority on the art marketplace. Estate valuations using the blockage principle, therefore, should rely upon appraisals by knowledgeable dealers and auctioneers; several appraisals for this purpose could be well worth the cost.

---

[9] In instances where valuation by appraisal is unreasonably high, valuation through sale may be preferable; but valuation by sale is generally inadvisable because it precludes the tax-saving device of blockage.

Insurance   The "fair market value" test is a tax test and does not necessarily apply to insurance valuations. Appraisals for insurance purposes are based on replacement value, the price at which an item may be reasonably replaced, at resale, within a reasonable time. "Resale" in this context is usually taken to mean "dealer" price, as opposed to auction price (assuming dealer price to be higher than auction price).

Insurance appraisals are more likely to be contested in the event of a loss than tax appraisals in the event of an audit. This is because the appraiser is regarded as the insured's agent, and the insurance valuation merely suggestive. But the insurance valuation may be supported with the same devices used for the tax valuation, the completeness of documentary data and the credibility of the appraiser.

What Happens If a Valuation Is Contested by the IRS?

In the event of a valuation contest, the IRS may merely contact the taxpayer for additional information; it may refer the valuation to one of its own appraisers; or an independent appraiser may be employed. If there is a valuation contest, the taxpayer or his representative attorney or accountant is entitled to a written statement from the IRS explaining the basis on which the IRS has determined, or proposes to determine, valuation of property which is different from the valuation returned by the taxpayer.

There has been much written on the recent IRS crackdown on inaccurate art valuations; most artists should not be intimidated by this so-called crackdown, which is directed primarily at non-artist donors to charitable institutions of greatly overvalued art. In order to help the IRS determine whether appraisals are realistic, a ten-person Art Advisory Panel was established in 1968. Unfortunately, if an art object (other than a print)[10] has a value of under $20,000, it is not reviewed by the panel, but left to the discretion of the usual IRS appraisers, who are basically real estate appraisers, ill equipped to contest a well-documented appraisal by a legitimate art appraiser.

The need for artists to ascertain and document the value of their work will grow as federal and state legislation increasingly recognizes tax relief and equity in the marketplace for visual artists. Be aware of the quantity of works in your possession and keep abreast of the legislation.

[10] The Art Print Advisory Panel was established on November 13, 1980. It will review and evaluate appraisals on art prints.

CHAPTER SEVENTEEN
GRANTS AND NONPROFIT CORPORATIONS

Lorin Brennan, Esq.
Robert L. Schuchard, Esq.

This article is a brief introduction to acquiring grants for the visual arts and to administering the grant funds once obtained in a nonprofit corporation. Despite the budget cuts won by the Reagan administration, there still exists a good deal of federal funding for the arts, and funding continues to be available from states and private sources. However, many artists and arts organizations are competing for the grant moneys which remain, so successful funding will demand careful preparation of the grant application and professional administration of the grant programs.

Grants are available for nearly any artistic project you can imagine. For a simple project, you can often obtain funding solely as an individual. But for a more ambitious project, you will often have to create an organization to convince the grantor that you can successfully administer the grant funds. The organization typically used is the nonprofit corporation.

Part I of this article will deal with acquiring grants. Part II will discuss administering the grant funds in a nonprofit corporation. Although these subjects appear separate, they can often affect one another. The chance to acquire a grant may be an incentive to form a nonprofit corporation, while, on the other hand, once a grant is awarded it may impose additional administrative requirements on the corporation. In reading the materials which follow, keep in mind that you must balance the advantages of grant funding or nonprofit incorporation against the additional restrictions they may entail.

PART I: GRANTS

Grantsmanship

"Grantsmanship" is the art of acquiring grants. It requires the ability to plan and present effective programs to the funding authorities. The related but nonetheless distinct field of "grant law" deals with the legal rights and obligations of grantees once they have obtained funding.

When preparing your grant application, two general principles should be kept in mind. First, make sure that you have the ability to complete the program for which you are seeking funding. The granting authorities want to make sure that their money is not misspent, and will not fund your project, no matter how worthwhile, if you do not have the capability to successfully administer it.

Reputation and personal contacts are therefore extremely important in giving grantors confidence in you. Second, remember that grants are given in order to accomplish the goals of the grantors, and, not unexpectedly, these goals can change with the political climate. For example, several years ago funding was readily available for programs helping disadvantaged minorities, usually with public sector employment. In recent years, the emphasis has expanded to include women and the disabled, although the programs now tend to emphasize job training rather than employment. The current watchwords of the Reagan administration seem to be "private sector incentives," and there is a great deal of interest in funding programs which provide skills needed to develop new businesses or manage existing ones. What all this means is that you should be flexible in selecting your grant project. Although your project may be quite original, the funding authorities are usually looking for specific activities to fund, and it may be necessary to adapt your project to the current funding desires.

An example of a successful grant for a "Biker Art" festival follows this article. Note how the grant emphasized (1) the applicant's administrative ability and (2) the intent of the grant to bring the work of non-traditional artists to a large segment of the population, both of which were very important to the funding authority.

An excellent source for grantsmanship information is the Grantsmanship Center in Los Angeles. It provides training in grant writing and nonprofit administrations and publishes a bimonthly magazine, *The Grantsmanship Center News.* Further information is contained in the bibliography following this article.

Private Grants

The traditional source of private sector grant funds has been the foundation. The projects which a foundation will fund are limited by the terms of its charter, so not all foundations will fund projects by visual artists. Excellent sources for researching private foundation funding are *The Foundation Center Source Book* and the *Taft Foundation Reporter,* which are contained in the bibliography. These texts list the major private foundations in the country, describe the programs that they fund and tell you how to apply.

Recently, private corporations have also entered the grant field. They tend to be more flexible than foundations in projects which they will fund, and on occasion will even provide money to assist in the routine operating expenses of an arts organization. Corporate funding sources are also described in the texts listed in the bibliography.

In the case of private grants, you determine your basic legal rights and obligations by looking at the terms of the grant agreement. This typically involves reclassifying the grant as either a gift, a contract or a trust.

If the grant is a gift, the issue will be whether you have satisfied all conditions necessary to receive the grant funds. If you have, your use of the funds after receipt will be largely unregulated, which means that you can even use the funds for purposes other than those for which they were given.

In the usual case, the grant will be considered to be a contract, so you must look carefully at the wording of the grant to determine your rights and responsibilities. What can a grantor do if dissatisfied with your performance under the grant? Well, first the grantor must prove that in fact you have failed to perform. This is not an easy job because grants are often defined in vague and general terms, making an exact specification of the required performance difficult. For example, assume that your gallery was funded to present a showing of "contemporary Indian art." If you only exhibited the work of one artist, would that satisfy the grant? How about ten? or twenty? If you only showed works from 1950 to the present, is that "contemporary"? What about from 1900? As you can see, a grantor could have great difficulty proving that any particular show did not fulfill the conditions of the grant. Faced with this kind of problematic evaluation, a court will not substitute its own opinions or taste for those of the parties, but instead will evaluate whether the grantee used "good faith efforts" in carrying out the terms of the grant. The use of "good faith efforts" is an elusive standard but, basically, it only requires an honest attempt to fulfill the grant conditions. Even if a lack of good faith efforts can be established, the grantor will usually be unable to prove any damages, so at best the grantor can only recover the grant funds. The likelihood of a dissatisfied grantor bringing a lawsuit against you is quite small, however, not only because of the legal complications involved, but also because of the grantor's desire not to lose the good will of the artistic community. As a practical matter, the grantor's best remedy for unsatisfactory performance is simply not to fund your future projects, which is in itself a severe enough sanction.

The final situation which can occur is the classification of the grant as a trust. In this case, the grantee will be held to the highest standards of honesty and care (called "fiduciary standards") in administering the grant. A grantee who fails to exercise the requisite honesty or care may be personally liable for all the grant funds. A true trust, however, is rare, and except in extreme cases will only be created by explicit terms in the grant agreement. This is another reason why you should read the grant agreement carefully—to make sure it is not making you a trustee of the grant funds.

Governmental Grants

Despite the size of many private foundations and corporations, the greatest amount of grant money still comes from governments, especially the federal government. For example, individual artists can receive up to $10,000 from the National Endowment for the Arts (NEA), and grants to nonprofit art organizations under the Job Training Partnership Act (JTPA) in excess of $100,000 are available. The materials in the bibliography contain a great deal of useful information on government funding. Of particular help is the *1981 Federal Funding Guide,* which lists numerous federal funding programs with simple directions on how to apply.

In the case of governmental grants, your legal rights and obligations are determined in a completely different manner than in the case of private grants. In order for any government to create a grant program, the legislature must pass a bill (technically called the "enabling statute") authorizing the spending of public money for the goals the grant is intended to achieve. The actual grant program is usually run by an administrative agency, such as the NEA for certain federal grants for artistic projects, or the federal Department of Labor and a local administrator for grants under JTPA. These administrative agencies publish their own sets of regulations to assist them in administering the program set out in the statute. Additionally, many general-purpose statutes apply across the board to large classes of government programs, including government grants. Such statutes include the administrative procedure acts, which tell administrative agencies how to operate, the civil rights acts, which foster the governmental policy of non-discrimination, and the labor standards acts, which establish minimum wage and working conditions for government employees. Many of these statutes are also administered by their own administrative agencies with their own regulations. They can all apply to your particular grant program. Your grant agreement, however, will not describe the vast majority of these rules and regulations. Nonetheless, they are the basic source of your rights and obligations under the grant, and if your grant agreement happens to conflict with them, the statutory rules or administrative regulations will control, regardless of what the grant agreement says. Many agencies administering government grants, however, will let you know where to look for the necessary rules and regulations in the grant application, and may even provide you with copies of them.

In the case of government grants, your basic right is to "due process of law." This means that before the government can take any action adversely affecting your rights under the grant, it must give you notice of the complaint against you and a reasonable opportunity to be heard at an impartial hearing. In the vast majority of governmental grants, the grantor has discretion to determine to whom to award grants and in what amounts. In that case, you have no right to a hearing (or funding) if your application is rejected. But it sometimes happens that grantees who meet the established statutory or administrative formulas acquire what is called a "legislative entitlement" to funding, and then the grantor is without discretion to withhold funds from a qualified grantee. If the grantor tries to do so, you have a right to a fair hearing. Once the grant is awarded, of course, you then have a protectable right to the funds, and your "due process" rights to notice and a hearing apply throughout the term of the grant.

To recap, finding the law applicable to your grant is of great practical importance. It will determine whether you have a right to a hearing in case your application is rejected, and the procedures to be used in conducting that hearing. It will establish the criteria which you must meet in administering the grant, the agency, and your remedies against the agency in case it cuts off your funds. Finally, the applicable law can also determine your right to refunding in case of a suspension or after a termination of the grant. Finding the law is often difficult, but it should not be ignored. A very helpful tool is Professor Cappalli's book, *Rights and Remedies under Federal Grants,* in the bibliography.

Specific Government Grant Programs

The Job Training Partnership Act　The Comprehensive Employment and Training Act (CETA), under which so many art agencies waxed fat, has been repealed. It has been replaced by the Job Training Partnership Act, a new law which has enacted not only radical changes in how federal grants are administered but also radical changes in their methods and goals. At the time of this writing, JTPA is too new for more than a few preliminary observations. Additional information should be available from local government officials, or from the National Alliance of Business referred to in the bibliography.

JTPA is another "block grant" program, like CETA. But there the similarities end. CETA was basically administered by the Department of Labor, who disbursed funds to local governmental units, or "prime sponsors." JTPA has funneled many of the DOL's responsibilities under CETA to state governors. They now have responsibility for establishing statewide job training and placement goals and objectives, which are revised every two years. The governor must share his authority with a State Job Training Co-ordinating Council, consisting of a set percentage of local legislators, business leaders and community activists. Once the governor and the Council set the statewide goals, they are very difficult to change until the two-year cycle runs out.

The state delivers JTPA funds to local "Service Delivery Areas," which are one or more local governments. SDAs are somewhat analogous to CETA "prime sponsors." However, each SDA must appoint a Private Industry Council, with which the local governmental body shares program responsibility. Basically, both the local governmental body (i.e., the Board of Supervisors, Board of Aldermen, City Council, etc.) must enter into a compact with the PIC for the administration of JTPA funds. In a new departure for federal legislation, JTPA gives local bodies great leeway in determining how power will be shared, what programs will be funded and who the grant recipients will be. Local bodies may also determine who will administer the grants, although the local PIC is given initial oversight responsibility. For established arts organizations, this new administrative system has been difficult. It means that elected officials no longer have the clout that they once had, forcing arts organizations to establish new lines of communication with the local businessmen, elected officials, labor leaders and community activists that comprise the PIC (although the compact in Los Angeles forbids local grant recipients from lobbying the PIC). On the other hand, it has allowed some new organizations to enter the process.

Another major change in JTPA has been in the type of programs it will fund. Although local agencies are given great latitude in selecting grant recipients, there are limits. Most JTPA funds must be spent on training, mainly for youth, high school dropouts and other hard-core unemployed. Under CETA, arts agencies tended to provide training and placement for artists, many of them highly educated (at least by JTPA standards), who were more underemployed than unemployed. It will be very difficult to shoehorn former arts-oriented educational or on-the-job training programs in under JTPA. JTPA's emphasis on training is backed up by a 15% cap on JTPA-allowed administrative costs, including salaries, and a 30% cap on the total of administrative costs, plus certain work experience expenditures, support services and needs based payments.

Most ominously, JTPA has introduced a new animal into the funding ecology: the performance contract. Under CETA, an agency was funded, for example, to train or place a certain number of people. As long as the agency actually served the designated number, it was considered to have met the grant requirements. Not so under JTPA. It's performance that counts. As the Act says, "Job training is an investment in human capital, not an expense." Return on that investment is measured solely by increased employment and decreased dependency on welfare. Grant recipients will therefore now be measured for grant eligibility based on their performance history. Moreover, although the grant period is for two years, funding may be for a lesser period of time, with continued funding based on meeting performance goals. Finally—and this may be the killer—there have been some attempts to hold grant recipients as organizations, and their officers and directors as individuals, liable for any funds which are spent for projects which do not meet performance goals.

JTPA has therefore dealt at least four body blows to arts organizations. First, it has decreased the importance of local politicians, thus undercutting long-standing relationships. Second, it has shifted the focus of services to the hard-core disadvantaged, who may be better served by training in other areas than aesthetics. Third, it has introduced performance contracts, with strong penalties for failure. And—the fourth blow—there is less money available.

As things shake out, JTPA may have a place for arts organizations, but it will take extra doses of creativity, organization and energy to find it.

National Foundation on the Arts and Humanities   The National Foundation on the Arts and Humanities has three components: the National Endowment for the Arts (NEA), the National Endowment for the Humanities (NEH) and the Federal Council on the Arts and Humanities (FCA). Typically, the NEA funds works of plastic, visual or musical arts, while the NEH funds works of writing or scholarship, although in special cases the NEA will fund research projects. For the visual artist, the NEA is usually the basic funding source.

The NEA is only authorized to assist projects or productions which (1) have substantial artistic merit, or (2) meet professional standards or standards of authenticity and would be otherwise unavailable without support; or (3) would assist artists to achieve a wider distribution of or further standards of excellence for their work. The projects or productions must be done in the United States. All grant applications to the NEA must therefore meet high standards of excellence, and the artist with an established professional portfolio will have a better chance of funding.

The NEA funds a wide variety of projects. Funding will be considered for individual painting, sculptures, films, audiovisual works, and for group exhibits, festivals, galleries, regional media centers and films. A complete list of available grants can be obtained by writing to the NEA or consulting one of the reference works in the bibliography.

The FCA is generally a planning organization for the NEA and the NEH. But, by special statute, the FCA is authorized to enter into indemnity agreements to protect certain works of art displayed in the United States. These essentially work like gallery insurance, and can be favorable. For further information, contact the FCA.

California Arts Council   The California Arts Council was established to promote works of art in the state of California. It is authorized to receive and distribute funds from the NEA, and also has a small operating budget of its own. Further information is available from the CAC in Sacramento.

PART II: NONPROFIT CORPORATIONS

Legal Form of Entity

The choice of the most appropriate form for doing business is one of the most important decisions you will make. Usually, a nonprofit organization is a prerequisite for obtaining funds from governmental agencies or private foundations. The exemption from state and federal taxation may also be a determinative consideration, because then private donations may be tax-deductible to the donor. Although nonprofit tax-exempt organizations may take a variety of legal forms—e.g., unincorporated association, trust, cooperative—we will assume that the advantages of doing business in corporate form outweigh the disadvantages. A further discussion of the advantages and disadvantages of incorporating are discussed in Chapter 13 of this Manual. The materials in this section will help you understand the mechanics of a nonprofit incorporation when you discuss the matter with your lawyer.

The California Nonprofit Corporation Law (NCL) recognizes three types of nonprofit corporations: public benefit, mutual benefit and religious. Public benefit corporations are those formed for charitable or public purposes: e.g., a museum, a private educational institution or a public art gallery. Most arts organizations will be public benefit corporations, so this article will only discuss them. However, many of the same principles will apply to the other types of corporations as well.

Organizing the Corporation

Selection of a Corporate Name   Your first step in organizing your corporation is to select a corporate name, one which is neither likely to mislead the public nor confusingly similar to the name of another corporation. To determine if your proposed name can be used, contact the California Secretary of State, Name-Availability Section (Tel.: (916) 322-2387). If it can, your corporation will be allowed exclusive use of that name when you file your articles of incorporation with the Secretary of State. Your name need not include the words "Inc." or "Corporation." However, you may not use "Bank," "Trust," "Trustee" or related words without the approval of the Superintendent of Banks. You can also reserve your name for up to 60 days by giving a written statement to the Secretary of State and paying a $4.00 fee ($7.00 in Los Angeles).

Preparing and Filing Articles of Incorporation   To bring your corporation into existence you must file articles of incorporation with the California Secretary of State. The NCL sets forth the following minimum mandatory requirements which must be contained in the articles: (1) the corporate name; (2) a required statement of corporate form; (3) a statement of the purpose of the corporation; and (4) the name and address of the initial agent for service of process, who must be a California resident. In the case of a public benefit corporation, the required statement of corporate form is: "This corporation is a nonprofit public benefit corporation and is not organized for the public gain of any person. It is organized under the Nonprofit Public Benefit Corporation Law for (public or charitable) (insert one or both) purposes." If the purposes include "public" purposes, the articles must, and in all other cases they may, include a further description of the corporation's purposes.

If the corporation intends to seek a California or federal tax exemption, the articles must also contain: (1) a clause irrevocably dedicating the assets of the corporation to one or more exempt purposes (as defined by the tax laws) or to another tax-exempt corporation upon dissolution; and (2) a restriction on the scope of activities of the corporation to those permitted tax-exempt organizations (e.g., not devoting more than an insubstantial part of its activities to political lobbying or campaigning). Other optional provisions are permitted.

The articles must be filed with the California Secretary of State either in Los Angeles or in Sacramento. The fee for filing the articles is $15.00 ($22.00 in Los Angeles). If the exemption from franchise taxation has not been previously secured, a $200.00 prepayment of the California franchise tax for the first year of operation must also be paid at the time of filing. This $200.00 fee is refunded upon receipt of the tax exemption from the California Franchise Tax Board.

Corporate Bylaws   The corporation's bylaws are an agreement between the corporation, the board of directors and the members of the corporation with respect to: (i) the rules and regulations for internal governance of the corporation—e.g., the manner of calling and holding meetings of members and directors, and election of members and directors; (ii) the determination of the rights and duties of the members—e.g., property and voting rights; and (iii) the definition of the rights, powers and duties of the officers and the board. The bylaws should be adopted by the board of directors or the incorporators shortly after incorporation.

The only required provision in the bylaws is one stating the number (or range for establishing the number) of directors, unless this is already set forth in the articles. It is advisable, though, that you adopt bylaws to enable the officials involved in the corporation to have a readily accessible guide as to how to take and administer corporate actions. The possibilities for variety as to the composition of the board or membership or limitations on corporate activities are virtually limitless. It is important, however, that bylaws be tailored to particular organizations and not simply copied from an unrelated organization.

Composition of the Board of Directors   The bylaws will generally establish the number, composition and qualifications of the members of the board of directors. Most organizations refer to their governing board members individually as "directors," but some refer to them as "trustees." You are not restricted in titles by which these officials may be described. The board of directors, however, will be the body ultimately responsible for running the corporation.

The NCL does contain restrictions as to the composition of the board. The directors must be natural persons. No more than one-third may hold office by designation or selection as provided in the bylaws (so called "ex officio" directors), as opposed to by election, except in certain circumstances. No more than 49 percent of the directors may be "interested persons"—i.e., persons currently being compensated by the corporation for services rendered to it within the past twelve months and certain relatives of these persons.

Members   Members are those persons or organizations that have the right to vote on the election of directors or the reorganization or dissolution of the corporation. A corporation is not required to have members, and if it does not, the rights and actions otherwise taken by the members are exercised by the board. If there is no compelling reason to have members (e.g., a specific legal requirement or a desire to have representation of a cross section of the public) it is better not to have them. In that way, the board can exercise all of the corporate authority, and corporate actions can be taken with a minimum of corporate bureaucracy. If a corporation does have members, the bylaws will generally set forth requirements for their qualification and admission.

Organizational Actions of the Board of Directors   The corporation must have a properly noticed first meeting of the board of directors, or take the necessary actions by written consent of the board of directors in lieu of a first meeting, signed by all directors then in office. At this meeting, or in the written consent, the officers of the corporation are elected, the corporate seal is adopted (although a seal is no longer statutorily required, many banks still require them to open corporate accounts), the principal executive office of the corporation is designated, the bank account and the signatory power are authorized, the accounting year is adopted and accountants are appointed, and such other general items are discussed or approved as may be required to commence the operation of a particular organization.

After these actions are taken, the corporation is essentially organized, but a few additional statements are required. A Statement by Domestic Nonprofit Corporation (Form S/O 100) must be filed with the Secretary of State, together with a $2.50 filing fee, within three months of the filing of the articles of incorporation. If the Statement is not filed within the three-month period, and thereafter annually within three months of the anniversary of the filing of the articles, a $50.00 fine is imposed on the corporation. If the nonprofit corporation will have employees subject to income tax withholding or social security (FICA), an Application for Employer Identification Number, Form SS-4, must be filed with the IRS no later than the seventh day after the first payment of wages. The corporation must also register with the California Employment Development Department within fifteen days of becoming subject to California income tax withholding (e.g., unemployment or disability insurance). All organizations holding property for charitable (as opposed to public) purposes (see above) must file a Form CT-1 with the California Attorney General pursuant to the Uniform Supervision of Trustees for Charitable Purposes Act within four months after the close of the corporation's first calendar or fiscal year, and within four months of the close of each succeeding year. Finally, any required local business licenses or permits, such as a city business license, must also be secured.

Application for Tax Exemption

To be tax-exempt, a nonprofit corporation must come within one of the provisions of the state and federal law declaring the exemption, and the corporation's purposes and activities can be no broader than those described in statutes. The California tax law is generally patterned after the federal law, and the available exemptions and procedures for filing applications for exempt status are very similar. Similar too is the treatment of what are called "private foundations" and "unrelated business income," matters which are beyond the scope of this article. Refer to tax specialists for an explanation and help.

In California, the exemption application is prepared on Form FTB 3500, which requires certain biographical information about the officers and directors, the proposed budget and the intended operations of the corporation. It is important that the statement of intended operations be carefully drafted. Many organizations encounter problems with their application because the statement is not fairly representative of the intended operations of the corporations. This is where it is helpful to have the advice of an attorney or accountant.

The federal application form is IRS Form 1023. Except in certain cases, all organizations claiming a tax exemption under Section S 501(c)(3) must file this form. The IRS uses this form to issue a "determination letter" recognizing your tax-exempt status. If your application form is filed within fifteen months of the month of incorporation, the exemption will be retroactive to the date of incorporation. If not, the exemption will be for the period after the determination letter is issued.

Both the California and the federal application must be signed by a principal officer or director of the corporation and must be accompanied by conformed copies of the corporation's articles of incorporation and bylaws, which will not be returned. The filing fee for the California exemption application is $10.00; there is no filing fee for the federal application.

The determination letters will be sent directly to you by the California Franchise Tax Board and the IRS. They should be retained in the corporation's minute book or some other place where they can be safely kept and readily found. You will often have occasion to refer to these letters—e.g., to show potential donors or to apply for various local licenses. The determination letters should also be read most carefully. They will explain the various forms which must be filed by the organization and the organization's liability for taxes (e.g., federal social security, unemployment taxes and other matters). The letters should also be reviewed with the corporation's accountant so that the organization may establish whatever books and records are necessary to comply with the reporting requirements.

Operation of the Corporation

The courts and the IRS will carefully scrutinize the operations of the corporation to determine whether proper corporate formality is being observed; if not, the directors and officers may be held personally liable for corporate debts. It is imperative, therefore, that the corporation be treated by the persons associated with it as a separate legal entity, e.g., that it hold regular meetings, that the corporation maintain separate bank accounts and file all required tax and information returns. Thus, it is important that the "corporate housekeeping" items discussed below be taken annually and properly documented.

Corporate Housekeeping As an easy "tickler" system, the annual "corporate housekeeping" matters can be taken care of each year upon receipt of the Statement by Domestic Nonprofit Corporation from the California Secretary of State's office. At that time, the corporation's members, if there are any, should elect the board of directors and ratify certain important acts previously authorized by the board (e.g., ratification of significant purchases, sales or leases; change of the corporation's accountant; change of the principal place of business). If there are no members, the board can do so. The newly elected directors should then elect the corporation's officers, reappoint or appoint a new agent for service of process and ratify certain important acts of the officers not previously approved by the board.

Corporations must keep minutes of proceedings of its board and membership in written form. They are usually kept in a loose-leaf book or binder, but no particular form of book must be used. When preparing minutes, the following practice should be observed. First, identify at the beginning of the minutes not only those persons who were present at the meeting but also those who were absent. Second, state whether or not a quorum was present and acting throughout the meeting and who served as the presiding officer (e.g., chairperson and secretary). Third, as one of the first items of business at each meeting, approve or correct the minutes of the last meeting, if necessary. Finally, indicate the vote count on each matter voted upon by the board or membership (e.g., unanimous approval; 20 for, 10 against, 5 abstentions).

Within 120 days after the close of the corporation's fiscal year, each nonprofit corporation having more than 100 members or $10,000 in assets must prepare and send to its members and directors an annual report setting forth assets and liabilities, changes in fund balances, revenues, receipts and expenses. If the corporation has indemnified any officer, director or agent, or entered into certain transactions involving "interested parties" (directors, officers or holders of more than 10 percent of the corporation's voting power), a description of the transactions must also be included in the annual report.

Directors' Standard of Care   Nonprofit organizations often try to persuade influential members of the community to be directors so that they can advise the organization and help with funding. These directors are sometimes concerned about their liability for their actions as directors, so following is a *very simple* overview of their obligations.

Generally, a director must act in what the director believes in good faith to be in the best interests of the corporation, with such care as an ordinarily prudent person would use in similar circumstances. This means that a director will not be held personally liable for a good faith judgment in conformity with the director's standard of care, even if the judgment turns out later to have been mistaken.

We can briefly expand on this "prudent person" standard. First, the requirement that a director act "in good faith" means that the director act with honesty of purpose and in a manner faithful to the corporation. Second, the requirement that a director act in what the director believes is in the best interests of the corporation relates to the director's *actual* belief rather than what the director ought to have believed. As applied to a public benefit corporation, a director is expected to act in a manner which will accomplish the public or charitable purpose of the corporation. Third, a director must exercise that degree of skill and attention, including reasonable inquiry, which an ordinarily prudent person in a similar position would use under similar circumstances. A director's actions will be judged by a hypothetical standard—the way in which another director in a like position would have acted under similar circumstances—thus preventing the harsher judgment which hindsight permits. Finally, the "prudent person" standard requires a director to make "reasonable inquiry" if the circumstances warrant. This requirement means that a director may not close his or her eyes to what is going on in the management of the corporation's business, if there is reason to suspect a problem.

Conflicts of Interest   Another area of concern for directors involves conflicts of interest. The NCL does not define "conflicts of interest" as such. Instead, it regulates "self-dealing" transactions, "material financial interests" held by a director and contracts between corporations with common directors. "Self-dealing" is defined as a transaction to which a public benefit corporation is a party and in which one or more of its directors has a material financial interest and which does not meet certain fairness tests and approval requirements. A director with such an interest is called an "interested director."

The NCL recognizes that a transaction in which a director has a material financial interest can nevertheless be fair and beneficial to a nonprofit public benefit corporation. However, the law requires that the board of directors make certain findings in approving such a transaction and that an interested director disclose his or her relationship and abstain from voting. Directors must meet the "prudent person" standard in approving a self-dealing transaction, and may incur personal liability to the corporation if they give their approval without observing the necessary formalities.

203

Grant law and nonprofit corporation law can be quite complex. This article only highlights some of the main issues you should be aware of, without discussing them in detail. If you have problems involving grant law or nonprofit corporation law, you should consult an attorney for assistance. If you are still in the planning stage, balance the costs of forming a nonprofit corporation against its benefits. A chance to acquire a lucrative grant can be a good reason to form one, but you should also consider the added administrative costs and inconvenience involved in running your nonprofit corporation. The materials in this article, and those in the bibliography, should help you make an intelligent evaluation of your chances to acquire grant funding and the value of administering those funds in a nonprofit corporation.

GRANTSMANSHIP SELECTED BIBLIOGRAPHY

Balkin, Jan E. (editor). *1981 Federal Funding Guide.* Describes more than 140 federal funding programs, with application instructions. Government Information Services, Inc., 1611 North Kent Street, Suite 508, Arlington, VA 22208.

Beek, Terry-Diane, and Gersumby, Alexis (editors). *The Foundation Center Source Book* (2 vols., Columbia University Press, 1975). An index to major private foundations, published by the Foundation Center in New York. The Foundation Center also publishes a Source Book Profiles series, a loose-leaf series describing funding sources, updated periodically.

Cappalli, Richard B. *Rights and Remedies Under Federal Grants* (B.N.A., 1979). The leading treatise on federal grant law, with an extensive bibliography.

Cultural Post. A bimonthly publication of the NEA carrying information on NEA activities and programs. Superintendent of Documents, U.S. Government Printing Office, Washington, DC 20402.

The Grantsmanship Center News. A bimonthly publication of the Grantsmanship Center in Los Angeles, containing excellent articles on granting sources and nonprofit administration. The Grantsmanship Center, 1031 South Grand Avenue, Los Angeles, CA 90015.

Guide to Programs (1981), National Endowment for the Arts. Describes the programs funded by NEA, with an appendix of regional arts agencies and selected publications. Information Office, National Endowment for the Arts, 7th Floor, West Wing, 2401 E Street, N.W., Washington, DC 20506.

Guide to the Job Training Partnership Act (Nov. 1982). National Alliances of Business, 1015 15th Street, N.W., Washington, DC 20005

McCallum, Tara (editor). *Taft Foundation Reporter* (1980 ed., 2 vols.). An extensive compilation of the major private foundations in the country, describing programs and application procedures, indexed by fields of interest. Taft Corporation, 1025 Vermont Avenue, N.W., Washington, DC 20005.

White, Virginia P. *Grants: How to Find Out About Them and What to Do Next* (Plenum Press, 1975). A good introduction to grantsmanship, including helpful information on grant writing.

Inter-Arts Program	Organization Grant Application Form NEA-3 (Rev.)

**Applications must be submitted in triplicate and mailed to: Grants Office/INTARTS,
National Endowment for the Arts, 2401 E Street, N.W., Washington, D.C. 20506**

I. Applicant Organization (name, address, zip)	II. Category under which support is requested:	III. Period of support requested:

Pasadena Community Arts Center
360 North Arroyo Boulevard
Pasadena, California 91103
	[ ] Presenting Organizations
	  [ ] Grants to Presenting Organizations
	  [ ] Services to Presenting Organizations
	[ ] Artist Colonies
	[X] Interdisciplinary Arts Projects
	[ ] Services to the Field
		Starting 10 1 80
		         month day year
		Ending 9 30 81
		         month day year

IV. Summary of project description (Complete in space provided. DO NOT continue on additional pages.)

The Pasadena Community Arts Center, founded in June 1973 through an NEA planning grant, is committed to: (1) Encourage the development of Visual/Performing artists with high-level professional skills; (2) Meeting the special needs of artists through: Employment, Skill development, Counseling, and Basic Marketing Techniques; (3) To demonstrate the role the Arts play in alleviating such problems.
Since 1977, PCAC has operated a COMMUNITY ARTS ACCESS PROGRAM the purpose of which is to identify/showcase Artist populations traditionally denied access to existing Arts programs. Among those identified were: BIKER ARTISTS. PCAC has co-sponsored 3 "Biker Art" events with the California Modified Motorcycle Association--reaching over 30,000 Los Angeles residents and receiving National/Local media coverage. PCAC proposes a pilot BIKER ART PROGRAM which would: (a) Identify/showcase 500 Biker Artists in both Visual/Performing Arts (State of California currently has 750,000 registered motorcycles); (b) Sponsor (in association with the MMA) two major Biker Art Events reaching 30,500 Los Angeles residents as well as receiving National/Local media coverage; (c) Orientation/Development of "Biker Art" events for both the Midwestern and Eastern regions. Case study would include: (1) identification of various Biker Art forms; (2) list of Biker Visual/Performing Artists; (3) list of California Biker Art Organizations. If awarded, the NEA BIKER ART PROGRAM would provide the community and Biker Artists access to new/innovative Arts programing and rural awareness.

V. Estimated number of persons expected to benefit from this project	30,500

VI. Summary of estimated costs (recapitulation of budget items in Section IX)

                                        Total costs of project (rounded to nearest ten dollars)

A. Direct Costs

Salaries and wages	$48,120
Fringe benefits	8,662
Supplies and materials	3,700
Travel	975
Permanent equipment	
Fees and other	6,330
Total direct costs	$67,787
B. Indirect costs	$ ------
Total project costs	$67,787

VII. Total amount requested from the National Endowment for the Arts $ 26,830

NOTE: This amount added to the total contributions, grants, and revenues from page 3 ($_____) must equal the total project costs in VI. above.

VIII. Organization total fiscal activity

		1980–81		1981–82 est.
A. Expenses	1. $	852,000	2. $	1,150,000
B. Revenues, grants, & contributions	1. $	852,000	2. $	1,150,000

Do not write in this space

[This grant was retyped from the original application for clearer printing].

CHAPTER EIGHTEEN
ISSUES IN ESTATE PLANNING FOR THE ARTIST

Allan B. Cutrow, Esq.

The purpose of this article is to list issues which should be considered by the artist and his or her professional adviser (whether it may be accountant, lawyer, insurance agent, financial planner or any combination thereof) in developing a comprehensive estate plan. Many of the areas covered within this article are of a very technical nature and should be considered and used by the artist *only* after consultation with his or her professional adviser. Notwithstanding this, the issues raised within the article should enable the artist to carefully review the tax and non-tax issues necessary to develop a comprehensive plan for the artist based upon his unique abilities and assets.

USE OF LIFETIME GIFTS

Prior to the Tax Reform Act of 1976, the incentive for making lifetime gifts was the removal of the asset and any subsequent appreciation from the decedent's estate. In addition, while a gift tax may have been imposed, the rates were lower than those for the estate tax. Under the Tax Reform Act of 1976 the rules were changed. Now, gift tax rates are the same as the estate tax rates. Thus, all gifts in excess of those qualifying for the *annual exclusion,* the *marital deduction* and *charitable deduction* will be a part of the estate tax computation at the fair market value on the date of the gift. Internal Revenue Code (hereinafter IRC) 2001(b). All that will be removed from the estate will be any future appreciation in the asset from the date of the gift. Despite this, there are still substantial planning opportunities in making lifetime gifts.

Many gifts may not generate any tax liability. Even if the annual exclusion and marital and charitable deduction are not sufficient to eliminate the gift tax, the unified credit may eliminate any gift tax. The unified credit is a credit against the gift tax on lifetime transfers, and to the extent it is unused at the date of death, a credit against a death tax on property in the estate at death. The amount of the credit and the property which would be sheltered from tax by the exemption increases from 1982 to 1986 and is as follows:

Year	Credit	Equivalent Exempt Property
1981	$ 47,500	$175,000
1982	62,800	225,000
1983	79,300	275,000
1984	96,300	325,000
1985	121,800	400,000
1986	155,800	500,000
1987	192,800	600,000

Below follows a discussion of some effective lifetime giving techniques. These techniques should be considered in light of the amounts that can be transferred during lifetime without tax (because of the unified credit) and without use of the following techniques.

Non-charitable Gifts

Annual Exclusion Gifts of assets worth less than $3,000 ($6,000 if the artist elects to "split" the gift with his wife or is in a community property state) can be made to non-charitable donees. This amount increases after 1981 to $10,000 per donee per year for federal (but not yet for California) purposes. No gift tax will be incurred on the transfer (if it is not in trust) and the gift will not be a part of the computation for the estate tax. Even if the gift is made within 3 years of death, it may be excluded.

Marital Deduction The artist may give works to his spouse. In addition to the annual exclusion, gifts to a spouse will be excluded entirely from the gift tax. This rule is now applicable to community property. IRC S2523. The only problem with this type of gift is that the gift may *create* an estate tax problem if the donee-spouse dies first.

Gifts to Trusts Gifts may provide a vehicle for shifting taxable income away from an artist who is in a high tax bracket to another family member (other than the spouse) in a lower bracket. But the artist will lose the use of the funds generated. Question: Can the artist assign income attributable to his personal services? See *Mark Tobey* 60 T.C. 227 (1973) and *Lucas* v. *Earl* (1930) 281 U.S. 111.

Gifts of artworks in trust may be impractical. Unless there is no prohibition on the sale of the works, the annual exclusion would probably be lost because the works are non-income-producing. However, if the beneficiary could withdraw a portion of the property transferred in the year of transfer, the annual exclusion may be available. See *Crummey* v. *Commissioner,* 297 F.2d 82 (1968). IRC SS2503(b) and 2503(c); *Fred Berzon,* 63 T.C. 601 (1975); but see *Rosen* v. *Comm'r,* 397 F.2d 245 (4th Cir., 1968). If the artworks can be sold, perhaps gifts in trust are a good idea, especially if to children. On the other hand, an alternative may be to have an installment sale to the trust (if property qualifies; see Duffy, *Art Law: Representing Artists, Dealers and Collectors,* Practicing Law Institute,

1977, pp. 190–92), and then allow the trust to sell the works for cash to potential purchasers in the future. See *Rushing* v. *Comm'r,* 441 F.2d 593 (CA-5, 1971). This would avoid the gift tax and enable the artist to realize proceeds in an orderly manner. But see IRC S644, which may cause the transferor to be taxed on the gain on sale if the property is sold within 2 years from the date of interest. See a similar rule under IRC S453 for sales on the installment basis.

Gifts with Retention of Control   Gifts with retained controls such as the right to revoke or to direct enjoyment or use of the property should be avoided. IRC S2036-2038. These gifts will cause inclusion of property in the donor's estate. Transfers in trust with right as trustee to use for the benefit of another where powers are limited (see IRC SS674-675) might work, unless little or no income is generated. However, when works of art are given, gifts may be a sham.

Gifts in Contemplation of Death   Prior to 1982, any transfer of property within 3 years of death (other than gifts qualifying for the annual exclusion) were still a part of the decedent's taxable estate. After 1981, transfers within 3 years of death are not a part of the decedent's estate unless the transfer is of insurance or in connection with prior gifts with retained interests. Therefore, gifts in contemplation of death may be very effective estate-planning tools.

Potential Disadvantages or Problems of Gifts
(a) Gift is irrevocable and there must be a complete parting with dominion and control over the gift.
(b) Increased estate of donee who dies first (where the gift is outright).
(c) Family disharmony.
(d) Gift may not be made in the legally required manner (i.e., forgetting to tell donee).

Charitable Gifts

(1) For income tax purposes, a charitable gift is not very advantageous, as the artist can only deduct the cost of the work. IRC S170(e). Thus, the artist can realize more by selling the work. In addition, prior to sale he can enjoy the work and direct its use.

(2) Charitable gifts do serve an estate-planning purpose by removing the asset from the artist's estate. IRC S2-01(b)(1)(B). There will be no gift tax (IRC S2522), and the transferred property will not enter into the computation of the estate tax.

(3) If the artist could at least direct the enjoyment of the work for a portion of his lifetime, perhaps the loss of the income tax deduction would be more than offset by the estate tax reduction through the removal of some portion of the value of the work at death. A gift of an undivided interest in the work directing that use and enjoyment be exclusive for certain specified times during the year should work. See IRC S170(f)(3)(b); Reg. S1.170A-7(b)(1) and Rev. Ruling 57-293, 1957-2 CB 153. (In this ruling a 25% interest in both title and possession of an art object was transferred by a collector/investor to a museum by deed of gift with the museum having a right to possess the work for the 9-month period. A deduction for 25% of fair market value of the art object was allowed. The rationale of the ruling should apply for exclusion of the property for death tax purposes, as the parties

held the property as tenants in common. Furthermore, the property given away would not enter into the tax computations since a charitable gift is not within the definition of "adjusted taxable gifts.") Where this type of gift is made, the initial possession by the donee should not be for more than one year from the transfer or the deduction may be lost. Reg. 1.170A-5(a)(2). See also Private Letter Ruling 7728046 and "Contribution of Partial Interest to Charity," *Journal of Taxation*, p. 112 (February 1980).

(4) Where a donor or decedent makes a qualified contribution of a copyrightable work of art to a qualified organization, the work of art and its copyright will be treated as separate properties for purposes of the estate and gift tax charitable deduction. Thus, a charitable deduction generally will be allowable for the transfer to charity of a work of art, whether or not the copyright itself is simultaneously transferred to the charitable organization.

A qualified organization is a public charity which is not a private foundation. A qualified contribution is any transfer to a qualified charitable organization provided the use of the property by the organization is related to its charitable purpose or function. This rule is only applicable to gifts made and estates of decedents dying after December 31, 1981.

Sales in Contemplation of Death

The artist taxpayer may wish to sell certain works to others in the family unit. As these items increase in value, the value will accrue to the other members within the family unit and be outside of the artist's estate. What is lost is the income tax that must be paid on disposition of the work. This tax can be avoided if held at death, because of the step-up in tax basis for the artist's heirs. Of course, the tax cost of this basis adjustment is the estate tax paid in the value of the asset in the artist's estate at death. In summary, this method will probably only be beneficial where the artist and his family are willing to bet on substantial future appreciation and the artist is willing to give up control of the work and the proceeds of future appreciation. This technique may not be as useful after 1981, since the gift in contemplation of death rules have changed.

TESTAMENTARY GIFTS—WHO GETS WHAT AND HOW

Are the Artist's Wife and/or Children to Be the Beneficiaries of the Estate? If so . . .

(1) Are they to benefit from the works themselves or the proceeds on sale?

(2) Will the gifts be in trust or outright?

(3) Will the gifts qualify for the marital deduction? After 1981, property left to a surviving spouse in a proper manner will qualify for an unlimited marital deduction. This means that through the marital deduction, a husband and wife can eliminate the federal death tax liability on the death of the first of them to die. IRC SS2056.

(a) If the gifts are outright, yes;

(b) If the gifts are in trust, is the trust drafted to qualify? What will be the effect of non-income-producing property on qualification? See IRC S2056(b)(7) and Treas. Reg. S20.2056(b)-5(f)(4).

(4) Who will manage the estate and trust and what will be the tax and administrative problems arising therefrom?

      (a) Will powers to invade principal have to be limited if the wife is in sole control? IRC S2041(b)(1)(A);

      (b) Flexibility in income distribution may be desired, but if the wife is the sole trustee, tax consequences may be undesirable. IRC S678;

      (c) What is the competency and trustworthiness of the persons selected? Is it consistent with the deceased artist's goals?

Is Charity to Be a Beneficiary of the Artist's Estate?

(1) Reduction of tax liability. IRC S2055.

(2) Is the charity to retain or sell the works? Does the charity have to exhibit the works? Are any of the artists' heirs to participate in these decisions?

(3) Will the charity be a public charity or a private foundation? IRC S509(a). The artist may determine that he wishes to create a new charitable organization to deal with the works. If the new organization is to be structured so that it will qualify under IRC S501(c)(3), the deduction will be allowed. The artist may select the directors or others responsible for management, while also establishing a thought-out plan for management and disposition of the works. The benefit of such a plan is to obtain flexibility for the survivors in control and disposition of the works and a charitable deduction for estate tax purposes, while directing the manner in which these items will be dealt with. The burden is that the new organization will more than likely be a private foundation. The provisions of the Internal Revenue Code provide for stringent rules with respect to the operation of a private foundation (i.e., prohibitions and taxes on self-dealing, failure to distribute income, certain expenditures and certain investments). See IRC SS4940-4946. The taxes to a large extent have a self-liquidating effect on the new organization, especially where works are not sold or contributed but are retained for whatever purpose. See sample language for such a foundation attached hereto as Exhibit A.

(4) In establishing the new charitable organization, the artist and his counsel should consider the consequences of the rules under the Internal Revenue Code regarding the taxation of private foundations. If these rules are not considered, the gift may qualify for the estate tax charitable deduction, but the artist's desires may not be carried out. Some of the rules and their consequences are as follows:

      (a) Taxes imposed on private foundations for failure to make current distributions of income. IRC S4942.

      (b) Excise tax on investment income. IRC S4940.

      (c) Taxes on unrelated trade or business income. IRC S511 *et seq.*

      (d) Taxes on taxable expenditures. IRC S4945.

      (e) Taxes on investments which jeopardize charitable purposes. IRC S4943.

      (f) Taxes on self-dealing. IRC S4941.

Combination of Familial and Charitable Beneficiary

If the artist wishes to provide a stream of income for his spouse, but also wishes to reduce his taxable estate and provide for an orderly scheme of distribution of his works, after 1981 the artist has two choices.

(1) The artist can leave property in a qualified charitable remainder trust. This probably assumes the sale of the works. The artist's wife and/or children will receive a fixed percentage of the value of the trust assets for their lives, and upon their death, property would be distributed to the designated charities. These gifts will generate a charitable deduction (and a marital deduction if the spouse is an income beneficiary) at the artist's death, but may be too restrictive for practical planning in most cases.

(2) A second alternative is to use a "Qualified Terminable Interest Trust"—see IRC S2056(b)(7)—under the new marital deduction rules with charity receiving the property on the spouse's death. Maximum flexibility will exist for income and principal distribution to the surviving spouse while he or she is alive, with a complete marital deduction in the deceased spouse's estate. Furthermore, although the property will be in the surviving spouse's estate at his or her later death, since the property is distributed to charity, a charitable deduction is then available.

In both cases, such a plan contemplates a disposition of the works of art so bequeathed. Without such a disposition, there may be no income or principal to support the surviving spouse. Furthermore, restrictions on disposition will cause loss of the marital and charitable deductions.

PLANNING FOR VALUATION

The first question is whether valuation is the kind of problem in an artist's estate which requires a solution. First, the artist's estate may not be in excess of the amount exempt from federal estate tax. The exempt amounts are:

Year	Amount
1981	$175,000
1982	225,000
1983	275,000
1984	325,000
1985	400,000
1986	500,000
1987	600,000

Second, if the artist is married all of the artist's estate may be exempt from the estate tax after taking into account the marital deduction and community property laws. See IRC SS2523, 2056, 2010. If valuation will be a problem:

A. The artist should keep a detailed record of transactions during his lifetime. It would seem that under the *Smith* case, sales prior to death can be used (rightly or wrongly) to reflect value. The artist's records should also reflect the nature of the works on hand. Are they major or minor works? Are the works interim efforts to achieve major works? Are they works of a kind which do not sell?

B. Realistic plans for marketing the artist's works during life and after death will provide assistance and a basis for valuation of works at the artist's death.

C. An arrangement with a gallery or dealer to purchase all or a portion of the works on hand at death at an appropriate sales price may assist in establishing value, as well as providing liquidity for the artist's estate. *Broderick* v. *Gore,* 224 F.2d 892 (10th Cir. 1955) and *Angela Fiorito,* 33 T.C. 440 (1959).

(1) The agreement should at least be binding upon the artist's estate. If there is only an option on the part of the estate, the agreement may not be completely binding on the IRS, but may only be a "depressing" factor in arriving at valuation. In addition, the price at death must be the same as the price during life. See *Minnie Caplan* 33 TCM 189 (1974).

(2) The agreement must be a bona fide business arrangement and not a sham to pass the works on to the artist's heirs for less than full consideration (i.e., are there other arrangements with the purchaser which might allow this to happen?).

(3) Potential income tax problems must be considered. With an agreement such as this, the sale of the works may be income in respect of a decedent under IRC S691. See *Estate of Peterson* 74 T.C. No. 49.

SELECTION OF ADMINISTRATORS

A. Are the works to be sold
  (1) At once?
  (2) Over time?
B. Are the works to be donated to charity?
C. Are the works to be retained?
D. Is the surviving spouse the primary beneficiary?

PLANNING FOR LIQUIDITY

In addition to the possible disposition of works, other methods of providing liquidity to pay death-related costs should be considered. These costs not only include the artist's federal and state death tax liability, but will include estate administration expenses (including legal and accounting fees), debts of the deceased artist which are due and funeral and last-illness expenses. Funds may also be needed to pay income taxes due upon the sale of works. Finally, liquid funds may be needed to provide for the artist's surviving heirs.

A. Insurance is one source of liquidity. Assuming that the artist obtains insurance coverage in a sufficient amount to provide for after-death needs, will the insurance be a part of the artist's taxable estate? Ways of excluding the insurance proceeds from the decedent's taxable estate should be considered so as to maximize the funds available. See Weinstock, *Planning an Estate* (Shepards, Inc.–McGraw-Hill, 1977, S10.11-10.17) Note that under the new marital deduction provision, ownership of the policy may not be as critical if the surviving spouse is the beneficiary. However, upon the death of the surviving spouse, there may be problems for the then heirs.

B. The artist should consider the establishment of a qualified retirement plan to accumulate funds tax-free to provide for retirement and liquidity on death.

(1) The plan can be a corporate plan where the artist has incorporated his business, or it can be a Keogh (H.R. 10) plan or Individual Retirement Account. In either event, if the proceeds are received in the proper manner, they will not be subject to estate taxation. See IRC S2039(c) and (e). However, this may subject the proceeds to unfavorable income tax consequences.

(2) The taxation of the receipt of such items for income tax purposes will vary depending on the manner in which they are paid out. This should be coordinated with the beneficiaries' tax bracket and the cash needs of the estate.

(3) Considerations:

(a) Is the beneficiary of the proceeds the beneficiary of the balance of the estate?

(b) Does the receipt of the proceeds coordinate with the disposition scheme of the estate plan?

(c) Does the taxation of the proceeds for income and estate tax purposes coordinate with the estate plan. Rev. Ruling 77-157, 1977-19 IRB 23.

(4) For a general discussion of these types of Employee Benefit Plans, see Duffy, *supra*, at pp. 197–200 and 205–7.

WHAT IF THE NON-ARTIST SPOUSE DIES FIRST?

A. Size of Estate

(1) Have gifts to the non-artist spouse created an estate?

(2) If a resident of a community property estate, half of works may automatically be a part of the non-artist spouse's estate.

B. Liquidity—if there is an estate, will tax liability require a disposition of works to raise needed cash? Is this desirable?

(1) May have to consider same devices in plan that you would consider for the artist spouse.

(2) Insurance may be very important.

PROBATE AVOIDANCE

The artist may wish to avoid the cost and delay involved in a formal court-supervised administration of his estate, including the works. Consider the use of a lifetime Revocable Trust.

Advantages

(1) Saving of legal and executor fees. These are normally determined by statute. The statutorily determined fee may exceed the normal hourly rate of the attorney or other person involved in administration. However, not all expenses can be avoided, as some expense or fee will be incurred to deal with estate at death. Furthermore, fees will be incurred at time of creation of trust (during artist's lifetime).

(2) Court-supervised proceedings may delay distribution to the artist's heirs. During administration, obtaining benefits for heirs may be cumbersome and inflexible.

(3) The Revocable Trust is easier than a conservatorship in dealing with possible senility or other incapacity of the artist.

(4) Privacy with respect to artist's plan.

Disadvantages

(1) A court-supervised proceeding provides an immediate and existing forum for resolving disputes among and between heirs and representatives regarding administration.

(2) Cost and inconvenience of maintaining a Revocable Trust during lifetime may make it impractical.

(3) There are several tax disadvantages or traps which must be considered.

(a) Loss of alternate valuation date if division among heirs at death is not postponed for at least six months. Rev. Ruling 73-97, 1973-1 CB 404. Postponement must consider effect on the marital deduction.

(b) May affect deductibility of "administration" expenses for death tax purposes.

(c) Possible loss of deferral available of IRC SS6166 and 6166A (after 1981, no longer applicable).

(d) Use of Flower Bonds—trustee must be directed to redeem.

(e) May lose the income tax benefit of income taxed in the estate (taxpayer). The throwback rules will not apply on distribution to beneficiaries.

USE OF CORPORATION— THE USE OF A CORPORATION BY THE ARTIST AS AN ESTATE PLANNING AND PRESERVATION VEHICLE MAY BE A REAL ALTERNATIVE FOR THE WEALTHIER ARTIST

A. Certain standard benefits of incorporation apply to artist (as well as any other professional). These include:

(1) Use of qualified corporate employee benefit plans.

(2) Use of medical reimbursement and group life insurance.

(3) Note: Make sure that upon formation, stock is issued for property and not services. IRC S351. But see discussion below regarding the *Mark Tobey* case.

B. A more important advantage of the corporation is to provide greater flexibility on disposition during life and at death or an opportunity to "freeze" existing asset value of an artist's estate.

(1) The concept is to establish the corporation with two classes of stock (common and preferred) and make gifts of one class of *stock* among family members, without losing control of specific *works.*

(a) Retention of preferred stock may isolate future appreciation in holders of common stock (heirs?). This may defeat certain goals regarding valuation. Normally, it is difficult to take a discount regarding the valuation of preferred stock with a preference on liquidation.

(b) Sale of stock by heirs normally will generate capital gain. (Problems of sale of stock may be the same as those encountered in a bulk sale of the artworks.) But see IRC S341 regarding collapsible corporations. In general, see Jordan, "How an Artist, Sculptor, Etc., Can Use a Corporation to Maximize His Overall Income," *Estate Planning* (January 1979), p. 40. (This article should be read in light of the repeal of the "carryover" basis rules.)

(2) The artist makes a determination that his or her estate is now of sufficient size such that any future increase in value can accrue to the benefit of his or her heirs. The artist therefore attempts to "freeze" the present value of his or her estate. This might be accomplished by the following scenario: The artist establishes a new corporation with most, if not all, of the stock in the corporation owned by the artist's heirs (in trust or otherwise). The artist enters into an employment contract with the corporation for his services, providing for reasonable compensation and perhaps a qualified employee benefit plan. All future appreciation in the value of the corporate assets (the works of the artist) accrue to the benefit of the corporate shareholders. At the artist's death, since he owns no stock in the corporation, none of the value of the corporate assets are attributable to the artist. As with all plans, this has some limitations and drawbacks.

(a) Does the corporation have cash to adequately compensate the artist?

(b) Is the compensation reasonable in light of the services to the corporation in producing the works? See IRC S482.

(c) Does the corporation have substance and carry on business or is it just a sham with all control resting with the artist?

(d) Will all of the income be "personal holding company" income? See IRC S543(a)(7) and *Thomas C. Byrnes, Inc.* 73 T.C. No. 36 (1979). Is this a problem since the artist is selling "goods" and not services? See *Tobey, supra.*

C. A possible disadvantage may result from the sale of works upon the death of the artist. The artist's heirs will now own stock in the corporation. The disposition of the stock will generate capital gain, and the heirs' basis in the stock inherited from the artist equals the fair market value of the works in the artist's estate.

(1) If the corporation sells the works, the sales will generate ordinary income.

(2) Selling the stock may be difficult because one may not want to purchase all of the shares of stock because this is, in essence, a purchase of all of the works in bulk.

(3) A liquidation by the corporation may not solve the problem, as the works of art may represent rights to ordinary income to the corporation. See *Judd Plumbing* v. *Commissioner,* 153 F.2d 681 (5th Cir. 1946), *Commissioner* v. *Kuckenberg* 62-2 USTC ¶9768 (9th Cir.); and *Schneider* v. *Commissioner,* 65 T.C. 18 (1975).

(4) If the stock in the corporation is part common stock and part preferred stock, and if the artist did not own all of the stock, the sale after death of the corporate stock owned by persons other than the deceased artist prior to death will have a very low tax basis and may generate a substantial capital gain.

D. The use of the corporation may have certain income tax advantages, but may not be the best vehicle to freeze the value of the artist's estate in the manner discussed above. The following is a list of problems that may exist with a corporate restructure and/or upon the formation of a new corporation to freeze asset value:

(1) Concern over IRC S306. Future sale of preferred stock may generate ordinary income. This might not be a problem if left to charity. Death solves this problem.

(2) Concern over IRC S305—deemed distribution—exposure. Depending on character of preferred stock, this could be a major problem.

(3) Ruling request considerations.

(4) Qualification for installment payment tests under IRC SS6166 and S6166A. If too much appreciation in transferred interests, retained assets may not meet percentage tests.

(5) Lack of cash to pay preferred dividends required by preferred stock issuance in a recapitalization.

(6) Double taxation at corporate and individual level.

(7) Possible exposure to asset inclusion under the new "Anti-Byrum" rules of IRC S2036 if voting control is retained by the transferor.

(8) Impact of stock classes on the tax attribute flow-through of Subchapter S. IRC S1371.

(9) Impact of stock classes on ordinary loss status. IRC S1244.

(10) Debt issuance by existing corporation unwise due to dividend exposure. IRC S354(a)(2)(B); Regs. S1.354-1(d), Ex. 3.

(11) In spite of a number of Revenue Rulings and published Private Letter Rulings finding in taxpayer's favor without application of attribution rules, concern exists in mind of some commentators that S306 exposure exists in all preferred stock recapitalizations. Cf. Lowell, "Section 306 Specter Hangs over E Recapitalizations Due to 1976 TRA," 47 *Journal of Taxation* 204 (April 1977).

(12) Valuation of common and preferred stock to be issued.

E. An alternative to the recapitalization might be combination of new corporation with concept of corporate restructuring. Current owners contribute existing stock to new corporation with preferred stock, common voting stock and possibly common non-voting stock. This may at least avoid IRC S306 problem. See 49 *Journal of Taxation* 318 (November 1978) and 50 *Journal of Taxation* 63–64 (January 1979).

F. Another alternative to the use of a corporation is the family partnership. This does not offer the income tax advantages of a corporation. On the other hand, it may be a much more favorable vehicle to take advantage of the concept of the estate freeze.

(1) Advantages:

    (a) Income and loss passed through to partners.

    (b) Avoid complexity of two-tiered corporate tax structure (dividends, unreasonable compensation, personal holding company tax, accumulated earnings problems).

    (c) Generally a more simple vehicle to operate.

    (d) Flexibility in dealing with tax attributes: special allocations, contributions of appreciated property, structuring buy-outs.

(2) Disadvantage: Loss of limited liability for all members (a limited partnership may provide some protection).

(3) Goal:

    (a) Ability to shift income to members in lower tax brackets.

    (b) Retention of control in managing partner (with compensation considered in light of additional desire to shift income), while shifting future appreciation among other members of family group.

(4) Steps necessary to have family partnership respected by IRC S704(e):

    (a) Family partnership will be recognized if each partner owns a capital interest (whether acquired by gift or purchase) where capital is a material income-producing factor. Is this the case with the artist? This may be more of income tax problem if some capital is contributed by heirs. See McKee, Nelson and Whitmire, *Federal Taxation of Partnerships and Partners* ¶14.06, Warren, Gorham & Lamont.

    (b) Income may still be allocated to donor partner to reasonably compensate for his or her efforts.

    (c) Income attributable to the donor cannot exceed pro rata share of income based upon capital interest. In this connection, interest purchased within the family unit is deemed to be a gift.

    (d) IRS can still disregard if the transfer was a sham or donor partner retains such incidences of ownership that he or she will be considered an owner for income tax purposes.

(5) Accomplishing the goal within the IRS guidelines: Is it possible to establish a partnership where donor partner retains control and substantial income flow, with most of capital interests (and future appreciation thereon) in other family members? Here not as concerned with income tax consequences since not really seeking to shift income. More important to remove future appreciation from the taxable estate.

    (a) Control over income and management as managing partner should not affect as long as reasonable fee paid to the managing partner and income that is retained relates to the reasonable needs of the business. In lieu of a management fee, reasonable compensation for production of works accomplishes the same result.

    (b) Where there is no direct gift to partner to provide the initial capital contribution, the estate tax rules will probably not cause inclusion. On the other hand, where the partnership interest is received by a gift, or where the funds to provide the capital contribution of the partners are received by gift, the estate tax rules may bring back some future appreciation into the donor partner's estate. This could be caused by any of the following aspects of the desired partnership arrangement: (i) retention of management powers, (ii) accumulation of income, (iii) use of income for support obligations, (iv) required sale of partnership interest at less than fair market value and (v) a combination of any of the foregoing with any other controls over the vehicle holding the partnership interest (trust or corporation). However, the following may be a basis for not including such interest in the donor partner's estate.

(A) The characteristics of each partner's general partnership interest are such that donor should not be deemed to have retained the right to possess or enjoy the income of the partnership. IRC S2036(a)(1) and *Byrum* v. *U.S.,* 408 U.S. 125 (1975). Furthermore, the donor's control, as managing partner, over partnership property and the stream of income (especially where a sizable management fee is claimed) should not cause inclusion. This is because the managing partner holds these powers, under partnership law, as a fiduciary and can only indirectly regulate the flow of income, subject to these fiduciary powers. IRC S2036(a)(2) and (B). It should also be noted that the managing partner cannot revoke, alter, amend or terminate the interest held by the donee partners, since control of the managing partner, subject to the partnership agreement, is over the partnership assets and not the partnership interest of the donee partner.

(B) If the entire arrangement is in reality a sham with no intent to have substantive partnership interests in one other than the donor partner, IRS under IRC S2033 may have a basis to cause inclusion in the donor's estate. *Commissioner* v. *Culbertson,* 337 U.S. 733 (1949).

(C) Depending upon how soon the donor partner dies after the transfer of property to create the interest in other family members, IRC S2035 may treat the transfer as a gift in contemplation of death.

(D) There may be a gift tax consequence to the creation of the partnership interest in the donee family members. In addition to the obvious problem of payment of a gift tax on the creation of such interest, there may be a real question of valuing the property gifted if the gift is other than cash.

(6) The concept also is applicable with a limited partnership. In fact, because control may be more readily centralized in the hands of the general partner, the limited partnership may be a more desirable vehicle. Since a limited partner is not entitled to management rights, some of the problems discussed above may be less relevant with a validly formed limited partnership. The key aspects may be (i) freedom to assign or otherwise transfer an interest and (ii) the right to distribution from the partnership unrelated to the support of a beneficiary. See IRC Regulation S1.704(e)(2) and Christenson, "Family Limited Partnerships and Their Role in Tax Planning," 117 *Trusts and Estates* 585 (September 1978).

(7) State inheritance tax results may not be the same as federal estate tax results. See *Estate of Huntzinger,* 38 Ca. App.3d 569 (1974).

(8) The family partnership may also provide a vehicle to qualify for the extended payment provisions of IRC S6166 and S6166A.

(9) Use of a Charitable Remainder Trust or other charitable beneficiary as the ultimate recipient of the preferred interests may provide significant tax benefits. The partnership would be established as described above. Some or all of the frozen interest can be donated to a Charitable Remainder Trust by the donor generation partners.

(a) Donor still retains the income interest.

(b) Current charitable deduction is allowed if during life; or if at death, for estate or inheritance tax purposes.

(c) Can also use with a charitable lead trust to shift temporarily the income benefits to charity.

In general see Comment, "The Partnership Capital Freeze: An Examination of Control Retention by Donor Partners," 59 *Nebraska Law Review* 709 (1980). Nash, "Family Partnerships: A Viable Planning Alternative," University of Miami Estate Planning Institute (1979); Stukenberg, "Estate Tax Problems in Retaining Controls of Gifts of Business Interests," 6 *Barristers* (Spring 1979); Abbin, "Partnership Capital Freeze: An Alternative to a Corporate Recapitalization," University of Miami Estate Planning Institute (1979), Ch. 17.

In summary, while the plan may have use in only limited circumstances, in those situations where applicable, it provides a unique tool to allow future growth and control, free of the imposition of taxes at the artist's death. For further comment, see Cooper, "A Voluntary Tax? New Perspectives on Sophisticated Estate Tax Avoidance," 77 *Columbia Law Review* (March 1977).

POSTMORTEM PLANNING

Disposition of Works

(1) Basic rules: The disposition of works would trigger a taxable gain to either the artist's estate or heirs upon the sale of the work. The character of the gain will apparently be capital gain rather than ordinary income. (See Tax Management Memorandum 78-18 8/29/78 and *Jacques Ferber* 22 T.C. 261 (1954) and *George Fullerton*, 22 T.C. 372 (1954).

(2) However, in certain instances the proceeds upon the sale may be income in respect of a decedent (IRD). If so, not only will full value of the work be in the artist's estate, the proceeds would be subject to an income tax, without any adjustment to an income tax basis. IRC S691. This may, in turn, reverse the characterization of proceeds under Section IX. A(1) above as capital gain rather than ordinary income. On the other hand, there are certain deductions available under IRC S691 which minimize to some extent the impact of the section. For instance, deductions in respect of the decedent and incurred to produce such income are allowable as an offset for income tax purposes. See IRC S691(b). Furthermore, there is a deduction allowed for a pro rata share of the incremental estate tax attributable to the inclusion of the IRD in the taxable estate. IRC S691(c). The computation only includes consideration of federal death taxes and not state death taxes. In addition, for items of IRD used to satisfy the marital deduction, the deduction under IRC S691(c) will be lost. The question here is whether works of the artist on hand at death represent income in respect of a decedent.

(a) Income in respect of a decedent is generally defined as an item that the deceased artist had earned at the date of his death and was otherwise entitled to, but had not yet recognized as income because of the artist's method of reporting income. Treas. Reg. S1.691(a)-1(b). This would generally include all payments attributable to personal services, sales and deferred compensation contracts, even though there was no right to payment prior to death. The characterization of the product of the artist's effort may therefore be important. If the paintings on hand are unsold "property," the IRD rules are probably not applicable. On the other hand, if the unsold works represent the result of the artist's personal services, the IRD rules may be applicable, and the subsequent sales proceeds received by the artist's heirs may be ordinary income.

(b) The *Mark Tobey* decision, 223 60 T.C. 227 (1973), may pose a problem in this regard. If proceeds from the sale of an artwork are considered payments for personal services at death, the taxpayer's heirs would not receive any adjustment in basis for the work and would not avoid a tax on a portion of the pre-death appreciation in value upon disposition of the work. Thus, the victory of the living artist in the *Tobey* case may affect the estates of deceased artists. The Tax Court stated that income generated from the sale of work should be treated no differently from that earned by a brain surgeon, movie star or certified public accountant. Therefore, like payments received by the brain surgeon's estate after his death and attributable to the brain surgeon's personal services—clearly IRD under Reg. S1.691(a)-2(b) (Ex. 1) (1960)—proceeds from the sales of an artist's works after death may also be treated as IRD.

(c) However, this should not be the case. The mere fact that the works are on hand does not place them in the same category as most items of IRD. The courts and the Internal Revenue Service do not look solely to the "economic activities" of the taxpayer. Compare Rev. Rul. 60-277, 1960-1 C.B. 262 and *Grill* v. *United States,* 503 F.2d 922 (Ct. Cl. 1962) with Rev. Rul. 57-544, 1957-2 C.B. 361. See also Berghe, "The Artist, the Art Market and the Income Tax," 29 *Tax Law Review* 491, 507–9, *supra* note 28, at 507–9. If further negotiations or activities are necessary to realize the proceeds on sale, the post-death proceeds of sale are not IRD. The courts have held that the proper test is whether the decedent had a right to the proceeds of sale at the time of death. For an excellent discussion of the current status of these rules, see *Estate of Peterson* 74 T.C. No. 49 and "Tax Court Enunciates Four Requirements for Determining Whether a Decedent Possessed the Requisite Right to Sale Proceeds at the Time of Death for Purposes of Section 691," *Estate Planning* (November 1980), p. 362. In summary, these four requirements are:

(i) The decedent must have entered into a legally significant arrangement for the disposition of the subject property so as to elevate the legal right beyond a mere expectancy.

(ii) The decedent must have formed the substantive acts required as conditions to the sale so that the subject matter of the sale was in a deliverable state at the date of the decedent's death.

(iii) Were there any economically material contingencies in existence at the date of the decedent's death which might have disrupted the sale?

(iv) The decedent would have eventually received the proceeds if he lived.

An artist's works usually consist of a group of unique items which the estate will dispose of over a period of time. The personal representative of the deceased artist's estate, or the artist's heirs, are faced with many difficult problems of judgment in attempting to maximize the gains to the estate upon sale of the works. The ability of these persons will have a substantial effect on the proceeds ultimately realized. It may, therefore, be appropriate not to classify the receipts negotiated and realized after death as IRD and to tax only a portion of the appreciation of the artist's work since creation.

(d) Notwithstanding the foregoing, should the works on hand (and not already sold and subject to IRD rules) become subject to classification as IRD, this would add a substantial tax burden to the artist's heirs. The works would receive no step-up in tax basis under present rules and this would place a substantial tax (income) and liquidity burden on the shoulders of the heirs.

Methods of Paying the Tax

(1) The tax is due 9 months after death of artist. IRC SS6018, 6075.

(2) Extensions of time for a reasonable period may be granted by the IRS for up to 12 months. The extension will be granted by the IRS, in its sole discretion, upon a showing of reasonable cause. IRC SS6161. This extension may be up to 10 years if proper application is made and the IRS determines that there is a sufficient reasonable cause. Reasonable cause may include (i) insufficient liquid assets to pay the tax, (ii) the estate includes substantial assets consisting of rights to receive payments in the future, (iii) assets subject to litigation claims or (iv) insufficient funds to pay family allowance and creditors' claims. Reg. S20.6161(a).

(3) There are also certain elections available to the representative of the artist's estate to pay the tax in installments. Under these elections, the tax is paid in installments over a period of time. Each installment will include interest on the outstanding tax liability. IRC SS6166; 6166A.

(a) The basic requirement is that the artist was operating an active trade or business of which the works are a part. If the artist is not held to be in a trade or business, this first requirement will not be met and the election to pay in installments will not be available. See *C. W. Churchman,* 68 T.C. 696 (1977); Rev. Ruling 75-365, C.B. 1972-2, 471; Rev. Ruling 75-366, C.B. 1975-2, 472; and Rev. Ruling 75-367, C.B. 1975-2, 472, for a discussion of trade or business requirements. See also Barcal, "IRS 'Active' Trade or Business Requirement for Estate Tax Deferral: An Analysis," 54 *Journal of Taxation* 52 (January 1981).

(b) One election allows the taxpayer to pay out the tax in ten annual installments. In this event, the works must be 35% of the gross estate or 50% of the taxable estate. IRC S6166A(a). The other election allows the tax to be paid in fifteen annual installments, with the first five installments consisting of interest only. For this election, the works must make up 65% of the artist's adjusted gross estate (the gross estate less all deductions other than the marital and charitable deductions). IRC S6166(a)(1).

(c) Under the ten-year deferred method, interest is computed at the current rate determined by the IRS (presently 12%). This rate is periodically adjusted. Under the fifteen-year deferred method, the interest on the first $345,800 ($1,000,000 worth of assets) of tax liability is limited to 4%, with the normal rate of interest on all amounts of tax in excess of $345,800. IRC SS6621, 6601(j).

(d) Disposition of the works by the heirs while the deferral provisions are operative may accelerate the tax liability to the year of disposition. Under the ten-year deferral, disposition of greater than 50% of the assets which qualified will trigger the acceleration of the tax liability to the year of disposition. IRC S6166(a)(b). With the fifteen-year deferral, a disposition of 33⅓% of the qualified assets will trigger acceleration. IRC S6166(a).

(e) *After 1981,* there is only one set of rules governing estate tax deferral. IRC S6166A (ten-year pay-out) has been deleted and the provisions of IRC S6166 (fifteen-year pay-out) will be modified as follows:

(i) The closely held business need only constitute 35% of the adjusted gross estate.

(ii) Disposition of 50% of the decedent's interest in the estate will accelerate the tax, rather than 35%.

(iii) Death of a transferee will no longer accelerate the tax if the property then passes to another family member (as defined in the code section).

(iv) The amount of tax deferred and subject to interest of only 4% is the difference between $345,000 and the then unified credit.

(f) *Planned lifetime gift giving and planned post-death disposition should take into consideration the possibility of qualification for the deferred pay-out provisions and the effect such transfers will have on these provisions.* This should include a consideration of whether a living Revocable Trust should be created to hold the works to avoid probate administration. Compare IRC S6166(g)(1)(D) with IRC S6166A(h)(1)(D).

Powers of the Legal Representative During Administration

Planning for administration allows the artist's estate to minimize the tax burden on the artist's estate and tax-plan for the beneficiaries.

(1) Giving the personal representative authority to make tax elections and directing how the effects of the elections shall be allocated:

(a) Elections on the final return:

(i) File a joint return with surviving spouse;

(ii) Deduction of medical expenses;

(iii) Redemption of U.S. Treasury Bond interest.

(b) Election of tax year for the estate.

(c) Deduction of administration expenses for income or estate tax purposes.

(d) Electing the alternate valuation date. IRC S2032.

(e) Election to defer paying taxes.

(f) Election to waive executor's fees.

In planning for these elections, consider whether the executor must make adjustments among those who benefit from such elections and those who are harmed by such election. See *Estate of Warms,* 140 N.Y.S. 2nd 169 (Surr. Ct., 1955); *Estate of Bixby,* 140 Cal. App. 2nd 326, 337–339 (1956) and Dobris, "Equitable Adjustments in Post-Mortem Tax Planning: An Unremitting Diet of Worms," 65 *Iowa Law Review* 103 (1979).

(2) Distribution planning: Give the executor the power to make non-pro-rata and in-kind distributions. This gives the executor the ability to fund the material deduction and residual gifts and tax-plan for beneficiaries without triggering a sale for tax purposes of the assets so split. See Calleton, "Non-pro rata Distributions by Estates and Trusts: Problems for the Careful Fiduciary," 109 *Trusts and Estates* 399 (May 1970).

Use of Disclaimers

A disclaimer is a refusal to accept benefits conferred by a will or operation of law. The Tax Reform Act of 1976 provides definitive rules for the effect of a disclaimer for federal estate and gift tax purposes. IRC SS2518 and 2045. If an effective disclaimer is made, the refusal to accept gifts at death will be disregarded for estate or gift tax purposes. The transfer to a successor beneficiary upon disclaimer will not be a gift subject to the gift tax. An effective disclaimer can be helpful in planning the artist's estate in the following situations:

(1) The surviving spouse may choose to disclaim the marital deduction.

(a) To avoid overloading the estate of surviving spouse;

(b) To shift property to satisfy the charitable deduction or pass to the non-marital trust and therefore decrease or otherwise not affect the tax liability of the estate.

(2) Children may disclaim gifts. Upon disclaimer, the works may pass to charity to reduce tax liability. Give children (or any heirs, including the surviving spouse) the opportunity to review the tax consequences at death and reduce tax burden by gifts to charity.

(3) Disclaimer of general powers of appointment gives the beneficiaries a better opportunity to plan their own estates subsequent to death of artist.

EXHIBIT A
ARTICLE SEVEN
ESTABLISHMENT OF TAX EXEMPT FOUNDATION

The residue of the estate shall be held, managed and distributed by the Trustee as hereafter provided: All paintings, sculptures, drawings, watercolors, monotypes, manuscripts, materials, tools, books and slides (the "COLLECTION") shall be distributed to the Directors hereinafter named for the purpose of establishing and incorporating under the laws of the State of California relating to nonprofit corporations, the _____ ARTS FOUNDATION ("FOUNDATION"). The FOUNDATION shall be established and incorporated to qualify as an exempt charitable or educational organization under Internal Revenue Code SS501(c)(3) and 2055 and shall be subject to the following terms and conditions:

1. The FOUNDATION shall be established to promote the visual arts by:

(i) aiding visual artists by the conduct of workshops, sponsorship of public exhibitions and the securing of paying engagements for such visual arts without a fee;

(ii) providing public education about the visual arts;

(iii) providing fellowship grants to young or unknown visual artists;

(iv) making the COLLECTION available for study by artists as a part of their education and training, and encouraging research in relation thereto; and

(v) distributing items from the COLLECTION to charitable organizations described in Section 170(c) of the Internal Revenue Code of 1954, as amended from time to time, as the Directors of the FOUNDATION shall select in their sole discretion.

2. There shall be _____ Directors of the FOUNDATION. The first Directors of the FOUNDATION shall be the surviving spouse, _____ and _____. If any one of the Directors shall fail or cease to so act, the remaining Directors or Director shall designate and select new successor Directors.

3. In stating the objective of the FOUNDATION, I do not intend to limit the purposes and powers of the FOUNDATION or the Directors to aid the visual arts and visual artists, provided, however, that (a) the FOUNDATION shall be organized and operated exclusively for charitable, literary or educational purposes, (b) the FOUNDATION shall not carry on any activities not exempt under Internal Revenue Code of 1954 Section 501(c)(3) or by an organization which can receive contributions deductible under Internal Revenue Code of 1954 Section 170(c)(2), (c) no part of the net earnings thereof shall inure to the benefit of any private shareholder or individual, and (d) no part of the activities thereof shall include the carrying on of propaganda or otherwise attempting to influence legislation. In this connection, I leave the details of the organization and maintenance of the FOUNDATION, and the rules and regulations concerning its activities, to the judgment of the Directors.

4. If, for any reason, the Directors are unable to cause the FOUNDATION to qualify as a charitable or educational organization described in Sections 501(c)(3) and 2055 of the Internal Revenue Code of 1954, as from time to time amended, the remaining portion of the COLLECTION shall be distributed to those charitable organizations which are described in Section 2055 of the Internal Revenue Code of 1954, as from time to time amended, as the Directors shall select in their discretion.

PART FIVE

PRACTICAL SAFEGUARDS FOR THE ARTIST, THE WORK AND THE STUDIO

CHAPTER NINETEEN

ARTIST'S STUDIO—BEWARE! HEALTH HAZARDS IN THE VISUAL ARTIST'S WORKING ENVIRONMENT

Shari Friedman

Almost 300 years ago, an artist complained to his doctor about paralysis in his fingers and hands, which eventually spread to his arms and feet. Then violent stomach pains began, and the patient did not respond to treatment. In searching for the cause of the mysterious ailment, the doctor focused on the painter's habit of wetting his paintbrush with his tongue and using his fingers to squeeze paint from the brush. The physician was Bernardino Ramazzini, the father of Occupational Medicine. He theorized that the violent stomach pains were caused by the artist's swallowing cinnabar, a red mercuric sulfide pigment—vermilion.

Although this puzzling medical case was recorded in the 17th Century, a modern-day artist might very well suffer from symptoms caused by the supplies he or she uses, particularly if the artist is not aware of the potential dangers lurking in the chemicals they use.

—Testimony of Congressman Fred Richmond before the House Committee on Interstate and Foreign Commerce and Finance Hearings on H.R. 6977, Washington, DC, September 17, 1980.

One area of growing concern to legislators, manufacturers and visual artists which has drawn increasing publicity in recent years is the vulnerability to health hazards prevalent among members of the art community. It is estimated that 56 million Americans use art and craft materials professionally or as students and hobbyists. What is now known fact is that these art and craft materials contain harmful chemicals which have caused serious, if not chronic, long-term damage to the user. Unfortunately, the labels on these materials do not inform the user on how best to protect against specific hazards.

The majority of visual artists are not aware that they are susceptible to the same kinds of exposure to dangerous chemical substances as those engaged in the industrial trades. The Occupational Safety and Health Administration (OSHA) rules and the Federal Hazardous Substances Act (FHSA) do not afford the visual artist adequate protection against the materials he or she may use or provide education on their use. OSHA rules do not apply to the visual artist engaged in individual enterprise and FHSA only addresses art materials that cause acute health problems.

Nor do visual artists receive recognition from the Consumer Product Safety Commission. For example, the amount of lead in artists' paints is not regulated by the Commission because these are considered "professional" and not "consumer" materials. As we know, lead content in many consumer goods is heavily regulated to avoid the horrors of neurological damage and mental impairment.

The visual artist is in a catch-22 situation since he/she also uses large quantities of "consumer" art materials which can be as lethal as professional materials, since they are not subject to adequate governmental regulation as to labeling of ingredients, health hazard warnings and proper usage. Labeling requirements as to long-term effects are not deemed necessary in these consumer products because the majority of art and craft supply manufacturers gear their product to the hobbyist or occasional user. This type of consumer does not have long-term exposure to the chemical substances contained in these products, and hence such labeling is viewed as unnecessary by the manufacturers.

Over three and a half years ago Congressman Fred Richmond, of the 14th District of New York, began studying the toxicity of artists' supplies. As a result of his study, he has proposed a bill (H.R. 443, formerly H.R. 6977, Chronic Hazards Labeling Act) (see reprint in Appendix 1 of this article) which would amend FHSA to include "chronic toxicity" under the definition of hazardous substances. In addition, H.R. 443 would provide the Consumer Product Safety Commission with the authority to issue regulations concerning substances that cause chronic illnesses.

The bill mandates, according to Congressman Richmond, that each product containing potentially harmful chemicals have a label clearly stating five pieces of information:

(1) The common name of each chemical found in the product;

(2) The potential hazards associated with misuse of these chemicals;

(3) How to avoid these health hazards;

(4) The antidotes to the health hazards; and

(5) How to dispose of the product safely.

Although art supply manufacturers may deem this a drastic government regulation, the mounting number of work-related injuries plaguing visual artists has necessitated this form of government action.

Barry Nickelsberg, Special Assistant for the Arts to Congressman Richmond since 1976, has stated that visual artists have suffered severe work-related illnesses.[1] The following are case histories of several artists exemplifying the common "professional" use of art and craft supplies.

G. Kaye Holden

Mr. Holden was a professional artist for nineteen years, during which time he had daily contact with oil paints, turpentine and mineral spirits for cleaning brushes. Gradually, over the years, Holden experienced increasing physical deterioration, which worsened to the point that he could no longer work and culminated in the loss of a kidney.

Holden contacted Dr. Theodore Ehrenreich, a kidney specialist, who had done research on the special relationship between solvents (including the solvent artists used when working with oil paints) and kidney disease. The hydrocarbons in petroleum spirits, solvents and paint thinners, when inhaled over a period of time, can cause kidney failure.

Holden was too late. By the time he received this information he had advanced kidney

[1] Telephone interview with Barry Nickelsberg, August 10, 1981.

failure. In 1977, at the age of forty-four, Holden received a kidney transplant. He then had to retrain himself and underwent a two-year process of learning to work with acrylics.

At one of the hearings on Congressman Richmond's bill, Holden testified that had he known in his early days as an art student that oil paint or paint thinner could possibly cause kidney failure, he would have protected himself more thoroughly, would have learned to work with other materials or not have become an artist at all.

Bruce Beasley

Mr. Beasley was a sculptor who used arsenic compounds to color aluminum sculptures. Over a period of about two years, Beasley began to lose his eyesight and was left almost blind. He consulted a pathologist, who came to Beasley's studio to examine the work surroundings. Ultimately, the pathologist suggested he stop using the arsenic compounds. He did and his eyesight was restored.

These are just two examples of the "chronic" illnesses that affect visual artists. Usually, the early symptoms of work-related problems are difficult to diagnose or are misdiagnosed. Common early symptoms can be manifested by depression, fatigue and headache. These symptoms have ultimately resulted in visual artists being afflicted with: chronic lead poisoning, toxic neuropathy (nerve damage), cancer of the chest cavity caused by exposure to asbestos, chemical pneumonia, mercury poisoning, asthma, blindness, kidney failure, aplastic anemia, nasal sinus cancer, miscarriages, heart attacks, permanent lung scarring and skin diseases.

Long-term use of art and craft materials has resulted in many cancer victims: Henry Bertoria, a metal sculptor, worked with copper and beryllium alloys for twenty years, and died of cancer in 1980 at the age of sixty-five; Eva Hesse died of brain cancer at the age of thirty-four—she worked with polyester resins and acrylics; Wilfried Zogbaum, a metal sculptor, died of leukemia at the age of fifty, after using spray lacquer which was contaminated with benzene.

Erica Barton: A Case History of Toxic Neuropathy[2]

Ms. Barton was trained as an easel painter. She began her art training at the age of thirteen and thereafter worked at mural art, architectural artwork, painting on fabrics, wall hangings, banners and painting silk materials for dresses. Through the years Barton perfected a technique working with masking for airbrushings. She used spray adhesives to affix maskings to fabrics and worked with this technique almost daily over a five-year period.

Barton began developing symptoms of fatigue, weakness, depression and falls. Suddenly, her feet became numb. The results of the tests performed by an internist were inconclusive and she was sent to a neurologist, who hospitalized her for more tests which screened for diseases from tumors of the spine to degenerative nerve disease. After fourteen painful and traumatic days of testing, no one was able to diagnose her problem.

Several weeks following the first fourteen-day barrage of tests, Barton saw a neurologist who had read about diseases afflicting industrial workers. These workers had sustained central and

[2] Telephone interview with Erica Barton, September 10, 1981.

peripheral nerve damage from exposure to chemical substances similar to those Barton used in her studio. Barton was retested in line with that theory and then definitely diagnosed as having nerve damage caused by exposure to toxic chemicals (toxic neuropathy). Toxic neuropathy occurs when one inhales fragments of certain materials. These fragments destroy the nerves. The solvent in the spray adhesives Barton was using consisted of a chemical called N-hexane, which kept the glue particles in suspension. N-hexane was the material believed to be the cause of Barton's nerve damage. Spray adhesive products containing N-hexane are available in art supply and hardware stores.

There is no treatment for toxic neuropathy. Barton's only recourse was to abstain from practicing her profession for two years in order to let the damaged nerves regenerate. Today, Barton still does not have normal strength and physical dexterity.

Most disturbing in Barton's case is that her studio was equipped with an exhaust-fan system. Nevertheless, long-term consistent exposure to the spray adhesives caused her to become highly sensitized to N-hexane, thus negating any safety precautions.

Erica Barton is one of the few visual artists who has sought legal redress. Barton contacted the law firm of Richard Frank, P.C., in New York City, and filed a lawsuit against the manufacturers of the spray adhesives for improper and inadequate labeling of their products. Robert Marcus, the attorney who handled her lawsuit, recently concluded a settlement of her claim with two manufacturers for a six-figure amount.

According to Marcus,[3] there were several inherent difficulties in prosecuting the lawsuit. First, the problem of enterprise liability. How do you prove which company's product caused the injuries when the injured party has used a product manufactured by different companies? Second, what is the standard of exposure? There are no general standards governing chronic exposure to chemicals outside the industrial setting. According to Marcus, "this is a result of the basic presumption on the part of manufacturers that their products are bought by the occasional user. Ignored by the manufacturers are the regularly working artists, photographers and handymen who use their products on a chronic basis." Marcus likened the Barton case to the black-lung disease cases. "One-time exposure to N-hexane is not dangerous, just as one-time exposure to asbestos won't cause lung disease. But systematic exposure to these substances is dangerous."

As Marcus stated, "Barton's situation is a classic example of inadequate labeling of a consumer product. The spray adhesives, as with most aerosol products, contain warnings of flame hazards but have minimal warnings regarding inhaling and general advice to use in a well-ventilated area." Marcus was of the opinion that many people have different conceptions of what a well-ventilated area means. Circulating fans, for example, only enhance the dangers of exposure to N-hexane and exhaust-fan systems like Barton's do not afford adequate ventilation. Users of spray adhesives should have been cautioned to wear filter masks similar to those now used by asbestos industry workers coupled with an industrial exhaust-hood system.

The most tragic loss for Barton, according to Marcus, is that she "has lost her gift of creating. An artist lives for and by art. When that is taken away the effects are catastrophic."

[3] Telephone interview with Robert Marcus, September 10, 1981.

DEALING WITH THE PROBLEM

Concurrent with the important efforts undertaken by Congressman Fred Richmond (see Appendices 1 and 2 for charts and reprint of Bill H.R. 443) there is now under way voluntary action concerning labeling of artists' supplies.

The American Society for Testing and Materials (ASTM) has already drafted proposed practices for labeling art materials for chronic hazards. ASTM is a nonprofit corporation for the development of standards on characteristics and performances of materials, products, systems and services, and the promotion of related knowledge. The ASTM standards are developed by those having expertise in specific areas, including producers, users, ultimate consumers and representatives of government and academia.

Congressman Fred Richmond, concerned about the need to address the problem of chronic toxicity and aware of the difficulties of further government regulation, forcefully urged manufacturers to act. Last fall some leading companies organized themselves into a Manufacturers Council and began a series of meetings with representatives of artists' organizations, toxicologists and industry hygienists. These companies have agreed to the precedent-setting program described below.

The new ASTM voluntary standard will require manufacturers to submit the percentage of all substances in their products to an industrial toxicologist who, after taking into consideration all government guidelines and the best current scientific information, will tell them which products must carry warning labels and exactly what the wording will be. These warnings have been coordinated with the Consumer Product Safety Commission.

These companies have also agreed to fund an institute which will hire the toxicologist and pay the costs of buying products each year off-the-shelf and analyzing them to make certain they contain the ingredients stated in the formulas. The institute's certifying committee will include artists' representatives and there will be a technical committee composed of the company chemists and, again, artists' representatives. Artists, and those they choose to represent them, will have direct input into decisions.

It is also important that the toxicologist, who is a medical doctor, consult regularly with company chemists who know the reason for, and form of, each ingredient. The toxicologist will consider possible interaction between different ingredients and even whether there might be increased hazard from combination with other products which may be used at the same time. As a further safeguard, the decisions of the institute toxicologist will be reviewed periodically by a panel of eminent toxicologists.

This arrangement provides flexibility and access to pertinent information which could never exist in a government program. Still another advantage to the voluntary program is that a separate standard for quality can also be administered by the certifying institute. Many paints today do not properly identify the pigments they contain and current lightfastness tests indicate that some pigments which will fade in a short time are being used in some major paint lines.

In addition to the standard and institute, this group of manufacturers have agreed to put details of their product formulations into Poisondex for distribution to local poison control centers. Grumbacher, Winsor & Newton and Binney & Smith have already begun sending information into Poisondex and other companies, including Hunt Mfg. Co. and Graphic Chemical and Ink, will follow as fast as Poisondex can handle the information. Since it will take eighteen months for new labels to appear on retail shelves, these companies wanted to demonstrate that they are not dragging their feet.[4]

This article has been written as an encouragement for the artist to examine his or her working environment. In all probability a casual inventory will include rubber cement, turpentine, thinners, colors, finishes, inks, clay and various sprays. When the perusal is completed, reference should be made to the chart in Appendix 2, which we believe speaks for itself.

[4] Joy Turner Luke, "The Case for Voluntary Labeling for Chronic Toxicity," copyright 1981, Joy Turner Luke.

APPENDIX 1

Congressional Record

United States
of America

PROCEEDINGS AND DEBATES OF THE 97th CONGRESS, FIRST SESSION

Vol. 127   WASHINGTON, THURSDAY, FEBRUARY 19, 1981   *No. 26*

House of Representatives

TOXICITY OF ARTISTS' SUPPLIES

HON. FREDERICK W. RICHMOND
OF NEW YORK

IN THE HOUSE OF REPRESENTATIVES

Thursday, February 19, 1981

Mr. RICHMOND. Mr. Speaker, 3 years ago, I began an investigation into the toxicity of artists' supplies after receiving letters from several artists who had developed serious, chronic illnesses while working with their art materials. Because of the lack of information in the labels of artists' supplies, these artists had no way of knowing the potential hazards of using these materials, or the proper precautionary measures to take to avoid misuse.

As I explored the problem further, I discovered that hundreds of artists and hobbyists are suffering from a number of illnesses, such as permanent nerve damage, liver and kidney damage, lung disease and miscarriages, as a result of their exposure to toxic art supplies. Conclusive evidence of the connection between the art materials and resulting illnesses was provided by research conducted by Battelle Laboratories of Ohio.

. To provide my colleagues with an idea of the scope of this problem, I have prepared a list to show a few of the professions which routinely use hazardous chemicals and the health-related problems associated with various degrees of use of the chemicals:

PAINTING

Cadmium Vermilion Red (Pigment Red 113) may cause mercury poisoning, which can severely damage the nervous system and kidneys.

Flake White (cremnitz white, white lead, Pigment White 1) may cause lead poisoning and birth defects, including mutations, through ingestion.

Turpentine (gum turpentine, gum spirits, spirits of turpentine, wood turpentine, steam-distilled turpentine) can cause skin irritation and allergies, sometimes years after exposure. Accidental entry into lungs through ingestion is common and can cause fatal pulmonary edema.

PRINTING

Chrome Yellow (lead chromate, Pigment Yellow 34) may lead to skin irritation, allergies and ulcers through direct contact. Chronic inhalation may cause lead poisoning and lung cancer. Ingestion may cause immediate chromium poisoning (Gastroenteritis, vertigo, muscle cramps and kidney damage).

Carbolic Acid (Phenol) may cause nervous system depression and liver, kidney and spleen damage with a single exposure. Direct skin contact can be fatal.

Toluene (Toluol, aromatic naptha) may cause menstrual disorders, skin defatting, narcosis and possible chronic liver and kidney damage. Inhalation of large amounts may cause heart sensitization and death.

CERAMICS, GLASSBLOWING, AND ENAMELING

Arsenic Oxide (used in glassblowing) can lead to skin ulceration and skin cancer through direct contact. Inhalation or ingestion may cause lung cancer, liver damage, permanent nerve damage, and kidney and blood damage.

Clays may cause silicosis, a disease involving severe lung scarring, through inhalation of clay dust.

Fluorspar (Fluorite, calcium fluoride, used in ceramics) may cause lung irritation, bone and teeth defects, and anemia through inhalation or ingestion.

Manganese Carbonate (used in enameling) can cause a serious nervous system disease resembling Parkinson's Disease.

SCULPTURE

Cedar Wood Dust (Western Red) can lead to severe skin allergies, asthma, bronchitis and conjunctivitis.

Methyl Ethyl Ketone (a peroxide hardener used with polyester resin) can cause immediate and permanent blindness upon contact with eyes.

Sandstone may cause silicosis through inhalation.

METALWORKING PROCESSES

Bronze often causes metal fume fever (chills, fever) through inhalation. May cause lead poisoning.

Lead may cause lead poisoning, affecting the gastrointestinal system (lead colic); red blood cells (anemia); and neuromuscular system (weakening of wrists, fingers, ankles, toes). May also cause liver and kidney damage and possible birth defects.

PHOTOGRAPHY AND PHOTOPROCESSES

Acetic Acid can cause severe skin corrosion and chronic bronchitis.

Catechin (catechol, pyrocatechol, o-dihydroxybenzene) can cause acute poisoning with symptoms of cyanosis (blue lips/nails), convulsions and anemia, through inhalation.

Tertiary-Butylamine Borane can cause nervous system damage.

CRAFTS

Oxalic Acid (used in fabric dying) can lead to severe skin corrosion, ulcers and gangrene through skin contact.

Ortho-Dichlorobenzene (used in leathercraft) causes narcosis, and possible hepatitis and kidney damage.

Zinc Chloride (used in stained-glassmaking) may cause chronic bronchitis through chronic exposure or pulmonary edema through large acute exposures.

Over the past 3 years, innumerable articles on this subject have appeared in the New York Times, the Los Angeles Times, the Washington Post, as well as regional and local papers throughout the country. Art Hazards News, Art Workers News, Ocular magazine for visual artists, and a host of

other trade papers have started regular series on this vital subject. One of the country's leading experts in the field, Dr. Michael McCann, has recently published a 378-page book entitled "Artist Beware" that explains in detail the dangers involved with the misuse of hundreds of artists products and chemicals.

In order to rectify this situation, which threatens the health and safety of the 36 million Americans who use art materials in the studio, the home, and the classroom, I introduced legislation that would require more comprehensive labeling information on artist supplies.

This legislation would require that the labels of potentially toxic artists' materials contain five pieces of information necessary to protect the consumer: a list of the common names of the chemicals contained in the product; the health hazards associated with misuse of the product; preventatiye measures to take to avoid misuse; measures to take in case illness occurs; and methods to safely dispose of the product.

In September 1980, our colleague, JIM SCHEUER, chairman of the House Subcommittee on Consumer Protection and Finance, held hearings on this legislation. During those hearings, testimony was given by artists and their physicians, toxicologists, artists' advocates and representatives from the art materials industry. At the conclusion of the testimony, Mr. SCHEUER suggested that, due to the serious consumer health risks created by the current situation, an appropriate resolution to the problem would be a cooperative effort between artists and industry representatives to draw up voluntary labeling standards for the art materials industry.

This discussion process has already begun, and I am happy to say that the art supply manufacturers have been very helpful and cooperative in attempting to work out a solution to our common problem.

Although I am reintroducing legislation that would set Federal standards for the labeling of art supplies, I am hopeful that more comprehensive labeling can be accomplished quickly through self-regulation of the industry. If industry self-regulation proves impossible, I believe it is the responsibility of Congress to recognize and address this issue that affects so many millions of Americans. I will continue to keep my colleagues up to date on this issue and will be happy to answer any questions they may have.

A summary of the legislation follows:

SECTION 1. Amends the Federal Hazardous Substances Act (FHSA) to include "chronic toxicity" under the definition of hazardous substances. This section also provides the Consumer Product Safety Commission with the authority to issue regulations concerning substances that cause chronic illnesses.

SECTION 2. Defines the term "chronic toxicity" as any substance which causes tumors or cancer, has an adverse reproductive or genetic effect, has an adverse effect on the central nervous system or peripheral nervous system, or any other chronic effects as determined by the Commission. The section goes on to add the word "chronic" to the term "toxic."

SECTION 3. Mandates that all labels of products containing substances that cause chronic or acute illness have: (a) a description of the physical side effects that could result from the misuse of the product; (b) a description of how to counteract the possible physical side effects resulting from misuse of the product; (c) a description of the proper precautionary measures to avoid misuse; and, (d) instructions for safely disposing of the product. Substances which may be carcinogenic must carry the following: Warning: Has Been Shown To Cause Cancer in Animals.

SECTION 4. Includes technical amendments to the FHSA and mandates that all labels of products containing substances that cause either chronic or acute illness provide instructions for procedures to counteract possible health side effects.

SECTION 5. Allows the Consumer Product Safety Commission two years to issue appropriate regulations under this Act.

The complete text of this bill follows:

H.R. 443

A bill to amend the Federal Hazardous Substances Act to establish labeling requirements applicable to substances which cause chronic health side effects, and for other purposes

Be it enacted by the Senate and House of Representatives of the United States of America in Congress assembled, That section 2(f)(1) of the Federal Hazardous Substances Act (15 U.S.C. 1261(f)(1)) is amended by adding at the end thereof the following new clauses:

"(E)(i) Any substance or mixture of substances which possesses chronic toxicity (as defined in paragraph (g)(2)(A)), if such substance or mixture is capable of being ingested, inhaled, or absorbed into the human body through any customary or reasonably foreseeable handling, use, or misuse (including any reasonably foreseeable handling, use, or misuse by children).

"(ii) The Consumer Product Safety Commission shall have the authority to issue regulations, in accordance with the procedures prescribed in section 553 of title 5, United States Code, which provide that any particular substance or mixture of substances shall not be classified as a hazardous substance under subclause (i) if the Commission determines that such substance or mixture does not present any risk to humans if such substance or mixture is ingested, inhaled, or absorbed into the human body through any customary or reasonably foreseeable handling, use, or misuse (including any reasonably foreseeable handling, use, or misuse by children).

"(F) Any substance or mixture of substances which the Consumer Product Safety Commission determines, in accordance with the procedures prescribed in section 553 of title 5, United States Code, or in accordance with the procedures established in section 3(a), to possess chronic toxicity (as defined in clause (B), clause (C), or clause (D) of paragraph (g)(2)), except that a substance or mixture shall not be considered to be a hazardous substance under this clause unless such substance or mixture is capable of being ingested, inhaled, or absorbed into the human body through any customary or reasonably foreseeable handling, use, or misuse (including any reasonably foreseeable handling, use, or misuse by children).

"(G) Any substance or mixture of substances which—

"(i) possesses chronic toxicity, as defined in subclause (A), subclause (B), or subclause (C) of paragraph (g)(2), or as determined under subclause (D) of paragraph (g)(2); and

"(ii) is present as a contaminant in any household substance or mixture of household substances;

if the Consumer Product Safety Commission determines, in accordance with the procedures prescribed in section 553 of title 5, United States Code, or in accordance with the procedures established in section 3(a), that such substance or mixture is capable of being ingested, inhaled, or absorbed into the human body through any customary or reasonably foreseeable handling, use, or misuse (including any reasonably foreseeable handling, use, or misuse by children).".

SEC. 2. Section 2(g) of the Federal Hazardous Substances Act (15 U.S.C. 1261(g)) is amended—

(1) by inserting "(1)" after the paragraph designation;

(2) by inserting ", and to any substance which possesses chronic toxicity" after "body surface", and

(3) by adding at the end thereof the following new subparagraph:

"(2) For purposes of this paragraph, substances which possess chronic toxicity include the following:

"(A) Any substance which causes tumors or cancer (or which is metabolized to a substance which causes tumors or cancer) in humans or other mammals, including—

"(i) any substance which—

"(I) the Secretary of Health and Human Services (or the head of any bureau, administration, or other organization unit in the Department of Health and Human Services) or

"(II) the International Agency for Research on Cancer;

reviews and determines to cause tumors or cancer in humans or other mammals, if any such determination is based upon valid studies and procedures; and

"(ii) any substance which is regulated by the Environmental Protection Agency, the Food and Drug Administration, or the Occupational Safety and Health Administration as the result of a determination that such substance causes tumors or cancer in humans or other mammals, if any such determination is based upon valid studies and procedures.

"(B)(i) Any substance which causes any adverse reproductive effect or any adverse genetic effect.

"(ii) For purposes of this clause, adverse reproductive effects and adverse genetic effects include any birth defect, toxicity to a fetus, sterility or impaired reproductive capacity, spontaneous abortion, any mutagenic effect, and any damage to genetic material.

"(iii) Any determination of the Consumer Product Safety Commission that a substance causes any adverse reproductive effect or any adverse genetic effect shall be based upon valid studies and procedures. Such studies and procedures may include the use of human subjects, experimental animals, micro-organisms, culture cells, or other test systems.

"(C)(i) Any substance which causes any adverse effect upon the central nervous system or any peripheral nervous system.

"(ii) any determination of the Consumer Product Safety Commission that a substance causes any adverse effect upon the central nervous system or any peripheral nervous system shall be based upon valid studies and procedures. Such studies and procedures may include the use of human subjects, experimental animals, or other test systems.

"(D) Any substance which the Consumer Product Safety Commission determines (in accordance with the procedures prescribed in section 553 of title 5, United States Code, or in accordance with the procedures established in section 3(a)) to possess any form of chronic toxicity, other than those forms of chronic toxicity specified in clause (A), clause (B), or clause (C), if such substance or mixture is capable of being ingested, inhaled, or absorbed into the human body through any customary or reasonably foreseeable handling, use, or misuse (including any reasonably foreseeable handling, use, or misuse by children).".

SEC. 3. Section 2(p) of the Federal Hazardous Substances Act (15 U.S.C. 1261(p)) is amended—

(1) in subparagraph (1) thereof—

(A) by inserting ", in the case of any substance other than any substance or mixture of substances which is defined as a hazardous substance under clause (E) or clause (G) of paragraph (f)(1) and other than any substance which possesses chronic toxicity (as defined in paragraph (g)(2)(A))," after "(1) which"; and

(B) by adding at the end thereof the following: "(K) in the case of any hazardous substance which causes any physical side effect, a statement which describes the nature of such side effect and explains procedures which may be followed to counteract such side effect;";

(2) in subparagraph (1)(I) thereof—

(A) by striking out "and storage" and inserting in lieu thereof ", storage, and disposal"; and

(B) by striking out "or storage; and" and inserting in lieu thereof ", storage, or disposal;"; and

(3) by redesignating subparagraph (2) as subparagraph (3), and by inserting after subparagraph (1) the following new subparagraph:

"(2) which, in the case of any substance or mixture of substances which is defined as a hazardous substance under clause (E) or clause (G) of paragraph (f)(1) and which possesses chronic toxicity (as defined in paragraph (g)(2)(A)), states conspicuously (A) the information required in clause (A), clause (B), and clause (I) of subparagraph (1); (B) the phrase 'Warning: Has Been Shown To Cause Cancer in Animals' on any substance which has been determined to possess chronic toxicity (as defined in paragraph (g)(2)(A)), based upon any valid study or procedure using experimental animals; (C) the phrase 'Warning: Has Been Shown To Cause Cancer in Humans' on any substance which has been determined to possess chronic toxicity (as defined in paragraph (g)(2)(A)), based upon any valid study or procedure using human subjects; and (D) precautionary measures which describe actions to be followed and actions to be avoided in connection with any use of the substance; and".

SEC. 4. Section 20(a)(1)(A) of the Federal Hazardous Substances Act (15 U.S.C. 1275(a)(1)(A)) is amended—

(1) by inserting ", 2(p)(2)," after "sections 2(p)(1)";

(2) in clause (i) thereof, by inserting "and section 2(p)(2)(D)" after "section 2(p)(1)(F)";

(3) in clause (ii) thereof, by striking out "and" at the end thereof; and

(4) by adding at the end thereof the following new clause:

"(iv) instructions for procedures to counteract side effects under section 2(p)(1)(K); and".

SEC. 5. The amendments made in the foregoing provisions of this Act shall take effect at the end of the 2-year period following the date of the enactment of this Act. The Consumer Product Safety Commission shall have authority to issue regulations (in accordance with the Federal Hazardous Substance Act, as amended by such foregoing provisions) during such 2-year period for purposes of carrying out such amendments, except that the effective date of any such regulations shall not occur before the end of such 2-year period.

APPENDIX 2

CHARTS PREPARED BY THE OFFICE OF CONGRESSMAN FRED RICHMOND

NAME OF PRODUCT	CHEMICAL	MANUFACTURER	HAZARD
Scotch Photo - Mount	Hexane	3M	Peripheral Neuropathy
Turpentine	Gum Spirits of turpentine	Grumbacher	Kidney damage, skin and respiratory allergies.
Thinner for Rubber Cement	Hexane	Sanford Corp.	Nerve damage
Rubber Cement	Hexane	Sanford Corp.	Nerve damage
Cold Water Fabric Dye Batikit	Hexane	AMACO	Severe respiratory allergies.
Cadmium Yellow Oil Paint	Cadmium	Grumbacher	Kidney damage, possibly lung and prostate cancer.
Manganese Blue Oil Paint	Manganese	Winsor & Newton	Manganese poisoing - similar to Parkinson's Disease.
Phthalo Green Oil Paint	PCB contamination	Speedball	Birth defects, cancer, chloracne
Flake White Oil Paint	Lead Carbonate	Grumbacher	Lead poisoning, kidney damage.
Cadmium-Vermillion Red Light Oil Paint	Cadmium Mercuric Sulfides	Permanent Pigments	Mercury poisoning
Celluclay Instant Paper Mache	Possibly Lead	Activa Products, Inc.	Lead poisoning
Flo-Paque Color	Xylene	Floquil-Polly S	Liver damage, menstrual irregularities.
Powdered Rosin	Rosin	Graphic Chemical & Ink Company	May cause asthma
Clear-Casting Polyester Resin	Styrene	Industrial Plastic	Liver damage, lung irritation, narcosis
Sta-Sharp Lacquer Thinner	Toluene	Ulano	Liver damage
Easy-Flo Silver Solder	Cadmium	Handy & Haromon	Kidney damage, possibly cancer and death
Acrylic Cement Quick-Drying	Methylene Chloride	Flex-Craft Industries	Skin irritation, heart attacks
Self-Flexing Acid-Core Solder	Lead	Lenk	Chronic bronchitis, burns
Flo-Master Opaque Ink	Aromatic Hydro-carbons, Naphthas	Faber-Castell	Liver damage
Chrome Yellow Ceramic Glaze	Lead Chromate	Ceramichrome	Chronic lead poisoning
Stained Glass Kit	Lead	Ernani Art Studio	Lead poisoning
Red Lead	Silica	Stewart Clay, Co.	Silicosis

NAME OF PRODUCT	CHEMICAL	MANUFACTURER	HAZARD
Rit Dye	Benzidine-Type Dye	Best Foods	Bladder Cancer
Star-Sheen Supreme One-Coat High Gloss Finish	Diisocynates	American Handicrafts Tandy	Chronic asthma at low levels of exposure
Royal-Coat Craft Accessories	Lead	Cunningham Art Products, Inc.	Lead poisoning
Parting Powder	Probably Talc & Asbestos	All-Craft Co.	Asbestosis, Mesothelioma, lung and other cancer
Leather Dye	O-Dichlorobenzene	Caldwell Crafts	Liver and kidney damage.
Jordan Clay	Silica	Baldwin Pottery Store	Silicosis
Strontium Oil Paints	Strontium	LeFranc Bourgeouis (import)	Strontium poisoning
Liquid Glaze For Oven-Firing	Unknown solvent, no contents label	Sculpture House	Unknown hazards

APPENDIX 3
CONTACTS

Dr. Michael McCann
Art Hazards Information Center
Center for Occupational Hazards
5 Beekman Street
New York, NY 10038
(212) 227-6220

Dr. Monona Rossal
Art Hazards Information Center
Center for Occupational Hazards
5 Beekman Street
New York, NY 10038
(212) 227-6220

Joy Turner Luke
Chairperson, ASTM Subcommittee DO1.57
Box 18, Route 1
Sperryville, VA 22740
(703) 987-8386

National Poison Control Center
University of Pittsburgh
School of Medicine
Pittsburgh, PA 15213
(412) 647-5600

Artists Equity Association, Inc.
3726 Albemarle Street, N.W.
Washington, DC 20016
(202) 244-0209

American Society for Testing and Materials
1916 Race Street
Philadelphia, PA 19103
(215) 299-5400

CHAPTER TWENTY

LIVING AND WORKING IN THE SAME SPACE: THE CASE FOR STUDIO LOFTS IN CITIES

David Paul Steiner, Esq.

All visual artists can attest to the pressing need for substantial studio space and acceptable housing quarters at affordable rental rates. While the housing problem is felt by everyone, regardless of profession or line of work, artists are hit hardest by this dilemma. They need especially large, safe spaces in which to work, perform, set up equipment, store materials and finished products, as well as live.

But as many of you already know, the very elements that attract artists to cities (the confluence of galleries, access to other artists, theater and other cultural benefits, potential buyers and markets for art) also make finding suitable places to work and live in the city environment very difficult. The pragmatic solution for many of you is a single space devoted to both residential use and work. Unfortunately, not all of us have the clout of the President, who lives and works in the same space in Washington, D.C.

Artists generally were unable to afford urban residential rentals with adequate space until recent developments in New York City and Los Angeles uniquely altered the legal alternatives for artist live/work space in those cities. Further, municipal zoning regulations (laws that dictate the types of use or non-use of property in specific areas of a city or town) traditionally prohibit or strongly restrict property uses which are not strictly residential or restrict residential use in commercial areas where rents are much more affordable.

This article will trace the history of live/work space and zoning, document the positive response by New York City to its artists and describe the similar steps that California, and most recently Los Angeles, has taken to provide artists the opportunity to live and work in affordable space in abandoned downtown factories, warehouses and the like. In addition, we will look at the results of the renovation of such areas, and how different business and legal plans by individual visual artists and groups can offset future headaches and heartaches.

HISTORY OF LIVE/WORK SPACE AND ZONING

The idea that artists should combine their place of residence with their place of work is hardly a revolutionary concept. The relationship between artists and craftspeople and government finds its roots in classical Greece, where artisans and artists tended to gather in the same districts of Athens near marketplaces. Later, during the Middle Ages, medieval cities saw the development of the guild system, whereby commercial, industrial and residential uses were mixed and often combined according to profession. Starting with the Renaissance in Florence, Italy, and later in France following the French Revolution, the artist's studio became a place for artists to work and live and express their independent lifestyle. It soon became more desirable to segregate groups like artists from the wealthier (more conservative) citizens who naturally controlled much of the regulation of public policy and decision-making processes. Thus evolved the concept of "zoning."

Zoning serves to spell out which activities are permitted in specific portions of a city, county or other legally defined area. Generally, zoning laws divide a city into residential, commercial or industrial zones with restrictions on use of the property in each area. You should remember that zoning laws create penalties, including fines, termination of prohibited activity and even eviction. San Francisco wrote the first zoning ordinance in the United States back in 1886, excluding Chinese laundries from white residential neighborhoods. Although the law was struck down, different versions directed against other activities like saloons and slaughterhouses soon appeared on the West Coast. These early California ordinances, together with pre-existing building codes from the East, were incorporated into the New York zoning law of 1916. This law became a prototype for the country, dividing cities into the three areas of use (industrial, commercial and residential) with building regulations for each section.

SoHo, NoHo and TriBeCa

The first and probably best-known city area to be predominantly taken over by artists requiring live/work space at initially low rental rates was SoHo (or *So*uth of *Ho*uston Street) in New York City. The SoHo area had been the mid-nineteenth-century commercial and entertainment center of the city, with largely cast-iron construction buildings that have proven remarkably durable and desirable over the years. Originally designed to withstand the huge floor loads and stresses of commercial activity and manufacturing, these buildings also have high ceilings and many windows in the upper floors (coincidentally perfect for visual artists who require unobstructed space and light in large quantities). SoHo began to deteriorate in the 1950s and 1960s as the larger-scale industries vacated smaller buildings which had become impractical for heavier manufacturing needs and was targeted for demolition and urban renewal. But as industry and commerce left SoHo, visual artists began to move into these sturdy spaces which afforded large square footage at such reasonable rent. More and more artists flooded into SoHo, first as studio users and then as residents, because of the rising rents in uptown Manhattan and the fact that SoHo lofts were large enough to provide space for both work and living. Not surprisingly, the landlords/owners of SoHo's vacated buildings were happy to rent these empty commercial spaces to artists who sought joint live/work environments. But letting visual artists reside in buildings subject to strictly commercial building codes was a violation of those codes. Consequently, landlords either ignored the fact that artists lived in the studio lofts or offered the artists a "commercial" lease. Tenancy under a commercial lease did not convey the safety requirements and amenities afforded to residential tenants under the laws, and still does not do so in any city. It was then the artist's job to convert an empty loft into joint live/work quarters.

The artists living and working in these studio lofts were illegal tenants, and could be forced to move out at any time, despite their improvements to the property, by landlords or city officials enforcing health, fire and building code regulations. These regulations were not strenuously enforced, and as the number of resident artists increased to massive proportions, the demand for social services (garbage collection, fire protection, schools) ordinarily not provided in a commercial neighborhood became a necessity.

By 1964, nearly 1,000 "artist households" existed in SoHo, enough to constitute a politically active force calling for sanitary services, fire protection and the like. City and state officials, recognizing the advantages of keeping resident artists in the city, attempted to accommodate the unique economic and space problems facing artists in that concentrated environment by passing an amendment to the New York State Multiple Dwelling Law (Article 7-B). The New York legislature basically authorized local governments (i.e., New York City's government) to zone joint live/work space for artists. It is useful to repeat the preamble of this 1964 amendment, as it illustrates the public policy behind all of New York's subsequent artist housing laws and reflects similar attitudes in California.

> It is hereby declared and found that persons regularly engaged in the visual fine arts require larger amounts of space for the pursuit of their artistic endeavors and for the storage of the materials therefor and of the products thereof than are regularly to be found in dwellings subject to this chapter, that the financial remunerations to be obtained from pursuit of a career in the visual fine arts are generally small, that . . . the high cost of land within such cities makes it particularly difficult for persons regularly engaged in the visual fine arts to obtain the use of the amounts of space required for their work as aforesaid, and that the foregoing conditions threaten to lead to an exodus of persons regularly engaged in the visual fine arts from such cities, to the detriment of the cultural life thereof and of the state.

The 1964 amendment did not clear up all the artists' problems. In fact, it created others. Legislators still wanted to preserve the SoHo area as a home for light industry, while allowing some residency by artists. Thus, artist occupancies were permitted only in those structures entirely abandoned by industry. Moreover, strict health and safety standards remained a deterrent to conversions by artists. Thereafter, in 1965 and 1971, a series of amendments expanded the usage of lofts as live/work space by liberalizing the structural changes required for legally sufficient conversions and easing up on the minimum light, air and fire protection requirements and building occupancy restrictions. Finally, in 1977, the legislature passed a revised version of Article 7-B, permitting general residential conversion of loft-style buildings as well as joint live/work space for artists. The safety standards, as revised, are strong but also make allowances for the special problems of converted older buildings found in SoHo and other areas like it.

You may ask, at this point, why wouldn't non-artists take advantage of the low rents and move into SoHo themselves? The New York legislature recognized the possibility but not the consequences when it also established a loose procedure for the "certification" of artists to prevent intrusion by non-artists and to prevent a natural rise in rent as desirability increased. The criteria for certification were: (1) an artist's need for space and (2) commitment to art. The newly developed cultural and creative environment of the SoHo district, coupled with a lack of zeal at enforcement of certification, led to a virtual inundation of young professionals, boutiques, cafés, fancy retail outlets and art patrons, all of whom drove rents sky-high. Many artists were driven out of SoHo, and in 1976 New York amended the zoning ordinance in the *No*rth of *Ho*uston area (NoHo). Since then another zone has been established for live/work space in the TriBeCa (*Tri*angle *Be*low *Ca*nal Street) area of Manhattan.

Sadly, the displacement of artists in the NoHo and TriBeCa areas is occurring even faster than it did in SoHo. Here we can view the recurring problem: the revitalization of recently vacated or unused portions of a city by an influx of mostly visual artists who then make the environment so attractive they price themselves out of the area.

A Look at Other Cities and Other Solutions

A more carefully structured definition of the term "artist" for certification, which many argue is either censorship or a violation of one's right to privacy, may not be the answer, especially with traditionally lax enforcement and avoidance by artists themselves. Acquiring "equity" positions in studio lofts through cooperative- or condominium-structured ownership may be a better method of maintaining such valuable space from an entrepreneurial perspective, and we will delve into those concepts a little later. But first, it is interesting to see how other cities have dealt with the problem and need for live/work space for their sculptors, photographers, graphic artists and the like.

San Francisco became the first city in the country to permit residential occupancies in all districts (November 1978). Live/work space for visual artists and other artists is allowed as a right in manufacturing (M) and commercial (C) zones of the city, but San Francisco has yet to spell out applicable housing and building codes. In Berkeley, California, the city zoning ordinance has been amended (as of October 1979) to permit live/work space in *all* non-residential districts. It is important to note that neither Northern California city has established a certification procedure, possibly because they use this all-inclusive geographic approach which tends to disperse and dilute the loft market, thereby avoiding the overcrowding which pushes rents skyward.

Seattle, Washington, passed zoning revisions in 1977 which may be more attractive to those of you who also favor the clean air of the Pacific Northwest. These laws permit artist studio dwellings as a *right* in all business zones, and the use is allowed as a special exception, with a two-year revocable permit from the building department, in industrial and manufacturing zones. An affidavit stating that the person is an artist, rather than a formal certification procedure, is used. Once again, the wide geographic possibilities have diluted the loft market, thus avoiding many of the economic results seen in SoHo, NoHo and TriBeCa. You must also consider, however, the advantages of working in an artistic community as opposed to being geographically separated from other visual artists.

BUILDING CODES/THE LOS ANGELES EXPERIMENT

Important to all visual artists who live in California is an understanding of the recent passage of State Bill 812 (sponsored by Petis and Sieroty), now codified as S17958.11 of the Health and Safety Code, and effective since January 1, 1980. (It is also a useful model to visual artists in other states without such legislation.) The new zoning statute *authorizes* cities and counties in California to rezone commercial and industrial areas for use as both living and working space by artists *and* to *adopt alternatives* consistent with that residential use. Under the new law, the space must include cooking space, sanitary facilities up to code and a working area regularly used by one or more persons in a family *or* one or more of four unrelated persons residing there. Additionally, the new housing law indicates that certain designated areas in the city/county (central city–downtown) should be chosen for these "work/live quarters." The California legislature also stated that the public would benefit from these conversions because (1) old/vacated buildings are upgraded by this program, (2) the conversion to this kind of space allows a revitalization of central city areas and (3) the cultural life of a city/county will be enhanced by greater numbers of people involved with the arts.

This strong legislative support has been coupled with an explosion of visual artists descending upon the warehouse/factory section of downtown Los Angeles (attracted, as always, by large spaces and low rents). Councilman Joel Wachs of Los Angeles has been responsible for the passage of a municipal ordinance adding a "conditional use" category to existing zoning regulations. It permits consideration of applications involving mixed residential and industrial or commercial uses for artists in the commercial and manufacturing zones of the city, and requires a minimum filing fee of $225.00. This ordinance was put into law in September 1981, and will legitimize the ongoing conversion of obsolete, abandoned and run-down loft buildings and warehouses by energetic visual artists and artisans. Yet as positive as this flurry of legislation appears, the fact that downtown Los Angeles loft space is becoming scarce and more expensive points to the SoHo syndrome again; now that you are being permitted to live and work in the same studio loft space, how can you keep the space without losing the proverbial arm and leg?

SOME PRACTICAL BUSINESS SOLUTIONS

After you have fought the building department and worked out all the health and safety requirements, such as structural design, entry and exit for fire protection, light and ventilation, electrical and plumbing standards, kitchen and bathroom facilities, and hidden any chemicals from inspectors, you are still not ready to turn to your craft. First, consult with other professionals concerning insurance (see the Insurance section in this Manual) and obtain any necessary business licenses. Second, after perusing the section on Taxes in this Manual, consult with an accountant or an attorney concerning your ability to deduct many of the expenses incurred in converting your studio loft. Whether you rent or own, those deductions are still open to you if you are willing to find out about them.

Third, consider your leasehold (rental) position in the studio. Is it for a substantial period of time (several years) with a set rent or set increases that you can live with, or does the landlord have many "outs" whereby he or she can raise the rent or remove you if your work disturbs his or her sensibilities or other tenants? If the lease (do not rent without a written lease) is confusing to you, consult an attorney of your choice and understand the terms of that lease.

Some factors to consider in a lease: (1) How long is the lease and can you get an option to renew it for a good number of years at the same price? (2) Are there any rent controls in effect? (3) What are the landlord's responsibilities and what are yours? (You want to avoid having to keep sidewalks clean, halls and roofs repaired, elevators operating, or promising to observe local statutes and ordinances.) (4) Make sure that you can add fixtures, air conditioning, heating and room dividers and that the lease doesn't automatically make these the landlord's property without your having a right to remove them or get paid for them. (5) Is the landlord aware of the ordinance allowing you to convert to live/work space and the fact that these standards may differ from those he/she is accustomed to?

(6) Make sure there are no restrictions that would conflict with your creative process, such as on noise created by equipment or drains on electrical systems or materials being used. (7) The landlord should have access only after a reasonable request is granted. Remember, you live there! (8) If applicable, obtain an option for the right to buy the space if it is converted into a co-op or condominium. Negotiating a good lease is as important to your work as your materials or your buyers, because without work space you cannot work. (This is not entrepreneurial wisdom, but plain good sense!)

An alternative to renting, which can completely offset the SoHo syndrome of pricing you out of your studio loft when the district becomes more attractive, is to own your live/work space either by yourself (as "fee simple" or condominium) or with other visual artists, through cooperatives or "limited partnerships." A fee simple means that you as the owner of a building receive a deed for that building and the land it occupies, usually subject to a mortgage. You pay tax on both, but tax benefits are extensive. The obvious drawback is cost—most artists cannot afford the mortgage payments, let alone the down payment. But if you are well heeled, this is the way to avoid landlords. In a condominium, the legal entity that owns a building subdivides the property and sells the pieces. Each unit (or studio loft) is individually owned and financed and benefits include important tax advantages and equity buildup instead of the outlay of rent. Disadvantages include financing common improvements and high mortgage costs, but you are again freeing yourself from the outside influence of higher rents—in other words, you are secure in your live/work space and, as the area improves, the value of your equity asset resale goes up in value.

Perhaps the most congenial and advantageous ownership/control is provided in cooperatives or co-ops. Cooperative ownership puts the building into the hands of a corporation, and all members of the corporation live in the building and have an exclusive right to occupy a specific area. (See the Tax section of this Manual for a full explanation about corporations.) Co-ops are simpler to set up than condominiums, permit flexible transfer and sale of ownership interests and offer the same tax benefits as to condominium and fee simple owners. Recently (1981), the mayor of New York gave his permission for the conversion of a number of abandoned city-owned tenement buildings on Manhattan's Lower East Side into cooperative lofts for artists, who will be eligible for low-cost mortgages.

This development may well herald the future for visual artists who want to live and work in the same space at reasonable prices, and it reflects the growing awareness that artists must deal in the real world as everyone else does—taking care of pragmatic living problems, making advantageous business decisions about where they live and work and then going about the business of creating.

CHAPTER TWENTY-ONE
PACKING AND SHIPPING ARTWORK

Marlene Weed

Space age technology has rapidly improved the art of preparing goods for transport. Packaging has become an engineering science with degree programs in such highly regarded universities as Michigan. But it's doubtful that this amazing progress has kept pace with the decline in the care given transported goods.

Three centuries ago great artworks, including a magnificent pipe organ, were transported from Spain to Mexico by galleons you would hesitate to take to Catalina Island. From the Mexican coast the organ was carried inland over the mountains to mile-high Mexico City. There it was installed in the cathedral being built on the site of the razed Aztec temple.

Carried on ship by sailors who could be whipped for negligence and hauled over the mountains by Indians who could be executed for breakage, the artwork arrived with negligible loss.

Today, a well-paid union member astride a forklift will force the lift blades under your airbound package when hand carrying would have been easier. One assumes there is a sociological advantage to the improvement in labor's status, but after seeing what an airline handler has done to a one-of-a-kind ceramic sculpture or a portfolio of illustrations, one has flashes of longing for the days of the whip and keelhaul.

Unless you're prepared to make the trip yourself, the artwork you ship is going to be handled roughly. This is a fact of life and it's up to you to handle and package the piece so that you diminish the likelihood of its destruction.

HANDLING

After considering all of the problems involved you may well decide to use a professional to crate and ship your artwork. Even so, you are going to be responsible for preparing the piece for packing. This preparation can determine the condition in which your piece ultimately arrives at its destination.

Much of what we suggest for proper handling of artworks is little more than common sense, but it may run counter to personal habits. At the handling stage you and your friends or employees may present as great a danger to the art as a disgruntled freight handler if you are not willing to observe the simple cautionary rules that expert art conservators have developed.

The first admonition is against smoking in the room in which you are handling artwork. The smoker no longer notices the odor that permeates everything in the room and may be only dimly aware of the implications of yellowed fingers. It is not only the possibility of fire that obliges you to prohibit smoking in any room in which you are handling the original artwork; it is the *certainty* of damage from the oily, yellowish film of tobacco smoke. Some work will suffer more immediately apparent or greater damage from tobacco smoke than others, but none can escape it.

Smoke is not the only airborne danger. Tar-lined paper should be kept out of any room in which you're preparing art for shipment. A change in atmosphere will cause the tar to melt and the vapor will damage paper and textiles. Insect repellents present the same danger. Be skeptical of the presence of any substance that produces a distinctive odor. If the air is carrying something to your nostrils, it may well be carrying a damaging substance to your work.

The room in which you prepare art for shipment should be clean and tidy. A vacuum cleaner (ideally the type that draws the dust-laden air through water, as with the old RexAire) should be used to reduce the dust which will damage fine fabrics and paper. Don't sweep the room while art objects are about. This will simply fill the air with dust and increase the possibility of damage.

Those same talented hands that enable you to be an artist can irretrievably damage a watercolor or etching or archival print photograph simply by touching. Hand smudges often do not appear immediately, but the damage from the oil, secretions and transferred residue on human hands will eventually appear, and the damage is irreversible.

Scroll and screen paintings are normally on silk or fibrous paper. Either substance will absorb the dampness from hands as readily as it absorbed the original ink. Once absorbed, that smudge is as permanent as that original ink.

Even hands that are well washed produce oil excretions. Fingerprints will not necessarily appear as you handle an early etching or original negative, but those prints will appear later and cannot be removed. The permanent damage that fingerprints do to damp old pewter is apparent immediately but slower with other metals.

No matter what type artwork you're preparing for shipment your first investment should be in a dozen pair of white cotton gloves such as those used by film editors in their daily handling of motion picture negative and print. These washable gloves are available from any motion picture supply house. J and R Film Company, 6820 Romaine, Los Angeles, CA (213) 467-3107, carries them at $3.90 per dozen.

Before you take up the art object that is to be shipped, consider the following: Did you remove all the sharp objects that the piece could rest on or bump against? Is the surface of the table washed clean and thoroughly dried? Is there any object whose surface could adhere to the piece on which you'll be working?

One last question before you uncover your art piece for pre-shipping examination. Do you want to draw the drapes to block out sunlight and turn off any fluorescent lights in the room? The degree of damage from sunlight or strong artificial light varies with the materials involved. The potential damage to inorganic substances (metal, metal alloys) is so slight as to make this precaution unnecessary, but light is extremely damaging to organic substances. Vegetable and animal dyes in tapestries suffer from the slightest exposure to any light and suffer greatly upon exposure to strong light. It is not just direct sunlight that will fade watercolors, destroy yellow dyes and discolor ivory. Reflected sunlight and fluorescent lighting will do as badly and will damage paper. High-quality paper resists light damage, but it will ultimately succumb.

You're now ready to examine the work and to prepare a written record of its condition. The written record should be thorough, detailed and accurate. Future disputes on condition may well be resolved on your written record. Comparison of your record with the piece may contribute to determining either the cause of damage or even the culprit. If your recipient complains, or a claim is to be made against the shipper or an insurance company, the record you made will be significantly more persuasive than your unsupported recollection.

If any damage or any weakness is noted prior to shipping, a copy of the report should accompany the artwork. When the receiving party is alerted to some weakness in the item precautions against damage are more easily taken.

It is a practice of the Los Angeles County Art Museum to X-ray artworks to determine structural flaws and weak points prior to shipping. You will not likely have the facilities for such thorough inspection, but you can certainly note previous repairs and restorations and, if the piece is framed, check the frame for breaks and open miters and make certain the painting is secure within the frame.

If someone has stapled or clipped the artwork that you are about to ship, remove the metal pieces immediately. A staple remover will only aggravate the damage, so use extreme care and tools with which you are skilled.

All tape, no matter how attractively named (water-soluble, pressure-sensitive or whatever), will damage artwork, especially art on paper. If you have to use an adhesive, use only rice or wheat flour paste. Avoid synthetic adhesives and rubber cement. They will indelibly stain.

When framing a work before shipping, avoid glass. Glass not only breaks easily, it will surely damage the work (whether painting, print, photograph, drawing, etc.) in the course of the break. If you desire a cover, use Plexiglas coated with antistatic film. Don't skimp here, buy the more expensive Plexiglas. It will give your surface unbreakable protection. It will *not,* however, protect the surface against sunlight.

Plexiglas is easily scratched, so you're going to have to protect it as carefully as you would have protected the surface of your painting. The notion that Plexiglas filters out harmful ultraviolet sun rays is firmly held throughout the land. It is not true.

Sometimes proper ways to handle artworks are not obvious. The Los Angeles County Art Museum prepared over 500,000 art objects for moving to the present location on Wilshire Boulevard. The only significant damage was to a Tuscan vase, broken because an employee did the obvious and picked it up by its handle.

CERAMICS should be carried single with one hand on the bottom supporting the weight and the other on the side, near the top but below the rim. Unless it's your own creation, in which event you presumably know its structural strength, never use the handles. Handles are the portions that most often have been broken and restored or replaced. The mending may not be apparent, but the mended portion will be structurally weak.

Other than handle misuse, ceramics usually do rather well in shipping. They are so obviously susceptible to breaks that even the most careless packer usually does a decent job with them.

GLASS shares the advantage of obvious breakability. It should be handled only on a padded table and carried in compartments separated by soft, resilient material or singly on a padded device.

FRAMED PAINTINGS should be carried with one hand at the midpoint of the bottom frame and the other hand on one side for balance. If the painting is so large that this handling would be awkward, two people must move it. Each must place the right hand at a bottom, weight-bearing corner with the left hand toward the top of the near side. No painting is sufficiently small to warrant different handling. There is no safe way for one person to carry two paintings.

FOLDING SCREEN PAINTINGS cannot safely be moved by hand. If you must move one to prepare it for shipment, call in assistance. You and your helper in clean clothes and gloves should cover the screen with acid-free tissue paper, fold it and gently move it onto a clean, padded hand truck.

Move only one screen at a time. The frames are not designed to bear weight and will not survive stacking.

TEXTILES, RUGS and TAPESTRIES are particularly awkward to handle in preparation for shipping because there is no way to move them without some folding or rolling and there is no way to fold or roll them without some damage to the fabric.

If it is your own work, the threads or fibers are new enough so that damage will not be apparent, but it will be there nonetheless. Careless handling can produce apparent fiber damage even in new products.

Fire and water take their toll, but the major destructive forces for fabric art are light, folding, dust, dry heat, insects and mold.

Prior to shipping you must examine the fabric for insects, larvae eggs, fungus and mold. Wool and silk are especially liable to attack by insects. The same silverfish that endangers your paper artwork will happily eat fabric if paper is unavailable. If the examination reveals any foreign substance, a good airing (in dry darkness) should be followed by fumigation. If it is a new or an older intact (unfrayed, unbroken threads, not restored) piece, it should be cleaned with a slow vacuum cleaner in even, vertical strokes, repeating each stroke in the opposite direction.

IVORY is not a medium you're apt to be using in your own work, but you may be asked to ship ivory art. The best thing would be to refuse. Ivory simply does not lend itself to being carted about and shouldn't be shipped.

Don't grasp any ivory piece by a projecting part, a rim or an edge. If it must be carried, examine all sides before touching it. Delicate carvings and fragile projections are often on the back or lower portion of carved ivory.

Sunlight damages ivory, as do sudden changes in temperature or humidity, which cause it to crack as you watch it. Your fingers will discolor ivory, and cotton lint will become lodged in the crevices of intricate carvings. If you're going to have to ship it, consult an expert and pray a little.

METAL OBJECTS that are small enough to be carried on a tray should be in separately padded compartments, as with glass, or cushioned by wadded acid-free tissue paper. SILVER and BRONZE can be wrapped in Saran Wrap for surface protection if it is certain they will remain dry and warm.

PHOTOGRAPHS and NEGATIVES require clean, dry hands and surfaces and a prohibition against paper clips or any object resting on the surface. Plastic sleeves will keep slides and negatives dust-free. Sunlight can be damaging.

If you've read this far, it's very likely that you're about to undertake the packing and shipping of one or more pieces of art, probably your own work.

Your next step in preparation, far more important than finishing this article, is to secure a copy of *Art Objects: Their Care and Preservation,* by Frieda Kay Fall. Ms. Fall was for many years Registrar of Collections at the Los Angeles County Art Museum. As such she planned one of the greatest art shipments of all time, the 1964 move of 500,000 art objects to the museum's present quarters on Wilshire Boulevard. Copies of the 1973 book are still available at $17.50 in sturdy binding from the publisher, Laurence McGilvery, P.O. Box 852, La Jolla, CA 92038.

PACKING

To some extent your method of packing will be influenced by the mode of transportation and the shipping personnel. If you're going to travel with the piece and it can be carried on board, sturdiness of crate can give way to ease of handling. If you have to ship by sea, the packaging must work against the serious problem of salt in the atmosphere. In planes that have no pressurized cargo hold, the package must survive extreme cold and rapid changes of temperature.

Economic factors will certainly influence some choices. The immediate or long-range importance of the particular artwork to your career is a legitimate factor in considering the cost of various forms of packing.

The type of work must also be considered. Before packing determine the conditions facing the work from the moment it leaves your studio until the moment it is unpacked at its destination. Will it travel through desert or mountains, or both? Will it go from Beverly Hills to Santa Monica by way of Memphis? (This is no joke. That's exactly the route it will take if you give it to Federal Express.) If it's going to New York you must know and prepare for the fact that the cargo is unloaded into an open-air shed at Kennedy Airport.

Rain is an obvious consideration. Dampness can be just as destructive. A short storage in damp quarters encourages the growth of mildew and mold. Unsealed work is constant prey to cockroaches (they love to eat pigment), silverfish (they prefer paper) and even termites. Don't ignore these pests, in transit or in the studio. One cockroach in one night can eat the better part of a watercolor surface.

Adapted Containers

The easiest packaging for your art object, if it will fit and withstand the expected handling, is an existing container adapted for your particular piece of art. The easiest of all is a sturdy suitcase or abandoned typewriter case, especially if you're going to deliver the item personally. You can carry it with you on plane or train, or securely packed into the luggage compartment of your automobile.

If the object is neither too bulky nor too heavy, you can convert the case by cutting two pieces of flexible urethane foam to completely fill each portion of the case as it is open. Glue each piece of urethane securely to the interior of the case. When the case is closed the two layers should touch.

Now wrap your small sculpture in tissue or plastic film and place it on the surface of the urethane. As the case is closed the urethane will give, cushioning your piece and holding it securely. If the size of the case or the object warrant it, you may wish to cut a bowl-shaped piece from one or both of the urethane surfaces.

Another adaptation for the case is to line the bottom with 2", 3" or 4" Ethafoam, spread a two- to three-inch layer of Pelaspan-Pac (commonly called peanuts because of the shape), place your glass sculpture or bronze on the spread peanuts and fill the case to overflowing. This will only work if you have a large and a very narrow side when the case is open, because it is important that the peanuts be pressed tightly when the lid is closed.

Old wooden soda cases are excellent adaptive containers for small objects. The twenty-four squares can be felt-lined and then tissue-wrapped objects simply nestled in each. Some of those wooden cases were for six-packs and have four larger compartments. They can be felt-lined for carrying or lined with ½" Ethafoam (two-pound density) for shipment. In the latter event a ⅜" plywood lid should be cut and also lined with ½" Ethafoam. The short ends of the case will be thick enough to handle small T bolts.

Jim Marshall, San Francisco photographer, advises that Kodak film boxes are the perfect mailing cartons for negatives and original slides. Marshall uses cardboard for filler and completes the package with simple brown paper and paper tape. He mails prints in manila envelopes between layers of cardboard. He ships all negatives by registered mail because the postal system (every person who handles the piece signs for it) makes it easy to trace a lost item.

Tubes

The least desirable, but occasionally the most practical, shipping container is a tube. When you use a tube you accept a certain amount of inevitable damage to the artwork you're shipping. Every year untold hundreds of paintings are pushed on their way to eventual destruction by shippers who maintain firmly that rolling is the best way to move an OIL PAINTING. You know, but many of their callers do not, that rolling squeezes the inner surface and stretches the outer surface. Squeezing oil paint causes wrinkles and chipping; stretching oil paint causes cracks.

If the painting you are shipping is so huge that it cannot be moved without rolling, give a lot of serious thought to leaving it where it is. If it has to be moved, carefully vacuum the front and back of the painting and thoroughly clean the surface on which you must lay it to roll.

Select the thickest possible pole of light wood or strong fiberboard. Never use a metal pole. Place a sheet of clear polyethylene on the cleaned tabletop (or, given the assumed size, the carefully scrubbed floor) and place the painting face down on the polyethylene. You have selected a pole at least a foot longer than the width of the painting so that a person on either end can hold the pole a quarter inch above the back of the painting as you now slowly roll the painting and the polyethylene onto the pole. The back of the painting is to the pole. The front of the painting and the covering polyethylene face outward as it rolls.

After the wrapping is complete the edges will be even if it has been done properly. Wrap the roll in waterproof paper and seal it. Don't tie the roll because it will pull the canvas unevenly and cause further damage.

The painting should be unrolled immediately after the move. It will have suffered some damage. If you're quite lucky and have done an excellent job, the damage will be imperceptible.

If they cannot be shipped perfectly flat and unfolded, the next-best way to ship TEXTILES, TAPESTRIES or RUGS is by tube. The rolling will weaken the fibers, but not as severely as folding would.

You have cleaned both surfaces. You carefully clean the floor or table on which the fabric will be rolled. You select as large a pole of light wood (for textiles and light tapestry it can be cardboard) as weight will permit. The pole must extend several inches beyond the fabric on either end. A metal pole cannot be used because it will oxidize and stain the fabric. The cardboard tube must be covered, preferably with acid-free tissue paper. Now roll slowly and carefully so that the edges are even and no crease is rolled in. Roll against the pile with the face inward (opposite the way you rolled the oil painting). It will be worth the effort if you take a cloth or rug of similar size and shape and have a couple of practice runs with your crew before undertaking the rolling of a valuable piece.

Lightweight Packing

If you're shipping something you've sold for a hundred dollars or less, you probably will want to gamble on something less sturdy than a wooden crate. A much more expensive SMALL TEXTILE, DRAWING or ARCHIVAL PRINT PHOTOGRAPH will justify a cardboard container if you've previously mounted it between sheets of Plexiglas. The Plexiglas will protect the work and the cardboard will prevent scratching of the Plexiglas surface. After delivery the Plexiglas mounting will be retained for both storage and show.

Three materials substantial enough to use in lightweight packing are cardboard, plywood and Masonite (a trade name; a similar product is called hardboard). Your choice may be influenced by what you have around the studio. Free material shouldn't be ignored. Cardboard from liquor store boxes serves perfectly well. You'll find most of the good lumberyards patient if you want to examine the different materials available. Remember that you'll need a saw for plywood or Masonite. A razor cutter will do for cardboard.

Both plywood and Masonite are sold in 4' by 8' sheets. If it's strictly a one-time venture and you have no saw, you can purchase 2' by 2', 2' by 3', 2' by 4' and 2' by 6' panels of plywood at most lumberyards. The panels are, of course, more costly per square foot than 4' by 8' sheets.

Masonite will cost approximately $7.00 for a ⅛" by 48" by 96" (4' by 8') sheet, or $11.00 for a ¼" sheet.

Plywood (ask for shop grade, it's cheaper and adequate for packing) will cost about $10.00 for a ¼" by 4' by 8' sheet, or $12.00 for a ⅜" sheet.

This light framing will be appropriate for PHOTOGRAPHS, ILLUSTRATIONS, MATTED WATERCOLORS, ETCHINGS, SIGNED PRINTS and SMALL MOUNTED OIL PAINTINGS.

Let us use a small mounted oil as an example for a typical light package. Take the following steps to package it:

(1) Measure the piece carefully. (Let's assume for the purpose of this example that you find it to be ¹⁵⁄₁₆" by 12" by 24".)

(2) If CARDBOARD is your choice of material, cut two 18" by 30" pieces with the grain or corrugation running horizontally. Then cut two pieces of the same size with the grain or corrugation

running vertically. Take one horizontally corrugated and one vertically corrugated and lightly paste together for each side of the package.

(2A) If you've chosen MASONITE or PLYWOOD, cut two 18″ by 30″ panels for the package.

(3) Wrap your painting in acid-free tissue or polyethylene film to protect it from dust and surface abrasion. Measure the inner pack again. (We'll assume for this example that the covering has added $\frac{1}{32}$″ to each surface.)

(4) If you're using CARDBOARD sides, cut Styrofoam for filler. Two strips 1″ by 30″ by $2^{31}\!/_{32}$″ plus two strips 1″ by $12\frac{1}{16}$″ by $2^{31}\!/_{32}$″ will be required. If you have free cardboard and plenty of patience you can cut enough cardboard strips in these two sizes to combine into one-inch-deep fillers.

(4A) If you've chosen PLYWOOD or MASONITE, coat the inner layer of each of the two panels with $\frac{1}{8}$″ Ethafoam or a layer of felt. This protective layer should be firmly glued to the hard surface. For your fillers you can forget the $\frac{1}{32}$″ tolerance and cut Ethafoam strips 30″ by 3″ and 12″ by 3″ (two each).

(5) When you've put your fillers in place on the underside of the developing package you will have a snug trench into which your framed painting with its protective wrap can be laid.

(6) Place the painting in the trench. You'll note that the frame gives the painted surface floating space. If you were packaging an unframed piece you would have to create this float with packing material.

(7) Place the second side on top of the painting (cushioned surface inward).

(8) Tape the package with gaffer's tape. Put the address on the surface of the container to ensure delivery in the event the covering is destroyed. Label the top side.

(9) Wrap with paper and seal with paper tape unless it is going by Greyhound, in which case you can seal it in a cloth bag if you wish. Mark the top side and add any special instructions for handling.

Wooden Crates

The drawings shown were prepared by James T. Kenion, Head, Art Museum Technical Services, Los Angeles County Museum of Art, for the use of his museum carpenters. Kenion has a strong sense of obligation to preserve art for future generations and insists that crates that go out of the Los Angeles County Museum of Art be built with the three-way corners which make the strongest possible wooden crate.

Each wooden crate constructed for art shipment is tailored for a particular artwork. There can be little standardization because of the unique characteristics of each piece that must be transported. This attention to the needs of each piece enabled Kenion to move over 500,000 pieces of art with but a single loss when he supervised the move of the museum to its present location.

A typical Kenion-designed art crate will have three 2-by-4 frame pieces overlapping at each corner, supporting sides of ¾″ plywood.

Immediately on the inside of the plywood will be a layer of waterproof paper covered by recompressed foam.

The side which will be opened to remove the artwork will be secured by metal screws that thread into a casement sunk into the frame. These screws can be repeatedly used without the eventual wearing away of the threaded hole as occurs with a wood screw.

Kenion shares the conviction of Bryan Cooke, owner of Cooke's Crating, that every crate should be built with cleats, 2-by-4s with one beveled edge nailed to the bottom of the crate. The primary purpose is to raise the crate from the floor so that the blades of a forklift will slide under it without opposition. Cooke points out that cleats serve the further purpose of raising the crate above small surface puddles of oil or water.

Both men have been in the business long enough to know that the work they ship out will be handled roughly. They try to build crates that will preserve the contents no matter how rough the handling. As Kenion remarks, "We build them to be handled by idiots."

If you're serious about doing your own packing, you must learn the properties of packaging materials. A good place to start is with the *Handbook of Package Materials,* by Stanley Sacharow, 243 pages, available at $26.50 from Avi Publishing Company, P.O. Box 831, Westport, CT 06881.

CRATE CONSTRUCTION DIAGRAMS

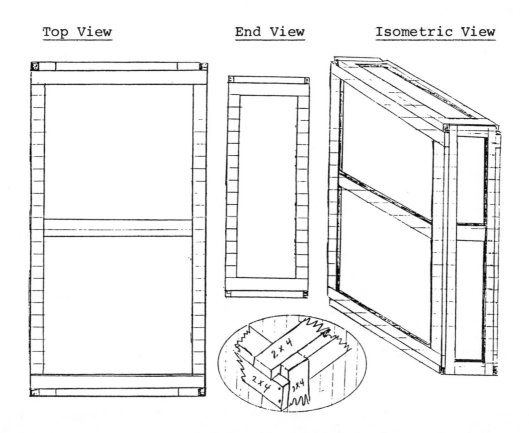

Top View   End View   Isometric View

Three-way Corner Detail

Diagrams drawn by Jim Kenion

A brief list of some materials used now or in the past for art shipment would include:

BUBBLEPAK has replaced Kimpak because it is more resilient and, if you can keep it from the children, easily reusable.

COTTON is still one of the best products for softly cradling fragile items. Keep it away from faceted glass or damaged enamel.

ETHAFOAM, a close-cell material that comes in densities from two to nine pounds, is now widely used by expert packers. It comes in varying thicknesses, $\frac{1}{8}''$ to $4''$. Non-abrasive and highly resilient.

EXCELSIOR is no longer used because it retains moisture and is highly flammable.

FELT, an old standard, is still ideal for lining crates and covering worktables.

GAUZE. The porcelains of the Chinese Exhibit were swathed in thousands of yards of gauze when they left Los Angeles.

KIMPAK has largely been replaced by Bubblepak.

MASONITE, a trade name; a similar product is called HARDBOARD. Some compressed boards of this type contain oil, so check before using.

PEANUTS, the common term for Pelaspan-Pac because of the peanut shape. An excellent cushioning material for fragile art objects, this is a Dow Chemical product.

PLYWOOD comes in 4' by 8' sheets and in thickness from $\frac{1}{4}''$ to $\frac{3}{4}''$. Order shop grade. It's cheaper and fine for packing. On an exhibit crate that will be painted you may want the higher grade.

POLYSTYRENE, a thermoplastic widely used with bronze because it is inert. It is resistant to acids and alkalis. You'll likely want to use this product a lot. Acquaint yourself with its characteristics by reference to the *Handbook of Package Materials,* by Stanley Sacharow.

POPCORN. Yes, the real thing. It too is excellent as a cushioning material, but has been replaced by the cleaner Pelaspan-Pac (peanuts).

QUILTED PADS are routinely used in the transport of bronze and other heavy artwork. Never send a pad out that has not been freshly laundered. The accumulated dust of a used pad will damage the art object.

SEEKURE is the trade name for waterproofing designed for the inside of your crate. An asphaltic is covered on both sides by Kraft paper. It is available in 100-yard rolls of widths from $24''$ to $96''$.

SHREDDED PAPER is no longer used. It has the drawbacks of excelsior plus the soiling from ink where, as often, newspaper is used.

URETHANE FOAM, manufactured by United Foam (213) 264-5600, is an excellent art-packing product. It is available in thicknesses varying from ⅛″ to 30″. A razor blade or knife-type cutter can be used to shape it. It is available from retail stores such as paint stores, home centers and handyman stores. A word of caution: The manufacturer warns that heat could cause the substance to stick to the oil in an oil painting. When used with an oil, make sure the surface is protected from the urethane.

Insurance

If you use a professional art packer, the packer can arrange insurance on your shipment. Various shippers offer varying amounts of coverage. However you choose to insure, you must know that your only satisfactory protection is proper packaging and careful handling.

Making an insurance claim is not a pleasant experience. Those nice chaps in the TV ads won't be the adjuster you'll deal with. Unless the shipment involved a provable sale, you'll have terrible times before you get agreement on the value of the lost art. If a controversy over value persists and the amount is significant, you'll soon learn about unpleasant inquiries being made into your lifestyle, economic situation and personal history.

One agency *does* insure working artists: Huntington T. Block, 2101 L Street, N.W., Washington, DC 20037, (800) 424-8830. The Block policy will cover the work in your studio and provide coverage equal to 25% of your total coverage for art in transit. The amount of premium will vary depending on where your studio is located (type of building, neighborhood, fire protection) and the medium in which you usually work. All else being equal, the artist who works in glass will have a higher premium than one who works in oil on canvas.

Block writes coverage in several companies. Insist on an American company, and don't get carried away by tolling ship's bells and exotic companies insuring starlets' legs.

PROFESSIONAL PACKERS AND SHIPPERS

Professional movers offer to pack and ship your artwork. Better you should do it yourself. However, there are companies that specialize in handling fine art and they should be seriously considered if you're making an important shipment. Importance doesn't necessarily relate to money. If it's your first show, or an important job, you'll want every piece to arrive just as it left your studio. Unless you've done a lot of art crating and know shippers and shipping problems, you'd better turn to a professional. Keep in mind that a well-constructed artwork crate is a permanent container, to be stored and used over and over as the piece or pieces for which it was constructed move about. It is also a model for you if you want to build additional crates.

Insurance adjusters, shippers, claim agents, freight handlers and cargo loaders are only nice on the surface, if at all. Professional art packers and shippers can insulate you from unpleasantness, frustration and anger that is devastating to your work.

If it's economically impossible to use one of the three professionals, learn all that you can about packing and shipping, take all the precautions and expect the worst. If you have a loss, absorb it and forget it! A four-year fight on an insurance claim will drain emotional energy that could more profitably be spent on creation of new art. You are an artist and entrepreneur, but first you're an artist. Successful executives hire high-priced secretaries to protect their emotional tranquillity. Do no less for yourself.

CHAPTER TWENTY-TWO
INSURANCE FOR THE WORKING ARTIST

Peter H. Karlen

Insurance has been defined as:

> An act, business, or system by which pecuniary indemnity is guaranteed by one party
> (as a company) to another party in certain contingencies, as of death, accident, damage,
> disaster, injury, loss, old age, risk, sickness, unemployment, etc., upon specified terms.[1]

In short, insurance is a financial arrangement whereby one party, the insured, is guaranteed compensation by another party, the insurer, for a specified loss. Typically, the insured party pays for this indemnification by remitting premiums to the insurer. These premiums are usually relatively small amounts of money payable in periodic installments.

Naturally, one can "insure" oneself merely by setting aside reserves of money to cover losses which may occur. One way of doing this is to put aside small sums on a periodic basis and build up a reserve. However, for most individuals, including artists, self-insurance makes little sense. Either one puts away a large sum to cover the loss, in which case one might as well not be insured at all, or one saves small sums and earns money on the savings when invested in the hope that no loss will occur at least until the fund has been built up to considerable proportions.

It makes more sense, of course, to pool one's contributions in an insurance fund along with the contributions of others; in other words, distribute the risks and liabilities and financial responsibilities among many insured persons. Such a system if established among many individuals, or perhaps even by associated artists, would be viable to insure against their losses. However, most persons, including artists, do not have the time to run insurance programs, to fill out policies, to pay out claims and to collect premiums. This is the justification for insurance companies. In exchange for the above services, the insurance company receives the monies of numerous subscribers. It invests the monies for its own benefit and makes a profit from investments and premiums and maintains a reserve to pay out on all valid claims. Or, put another way, the insurance company acts as a conduit for the monies of subscribers and claimants, and acts as the mediator in this system of allocation of risks and benefits.

In the case of artists, insurance protects against many losses. Naturally, artists, like other persons, may procure life, disability and medical insurance. They may also insure their inventory just like any other businesspersons. However, even ordinary insurance policies for artists present special

[1] Funk & Wagnalls Standard Dictionary (International ed., 1960).

considerations, and, of course, artists may have special types of insurance policies which are not common to other occupational groups.

The purpose of this article on insurance is primarily to discuss the insurance needs of working artists, including painters, sculptors, graphic designers and photographers.[2] The topics covered are insurance for one's work, liability insurance and disability insurance.

Insuring One's Work

Most artists do not command relatively high prices for their work, and perhaps they do not need insurance policies and the burden of premiums when they start their careers. Nevertheless, many artists have a deep attachment to their works because the works may be considered expressions of their personalities or emotions, or simply because the works are the products of considerable time and effort. Therefore, artists are concerned with protecting their works against loss or damage.

There are several ways in which the works may be lost or damaged. In geographic and temporal terms, loss may occur in the studio; in transit to or from a purchaser, dealer, museum, agent, publisher, advertising agency, licensee or printer (hereafter collectively referred to as "client or user"), or on their premises.

Studio Insurance

If the artist works at home, and perhaps enjoys the "home office" income tax deduction, insurance problems are not necessarily complex, especially if the artist does not have many visitors to the studio. Fire insurance, extended to cover other perils such as lightning and explosion, plus theft insurance, should protect the works of the artist as well as his/her equipment, supplies and library. Even a package policy such as a homeowner's or commercial package policy may be adequate in some cases. Of course, one must bear in mind that a shortcoming of the homeowner's policy is that it will not cover property held for sale or sold but not delivered; nor will it cover business property away from the premises. This means that the artist who holds a homeowner's policy while maintaining a home studio is taking a chance when it comes time to make a claim for loss occurring in the studio. Moreover, the artist may not be able to gain protection from a "floater" policy, covering personal property which is subject to removal from one place to another, because the artist's works may be considered "inventory" not protected under personal property "floater" policies.[3] Nonetheless, the floater policy would cover works of other artists collected by the insured artist, who is considered a collector just like any other collector.

In any case, the insurance policy for the home studio should at least cover loss by fire, theft and vandalism. In addition, some artists may want to carry "valuable papers" insurance, an "all-risk" policy for almost all perils. This type of insurance may be recommended for photographers, graphic designers and architects whose plans, drawings, negatives or blueprints are particularly valuable. One

[2] The term "artist" as used hereafter shall refer to painters, sculptors, graphic designers, photographers and other "visual" artists.

[3] The term "floater" is used to describe a policy under which specific listed articles of personal property are protected while they "float" from one location to another.

drawback of valuable papers insurance is that it will usually cover only reproduction costs of the "papers" in question, and will not provide reimbursement for the full value of the papers. No matter what type of policy the artist procures for works in the home studio, he/she should ascertain what types of damage give rise to proper claims under the policy. Many policies will not cover minor damage to the work such as scratches or chipping unless the artist demands such coverage, in which case the premiums will rise sharply. Also one cannot expect to be covered for all perils, such as earthquakes (unless one has earthquake insurance), wars, insurrections or certain "acts of God."

If the studio is not located at or about the home but in separate business premises, a commercial package policy will be required. The commercial package policy, unlike the homeowner's package policy, can be structured to cover inventory and business property. It is possible, of course, to procure separate fire, theft and vandalism policies, but once again the package policy will cover more perils and will be relatively cheaper and easier to administer than the separate policies. The comprehensive commercial package policy can cover the artist's works, library, equipment and supplies.

When the studio insurance is procured the artist should mention to the agent that his/her works are to be covered so that both parties are aware of the extent of coverage desired and provided. If the works reach a certain value the insurer will probably request an inventory of the works to be protected. Thus, the artist will have to provide a list of the titles, descriptions and values of the works. Of course, the artist should maintain photographs of the works, preferably transparencies, not only because they may be requested but also to prove his/her claims, and for other purposes including preservation of moral rights and other intellectual property rights. The descriptions of the works should at least include dimensions, year of creation, medium and materials and colors, if any. The value of the work should be its selling price, or at least its "fair market value," i.e., what a willing purchaser would pay for the work in an arm's-length transaction. The artist should not underestimate value because, if valuation is to be negotiated at the time of making a claim, the insurer may attempt to lower the valuation. Past sales proceeds for similar works are a good gauge for valuation. Evidence will include gallery records, sales slips, invoices and contracts for sales or licensing. If new works are placed in the studio they, too, should be included on supplements to the inventory, which should be kept updated at all times.

Works in Transit

Many times losses take place not at the studio but in transit from the studio to other locations. For example, a work may be lost or damaged while being delivered to a client or user. The results may not only be calamitous but also embarrassing, and the ordinary policies for home or office studio will not cover these losses. The artist may try to compensate for these losses in certain cases by making claims against other parties or by resisting the demands of purchasers. For instance, the artist may sue the carrier which transported the work. Also the risk of loss passes to the purchaser who buys a work in the artist's studio and leaves it there for later pickup or delivery, and the artist could keep the purchase price even though the work was later lost in transit. However, this is no way to conduct business in the absence of insurance. The artist must either make the carrier, client or user liable for the loss in an explicit prior agreement or must insure works that are being delivered.

The usual policy, before the advent of specialized policies to protect artists, was "inland marine insurance," a species of floater policies used to cover merchandise in transit, including artworks to be sold on consignment. Other alternatives for those who have infrequent shipments, and who do not need a policy which is in force continuously, are parcel post insurance, trip transit policies, registered mail and express shipment insurance and other minor policies which cover only the shipment in question. The transaction costs and premiums per shipment are probably higher, in the aggregate, for such limited insurance, and the broader transit insurance policy may be justified for artists who ship too many works to be bothered by constant paperwork.

With transit insurance complete records must be kept which not only indicate the title, description, medium and value of the work but also its destination and mode of shipment. The insured must also be aware that the transit policy may cover only works shipped in a certain manner by specified channels, packaged in specified ways, to limited destinations (e.g., in the United States only).

Unlike the insurance policy that covers the studio, which in a few cases may come under the rubric of a home or office package policy, the policies which cover art in transit may not be procurable from every insurance agent. In fact, if high valuations or unusual risks are involved many agents may duck the policy or ask for policies which carry exorbitant premiums. It is best in some cases, therefore, to deal with those agents and companies which routinely insure works of art. Transit insurance is usually procurable from agents and brokers who deal heavily in commercial insurance.

The problem of loss during shipment, of course, is particularly acute when purchasers are involved because money has often changed hands and the purchaser has a strong interest in receiving a particular piece. And usually there is no diplomatic way to foist insurance costs upon the buyer unless they are surreptitiously included in the purchaser price. However, in the case of museums the situation may be remedied somewhat. With a museum which wants to grace its interiors with the artist's work, the artist may be able to insist upon "wall-to-wall" insurance carried by the museum. This insurance protects the works in question beginning at the time of removal from the artist's studio until after their exhibition and return to the studio. Thus, the museum's policy should guarantee payment for the full value of the work as stated by the artist. If the museum refuses to insure, the artist either should not lend the work or should have a provision in a written lending agreement making the museum absolutely liable for all damage during exhibition and transit both ways. In the case of original graphic artwork being shipped for reproduction, the artist should at least ask the advertising agency or other user to pay for insurance or be responsible for loss. After all, the loss of a work not only deprives the artist of the full sales price of the work but also effectively destroys the copyright in the work and, if applicable, the right to resale royalties.

Artists, however, may not be in the same position with respect to galleries and dealers. Normally most museums and large advertising agencies have broad and effective insurance policies. But gallery owners who may wish to economize and reduce overhead may not carry insurance policies or may try to shift the burden of insurance to the artist. Again there are alternatives. The artist should either bargain for an insurance clause in a written consignment agreement or insist upon a clause making the dealer absolutely liable. Sometimes the artist and dealer arrive at an agreement whereby they will split the costs of insurance to and from the gallery. That is, they will divide the costs of insurance payments for individual shipments, not the cost of a long-range policy unless there is to be a long-term relationship. Or the artist may insure the work on its way to the gallery while the gallery pays the premium for the return shipment, or vice versa. If the dealer will not pay for insurance he may be persuaded to accept responsibility for loss in transit, although this may be limited to the return shipment, for which he/she will be in control of the manner of shipping. Probably in most cases the dealer will not accept responsibility. Nevertheless, the special statutes that regulate artist-dealer relationships and consignment sales, which are discussed below, may automatically place the responsibility for the return shipment on the dealer.

Works on Display or in Process of Reproduction

Once the work is actually on the premises of the client or user, the artist's problems may be eased. In most cases, museums, dealers and advertising agencies have insurance for property on their premises, although in all cases it is wise to obtain some written promise that the insurance is in force and covers the artist's works adequately. Again, in the case of a museum, the artist should not lend the work if there is neither insurance nor an agreement to accept absolute liability. If the work is to be reproduced and is valuable and irreplaceable, the artist should not let it remain on the premises of the advertising agency, printer or publisher without similar assurances. Although some dealers may carry an art dealer's floater policy on an all-purpose floater policy, with an uninsured dealer the situation is slightly different. Naturally, a dealer may not want to accept absolute liability in the absence of insurance, but he/she may have no choice under the California artist-dealer statute which calls for absolute liability of the dealer.[4] The Uniform Commercial Code, which deals with consignment sales in general, also shifts the responsibility to the gallery.[5] Moreover, under the special artist-dealer statute the artist cannot even be forced to waive his/her statutory rights, and any agreement which shifts the responsibility for loss or damage is unenforceable.[6] Nevertheless, despite these statutory rules, where there is no insurance all that the artist can do is demand compensation from the dealer. If the dealer refuses, the artist must go to court, and although he/she must certainly win, litigation is an unpleasant prospect. Perhaps a comprehensive insurance policy which covers business property or inventory off premises would be a more appropriate alternative.

Casualty/Liability Insurance

The artist who runs an active studio with many visitors may want to consider a policy which covers personal injuries to other persons. Of course, personal injuries are covered under most home and office package policies, so that there need be no new policy if the artist is already using the home or office policy to insure his/her works. However, as mentioned above, the homeowner's policy will usually not cover inventory or business property, and it will not cover the artist for injuries sustained on business premises.

If the artist is not protected by a package policy, a separate liability policy should be secured, especially for artists who work in hazardous areas or with materials which present dangers to visitors. For instance, the artist who runs a small "foundry" on his/her premises or who produces

[4] California Civil Code SS 1738-38.9.
[5] Uniform Commercial Code S 2-309.
[6] California Civil Code S 1738.6(c).

large sculptures may wish to have fairly high coverage for personal injuries. Sometimes even chemicals in a darkroom may be potential hazards. Failure to procure such insurance will result in exposure to enormous claims. A very large judgment against an artist can burden the artist for the rest of his/her life. And coverage is relatively inexpensive.

The problems of personal injury insurance are particularly vexing for performance artists, especially those who are not covered because they do not perform in traditional venues such as auditoriums and theaters whose proprietors carry insurance. Artists, such as Chris Burden of Los Angeles, who perform dangerous works of performance art outdoors, should either be judgment-proof, have accommodating relatives who live abroad or somehow obtain insurance to cover their performances. Strange as it may seem, insurance to cover the risks of daring performance art may be available. There is always a species of public liability insurance reserved for performers or theater owners, at least if one is willing to pay for it.

Artists are not only liable for "slip and fall" accidents on their premises or for injuries caused by their performances but can be held liable for injuries resulting from defects in their products. The sculpture which tips over, the mobile which falls from the ceiling or the electric work which starts a fire may cause claims against the artist.

These types of claims ordinarily cannot be referred to one's home, office or personal liability policies unless the incident occurs on the insured's premises. What is first indicated is a products liability policy. However, the artist who just paints oil paintings or manufactures small sculptures may not need a products liability policy to insure against such claims. Probably these types of works will not cause injury, and the artist, after all, is not responsible if someone else uses the work as a weapon or projectile. Nonetheless, if the artist's works are incorporated in useful articles, such as furniture or kitchenware, where they are in physical contact with people, or if the works are large and made to hang from walls or ceilings, a products liability policy may be recommended. If the artist is mass-producing a work for use in many locations it is imperative to procure such a policy.

The artist should remember that in products liability cases the court may impose "strict liability" so that the artist will not be able to avoid financial responsibility for the injury if the claimant can establish that a defect in the work contributed to his/her injuries.[7] The best thing is to get insurance, which in most situations is relatively inexpensive. The expense must be viewed only as another cost of doing business. The artist should ensure that the policy covers all of his/her line of products for all their intended uses. It does not help to have a policy if it does not apply to a particular work used in a certain fashion. If there are any doubts about the coverage, check with one's agent, and broaden the scope of the policy with a rider to the policy, if necessary. Where the artistic works are mass-produced, the marginal cost per item is very small in any case.

Another type of insurance needed by some artists is "completed operations" liability insurance, which is akin to the products liability insurance. Unlike the products liability policy, which covers injuries resulting from defects in the goods produced and sold by the artist, the completed operations policy covers injuries arising from use of the goods by others. For instance, the artist whose large hanging mobile fell on someone may be covered by a completed operations policy.[8]

---

[7] Where "strict liability" is imposed, the claimant need not even establish that the artist was negligent or at fault in any way.
[8] Completed operations insurance, therefore, covers injuries which are caused by the use of the artist's product even though no defect in the product contributed to the injury.

If the artist is one who subcontracts others to work for him/her, an independent contractor's liability policy will cover him/her for claims arising from operations by subcontractors on his/her behalf.

Where the artist is running a large business, such as a manufacturing enterprise, a comprehensive general liability policy is recommended which will cover most of the liabilities faced by the business.

Disability, Dismemberment Insurance

Many professionals are solicited by insurance agents to buy disability and dismemberment insurance policies. One often associates this type of coverage with well-to-do physicians, lawyers and corporate executives. However, artists, especially the chosen few who make their living almost exclusively from their art, must consider certain types of insurance to cover them for their own injuries. Just because Betty Grable obtained insurance for her legs, which were considered income-producing assets, does not mean that every artist should immediately insure his/her hands. Nevertheless, certain artists who receive a high return for their work must view their hands as capital assets, and insurance for severe injury or dismemberment, which would compensate them for a catastrophic accident, may be considered.

The Artists Equity Policy

For many years concerned artists have bemoaned the fact that there seemed to be no comprehensive policy which covered them for the most common perils and liabilities which they faced. As explained above, the homeowner's policy or even other package policies excluded coverage for the artist's works, either because they were considered business property or because they were subject to off-premises risks. Because of this apparent void in the insurance market for artists, Artists Equity, the national organization of artists dedicated to promoting artists' rights, developed the concept of a comprehensive all-risk fine art insurance program for visual artists.

Developing the concept of a comprehensive policy for artists was an easy task compared to finding an insurance company to underwrite the policy.[9] After years of bargaining with insurance carriers who were loath to carry such a policy because of the lack of reliable information on the number of losses and amounts of compensable claims, Equity finally persuaded St. Paul Insurance Company to underwrite such a policy, which is now administered by Huntington T. Block Insurance Company.

This Artists Equity policy, which is available for both Equity members and other visual artists, has been touted as a panacea for the insurance woes of artists. Indeed, as far as the artist's works are concerned, the policy is almost all that one could hope it would be and represents a significant advance in insurance for working artists. However, the Equity policy is *not* a comprehensive liability policy, so that if the artist wants products liability insurance, completed operations insurance or any type of public liability insurance, these must be purchased in addition to the coverage of the Equity policy. Further, ostensibly it covers only "fine artists" and perhaps may exclude some commercial photographers and graphic artists.

[9] All-risk fine arts floater policies can be purchased from good commercial insurers which deal in multi-line products, and in some sense, therefore, the Equity policy is not exactly unique.

In more detail the Equity policy offers the following coverage and is restricted by the following exclusions.

Coverage is "all risk" including but not limited to loss or damage by fire, windstorm, breakage, water damage (including flood), earthquake, burglary, theft, damage caused by handling and while being transported, punctures, and rips or tears. The insurance covers within the 50 states of the United States and Canada. . . .

Works of art are covered while in your studio and/or storage location, while in the hands of others for approval to purchase, for restoration, for framing, for casting, and if necessary, at galleries and museums—but it is recommended that the galleries and museums be asked to insure.

The insurance is not meant to cover your studio furniture, fixtures, art supplies or art library; nor is it intended to cover your responsibility for the care of the property of others, such as other members of a co-op.

The exclusions in the policy are: (a) wear and tear, gradual deterioration, moths, vermin, inherent vice or damage sustained due to or resulting from any repairing, restoration, or retouching process; (b) war risks and nuclear radiation; (c) inventory shortage, mysterious disappearance and misappropriation, secretion, infidelity or any dishonest act on the part of others to whom the insured property may be entrusted (carriers for hire excepted); (d) loss due to bankruptcy of yourself or others.

Coverage at art and book fairs or international expositions is limited to $10,000 or the amount provided under your policy "at any other location," whichever is less, with a mandatory $500 deductible applying.

Valuation of works of art is based on 60% of the selling price, or if the work has been sold, but not delivered to the purchaser, then the work would be insured for the full selling price. Commissioned works of art are insured for the commissioned price.

50% of the amount of insurance at your studio will apply "at any other location" or "while in transit in any one shipment" within the United States and Canada, except there is a limit of $1,000 on any parcel post shipment. Mail shipments must be either registered first class or parcel post. . . . All property must be packed by competent packers. If you must transport in your own vehicle, a borrowed or rented vehicle, the property must never be left unattended (whether or not the vehicle is locked).

A mandatory $100 deductible clause applies per loss (not per item), except a mandatory 2% of the policy amount with a minimum $250 deductible applies to all earthquake losses in California. . . .[10]

Finding Insurance

Because the Artists Equity policy is now available, at least some of the problems of finding proper insurance have been dispelled. However, because the working artist may have other needs, perhaps they must be met elsewhere. Where does one look?

In the first place, one must find the right agent or broker. Agents fall into two categories: independent and employed. Although both types sell insurance, the independent agent works with only as many companies as he/she wants, and he/she sells policies to his/her clients which are written only by the companies he/she represents. The employed agent works only for one insurance company as

[10] Selected excerpts quoted verbatim from the current flyer accompanying the application form for the Equity policy. For further information about this insurance policy, contact Ms. Gail Simmons, Artists Equity Association, Inc., 3726 Albemarle Street, N.W., Washington, DC 20016, (202) 244-0209.

an employee and writes only the insurance policies carried by that company. On the other hand, brokers are not necessarily associated with any particular company or companies and are free to negotiate insurance with any company which is willing to write it.

Unless the artist wants insurance issued by a particular company, perhaps because that company has the right policy, he/she should go to an agent or broker who is familiar with insurance for artists and who has access to policies handled by several companies. One way to find such an agent or broker is to ask other agents or brokers, or to make inquiries with artists and dealers who carry the type of insurance that is desired. Once a working relationship is established with an insurance representative, the artist should insist on shopping around for the best policy and should not snap up the first policy that is proffered. The artist should remember that not all policies have identical coverage in terms of perils, exclusions, deductibles and the like. Moreover, not all insurance companies are the same. Some have much better reputations for attending to and paying out on claims.

Making the Claim

Once a compensable loss occurs the insured artist should make a claim forthwith. Assuming that the artist has paid his/her premiums on time and has maintained adequate records, he/she should expect some compensation. However, before an insurance company will pay out on a claim it will want to be assured that the claim is genuine and well founded. The artist, therefore, may have to comply with some further requirements. In the first place, most policies require that the claim be filed within a certain period of time. This filing requirement in part is to eliminate stale claims which are filed after most of the original information about the loss or injury has evaporated or is not fresh in the minds of the parties concerned. The artist in furnishing a timely notice of loss or injury will also have to provide information about the time and cause of the event.

If there is a loss, the artist may also have to establish his/her interest in the property, and in some cases may even have to prove ownership with written documents. The artist must also declare the value of the destroyed work. In a few instances the claimant will be required to prove the loss by showing, for example, that the police were summoned and that a police report was actually made. Assuming that there is no squabble about whether the work is covered, the next issue is the amount of compensation to be paid. If no agreement can be reached an appraiser may be appointed. Ultimately the question may be settled in court. Most of the time the settlement or payment will be made by the local agent or adjuster, but sometimes the artist may wind up dealing with representatives from the principal offices of the insurance company.

Many of the same considerations apply to liability policies. The artist must be quick to report the incident giving rise to the claim and to gather all the evidence he/she can about the accident. In every way the artist will have to cooperate with the insurer in settling or defending against the claim, or otherwise he/she will find himself without coverage.

Alternatives to Insurance

The artist may avoid purchasing insurance, for example, by "self-insuring" as discussed above. However, there are other means to avoid insurance which have also been mentioned in passing.

For instance, the artist may enter into written contracts for indemnification. That is, the client or user may guarantee compensation for loss of a work, or a distributor may agree to indemnify and defend an artist in products liability cases. These arrangements are acceptable only if the indemnitor is reliable and solvent and there is no need to bring suit to enforce the agreement. Perhaps most museums, large agencies and corporate clients may be considered proper parties for such agreements. However, such an agreement with a client or user creates problems if one must sue them and thus establish a bad reputation as a "litigant." It is easy to imagine situations where the client or user will refuse to compensate the artist because the work was destroyed by accident. Should the artist thereafter commence legal proceedings? In any case, if the artist is serious about indemnification agreements which are enforceable he/she must ensure that each such agreement contains a provision for an award of attorney's fees should he/she have to enforce the agreement.

The second alternative for avoiding the purchase of insurance is to become the beneficiary of an insurance policy purchased by another. For example, with products liability insurance, a distributor or even a retailer can buy a policy naming the artist as an insured party. Thus, if the artist is sued because of injuries caused by a defect in his/her product, he/she may avail himself/herself of the insurance protection purchased by another. In other words, the artist becomes a direct beneficiary, i.e., a "third-party beneficiary," of the insurance contract between the insurance company and the purchaser of the insurance policy. This means of protection is a viable alternative, especially if a commissioned project is undertaken or if a continuing series of commercial transactions are involved. However, the transaction costs and inconvenience of buying a policy which names the artist as a beneficiary may deter the potential purchaser of insurance from dealing with the artist if the artist insists on such a policy.

If the artist can persuade the party he/she is dealing with to carry insurance which protects the artist, it is incumbent upon the artist to examine the policy. In many cases artists will have a contract which provides that they will be covered by insurance, and sometimes the amounts of coverage are specified. However, unless the artist actually insists upon the right to examine the policy, the artist may be left with a skimpy policy which has numerous exclusions and deductibles. In other words, effectively the artist will not be insured for the broad range of risks and perils for which he/she intended to be covered.

Insurance, self-insurance, indemnification agreements and third-party beneficiary insurance policies are just some of the alternatives available to artists. Furthermore, the artist, if he/she has the time and resources, can engage in "creative" insuring. Many of these alternative solutions may be combined so that when loss or liability occurs the artist will have a number of collateral sources of compensation.

For many artists, insurance and art are like oil and water. Artists are persons often characterized by daring and unconventional ways, and by their willingness to forgo financial rewards and comforts in favor of their work. For the artist to be burdened by the thoughts of innumerable risks, liabilities and contingencies, and further by the prospect of insuring against them, takes away energy and concentration from his/her work. To be an innovative artist and a prudent businessperson at the same time is no easy task.

Nevertheless, at a time when the law is expanding to recognize new wrongs and remedies and when claimants do not hesitate to bring suit, can the artist ignore the risks which are covered by liability insurance? Perhaps the artist may dispense with protection for his/her works and his/her studio, because a studio may be renovated and new works created. But liability insurance cannot be ignored by any practicing artist whose operations present risks of injuries to others. As is the case with automobile insurance, liability insurance in some way also represents a social responsibility. Moreover, although most losses involving the artist's works or studio will not be catastrophic,[11] even the "all-risk" insurance plans may allay the fears of those who continually worry about the safety of their workplace and the products of their labor. Insurance, after all, is not only evaluated in terms of dollars and cents but may bring a sense of security to the artist in an otherwise insecure world.

[11] Note that there is insurance which will provide compensation for lost income suffered as a result of the destruction of the artist's studio.

PART SIX

APPENDICES

VISUAL ARTIST RESOURCE APPENDIX

Compiled by Gregory T. Victoroff, Esq.

The following array of organizations, associations, clubs, guilds, museums, schools and agencies provides a panoply of assistance for visual artists of all types. Organizations nationwide are listed alphabetically in six categories of assistance rendered.

Organizations marked with an asterisk (*) render two or more types of services, as designated by the following symbols:

I – Information, reference and educational services and resources for visual artists.

$ – Grant sources and grant information, scholarships, direct economic aid, financial assistance.

L – Legal information and assistance; lawyer referrals for visual artists.

GV – Governmental arts agencies; civic, state, regional and federal offices, commissions, councils and legislative caucuses.

T – Technical assistance in art or arts management.

M – Membership organizations; unions, guilds, clubs.

I
INFORMATION, REFERENCE, EDUCATIONAL

Following is an alphabetical list of organizations which provide arts information. Included are reference sources, educational opportunities, information clearinghouses and community arts centers.

American Council for the Arts*
570 Seventh Avenue
New York, NY 10018
(212) 354-6655   I, GV

Arts for Communities, Inc.
9850 Terra Dell
Pico Rivera, CA 90660
(213) 949-3866

Arts and Humanities Center of Los Angeles*
2405 Echo Park Avenue
Los Angeles, CA 90026
(213) 664-2483   I, T

California College/Arts and Crafts*
Center for the Visual Arts
Oakland, CA 94618
(415) 653-8118   I, T

California Confederation of the Arts*
6253 Hollywood Boulevard, Suite 922
Los Angeles, CA 90028
(213) 469-5873   I, GV

California Institute of the Arts
24700 West McDean Parkway
Vallencia, CA 91355
(805) 255-1050

Center for Arts Information
625 Broadway
New York, NY 10012

Craft & Folk Art Museum*
Contemporary Craft Council
5814 Wilshire Boulevard
Los Angeles, CA 90036
(213) 937-5544   I, T

Foundation for the Community of Artists
220 Broadway
New York, NY 10007

Inland Empire Cultural Foundation
11161 Santo Antonio Drive
Suite J
Colton, CA 92323

Intercultural Council of the Arts
415 West Broadway
San Diego, CA 92101

LACE
240 South Broadway
Los Angeles, CA 90012
(213) 620-0104

Los Angeles Center for Photographic
  Studies*
P.O. Box 74381
Los Angeles, CA 90004
(213) 661-5290   I, T

Los Angeles Public Library*
Art, Music and Recreation Department
630 West Fifth Street
Los Angeles, CA 90071
(213) 626-7461   I, T

Management in the Arts Program*
Graduate School of Management
University of California, Los Angeles
Los Angeles, CA 90024
(213) 825-4488   I, T

Maryland Summer Institute for the Creative and
  Performing Arts
University of Maryland
College Park, MD 20742
(301) 454-5910

Museum of Modern Art
11 West 53rd Street
New York, NY 10019
(212) 956-6100

Neighborhood Arts*
522 North Salsipuedes Street
Santa Barbara, CA 93103
(805) 965-3559   I, T

New York Artists Equity Association*
225 West 34th Street
New York, NY 10001   I, M

Otis Art Institute/Parsons School of Design*
2041 Wilshire Boulevard
Los Angeles, CA 90057
(213) 387-5288   I, T

Pasadena Arts Council*
780 South Arroyo Parkway
Pasadena, CA 91105
(213) 795-0825   I, $, GV

Public Corporation for the Arts*
130 Pine Avenue
Long Beach, CA 90802
(213) 432-8708   I, T

Regional Arts Council, Turlock*
2690 El Capitan
Turlock, CA 95380   I, GV

San Jose Fine Arts Commission*
2064 Alameda Way
San Jose, CA 95126
(408) 998-3020   I, GV

Santa Barbara Artists Equity
127 W. Ortega Street
Santa Barbara, CA 93101

Sonoma County Arts Council*
P.O. Box 509
Occidental, CA 95465   I, GV

Sonoma State University
Rohnert Park, CA 94928
(707) 664-2880

Southern California Women's Caucus for Art
9127 Encino Avenue
Northridge, CA 91325

Visual Artists and Galleries Association
(VAGA)*
One World Trade Center
Suite 1535
New York, NY 10048   I, $, L, T

Visual Arts Resources
Museum of Art
University of Oregon
1802 Moss Street
Eugene, OR 97403

Western States Art Foundation
P.O. Box 8289
Denver, CO 80201

The Woman's Building*
1727 North Spring
Los Angeles, CA 90012
(213) 221-6161   I, T

Women in Design
4240 Stern Avenue
Sherman Oaks, CA 91423

$

GRANTS, SCHOLARSHIPS, DIRECT ECONOMIC AID

These organizations render direct financial assistance through grants and funding, grants information, loans, scholarships and competitions. Amounts available vary according to need and the specific project being funded. Contact organizations directly concerning application deadlines and specific requirements.

Artists Equity Association, Inc.*
3726 Albemarle Street, N.W.
Washington, DC 20016 $, I, GV, L

Change, Inc. West*
P.O. Box 480027
Los Angeles, CA 90048
(213) 652-9172 $, I

Judith Selkowitz Fine Arts, Inc.*
65 East 55th Street
Suite 504
New York, NY 10022
(212) 838-3706 $, I

Los Angeles, City of*
Municipal Arts Department
Room 1500, City Hall
Los Angeles, CA 90012
(213) 485-2433 $, I, GV

National Endowment for the Arts*
Washington, DC 20506
DC (202) 634-1566
LA (213) 385-3990 $, GV

L
LEGAL INFORMATION, REFERRALS

These organizations comprise a nationwide network of legal assistance services for artists. Most provide legal information important to artists, and referrals to lawyers who practice in art law, copyright and related areas. Most offer legal aid on a reduced-fee, "ability-to-pay" or *pro bono* (free) basis. Some provide group legal services for artists' membership organizations and conduct seminars and symposia on legal issues confronting visual arts.

Advocates for the Arts
UCLA School of Law
405 Hilgard Avenue
Los Angeles, CA 90024

Arts and the Lawyer*
6420 West 95th Street
Suite 202
Overland Park
Lawrence, KS 66212
(913) 648-0500   L, I, GV

Bay Area Lawyers for the Arts (BALA)*
Fort Mason Center
Building B
San Francisco, CA 94123
(415) 775-7200   L, I, T

Beverly Hills Bar Association*
Barristers' Committee for the Arts
300 South Beverly Drive
Suite 201
Beverly Hills, CA 90212
(213) 553-6644   L, I

Chicago Bar Association*
Creative Arts Committee
1130 South Wabash Avenue
Chicago, IL 60605
(312) 922-3106   L, I

Connecticut Volunteer Lawyers for the Arts
Connecticut Commission on the Arts
340 Capitol Avenue
Hartford, CT 06106
(203) 566-4770

Florida State Bar Association*
"Lawyers and the Arts"
1915 Harrison Street
Hollywood, FL 33020
(904) 222-5286   L, I

Kansas Bar Association
Committee on the Arts
1200 Southwest Harrison
Topeka, KS 66612

Lawyers for the Arts Committee*
Young Lawyers Section
Philadelphia Bar Association
260 South Broad Street
Room 1302A
Philadelphia, PA 19102
(215) 864-0400 (Attorney Referral)
(215) 545-3385 (Committee for the Arts)   L, I

Lawyers for the Creative Arts*
Suite 1404
220 South State Street
Chicago, IL 60604
(312) 987-0198   L, I

Los Angeles County Bar Association*
Barristers' Committee for the Arts
Artists and the Law
606 South Olive, Suite 1212
Los Angeles, CA 90014
(213) 627-2727   L, I

Los Angeles Lawyers for the Arts*
617 South Olive Street
Suite 515
Los Angeles, CA 90014
(213) 614-0972   L, I

Volunteer Lawyers for the Arts*
36 West 44th Street
Suite 1110
New York, NY 10036   L, I, T

GV
GOVERNMENTAL ARTS AGENCIES

These organizations are primarily municipal, state, regional and federal governmental agencies which administer public arts projects and provide information on local arts legislation.

California Alliance for Arts Education*
18401 Blackhawk Street
Northridge, CA 91326
(213) 363-0558

California Arts Council*
2022 J Street
Sacramento, CA 95814
(916) 445-1530   GV, I

California State Board of Equalization*
1020 N Street, Room 118
Sacramento, CA 95814
(916) 445-6479   GV, T, I

Congressional Arts Caucus*
1707 Longworth House Office Building
Washington, DC 20515
(202) 225-5936   GV, I

Florida Secretary of State*
Division of Cultural Affairs
Capitol Building
Tallahassee, FL 32301
(904) 488-6346   GV, I

Illinois Art Council*
111 North Wabash
Chicago, IL 60602
(312) 793-6750   GV, I

Iowa Arts Council*
State Capitol Building
Des Moines, IA 50319   GV, I

Kansas, State of*
Arts Commission
112 Sixth Street
Topeka, KS 66603
(913) 296-3335   GV, $

Massachusetts Council on the Arts and
   Humanities*
One Ashburton Place
Boston, MA 02108
(617) 727-3668   GV, I

Minnesota Citizens for the Arts*
709 Pioneer Building
St. Paul, MN 55101   GV, I

National Assembly of State Arts Agencies
1010 Vermont Avenue, N.W.
Washington, DC 20005
(202) 347-6352

Oregon Arts Commission*
835 Summer, N.E.
Salem, OR 97301
(503) 378-3625   GV, I

Sacramento Metropolitan Arts Commission
1221 J Street
Sacramento, CA 95814
(916) 449-5320

Sacramento Regional Arts Council*
Downtown Plaza
Sacramento, CA 95818
(916) 441-1044   GV, I

San Francisco Arts Commission*
City Hall
San Francisco, CA 94102
(415) 648-4744   GV, I, $

San Francisco Arts Department*
1306 Mission
San Francisco, CA 94103
(415) 861-0938   GV, $, I

M
UNIONS, GUILDS, CLUBS

These organizations invite artists to receive the benefits of membership. They include unions, guilds and clubs which provide opportunities for artists to participate in group projects and to interact with other artists, as well as providing informational assistance to their members.

Allied Craftsmen*
13063 Via Grimaldi
Del Mar, CA 92014   M, I, T

American Society of Magazine Photographers*
205 Lexington Avenue
New York, NY 10016   M, I, T

Artists for Economic Action*
974 Teakwood Road
Los Angeles, CA 90049
(213) 472-8008   M, I, GV

Artists Foundation*
100 Boylston Street
Boston, MA 02116
(617) 482-8100   M, GV, I, T

Arts Council of Kern*
P.O. Box 1244
Bakersfield, CA 93302   M, GV, I

Association of Artist-Run Galleries*
c/o Pleiades Gallery
152 Wooster Street
New York, NY 10012   M, I, T

Association of International Photography Art Dealers, Inc.*
60 East 42nd Street
Suite 2505
New York, NY 10165   M, I

Boston Visual Artists Union, Inc.*
77 North Washington Street
Boston, MA 02114
(617) 227-3076   M, I, T

Chicago Artists Coalition*
5 West Grand Avenue
Chicago, IL 60610   M, I

Cultural Alliance of Greater Washington
805 15th Street, N.W.
Washington, DC 20005
(202) 638-2406

Graphic Artists Guild*
330 East 20th Street
New York, NY 10003   M, I, T

SELECTED BIBLIOGRAPHY

(Listed by Subject Matter)[1]

BUSINESS AND MARKETING

Cochrane, Diane, *This Business of Art,* Watson-Guptill Publishers, New York, 1978, 256 pp. Written particularly for the artist, this book covers such areas as copyright, income and estate taxes, insurance, bookkeeping, cooperative galleries, arrangements with publishers, dealers and museums. The book includes some contracts and forms, and is written in question-and-answer style. Includes an appendix listing of Volunteer Lawyers for the Arts Organizations.

Crawford, Tad, and Kopelman, Arie, *Selling Your Graphic Design and Illustration* and *Selling Your Photography,* Graphic Artists Guild, 30 East 20th Street, New York, NY 10003. These two volumes set down, in a practical format, the markets, standard contractual terms, billing and pricing, "the going concern," business records, libel, obscenity, invasion of privacy, releases and legal concerns.

Follis, John, and Hammer, Dave, *Architectural Signing and Graphics,* Whitney/Watson-Guptill, New York, 1979.

Foote, Rosslyn F., *Running an Office for Fun and Profit: Business Techniques for Small Design Firms,* McGraw-Hill, New York, 1978.

Goodchild, Jon, and Henkin, Bill, *By Design: A Graphics Sourcebook of Materials, Equipment and Services,* Quick Fox, 1979.

Goodman, Calvin J., "Every Artist Is a Dealer," 40 *American Artist* 47 (February 1976).

Gordon, Barbara, and Gordon, Elliott, *How to Survive in the Free Lance Jungle,* Executive Communications, 400 East 54th Street, New York, NY 10022. Mail order: $9.95 including handling.

Klimet, Stephen A., *Creative Communications for a Successful Design Practice,* Watson-Guptill, New York, 1977.

Paetro, Maxine, *How to Put Your Book Together and Get a Job in Advertising,* Executive Communications, 400 East 54th Street, New York, NY. Mail order: $9.95 including handling.

[1] Complete information on magazines, periodicals and arts organizations can be found in the Magazines, Newsletters and Subscriptions section of this Bibliography and in the Resources section of this Manual.

Scott, Michael, *The Crafts Business Encyclopedia: Marketing, Management and Money,* P.O. Box 1992, Wilmington, DE 19899. Covers everything you ever wanted to know about the field alphabetically, from accounting to zoning.

Travers, David, *Preparing Design Office Brochures: A Handbook,* Management Books, Santa Monica, CA.

Witteborg, Lother P., *Good Show: A Practical Guide for Temporary Exhibitions,* Smithsonian Institution.

"Art and Money: The Artist's Royalty Problem," 62 *Art in America* 20 (March 1974).

Banking for Nonbankers, D.H.A. Associates, P.O. Box 1861, Seattle, WA 98111.

Borrowing Basics for Women, Citibank, Public Affairs Department, P.O. Box 939, Church Street Station, New York, NY 10008.

The Graphic Artists Guild Handbook: Pricing and Ethical Guidelines, Fourth Edition. This 144-page book outlines in great detail the standard prices and trade customs for artists and free-lance and staff art directors based on our 1981 nationwide survey. Also includes model contracts and principles of buying and selling art.

Professional Business Practices in Photography, American Society of Magazine Photographers, 205 Lexington Avenue, New York, NY 10016. A nuts-and-bolts approach to the business of doing business for professional photographers. Sample form contracts, copyright, insurance, trade definitions, agent relationships.

COLLECTING

Carter, "The World Art Market Conference," 75 *Art News* 46 (December 1976).

Duffy, Robert E., *Art Law: Representing Artists, Dealers and Collectors,* Practicing Law Institute, New York, 1977.

Graves, Harmon S., "The Art Collector and the Tax Collector," 32 *Art L. Journal* 426 (Summer 1973).

Hodes, Scott, *The Law of Art and Antiques,* Oceana, Dobbs Ferry, NY, 1966, 112 pp. This book is divided into two parts: the first covering areas of concern to the artist such as sales, copyright and taxes, and the second dealing with the collector—purchases, customs, taxes and insurance.

Hodes, Scott, *What Every Artist and Collector Should Know About the Law,* E. P. Dutton, New York, 1974, 268 pp. Expanded and updated materials from earlier book. Half the book deals with the concerns of the artist while the other half treats the concerns of the collector. Appendices contain form contracts, including gallery rental agreement, museum loan, assignment of copyright.

"Acquisition and Disposition of Art Objects," *Art & the Law,* Vol. IV, No. 3 (1979).

"Art Collector as Investor: Tax Considerations," *Art & the Law,* Vol. III, No. 4 (August–September 1977).

COPYRIGHT

Cochrane, "The New Copyright Revision Act," 42 *American Artist* 92 (April 1978).

Crawford, Tad, "Copyright for Graphic Design," 44 *American Artist* 74–77 (June 1980).

Crawford, Tad, "Copyright Law Update: A Revised Opinion," 66 *Art in America* 11 (May–June 1978).

Crawford, Tad, "The New Copyright Law," 67 *Art in America* (September–October 1977).

Crawford, Tad, *Visual Artists' Guide to the New Copyright Law,* Graphic Artists Guild, New York, 1978, 63 pp. An excellent overview of the impact and use of the copyright law as it relates specifically to the visual artist.

Glassman, David, *Writers and Artists' Rights,* Writers Press, Washington, DC, 1978, 104 pp., ill. Treatment of the basic benefits and protections extended to authors, artists, composers, sculptors, photographers, choreographers and moviemakers under the new Copyright Act.

Knoll and Drapiewski, "Knowing Your Copyrights," 55 *Museum News* 49 (March–April 1977).

Koenigsberg, Fred I., "1976 Copyright Act: Advances for the Creator," 26 *Clev. St. L. Rev.* 479 (1977), Art and Law Symposium.

Millinger, Donald M., "Copyright and the Fine Artist," Associate, Wolf, Black, Schorr & Solis-Cohen, *Phil. Geo. Wash. L. Rev.* 354 (March 1980).

Oppenheimer, G., "Originality in Art Reproductions: 'Variations' in Search of a Theme," The Copyright Society of the USA, NYU Law Center, 40 Washington Square South, New York, NY 10012.

Thorkelson, Howard, "A Lawyer's Commentary on the New Copyright Law," 41 *American Artist* 40 (January 1977).

"Copyright Revision Bill's Impact on the Visual Artist," 1976 by Visual Dialog, *Art & the Law,* Vol. II, No. 6 (September–October 1976).

"Courting the Artist with Copyright: The 1976 Copyright Act," 24 *Wayne L. Rev.* 1685–1704 (Summer 1978).

"The Evolving Law of Artists: The Search for an American Law of Personalty," *Art & the Law* (December 1974).

"Exhibiting Without Copyright: The Visual Artist's Dilemma," *Art & the Law* (January 1975).

"Fine Artist's Right to the Reproductions of His Original Work," 23 *L. Sym.* 81–87 (1977).

An Introduction to the New Copyright Law, Bay Area Lawyers for the Arts, San Francisco, 1978. This work discusses the new Copyright Revision Act of 1976 and provides basic information to artists in any medium.

"A New Weapon for Artists' Rights: Sec. 439(a) of the Lanham Trademark Act," *Art & the Law,* Vol. V, No. 2 (1980).

"The Omnibus Copyright Revision," *Art & the Law,* Vol. II, No. 3 (February–March 1976).

What Every Artist Should Know About Copyright, Volunteer Lawyers for the Arts, New York, 1978. Describes recent changes in the copyright law which affect every visual, literary and performing artist.

ESTATE PLANNING AND ADMINISTRATION

Ashbury, Edith Evans, "The Rothko Decision," 75 *Art News* 42 (February 1976).

Carter, Malcolm N., "The Impact of the Rothko Case," 76 *Art News* 78 (October 1977).

Conrad, A., "Artful Trust: A Breakthrough in Estate Planning for Artists," 43 *American Artist* 88 (July 1979).

Crawford, Tad, *Protecting Your Heirs and Creative Works: An Estate Planning Guide for Artists, Authors, Composers and Other Creators of Artistic Works,* Graphic Artists Guild, New York, 1980. An excellent, easy-to-read guide.

Harrow, Gustave, "Reflections on the Estate of Rothko," 26 *Cleve. St. L. Rev.* 479 (1977), Art and the Law Symposium. A thorough, reflective and informative examination of the responsibilities of advisers, attorneys, executors and trustees to the artist and the artist's estate.

Hess, John L., "The Rothko Donnybrook," 71 *Art News* 24 (November 1972).

Lerner, Max K., and Taubman, Joseph, "The Significance of Rothko," 6 *Performing Arts Rev.* 187 (1976).

Lieb, Charles, and Schaaf, David, "Estate Planning for Creators of Intellectual Property," *U. Ill. Law Forum* 373 (1979).

Merryman, John Henry, "The 'Straw Man' in the Rothko Case," 75 *Art News* 32 (December 1976).

Seldes, Lee, *The Legacy of Mark Rothko,* Holt, Rinehart and Winston, New York, 1978, 372 pp. Written by a journalist who covered the entire trial of Mark Rothko, this book describes the intricacies of the case and the people involved, in light of Rothko's life and position as an artist.

"Effect of the 1976 Tax Reform Act on Artists' Estate and Gift Tax," *Art & the Law,* Vol. II, No. 8 (January–February 1977).

"The Final Word in the Rothko Case: Salient Legal Holdings of the Court of Appeals," *Art & the Law,* Vol. IV, No. 2 (1978).

"Nothing in It for the Artist: Estate of *Friedman* v. *Egan,* " *Art & the Law,* Vol. V, No. 2 (1980).

"Rothko Continued," 73 *Art News* 46 (May 1974).

"The Rothko Estate: The Case of the Beleaguered Executor," *Art & the Law,* Vol. II, No. 5 (Summer 1976).

"The Rothko Trial," 73 *Art News* 72 (April 1974).

"Valuing Artists' Estates: What Is Fair?" *Art & the Law,* Vol. II, No. 5 (Summer 1976).

GRANTS AND FUND RAISING[2]

Brownrigg, W. Grant, *Corporate Fundraising: A Practical Plan of Action.* American Council for the Arts (ACA), 1978. Detailed practical and systematic approach to soliciting contributions from business.

Coe, Linda; Denny, Rebecca; and Rogers, Anne, *Cultural Directory II.* A source for locating grants and assistance available from the federal government for cultural activities. Includes details on more than 300 federal programs, activities and resources, and describes the assistance each offers to individuals, institutions and organizations.

"Fund Raising Ideas Catalog" comes from the Center for Non-Profits, 155 West 72nd Street, New York, NY 10023, free (send SASE).

Guide to Corporate Giving in the Arts. A 378-page book listing over 500 *Fortune-* ranked companies and details of their arts support programs.

"A Modern Medici for Public Art," *Art & the Law,* Vol. III, No. 2 (May–June 1977).

Money Business: Grants and Awards for Creative Artists. A directory of more than 300 organizations that offer assistance to individual artists. Contains listings for painters, sculptors, printmakers, video artists and choreographers. Includes information on whom to contact, amount of the award and application process.

Raising Money for the Arts. Summarizes the speeches and sessions of ACA's 1979 conference on fund raising, conducted with the United Way. Contains information on basic fund-raising principles and organization, recruiting and training volunteers and developing a case for giving.

[2] The books marked with an asterisk are available from the American Council for the Arts (ACA), 570 Seventh Avenue, New York, NY 10018.

"Recent Developments in Federal Regulation of Recipients of Federal Financial Assistance," *Art & the Law,* Vol. V, No. 1 (1979).

*United Arts Fundraising Manual. Seven directors from leading united arts funds share their expertise on the rudiments of organizing and running a united arts campaign. Collectively, their organizations raised nearly $12 million for the arts in 1979. Covers such topics as starting up a united arts fund, campaign techniques and promotional materials and allocation of funds.

*United Arts Fundraising Policybook. Contains a copy of the bylaws, policies and procedures from thirteen large and small united arts funds around the country. Provides examples for people interested in setting up a united arts fund or improving an existing one.

Washington International Arts Letter. A letter and digest concerning 20th Century Patronage, support programs and developments, books and publications. P.O. Box 9005, Washington, DC 20003.

Wherewithal: A Guide to Resources for Museums and Historical Societies in New York State. A 96-page softbound volume describing 145 organizations and government agencies offering funds, consultant and legal services, technical assistance, circulating exhibitions, workshops and research facilities. Available from Center for Arts Information, 625 Broadway, New York, NY 10012.

HEALTH HAZARDS, WORKER COMPENSATION AND PRODUCTS LIABILITY

Barazani, Gail Coninply, *Safe Practices in the Arts and Crafts: A Studio Guide,* 1977, available from the College Art Association, 16 East 52nd Street, New York, NY 10022, $3.00 plus $0.75 postage and handling.

"Beware Artists—Products Liability," *Art & the Law,* Vol. V, No. 2 (1979).

Center for Occupational Hazards publishes a newsletter on hazards in the arts, 5 Beekman Street, New York, NY 10038, $10 per year.

Kotz, Mary Lynn, and Kotz, Nick, "Can Making Art Be Hazardous to Your Health," *Art News,* Vol. 80, No. 4 (April 1981).

Luke, Joy Turner, "The Case for Voluntary Labeling for Chronic Toxicity." Contact Ms. Luke at Box 18, Route 1, Sperryville, VA 22740.

McCann, Michael, *Artist Beware: The Hazards and Precautions in Working with Art and Craft Materials,* Watson-Guptill, New York, $10.95.

McCann, Michael, *Health Hazards Manual for Artists,* Graphic Artists Guild, 30 East 20th Street, New York, NY 10003, 1978. This 40-page book tells you what job-related materials can cause serious health problems and includes information on rubber-cement solvents, markers and proper ventilation in work areas.

Moses, Cherie; Purdham, James; Bowhay, Dwight; and Hosein, Roland, *Health and Safety in Print-making: A Manual for Printmakers,* Alberta Labour, Occupational Health and Safety Division, 2nd Floor, Oxbridge Place, 9820 106th Street, Edmonton, Alberta, (403) 427-2687. An intensive study aimed at increasing printmakers' awareness of hazards associated with the chemicals they use and how to protect themselves.

Pinney, Zora, and Lasaraow, Bill, "Materials Standards and Labeling: Artists and Manufacturers Working Together," *Los Angeles Artists Equity News,* Vol. II, No. 2 (May 1981).

HOUSING, LIVE/WORK SPACE, THE STUDIO LEASE

Kern, Kogon, and Thallon, *The Owner-Builder and the Code,* Owner-Builder Publications, 1976.

Artist Housing Conference Materials, Volunteer Lawyers for the Arts, New York. Includes materials on artist certification, building and zoning regulations, duties of tenants and landlords.

Artists Live/Work Space: Changing Public Policy, Artists Equity Association's Northern California Chapter, 81 Leavenworth Street, San Francisco, CA 94102, $5.00 plus $1.00 for shipping. It covers zoning, building codes, political action and other pertinent topics.

"ART Matters" contains information about the International Visual Artists Exchange Programme (living/studio space), which is growing. Contact Margo Rish, Box 71011, Los Angeles, CA 90071.

Special Space: A Guide to Artists' Housing and Loft Living, Volunteer Lawyers for the Arts, New York, 1981. A comprehensive, information-packed book which takes its facts from artists' live/work space experiences in New York.

Workstead, Dolphin Books, 1981.

"You Can't Take It with You: Law of Fixtures and Loft Leases," *Art & the Law,* Vol. III, No. 8 (January 1978).

LEGISLATION

Chamberlain, Betty, "Prints: Can We Legislate?" 40 *American Artist* 26 (April 1976).

Crawford, Tad, "Legislation: Art Resale Proceeds," 48 *American Artist* 82 (June 1979).

Green, Dennis, *% for Art: New Legislation Can Integrate Art and Architecture,* American Council for the Arts, 570 Seventh Avenue, New York, NY 10018. History and analysis of state and local laws setting aside a percentage of public construction costs for works of art. Contains examples of legislation, contracts and guidelines for communities and states trying to start percent for art.

Karlen, Peter, "Law of Artificial Rarity: Fine Print Legislation," 110 West C Street, Ste 714, San Diego, CA 92101. 10 *Art Week* 21 (December 29, 1979).

Kriesberg, Luisa, *Local Government and the Arts,* American Council for the Arts, 570 Seventh Avenue, New York, NY 10018. Written in plain language, illustrated and organized in an easy-to-use loose-leaf binder format, the volume places the arts within the context of such municipal priorities as economic development, transportation, human resources and urban design. Highlights successful civic programs using the arts that can work in any city. An excellent manual showing what the arts can do for a city and what a city can do for the arts.

Wayne, June, and Sandison, Hamish, "On Print Disclosure Legislation," 40 *American Artist* 58 (April 1976).

"The California Art Preservation Act," *Art & the Law,* Vol. V, No. 3 (1980).

"California Art Preservation Act: Statutory Protection of Art Work Against Intentional Alteration or Destruction," 49 *U. Cinn. L. R.* 486 (1980).

Legislative Masterpieces: A Guide to California Arts Legislation, Bay Area Lawyers for the Arts, Fort Mason Center, Building B, San Francisco, CA 94123, 1980. Covers six different laws which have recently been passed in California.

LAW, CONTRACTS, ARTIST/DEALER/REPRESENTATIVE RELATIONSHIPS

Cochran, D., "When Commissioning Fine Art, Don't Forget the Fine Print: Commission Agreement Between Artists and Clients," *Contract Int.* 138 (Summer 1978).

Crawford, Tad, and Melon, Susan, *The Artist-Gallery Partnership,* American Council for the Arts, 570 Seventh Avenue, New York, NY 10018. Practical guide to drafting your own consignment contract.

Crawford, Tad, *Legal Guide for the Visual Artist.* Hawthorne Books, New York, 1977, 257 pp. This work deals with many areas of the law which are of interest to artists, collectors and dealers, and provides a reasonable and accurate overview of the law. Subjects include the 1976 Copyright Act, relations between artists and galleries, contracts, tax problems, loft leases, publishing and dealer contracts, First Amendment rights, relations between artists and museums and public support of the arts.

Davidson, Marion, and Blue, Martha, *Making It Legal,* McGraw-Hill Paperback Division, 1221 Avenue of the Americas, New York, NY, 1979. An overall view for visual artist and craftsmaker for setting up business, paying taxes, making contracts, avoiding liability and protecting creative work.

Duboff, Leonard D., and Crawford, Mary Ann, *Law and the Visual Arts,* 1974, 372 pp. Handbook from a conference at Northwestern School of Law, Portland, Oregon. A good overview, geared to lawyers, museum officials and art historians, on counseling the artist, artist's property rights, copyright law, international trade in national art treasures, scientific authentication of art and museum acquisition policies.

Duffy, Robert E., *Art Law: Representing Artists, Dealers and Collectors,* Practicing Law Institute, New York, 1977.

Elsen, Albert, and Merryman, John Henry, *Law, Ethics and the Visual Arts,* Matthew Bender, New York, 1979. An excellent compendium of materials, articles, contracts and annotations from a wide variety of sources around the country.

Feldman, Franklin, and Weil, Stephen E., *Legal and Business Problems of Artists, Art Galleries and Museums,* Practicing Law Institute, 1973. The original source and reference book on the visual arts. A vast collection of essays, articles and related information. Aimed at the artist, lawyer and art administrator.

Freedman, Robert, *Basic Law for the Artist,* Bay Area Lawyers for the Arts, San Francisco. Covers selecting the form of doing business, licensing and registration requirements, fundamental concepts of contract law. Appendices contain sample tax and business forms as well as form contracts—Projansky, Artists Equity and BALA model contracts.

Rosenbaum, Lee, "Artist-Gallery Contracts: Scenes from a Marriage," 65 *Art in America* 10 (July–August 1977).

Stone, Norman, *An Introduction to Contracts for the Visual Artist,* Bay Area Lawyers for the Arts, San Francisco, 1980, 34 pp. Included here are agreements for sale, transfer of rights, commission, consignment and other important aspects of contract law.

Warshaw, Robert S., "Law in the Art Marketplace," 53 *Museum News* 18 (May 1975).

Weiner, Richard M., "The Artist and His Gallery," 2 *Performing Arts Rev.* 91 (1971).

Art Works: Law, Policy, Practice, Practicing Law Institute, 1974.

Law and the Arts—Art and the Law, Lawyers for the Creative Arts/Chicago, T. Horwitz, Editor, 1979, 229 pp. A handbook/sourcebook for artists, craftspeople, arts attorneys and arts administrators. Deals with the legal and financial concerns of practicing in each artistic medium. Income taxes and record keeping, real estate, management, budgeting and bookkeeping and not-for-profit, tax-exempt corporate structure.

"Life-time Agency Contract Between O'Keeffe and Representative," *Art & the Law,* Vol. V, No. 1 (1980).

The Visual Artist and the Law, Associated Councils of the Arts, the Association of the Bar of the City of New York, Volunteer Lawyers for the Arts, 1974, 87 pp. Deals with the legal problems of the visual artist. It is a well-written, scholarly and well-documented introduction to the field, covering such topics as copyright, gallery agreements, publishers and museums, tax problems and art legislation. Aimed at the artist and the lawyer.

LITIGATION AND LEGAL PROBLEMS FOR THE VISUAL ARTIST

Adams, Laurie, *Art on Trial: From Whistler to Rothko,* Walker & Co., New York, 1976, 236 pp. Introduction by Tom Wolfe. Covers the most famous art trials of the past hundred years. Six trials in which the works of art themselves were the most predominant factors in the courtroom proceedings include the libel case of *Whistler* v. *Ruskin,* the customs case of *Brancusi* v. *United States,* the free speech decision of *New York* v. *Radich* and the recent headlines case of *The Estate of Mark Rothko.* The principal figures of interest are the artists, the critics and dealers.

Baldwin, Carl R., "Art and the Law: The Flag in Court Again," 62 *Art in America* 50 (May 1974).

Hochfield, Sylvia, "Artists' Rights: Pros and Cons," 74 *Art News* 20 (May 1975).

Karlen, P. H., "Legal Aesthetics," 19 *Brit. J. Aesthetics,* No. 3 (Summer 1979).

Meyer, Karl E., *Plundered Past,* Atheneum, New York, 1973, 353 pp. An absorbing study of the illegal international traffic in works of art, with special emphasis on archaeological works. Methods used by traffickers as well as the underlying philosophical and ethical problems of theft of artwork.

Schultz, E. H., "Joint Ethics: The Case of the Unauthorized Album Cover Art," 31 *Art Direction* 12 (Summer 1979).

Stella, Frank, "Duty of an Artist to Inform Purchaser of Duplicate Work," *Art & the Law,* Vol. IV, No. 4 (1979).

"Fraud à la Française? Bicentennial Arts Exhibition in Paris Results in Unsatisfied Claims," *Art & the Law,* Vol. IV, No. 1 (1978).

"The Print's Progress: Problems in a Changing Medium," reprinted with permission from *Art News* (Summer 1976), *Art & the Law,* Vol. II, No. 8 (January–February 1977).

"Stolen Art Ruling—Georgia O'Keeffe," *Art & the Law,* Vol. IV, No. 4 (1979).

"Theft, Wills and Moral Rights—Recent Court Rulings Regarding Georgia O'Keeffe and Jean Dubuffet," 77 *Art News* 40 (Summer 1978).

MUSEUMS AND ART ADMINISTRATION

Knoll, Alfred P., and Sandison, Hamish, "Museums: A Gunslinger's Dream," Bay Area Lawyers for the Arts, San Francisco. The relationship between artist and museum is explained, as well as the museum as a charitable trust, acquisition problems, museum management, an artist/gallery agreement.

Reiss, Alvin H., *Arts Management Handbook,* Second Edition, Law-Arts, New York, 1974.

Weintraub, Henry, "Museums with Walls—Public Regulation of Deaccessioning and Disposal," *Art & the Law,* Fall 1975.

A Survey of Arts Administration Training in the United States and Canada: 1979–80, American Council for the Arts, 570 Seventh Avenue, New York, NY 10018. Includes descriptions of university programs in arts administration, general arts and museum internships, special programs and seminars. For present and future arts administrators or for prospective employers who want an idea of the content of arts administration programs.

MORAL RIGHTS

Baldwin, Carl R., "Art and the Law: Property Right vs. 'Moral Right,'" 62 *Art in America* 34 (September 1974).

Baldwin, Carl R., "Whitney Flap: More on Artists' 'Moral Rights,'" 64 *Art in America* 10 (September–October 1976).

Crawford, Tad, "Moral Rights and the Artist," 42 *American Artist* 98 (April 1978).

Kirby, James R., "An Artist's Personal Rights in His Creative Works: Beyond the Human Cannonball and the Flying Circus," 9 *Pac. L.J.* 855 (1978).

Merryman, John Henry, "Bernard Buffet's Refrigerator and the Integrity of the Work of Art," 76 *Art News* 38 (February 1977).

Rose, Diana, "Calder's Pittsburgh: A Violated and Immobile Mobile," 77 *Art News* 38 (January 1978).

Sandison, Hamish, "California Enacts *Droit Moral* and *Droit de Suite,*" *Art & the Law,* Vol. III, No. 1 (March–April 1977).

Weil, S. E., "Moral Right Comes to California," 78 *Art News* 88–92 (December 1979).

PHOTOGRAPHY

Chernoff, G., and Sarbin, H., *Photography and the Law,* Fifth Edition, Amphoto Publishing, Garden City, NY, 1977, 160 pp.

Crawford, Tad, *Selling Your Photography,* St. Martin's Press, New York, 1980, 256 pp. Legal and financial concerns of the photographer. Deals with the various aspects of marketing photographs, materials and skills, choosing an agent or gallery representative, pricing, contracts, taxes, insurance, copyright, right to privacy, releases and choosing a lawyer. Appendices offer information on grants and professional organizations and associations.

The Garlic Press (Box 24799, Los Angeles, CA 90024) has a list which they sell for $30 of 400 galleries and museums which show/sell photography in the United States and 200 abroad.

Professional Business Practices in Photography, American Society of Magazine Photographers (ASMP), 205 Lexington Avenue, New York, NY 10016.

RESALE ROYALTIES

Ashley, Stephen S., "Critical Comment on California's *Droit de Suite,* Civil Code Sec. 986," 29 *Hastings L.J.* 249–60 (November 1977).

Boe, Kathryn L., "*Droit de Suite* Has Arrived: Can It Thrive in Califnia as It Has in Calais?" 11 *Creighton L.R.* 529–62 (December 1977).

Bolch, B. W., Damon, W. W., and Hinshaw, E. E., "An Economic Analysis of the California Art Royalty Statute," 10 *Conn. L. R.* 545 (Spring 1978), Nonprofit Arts Institutions: A Symposium.

Clack, "Artists' Rights," *The Cultural Post,* Issue 10 (March–April 1977), p. 1. Published by NEA, Washington, D.C. 20506.

Duffy, R. E., "Royalties for Visual Artists," 7 *Performing Arts Rev.* 560 (1977).

Elsen, Albert, "California Artists' Resale Law: Failure of Innocence," 65 *Art in America* (March–April 1977).

Gorewitz, Rubin, and Elsen, Albert, "Discussion on the California Royalties Law," 55 *Museum News* 7 (May–June 1977).

Gorewitz, Rubin, "Artists' Royalties: Should There Be a Law?" 62 *Art in America* 22 (March 1974).

Hochfield, Sylvia, "Legislating Royalties for Artists," 75 *Art News* 52 (December 1976).

Merryman, John Henry and Sandison, Hamish, "The California Royalty Bill: Milestone or Mistake?" 41 *American Artist* 60 (February 1977).

Price, Monroe E., "Economic Security for Artists: The Case of the *Droit de Suite,*" 77 *Yale L. J.* 1333 (1968).

Soloman, L. D., and Gill, L. V., "Federal and State Resale Royalty Legislation: What Hath Art Wrought?" 26 *UCLA L. R.* 322–59 (December 1978).

Weil, Stephen E., "Resale Royalties: Nobody Benefits," 77 *Art News* 58 (March 1978).

TAX

Abouaf, Jeffrey B., *Tax and the Individual Artist,* Bay Area Lawyers for the Arts, San Francisco.

Anthoine, Robert, "Deductions for Charitable Contributions of Appreciated Property—The Art World," NYU Law School, 35 *Tax L. Rev.* 239 (1980).

Baldwin, Carl R., "Art and Money: Acting to Reform the Tax Reform Act," 64 *Art in America* 40 (May 1976).

Chamberlain, Betty, "Artists' Tax Bills," 42 *American Artist* 18 (January 1978).

Crawford, Tad, "Is the Internal Revenue Service Unfair to Artists?" 41 *American Artist* 8 (March 1977).

Crawford, Tad, "The Hobby-Loss Challenge: For Many Artists, Their Biggest Headache," 40 *American Artist* 61 (February 1976).

Feld, A. L., "Artists, Art Collectors and Income Tax," Boston University School of Law, 60 *B. U. L. Rev.* 625 (1980).

Gray, Arnold L., "Income Tax and the Artists," 41 *American Artist* 43 (January 1977).

Helleloit, Richard, *The Tax Reliever: A Guide for the Artist,* Drum Books, Box 1651, St. Paul, MN 55116.

Holubowich, Alexandra, "Pension Plans for Artists," 41 *American Artist* 47 (January 1977).

Lidstone, Herrick K., *A Tax Guide for Artists and Arts Organizations,* Lexington Books, 1979. A highly informative, well-written, understandable guide to taxation, deduction, pension and profit-sharing plans and financial planning. Appendix contains sample cases and sample tax returns.

Murphy, "The 1976 Tax Reform Act: It Could Have Been Worse," 55 *Museum News* 30 (July–August 1977).

O'Connell, M. F., "Defending Art Valuations for Tax Purposes," 115 *Trusts & Est.* 604–7 (Summer 1976).

Rosenbaum, Lee, "More on Tax Reform: Artists Strike Out," 64 *Art in America* 23 (November–December 1976).

Skindrud, Michael, "Recognition Under Sec. 501(c)(3) of IRS as Prerequisite to Art Grants: Special Problems for Literary Publishers and Art Galleries," 26 *Cleve. St. L. Rev.* (1977), Art and the Law Symposium.

Sloane, Leonard, "Valuing Artists' Estates: What Is Fair?" 75 *Art News* 91 (April 1976).

Wasson, H. Reed, "Tax Reform Act Changes Deduction for Business Use of Home," 3 *Art & the Law* 1 (December 1977).

The Art of Deduction, Bay Area Lawyers for the Arts, San Francisco, 1980, 28 pp. This is a guide through the tax maze, covering what is taxable, what is deductible, guidelines for record keeping and more.

Fear of Filing—1980 Revision, Volunteer Lawyers for the Arts, New York. Designed to help the artist understand the federal tax system and cope with the variety of tax categories, as well as to become familiar with the 1040 form.

"Is There Art After Death?" 41 *American Artist* 35 (January 1977).

"The New Tax Law and Studio Deductions," 42 *American Artist* 112 (April 1978).

"Tax Treatment of Artists' Charitable Contributions," 89 *Yale L. J.* 144 (1979).

MAGAZINES, NEWSLETTERS, SUBSCRIPTIONS[3]
Compiled and edited by Estelle Bern and Gregory T. Victoroff, Esq.

Ceramics, Glass

Ceramic Industry, 270 Saint Paul Street, Denver, CO 80206

Ceramic Review, Craftsmen Potters Assn. of Great Britain, 17A Newburgh Street, London, W.1, England

Ceramics Monthly, Professional Publications, Inc., Box 12448, Columbus, OH 43212

Glass Studio, 408 South West Second Avenue, Portland, OR 97204

Stained Glass, 1125 Wilmington Avenue, St. Louis, MO 63111

Studio Potter, Box 65, Goffstown, NH 03045

Crafts, Jewelry

American Craft, 22 West 55th Street, New York, NY 10019

Artisan Crafts, Star Route 4, Box 179F, Reeds Spring, MO 65737

Contemporary Crafts Marketplace, American Crafts Council, R. R. Bowker Co., Publishers, Box 1807, Ann Arbor, MI 48106

Craft International, 24 Spring Street, New York, NY 10012

The Crafts Report, monthly all-around informant on law, legislation, business and related concerns. Write for current subscription information to 3632 Ashworth North, Seattle, WA 98103

Crafts, 8 Waterloo Place, London, SW1Y 4AW, England

Lapidary, 3564 Kettner Boulevard, P.O. Box 80937, San Diego, CA 92138

Ornament, 1221 South La Cienega Boulevard, Los Angeles, CA 90035

Ethnic Art

African Arts, African Studies Center, UCLA, 405 Hilgard Avenue, Los Angeles, CA 90024

American Indian Art, 7333 East Monterey Way 5, Scottsdale, AZ 85251

Black Art, 137–55 Southgate Street, Jamaica, NY 11413

Oriental Arts, 12 Ennerdale Road, Richmond, Surrey, England

Fashion, Fiber

American Fabrics & Fashion, 24 East 38th Street, New York, NY 10016

California Apparel News, 945 South Wall Street, Los Angeles, CA 90015

Dress, The Costume Institute, Metropolitan Museum of Art, Fifth Avenue at 82nd Street, New York, NY 10028

Fiberscope, Interweave Press, 306 CI North Washington Street, Loveland, CO 80537

Interweave, Interweave Press, 306 CI North Washington Street, Loveland, CO 80537

Shuttle, Spindle & Dyepot, Handweavers Guild of America, 65 La Salle Road, P.O. Box 7-374, West Hartford, CT 06107

The Tie Up, So. Cal. Handweavers Guild, 1717 North Gramercy Place, Hollywood, CA 90028

Women's Wear Daily, P.O. Box 1005, Manasquan, NJ 08736

General Art and Design

AfterImage, 31 Prince Street, Rochester, NY 14607

American Artist, 1 Astor Plaza, New York, NY 10036

American Artist Business Letter, 2160 Patterson Street, Cincinnati, OH 45214

American Arts, published bimonthly by the American Council for the Arts, 570 Seventh Avenue, New York, NY 10018

American Art Journal, 40 West 57th Street, 5th Floor, New York, NY 10019

American Art Review, Box 689, Old Lime, CT 06371

Art & the Law, Volunteer Lawyers for the Arts, 36 West 44th Street, New York, NY 10036

Art Direction, 19 West 44th Street, New York, NY 10036

Art Express, 964 Arts Plaza, Farmingdale, NY 11737

Art Forum, 667 Madison Avenue, New York, NY 10021

Art in America, 850 Third Avenue, New York, NY 10022

Art Letter—Artworld Intelligence for Professionals, published monthly by Art in America, Inc., 850 Third Avenue, New York, NY 10022

Art Magazine, 234 Eglinton Avenue, East No. 408, Toronto, Ontario M4P 1K5, Canada

Art Week, 1305 Franklin Street, Oakland, CA 94612

Artists Equity News, quarterly publication of the Visual Artists Guild, P.O. Box 4103, Los Angeles, CA 90028

Artists Market, 78, Craftsworkers Market, 78, 9933 Alliance Road, Cincinnati, OH 45242

Artists News, P.O. Box 671, Topanga, CA 90290

Art News, 122 East 42nd Street, New York, NY 10017. Subscription service: P.O. Box 969, Farmingdale, NY 11737

Arts Magazine, 23 East 26th Street, New York, NY 10010

Arts Matters, California Confederation of the Arts, 6253 Hollywood Boulevard, Suite 922, Los Angeles, CA 90028

Artworker News, published by the Foundation for the Community of Artists, 220 Broadway, New York, NY 10007

Boston Visual Artists Union publishes excellent publications and a newsletter that includes articles pertinent to craftspeople as well as fine artists. 77 North Washington Street, Boston, MA 02114.

Bulletin, Advocates for the Arts, UCLA School of Law, 405 Hilgard Avenue, Los Angeles, CA 90024 (10 issues annually)

Chicago Artists Coalition, 5 West Grand Avenue, Chicago, IL 60610. Publishes a survey of galleries for artists seeking affiliation. Describes how to get in touch with galleries, handle the media, contracts, commissions, insurance, etc.

Communication Arts, 410 Sherman Avenue, P.O. Box 10300, Palo Alto, CA 94303

Design Quarterly, Walker Art Center, Vineland Place, Minneapolis, MN 55403

Domus, 6725 Allott Avenue, Van Nuys, CA (U.S. correspondent)

Flash Art, 36 Vin Donatello, 20131 Milan, Italy

Illustrator Magazine, 500 South Fourth Street, Minneapolis, MN 55415

Illustrators Annual, 10 East 40th Street, New York, NY 10016

Images & Issues, 1651B 18th Street, Santa Monica, CA 90404 (quarterly)

Industrial Design, 830 Third Avenue, New York, NY 10022

Interior Design, 1515 Broadway, New York, NY 10036

Interiors, P.O. Box 13811, Philadelphia, PA 19101

Modo, Via Brera, 11 20121 Milan, Italy

Museum News, American Association of Museums, 1055 Thomas Jefferson Street, N.W., Washington, DC 20007

National Murals Network Newsletter, P.O. Box 40383, San Francisco, CA 94140. About the technical, legal and artistic elements

Ocular, 1549 Platte Street, Denver, CO 80202

Portfolio, P.O. Box 2716, Boulder, CO 80322

The Working Arts, quarterly publication of the Bay Area Lawyers for the Arts (BALA), Fort Mason Center, Building B, San Francisco, CA 94123. Art news, specialized-interest articles on all aspects of visual arts

Upper Case lower case, ITC 2 Hammarskjold Plaza, New York, NY 10017

VAGA—Visual Artists and Galleries Assoc. Newsletter, One World Trade Center, Suite 1535, New York, NY 10048

Vanguard, Vancouver Art Gallery, 1145 West Georgia Street, Vancouver, British Columbia, Canada, V6E 3H2

Washington International Arts Letter, P.O. Box 9005, Washington, DC 20003. Arts support programs, funding, developments, books and publications

Women's Art Journal, P.O. Box 3304, Grand Central Station, New York, NY 10063

Graphics

Adweek, 514 Shatto Place, Los Angeles, CA 90020

Graphik, Pilgersheimer Strasse 38, Pastfach 90 07 40, D-8000 Munich 90, Germany

Photographis: International Annual of Advertising & Editorial Photography, 10 East 40th Street, New York, NY 10016

Print, American Graphics & Design, 355 Lexington Avenue, New York, NY 10017

Push Pin Graphics, 207 East 32nd Street, New York, NY 10016

Graphics Novum, Pennsylvania State University, School of Visual Art, 102 Visual Arts Building, University Park, PA 16802

Marketing; Materials

Art Hazard News, Center for Occupational Hazards, 5 Beekman Street, New York, NY 10038

Art Material Trade News, 6 East 43rd Street, New York, NY 10017

Artists and Photographers Market, 1180 Avenue of the Americas, New York, NY 10036

Contemporary Crafts Market, 1180 Avenue of the Americas, New York, NY 10036

Fine Arts Marketplace, 1180 Avenue of the Americas, New York, NY 10036

Performance Art

High Performance, 240 South Broadway, 5th Floor, Los Angeles, CA 90012

Performance Art Journal, P.O. Box 858, Peter Stuyvesant Station, New York, NY 10009

Photography

Camera, Zurichstrasse 3, CH 6002 Lucerne, Switzerland

Center for Creative Photography, University of Arizona, 843 East University Boulevard, Tucson, AZ 85719

Creative Camera, P.O. Box 3012, Rochester, NY 14614

Exposure, P.O. Box 1651, FDR Post Office, New York, NY 10022

Image Nation, 401 Huron Street, Toronto, Ontario, Canada M5S 2G5

Latent Image, P.O. Box 1695, Palo Alto, CA 93402

Ovo, P.O. Box 1431, Station A, Montreal, Quebec, Canada H3C 2Z9

Photo Forum, P.O. Box 10-163, Auckland 4, New Zealand

Photographer, P.O. Box 24954, Postal Station C, Vancouver, British Columbia, Canada V5T 4G3

Photographis: International Annual of Advertising & Editorial Photography, 10 East 40th Street, New York, NY 10016

Picture Magazine, 4121 Wilshire Boulevard, Suite 110, Los Angeles, CA 90010

The Working Craftsman, P.O. Box 42, Northbrook, IL 60062

GLOSSARY

Compiled and edited by Richard M. Ross, Esq., and Tina D. Pasternack, Esq.

ACCOUNTS RECEIVABLE: A statement of what others are obligated to pay for services or materials rendered or furnished.

ADVANCE: A payment, sometimes in the form of materials, which is made before delivery or performance, and usually credited against the total sales or purchase price or royalties.

AGENT: One who is given the power to act for another. Many of the agent's responsibilities, duties and obligations are imposed by law and include the duty to act in the best interests of the individual represented.

ALLOCATION: The share or proportion of value of the whole assigned to individuals or entities based on their respective interests.

ARBITRATION: A method for settling disputes outside of court by submission to one or more disinterested persons knowledgeable about the subject matter, either by mutual consent (voluntary arbitration) or by law (compulsory arbitration). Generally the arbitration procedure is faster and less costly than adjudication in a trial court.

ARTICLES OF INCORPORATION: Also known as a corporate charter, this states the business purposes and powers of a corporation and some of the rules which it follows in the conduct of its business and is filed with the Secretary of State of the state in which the corporation is located.

ARTIST (VISUAL): One who creates forms and/or images in any media, whether fine or commercial, including painters, sculptors, graphic artists, animators, photographers, etc.

ASSET: Something of value which is owned or controlled by a person or a business, as opposed to a liability or a debt.

ASSIGNMENT: A legal transfer of all or any portion of an interest, right or obligation (except performance of personal services), such as the outright sale of a work of art including the copyright, or the limited right to reproduce a work of art where the owner retains or reserves all other rights.

AUDIT: A formal examination of a statement of financial transactions (such as royalty statements), usually done according to generally accepted accounting principles.

BAD DEBT: An uncollectible obligation (e.g., because the debtor is insolvent).

BALANCE: The amount of money remaining or owing in an account.

BALANCE SHEET: A statement which summarizes the assets and liabilities of a business at a particular point in time.

BOILER PLATE: A catchall phrase referring to the standard and technical provisions generally contained in most contracts which do not address the "material terms" negotiated and agreed upon in connection with and unique to a particular contract, such as the compensation structure.

CAPITAL: Money (or other assets which can be easily turned into money) which is free to be used for the establishment and conduct of business.

CAPITAL REQUIREMENT: A schedule of the amounts for which funds must be available to meet the initial start-up and operating costs of a business, such as the cost of acquiring equipment and promoting the business.

CASH RECEIPTS: Money received by a business from customers in the ordinary course of operation.

COMMERCIAL RIGHTS: The rights or interests in a work of art which are available for commercial use and which may be granted or sold (or retained) in the ordinary course of business, which are separate from the ownership of the physical object or work of art.

COMMERCIAL USE: Exploitation of a work of art for business or trade purposes (e.g., reproductions, posters, advertising and merchandising items).

COMMISSION: A fee paid to an agent, dealer or representative as compensation in connection with a purchase or sale or other transfer of rights, generally expressed in terms of a percentage of the "gross" sum (without deductions for taxes, expenses, etc.) or the "net" sum (including some deductions).

COMMISSIONED WORK: A work which is specifically assigned or contracted to be created and delivered, such as a "work made for hire" under the copyright law. (See WORK MADE FOR HIRE.)

CONSIDERATION: That which the parties to a contract give up to and get from each other.

CONSIGNMENT: Giving a work of art to someone who agrees to try to sell it on behalf of the artist. The artist retains ownership and legal title. (See TRANSFER.)

CONTRACT: An agreement, oral or written, imposing duties and creating privileges for both sides and expressing the mutual approval of all parties as to each of the important terms of the relationship, such as the act to be performed, the time of the performance, the price to be paid and the time for payment.

COPYRIGHT: The legal ownership, regulated by statute, of the exclusive right to reproduce, copy and/or exploit a work of art for a limited period of time.

COPYRIGHT REGISTRATION: The official written recordation of the ownership of a copyright with the United States Copyright Office in Washington, D.C., which usually requires the submission of a copy of the work of art.

CORPORATION: A business organization which is a legal entity made up of stockholders and which has an existence separate and distinct from the stockholders themselves.

DAMAGES: Compensation, generally monetary, paid to a person who has incurred loss or injury to his rights, property or person (e.g., reputation) through the unlawful act of another (e.g., breach of contractual obligations).

DEBTS: The fixed amounts owed to a business entity or an individual for goods furnished or services rendered in the ordinary course of business.

DEFAULT: Non-payment or non-performance in accordance with the terms of a contract or an independent legal duty.

DELIVERY: The transfer of physical goods or the right to goods, or the performance of a service at the agreed-upon time and place.

DEMAND: A formal request to comply with a contractual obligation, usually a prerequisite to commencing legal action to enforce the contract or to seek damages for a default.

DEPRECIATION: A diminution in value because of use or passage of time, which is sometimes arbitrarily determined by regulation or statute for accounting or tax purposes.

DERIVATIVE WORK: A work based upon one or more pre-existing work(s).

DESIGN: A decorative pattern or distinctive mark; it also refers to a preliminary sketch or outline highlighting or indicating the main artistic features to be executed in the final work of art.

DISTRIBUTION: The arrangements or method by which works of art are disseminated and exploited.

EMPLOYEE: One who is hired to perform services for another (employer), who usually controls and directs the manner in which the services are performed.

ENTERPRISE: The actual form of a business, which may be a corporation or partnership, or conducted individually under an actual or assumed (fictitious) name.

ENTREPRENEUR: The individual who creates, operates and controls a business.

EQUITY CAPITAL: Venture-risk or "start-up" money which is invested usually by an individual or entity in starting a business enterprise.

EXHIBITION: The presentation or display for viewing by the public, which might constitute a "publication" for purposes of copyright law, depending upon the nature and extent of the exhibition, whether there is an entrance charge or whether the exhibition is for purposes of generating sales.

EXPENSES: Costs and charges outlaid or incurred which may be chargeable against revenue.

EXPIRATION: The natural or designated end of a period of time, such as the term of a contract or the duration of a grant of rights.

FAIR MARKET VALUE: The price that a willing buyer and seller in an arm's-length transaction agree upon with respect to goods or services, sometimes referred to as the "going price."

FAIR USE: Under copyright law, a limited right to use copyrighted material for specified purposes without the consent of or payment to the copyright owner, such as critical comment, research, news, etc. The rules regarding "fair use" are very complicated and require expert advice for application.

FIDUCIARY: Someone charged with a high duty of trust and care in acting for the benefit of another.

FINANCIAL STATEMENT: A record of total assets and liabilities, including all forms of real and personal property owned and all debts which are owed. A financial statement is usually required by a financial institution or other lender for the purpose of extending credit or making a loan.

FINANCING: Obtaining money from others to operate a business or for a purchase, sale or other commercial transaction.

FIXED EXPENSE: Those costs which are necessarily incurred on a regular basis, do not vary substantially from one period to the next and are not affected by the amount of business transacted or the cash receipts obtained.

GROSS or GROSS RECEIPTS: The total amount of money or other things of value received as the proceeds from the sale or exploitation of a work or the operation of a business, before deducting charges and expenses such as taxes, commissions and the other costs of the transaction.

HOUSE ACCOUNT: An existing account which an artist retains completely and on which no commission is paid to an artist's representative or agent.

ILLUSTRATOR: One who provides visual features or designs to explain or decorate ideas or objects.

IMAGE: A term which may describe either the work of art (which may then be duplicated in a series) or an individual visual component within a work of art itself.

IMPLIED CONTRACT: A set of legal rights, duties and obligations which may flow from the normal expectations of two or more parties by reason of their dealings with each other and their natural assumptions, even though never formally expressed or reduced to writing.

INDEPENDENT CONTRACTOR: One who is commissioned or engaged for a particular task, retaining the right to determine and control the manner, time and/or conditions of his or her performance (as contrasted with an employee).

INSTALLATION: The fixed setting or display of a work of art in a gallery, museum or other place of public exhibition.

JOINT VENTURE: A business combination (a form of partnership) comprised of two or more parties acting together to achieve a common goal or objective. (See LIMITED PARTNERSHIP and PARTNERSHIP.)

JURISDICTION: The place in which a transaction occurs; also, the power of a forum or tribunal to exert control over parties who may come before it and to render binding decisions, such as a court of law or an arbitration panel.

LEASE: A contract which transfers the use or enjoyment of tangible items (real or personal property) for a specified period of time and for a specified amount of money, and which usually requires the property to be returned to the owner or landlord in the same condition at the end of the term, normal wear and tear excepted.

LIABILITY: Something which is owed or for which one has a financial or other obligation, as opposed to an asset. A contingent liability is a liability which may arise in the future but has not yet been fixed, such as a lawsuit which has not yet been decided.

LIABILITY INSURANCE: Insurance which protects against accidents and obligations to third parties for personal and property injuries for which an artist or a business may be liable, including those with respect to employees and customers.

LIMITED PARTNERSHIP: A form of partnership in which some principals (the general partners) assume managerial control and financial responsibility for unlimited liability, and certain others (the limited partners) have no or very little decision-making authority and assume specific financial responsibility usually limited only to the actual amount initially agreed to be invested. (See JOINT VENTURE or PARTNERSHIP.)

LIQUIDATE: To satisfy a debt or convert assets to cash.

NEGLIGENCE: Failure to exercise the ordinary degree of care required of the average person, according to what is reasonable or customary under the circumstances.

NEGOTIATION: The process of bargaining or coming to an agreement.

NET or NET RECEIPTS: That which remains from gross receipts over and above all charges, costs and expenses.

NON-RECURRING EXPENSE: One-time or extraordinary, as distinguished from a fixed expense, which is of a repeating nature.

OPERATING COSTS: Day-to-day expenses resulting from normal operations of a business, differing from fixed expenses in that they may vary up or down depending upon changing circumstances and the level at which business is conducted.

OPTION: An agreement with respect to the right to do something in the future pursuant to specified terms and conditions established in advance, which may or may not be exercised at the discretion of the party having the option.

ORIGINAL: The initial, unique physical object from which copies or reproductions may be made or which may form the basis for the creation of derivative works of art.

PARTNERSHIP: A form of joint business undertaking in which individuals share responsibilities, resources and profits in accordance with legal relationships and in which each partner is fully liable for the debts of the partnership. (See JOINT VENTURE and LIMITED PARTNERSHIP.)

PATENT/DESIGN PATENT: A statutory form of protection for a term of years, similar in certain respects to a copyright but usually for a shorter period of protection, which gives the owner the exclusive right to exploit a device or process which is the subject of the patent.

PATERNITY: The right of an artist to claim authorship in his or her artwork.

PER DIEM: Payment of compensation for specified expenses (e.g., food, transportation, hotel) on a daily or time basis in connection with employment or a commission.

PERFORMANCE: The legal satisfaction of a duty under a contract which constitutes the consideration flowing to the other party. Non-performance is usually a breach or default under the contract and may entitle the injured party to recover damages or seek other remedies.

PRINCIPAL: Money or property which is invested or physically incorporated in a business, as opposed to interest or income; also, the one who is directly concerned or the actual owner in a business enterprise or undertaking, as opposed to an agent or representative of such persons.

PRINT: A reproduction of an original work of art made by a photomechanical or other process and which may consist of one or more copies in a series.

PROFIT: Financial gain, or the amount of return from an enterprise after deducting expenditures. (See PROFIT AND LOSS STATEMENT.)

PROFIT AND LOSS STATEMENT: A schedule of the total amount of sales made and other income, less expenses and costs, including fixed expenses, operating costs and non-recurring items, to show the amount of "profit" or "loss" for doing business.

PROFIT MARGIN: An allowance over expenditures in determining a sales price, usually calculated as a percentage of the costs and expenses of producing a certain work.

PROVENANCE: The history of the ownership and/or custodianship of a work of art.

PUBLICATION: Distribution of copies of a work to the public by sale, lease, license or other transfer.

RECEIVABLE: Something which awaits payment or collection.

RECOUPMENT: The recovery of all expenses incurred in connection with the investment in a work, a project or a business.

RELIANCE (RELIANCE INTEREST):   With regard to a contract, the reasonably or justifiably expected change in one party's financial or material position based upon that party's belief that the other party to the contract will keep his bargain.

REPRESENTATION: A statement of truth or fact or intention which is meant to be relied upon by the person to whom it is made. (See WARRANTY.)

REPRODUCTION/REPRODUCTION RIGHTS: The right to use or make copies of, in whole or in part, an original work of art, usually licensed by contract between an artist and a publisher or other user.

RESALE ROYALTY: A royalty payable each time a work of art is sold after its initial sale, usually only at a price exceeding a minimum level provided by law.

RESCIND: To place the parties to a contract in their original positions as if the contract had never been made, which may be available as a remedy in certain cases of breach of contract.

RESERVE: A sum of money which is set aside for a specified purpose or for a general fund for unknown obligations, such as for contingent liabilities.

RESERVED RIGHTS: Those rights which are held or retained by the owner (such as the copyright owner) and which are not granted by license or other transfer of partial interest in the rights to the user.

RETAIL: Selling to the actual user, and not for further sale to others. (See WHOLESALE.)

RIGHT: A legal interest in something of value which one has the power to use, exercise, transfer or grant to others or to refrain from so doing. Rights may be non-exclusive or exclusive (i.e., allowing third parties also to exercise or enjoy the rights or preventing them from doing so) and may be for an unlimited or a limited period of time.

ROYALTY: A payment made to the creator or the owner of a work of art for each copy of his or her work sold or for each use of any of the rights in his or her work. This is usually expressed as a percentage of the gross or net price obtained from the sale or other use, and accounted for and paid on a periodic basis.

STATUTES OF LIMITATION: Laws which are designed to encourage persons to pursue their legal remedies promptly and to penalize those who "sleep on their rights," by providing a certain maximum period of time (depending upon the rights involved; e.g., a contract claim or a personal injury) within which a lawsuit must be brought in order to vindicate such rights.

STUDIO SALES: Sales which are made from or in the artist's workplace or studio.

SUBSIDIARY (ANCILLARY) RIGHTS: Those rights in a work which may be exploited secondarily to the main exploitation of a work, including the creation and exploitation of derivative works, and which may have great value independently of the value of the main exploitation.

TERMINATION: The end, by means of normal expiration, default or affirmative act, of an allotted period of time or the term of a lease, license, agreement or contract.

TRADEMARK: A mark, symbol or series of words pointing distinctly to the origin or ownership of merchandise or objects of commerce to which it is applied or affixed and which is legally reserved to the exclusive use of the owner, usually requiring filing and registration with the state and/or federal government.

TRANSFER: The passage of legal rights (e.g., from an artist to a buyer). A consignment or delivery of goods or objects to an agent does not constitute a legal transfer.

WARRANTY: A legal guarantee, such as to the ownership, originality, safety or fitness for use for a specific purpose of a work or of goods. Some warranties may be implied by law and cannot be waived or relinquished by the party for whose benefit the warranties exist. (See REPRESENTATION.)

WHOLESALE: Selling chiefly to retailers, other merchants or industrial, institutional or commercial users, primarily for resale or for business use, as opposed to sales to the general public or ultimate users themselves. (See RETAIL.)

WORK MADE FOR HIRE: A work prepared by an employee within the scope of his or her employment, or specially ordered or commissioned under certain circumstances, and in which the employer or person commissioning the work is considered the owner for copyright purposes.